American Evangelicals and Religious Diversity

Subcultural Education, Theological Boundaries, and the Relativization of Tradition

A volume in
Research on Religion and Education
Stephen J. Denig and Lyndon G. Furst, Series Editors

Research on Religion and Education

Stephen J. Denig, *Niagara University*
Lyndon G. Furst, *Andrews University*
Series Editors

Religion, Education, and Academic Success (2003)
  by William Jeynes

*American Evangelicals and Religious Diversity: Subcultural Education,
Theological Boundaries, and the Relativization of Tradition* (2006)
  by Kevin M. Taylor

American Evangelicals and Religious Diversity

Subcultural Education, Theological Boundaries, and the Relativization of Tradition

by

Kevin M. Taylor

INFORMATION AGE
PUBLISHING

Greenwich, Connecticut • www.infoagepub.com

Library of Congress Cataloging-in-Publication Data

Taylor, Kevin M.
  American evangelicals and religious diversity : subcultural education,
theological boundaries, and the relativization of tradition / by Kevin M.
Taylor.
      p. cm. – (Research in religion and education)
  Includes bibliographical references.
  ISBN 1-59311-517-2 (pbk.) – ISBN 1-59311-518-0 (hardcover)
  1. Church and education–United States. 2. Toleration–United
States–Case studies. I. Title. II. Series.
  LC368.T39 2006
  371.071–dc22

                                                  2006007224

To my wife Heather, for her unfailing and sustaining love

To Tonya Huber, for encouragement and synergy

To the students of Midwestern Christian Academy, for a delightful 9 years
¡Qué Dios les bendiga ricamente!

CONTENTS

Appendices

FOREWORD

Kevin Taylor's book, *American Evangelicals and Religious Diversity*, is the second book in Information Age Publishing's series *Research on Religion and Education*. The series seeks to unveil the relationship of religion and education as two major factors in the socialization of citizens and future citizens in the American scene. The first book in the series, *Religion, Education, and Academic Success* by Professor William Jeynes, documented the nexus between the religious experience of American youth and their success in school. His carefully conducted meta-analysis provides a solid scientific base for the study of religion and education.

From colonial times, the interests of religion and education have intersected. The first schools had decidedly religious purposes: to teach people to read the bible so that they might be better equipped to fend off the temptations of the devil and to train native clergy for ministry in the colonies. For the first fifty years of the Republic, all schools were seen as serving a public purpose and many schools, even those sponsored by religious denominations, received public funding. To this day all schools, even those considered to be "sectarian," serve the public purpose of forming a literate citizenry, able to partake in the public debate so necessary to our democracy.

In recent years, the intersection of religion and education has often been a collision. Should religious schools receive funding to help them continue to serve the public good of literacy? Can vouchers be used at religious schools? Can opportunities for prayer be provided during the public school day? Can athletes in public schools, with or without the leadership of their coaches, be permitted to pray before a competition? To what extent may religious music and icons be part of assemblies and performances in public schools? What provisions are made in public schools for

American Evangelicals and Religious Diversity, pages vii–viii
Copyright © 2006 by Information Age Publishing
All rights of reproduction in any form reserved.

religion-based dietary needs of students and faculty? To what extent do the rights of students and faculty to pray during the day clash with the First Amendment? These are only a few of the ways in which religion and education intersect to this day. The research based series of which this volume is a part critically explores this intersection.

American Evangelicals and Religious Diversity is a qualitative study of how religion and education intersect at one conservative Christian school. The school is evangelical and American. The school's curriculum is bible-based and fulfills its state's educational requirements for high school graduation. While the school has an environment that is evangelical, the students live in a religiously diverse world. This book documents how three students and their teacher struggle to understand a world that challenges their faith. The context for this understanding is how the teacher presents and the three students come to understand Catholicism, Islam, and the indigenous religions of the Americas.

Americans continue to debate whether religious schools are too parochial and do not prepare students to live a diverse society. It is the opinion of the editors that this book should put to rest some of this fear. We read the manuscript with a critical editorial eye but found the story a compelling one which challenged us to review the tenets of our own faith. The author's style of presentation is consistent with good scientific discourse yet impels the reader to a view inside the experience of the subjects of the study. Reading the manuscript was not only an informative experience but a faith-affirming one too. We are very pleased to present Kevin Taylor's book, *American Evangelicals and Religious Diversity* as an important part of our series on research on religion and education.

—Stephen J. Denig, Niagara University
Lyndon G. Furst, Andrews University

CHAPTER 1

CHRISTIAN SCHOOLS AND THE IMPLICATIONS OF IDENTITY

PERSONAL AND COLLECTIVE IDENTITY IN A MODERN, PLURALISTIC WORLD

For many of us who live in the United States or other parts of the modern-ized West, a burgeoning worldwide population, record life expectancies, and previously unimaginable medical advances make it easy for us to lose sight of the fact that our existence on this earth is precarious. When it comes to issues such as the overconsumption of natural resources or the threat of biological weapons and nuclear arms proliferation, the decisions we make as individuals and as communities have profound and sometimes deleterious consequences. We do live with the fearful prospect that, with our development of technology often outpacing our wisdom in knowing how to apply it, we are perfectly capable of destroying one other. In fact, there exist some in our world who would like nothing better than to do just that. Recent history is replete with examples of ethnic cleansing, interna-tional warfare, racism, sexism, and a host of other conflicts illustrating how the numerous communities in our modern world often find themselves at odds with one another.

It is in this context that the study of individual and group identity has come to the forefront in recent years. Barring some disability, each adult person alive today shares with other members in the history of the human race qualities such as language, bipedality, opposable thumbs, self-con-

American Evangelicals and Religious Diversity, pages 1–11

sciousness, and a number of other characteristics that make us human, even if we can't always agree on what those items are. Each of us is also unique, inhabiting a particular conjunction of time and space and possessing distinctive combinations of physical, behavioral, and psychological features and a personal life-story that makes each of us "who we are." Out of these "self-aspects" (Simon, 1997) we fashion, interpret, and maintain our identities, not just individually, but also collectively (Schwalbe & Mason-Schrock, 1996). As humans we inhabit our planet with those we deem as "like us" or "not like us," groupings whose membership changes depending on the criteria employed to determine inclusion or exclusion. We band together with people who share boundary markers such as race, nationality, clan, gender, and religion, all of which serve to differentiate "us" from "them."

Regardless of whether or not one fully agrees with social constructivist theories, it is apparent from historical and anthropological study that these identity markers and the significance attached to them are, if not entirely cultural products, at least greatly shaped by culture. Of course, this does not mean that we are deterministically bound to use the categories in exactly the way they are presented to us, since individual agents influence culture at the same time that culture influences individuals. Nevertheless, people do latch on, to greater or lesser degrees, to those items that are given expression in particular eras and geographical regions. For example, it has been argued from recent exploration of the human genome that the concept of race is biologically unfounded, yet it is impossible to dispute the tremendous power it has held and continues to hold in American society (American Anthropological Association, 1998; Graves, 2004; Smedley, 1998; Templeton, 1998). In a similar fashion, scholars debate the extent to which "gender" is bound up with our physiology, yet what it means to be "masculine" and "feminine" does vary considerably from culture to culture (Bonvillain, 1998).

Moreover, identity markers provide meaning in a cultural setting by demarcating a plurality of possibilities. For example, it would make no sense to call oneself "American" if there were no other countries to which one could belong. If there were only one country, then there would be no purpose in naming it or even thinking of it as a "country." To use another illustration, it is absurd to refer to oneself as the type of human being that has an endoskeleton. Since all humans have an endoskeleton, this biological feature does not serve as a basis of identity among humans, although it obviously takes on some meaning in comparison to certain other life forms. Within the human realm, it would be meaningful for personal and group identity only if there were humans that lacked an endoskeleton. Thus, when one speaks of identity, characteristics hold significance only in the presence of individuals or groups that do not share them, which scholars of identity have designated the "Other."

These defining traits are multifarious, including items such as physical qualities, economic status, social roles, behavioral patterns, aptitudes, personality traits, interests, political views or, as in the context of this book on evangelical Christians, religious beliefs. Which of these descriptors becomes salient at any given moment depends on the social context and on our relative levels of commitment to each of them (Stryker & Serpe, 1982; Turner, Oakes, Haslam, & McGarty, 1994). Additionally, the way we view these self-aspects are heavily influenced by our upbringing, since

> People do not acquire the languages needed for self-definition on their own. Rather, we are introduced to them through interaction with others who matter to us. . . . The genesis of the human mind is in this sense not monological, not something each person accomplishes on his or her own, but dialogical. (Taylor, 1994, p. 32)

In fact, not only is our identity shaped by our parents and others who participate in our upbringing, along with voices from society and culture at large, but also by the Other itself. In a sense, both individuals and groups are not culturally isolated from the Other, but rather defined in relation to it. As Paul Ricoeur (1990/1992) has stated, "the selfhood of oneself implies otherness to such a degree that one cannot be thought of without the other" (p. 3). Hence, not only are we defined and define ourselves as separate from others, but our cultural juxtaposition means that we ourselves are shaped in significant ways by our relationship with them (Volf, 1996).

Even if culture defines us, it does so only partially, since we are also active participants in the process of cultural definition. In fact, much cultural identity work is often necessary to reinforce the saliency of boundaries that ensure the continued existence of a psychological group or subculture (Lamont, 1992; Lamont & Fournier, 1992; Schwalbe & Mason-Schrock, 1996). According to Turner (1987), a psychological group is "one that is psychologically significant for the members, to which they relate themselves subjectively for social comparison and the acquisition of norms and values that they privately accept membership in, and which influences their attitudes and behavior" (pp. 1–2). Although sometimes used unreflectively or reductively by scholars (Fine & Kleinman, 1979), the concept of subculture is also a valuable model, and plays an important role in the present study. Claude Fischer (1995) defines subculture as

> a large set of people who share a defining trait, associate with one another, are members of institutions associated with their defining trait, adhere to a distinct set of values, share a set of cultural tools (Swidler, 1986), and take part in a common way of life. (p. 544)

Even as it is acknowledged that subcultures are not entirely "homogeneous, static, and closed" (Fine & Kleinman, 1979, p. 2) and that "subcultures' boundaries may be vague and overlapping" (Fischer, 1995, pp. 544–545), they do derive their identities from the particularistic narratives, cultural values, traits, and behaviors that distinguish them in some degree from society as a whole and the other subcultures found therein. As Charles Tilly (2003) puts it,

> Categorical boundaries need not separate homogeneous populations from each other. Away from the boundary, great heterogeneity can prevail within...categories....But boundaries exist to the extent that participants on each side employ similar uniform practices and representations of themselves and of those on the other side.

For some people, such as the evangelical Christians of this book, the defining traits are primarily theological and moral (Hunter, 1987; Reimer, 1996; Swidler, 2001). In this case, a subculture

> entails a distinctive set of norms and values plus mechanisms for sustaining these values among group members and transmitting them to new members. According to this view, subcultures harbor values that deviate from those of the societal mainstream, and their participants will be *relatively* cohesive and homogeneous in espousing those values. (Gay & Ellison, 1993, p. 312, emphasis added)

In America in recent years, multiculturalism has arisen as a political and social force, as proponents engaged in the "politics of recognition" call individuals and groups within society to both recognize and value the distinctiveness of various subcultures, allowing them to retain their uniqueness instead of requiring their total assimilation into a homogenized civil order (Taylor, 1994). Of course, this vision of society is quite frightening for some liberal scholars, who wonder what is going to hold us together as a nation if every subgroup is allowed to do its own thing. If all groups are left to pursue their own ends, is anarchy not just around the corner? One of the fears of the postmodern age is that, without an overarching meta-narrative to unite us, all that remains is a power struggle between rival communities. One need study only a very little history or watch the evening news to know how ugly such conflict can become, and religious communities are sometimes prime examples of this. Perhaps in recognition of this tendency, individuals such as theologian Don Cupitt (1997) express the following desire:

> [W]e no longer actually need roots, identity, stability, or a provenance. We can live without those things. Me, I don't want them anymore. I'd prefer to

be without identity. I'd like to belong to no ethnic group, and to have no Other. (p. 99)

Such sentiments, however, are fantasies. To make sense of things, we categorize them (McGarty, 1999; Tajfel, 1981). To speak, we must use names and labels. As the process goes, before long a term undoubtedly develops to describe this "freeform" way of life, and it finds meaning primarily in contrast to "traditional" or "subcultural" modes of existence. Soon "freeformers" find themselves banding together with others "like them" to advance their cause in the face of their "traditionalist" competitors and we end up right back where we started.

Of course, identity is not simply an either/or thing. "[A]ll individuals have multiple identities available to them, and most individuals switch incessantly among identities as a function of the settings they enter, the others with whom they interact, and the activities they are currently carrying on" (Tilly, 2003). Much of this depends on the way in which individuals align their own autobiographical narrative with the various social narratives available in the communities in which they live (Altena, Hermans, & van der Ven, 2000; Ammerman, 2003; Somers, 1994). Thus, a white Christian can see him- or herself as both "oppressor" and "oppressed" depending on whether he or she has in mind the enslavement of blacks in the American South or the persecution of the early Christian church. Indeed, within the single Christian meta-narrative of sin, redemption, and sanctification, an individual takes on an identity that manages to hold together both "saint" and "sinner" at the very same time.

Although personal identities are multiple in nature, collective identities are generally centered on a single self-aspect and the secondary characteristics directly implied by it (Simon, 1997). It is proposed that this common self-identification with categorical descriptors is what makes social life possible (Turner, 1982; Wuthnow, 1988a). When groups relate to one another, it is this descriptor that forms the boundary between them and distinguishes "ingroups" from "outgroups" (Conover, 1988). It is theorized that out of a desire to establish a positive social identity and possibly also to boost self-esteem, one is prone to evaluate one's own group more favorably than others' and to work to benefit the ingroup, sometimes at the expense of outgroups, who may be denigrated in the process (Hogg & Abrams, 1990; Oakes, Haslam, & Turner, 1994; Tajfel & Turner, 1979). In fact, in certain threatening or competitive contexts such as war, team games, or political feuds, ingroup solidarity can be said to increase the more that emphasis is placed on the boundary between "us" and "them" (Hogg, 1992). In these instances, the ingroup comes to represent everything that is good, true, and right while outgroups represent everything that is evil, false, and wrong with the world.

On the individual level, stereotyping comes into play when individuals are encountered as group members, and are therefore described in terms of that single defining descriptor and the secondary characteristics associated with it (Oakes et al., 1994). Although seen by scholars of individual-level processes as limiting and misrepresentative in that it reduces the complex nature of individuals to a single dimension, stereotyping is seen by scholars of group-level behavior as a requisite part of collective life and not necessarily inaccurate. In function, stereotyping has both a cognitive component that brings the world into focus and a value component that contributes to individuals' value systems (Hogg & Abrams, 1988). "Where the category is value-laden and has direct and crucial relevance to one's own value system and conceptualization of self," social psychologists Michael Hogg and Dominic Abrams state, "there is a personal investment in preserving and accentuating intergroup distinctiveness" (p. 76). Because of the vested interest with which we hold our values and identity, others who display characteristics that could potentially disconfirm the distinctiveness drawn between "us" and "them" are more likely to be disregarded if the categories are formed on the basis of some deeply held value than if the divisive characteristic is only peripheral to one's identity.

With all of this in mind, how should we, with our similarities and our differences, relate to one another? How do we educate our children to live in a pluralistic world, to remain true to their upbringing and traditions, and yet coexist with others who may not share their convictions? Do we tell them that violence is justified to protect "our" interests? Should we be suspicious of intercultural and interreligious dialogue, fearing a cloaked and lurking imperialism eager to oppress us? Should we trust those who are different than us, assuming that they have our best interests at heart as well as their own? Does making room in one's tradition for the Other mean that one must give up the core of one's identity? Must one compromise the truth in the quest for peace? These questions weigh heavily on the minds of many in our world today, a world that finds an increasing part of its identity in its pluralistic condition. As theologian Raimundo Panikkar (1979) has noted,

> Pluralism is today a human existential problem which raises acute questions about how we are going to live our lives in the midst of so many options. Pluralism is no longer just the old schoolbook question about the One-and-the-Many; it has become the concrete day-to-day dilemma occasioned by the encounter of mutually incompatible worldviews and philosophies. Today we face pluralism as the very practical question of planetary human coexistence. (p. 201)

Although there has always existed in human societies a wide range of belief patterns, and modern scholars of religion have in many ways exaggerated the differences between modern and premodern social systems (Douglas, 1973, 1982), in a preindustrialized and preurbanized world one may have found oneself living in relative isolation from the Other. The interconnectedness of the modern world has made it much less likely, so the story goes, that individuals in a given cultural group will remain separate from those who think, believe, and behave in a different manner (Berger, 1998).

The classical sociological theorists of the 19th century contend that modernization, through the vehicles of industrialization and urbanization, "greatly increases the variety of identities within society and the potential for contact among persons of differing identities" (Olson, 1993, p. 33). Defined by sociologist Peter Berger (1998), cultural pluralism is simply "the coexistence and social interaction of people with very different beliefs, values and lifestyles" (p. 782).[1]

On an individual religious level, exposure to those with different beliefs and practices can lead to radically divergent consequences regarding the establishment of personal identity. In some cases, people recoil from the existence of the Other and reinforce their position within the faith of their heritage. In other cases, people reconsider their own faith in light of the Other, modifying their beliefs in significant ways. Sometimes individuals abandon their original faith altogether, even if the new faith is always partially understood in light of the former one.

RELIGIOUS SUBCULTURAL EDUCATION

In the realm of religious education, differing visions of the good life and the good society shape both curriculum and instructional practice. At the intersection of communal and individual interests, one finds liberal educators proposing a form of instruction in which students are acquainted with various religious traditions in a value-neutral, objective fashion (Schweitzer, 2000). Once taught to think critically and rationally about the various religious values, students are given the freedom to do with them what they please (Hirst, 1972, 1981). In this way, instructors withhold their own views and do not impinge upon the moral autonomy of individual students by mandating a single authoritative position or viewpoint, since to teach

---

1.   Strictly speaking, the term "pluralism" is not synonymous with either "plurality" or "diversity," but is instead a philosophical and theological position with respect to the phenomenon (Hall, 1998; Wuthnow, 2004). Since such large numbers of social scientists use the terms interchangeably, however, this work will do likewise.

from a particular vantage point in an effort to transmit a particular set of values restricts individual choice and is tantamount to indoctrination (Hermans, 2000a, 2000c). Communitarian pedagogues, on the other hand, argue that neutrality is a myth, and that this supposedly value-neutral and objective approach is itself based on a particular value system (van der Ven, 2000). Since someone's values are always being taught, educators should not be ashamed to instruct from the vantage point of their own religious tradition (Hermans, 2000a; Schweitzer, 2000). One can see this approach in many private Christian schools, in which "formation of the self based on a specific religious tradition is their core business" (Hermans, 2000b, p. 2). To bring their children up in heritage of the true faith and to enable them to take their place in the Christian community is the goal of many Christian parents and educators (Astley, Francis, Wilcox, & Burton, 2000; Balmer, 1989; Francis, 2000; Furst, 2000; Goldman, 1965; Hermans, 2000c).

At the junction of community and society, the views of communitarians and liberals diverge yet again. Whereas communitarians see the goal of religious instruction as strengthening subcultures, liberals see one of the purposes of education as social and political integration as a nation (Macedo, 2000; Schweitzer, 2000). Communitarians envision society as a "community of communities," each contributing its uniqueness to the enrichment of the whole (Etzioni, 1995). Only when they are strong, however, do subcultures have something to give. Liberals, however, insist that what may be good for particular communities can be bad for society. In this light, private educational settings are viewed as exclusive, segregated, and escapist—as controlled environments that restrict contact with and foster distrust of the outside world (Gutmann, 1987; Miedema, 2000). Not only is there little room within for students to construct their own identities (Miedema, 2000), but indoctrinated students make poor citizens since they "do not learn skills to handle the moral pluralism of our society" (Hermans, 2000c, p. 283). For that reason, the more those religious subcultures establish their own educational institutions, the more the country will be pulled apart by "divisive sectarianism" (Francis, 2000).

AN OVERVIEW OF THE PRESENT STUDY

The purpose of this book is to examine a particular subset of the American religious field, namely evangelical Protestant Christians, to see how theological views lead them to view the Other and affect the way in which they establish and maintain individual and collective identity boundaries. The initial chapters provide a depiction of evangelicalism, its history, and some of the issues it faces today as one religious option among many in contemporary America. Following this is an in-depth case study documenting how a particular group of students at an American evangelical high school experienced and responded to the Other during a presentation of other religious traditions that was more balanced in its approach than is often found in such a school. In this case, the traditions studied were (1) Islam; (2) the Roman Catholicism of Spain and Latin America (both historical and present-day); and (3) the worldviews of the Mayan, Aztec, and Incan civilizations. Finally, the book concludes with two chapters in which I offer some observations and challenges for both a general audience and for evangelical educators.

As a product of the American evangelical Protestant Christian heritage myself, I have a keen personal interest in this subject. Growing up as a member of a specific religious community, I have felt both the delightful and the disorienting effects of American religious pluralism on my own faith journey as I have encountered those who do not look, think, or act like me. How much room should we allow within our own tradition for the Other? How does that change how we see ourselves? How much change can be made in one's beliefs before one is no longer considered an evangelical Christian? These are a few of the questions with which I and many others have had to wrestle as we try to make sense of both the world around us and of who we are within both our own faith tradition and that wider world.

Second, I realize that the current state of thought within the evangelical subculture vis-à-vis the establishment of personal identity and group boundaries greatly affects the way my students perceive those of other cultures. As a Spanish teacher I have seen this manifested in the way my students view both (1) the people who currently speak the Spanish language and (2) those who have contributed historically to the shaping of present-day Spain and Latin America. After all, the theological narratives according to which my students live and find their place in the world also contain a place for the people of these cultures as well as for other non-evangelicals that they will encounter throughout their lives.

Because the primary informants in the case study comprised a small, purposive sample drawn from a specific age group, geographical location, and socioeconomic status, the experiences and views encountered are limited in their generalizability to the greater evangelical population. For this reason, overreaching claims will not be proffered regarding the current state of the whole of American evangelical Protestantism. However, as one who was raised in the evangelical church and has taught for many years in an evangelical school, I feel qualified to say that most of the views expressed by each of the primary informants are either widely held in evangelical circles or enlightening because of their divergence from more commonly held views. They provide a vivid illustration of the internal dialogue present as those within the evangelical subculture try to decide on the proper way of dealing with people of other faiths.

Due to the fact that the exploration of Islam, Roman Catholicism, and the worldviews of the Mayas, Aztecs, and Incas took place during a 3-month period (excluding one member check session that occurred a year later), the case study was also limited in its ability to measure changes over an extended period of time. Obviously, individual responses to cultural pluralism can take many years. In fact, it can be said that, on an individual basis, one is never finished revising or reinforcing (consciously or unconsciously) one's beliefs. This study, however, attempts to examine only (1) that narrow window in which one can see either the effects of previous student experiences with other religious traditions or (2) the initial stages of change (or lack thereof) due to the brief encounter with the specific traditions presented in a high school classroom.

Unlike what often happens in evangelical Christian schools, I sought during the presentation of the other faith traditions to stress both similarities and differences between the other religious traditions and evangelical Christianity. I am aware, as an educator, that introducing students to previously unexplored interpretations of reality, some of which contradict the explanations commonly provided by evangelical Christianity, can lead to unpredictable results. As a person of faith myself, I take very seriously the spiritual well-being of those entrusted to my care. Therefore, I must stress that, although there existed during the encounter with the various cultures and religions the possibility that a shift might occur in the thinking of the students, there was no desire on my part to effect change apart from an instructor trying to bring about comprehension of the subject material. My only objective was to document how students processed and responded to the information we covered. As we explored different sacred texts of the various traditions, none of them were taught as religious instruction. That is to say, at no point were students encouraged either to reject what was presented or to adopt the beliefs of other faith traditions as their own.

Some educators committed to the appreciation of diversity may consider such an instructional approach inappropriate, thinking that measures should be taken to emphasize those features of other traditions that evangelicals might find attractive in an attempt to promote religious tolerance and better relations between those of differing backgrounds. However, that was not the purpose of this study. My purpose was not to encourage students to adopt a particular position, but to see how they fit the new information into their preexisting intellectual frameworks.

Likewise, some evangelical Christians may also consider such an instructional approach inappropriate, thinking that I should rather have advocated on behalf of evangelical Christianity over and against the other religious traditions. I sincerely understand why adults may want to shelter their students from taking seriously alternative explanations of reality, especially if they deem high school students as not yet sophisticated enough to discern truth from error. For some of the parents and staff at my school, one of their greatest fears is that their young people will leave for college, encounter the wider world, and "lose their faith," a spiritual disaster with both temporal and eternal implications. To these people I can say two things: (1) for their age, the students in my classroom were quite advanced in their ability to think critically, and (2) they will find the approach I took markedly better than that of the hypothetical college professor who may not be sympathetic to religion in general or to evangelical Christianity in particular.

However, I must also say that to promote evangelical Christianity in the way that is often done, by exclusively emphasizing the perceived difficulties or shortcomings of other religions, was not on my agenda either. In fact, I find this approach to be dishonest. Strengthening and maintaining one's faith is, on the whole, a very good thing. However, I believe that faith is not something that one locks away in a box for fear of losing it, but rather something that grows, adjusts, and hopefully deepens as one's life experience increases. A faith that is artificially propped up by presenting it as the sole repository of reason and morality is not much of a faith, and such an instructional approach may backfire when students end up someday meeting those of other faiths who appear to possess both generous hearts and perceptive minds.

CHAPTER 2

A THEOLOGICAL OVERVIEW OF AMERICAN EVANGELICAL PROTESTANT CHRISTIANITY

DESCRIPTION OF PRESENT-DAY EVANGELICALISM

Protestant evangelicalism, derived from the Greek word *euangellion,* meaning "good news," is a significant part of the American religious scene today (Noll, 2003). Depending on the measures one uses to identify who is an evangelical, it is estimated that evangelicals comprise anywhere from 5 to 46% of the population of the United States (Kellstedt & Green, 1996), although most studies place the number in the 15–25% range (Schmalzbauer, 1999).

Evangelicalism is not a monolithic entity, but rather a very diverse coalition encompassing a broad spectrum of denominations, geographical regions, and social classes (Barna Research Group, 2000; Blomberg & Robinson, 1997; Greenberg Quinlan Rosner Research, 2004; Hunter, 1987; Jelen & Wilcox, 1991). It has been called a "mosaic" (Askew, 1987), a "kaleidoscope" (T. L. Smith, 1980), a "company" (Hill, 1989), an "umbrella" (Webber, 1978), a "vast tent" (Murphy, 1981), a "conglomerate" (Stransky, 1988), a "patchwork quilt" (Balmer, 1989), and an "extended family" (Johnston, 1991). In fact, due to its diverse nature, it is frequently difficult to agree on how to define evangelicalism or categorize those within its fold (Moberg, 1975; Weber, 1991). Scholars have numbered the subgroups within evangelicalism from as few as 3 (Wilcox, 1990) to as many as 14 (Webber, 1978), with the rest settling on a number somewhere in between

American Evangelicals and Religious Diversity, pages 13–23

(Askew, 1987; Dayton & Johnston, 1991; Hunter, 1983; Murphy, 1981; Quebedeaux, 1974; Weber, 1991).

At its most basic level, the larger evangelical field is divisible into three historically distinct subsets, namely *fundamentalism, Pentecostalism,* and *neo-evangelicalism.* Unfortunately, the latter of these is nearly always abbreviated as "evangelicalism," to the great consternation of those trying to keep straight whether reference is being made to conservative Protestantism as a whole (which is the way the term will be used in this book) or merely one of its constituent parts. Compounding things further is the difficulty in determining whether individual survey respondents are indeed evangelicals. One can find both subtle and not-so-subtle variations between studies depending on whether researchers have used self-identification, association with historically linked church denominations or movements, doctrinal confession, or a combination of the above to operationalize the tradition (Kellstedt, Green, Smidt, & Guth, 1996; Kellstedt & Smidt, 1996; Woodberry & Smith, 1998). For example, the majority of black churches in the United States today are very conservative theologically and would probably fall within the fundamentalist branch of conservative Protestantism (Woodberry & Smith, 1998). However, the black church has been shaped historically by a much different set of social circumstances than their white counterparts and politically are far more progressive. Therefore, whether one is studying theology or politics can determine who is included in one's sample.

For many evangelicals themselves, it seems that the identity marker "evangelical" is only a secondary label. Although many have no problem identifying themselves as such (Kellstedt, Green, Smidt, & Guth, 1996; C. Smith & Sikkink, 2003), it has been shown that when they use the term they do not always have in mind the broad national grouping perceived by scholars (Sikkink, 1998). In fact, it is partly the local character of evangelicalism that contributes to the plethora of evangelical subgroups and gives them their grassroots character (Balmer, 1989; Galli, 2004; Warner, 1988). Although they may associate with prominent national church denominations such as Southern Baptist, Church of the Nazarene, Missouri Synod Lutheran, Churches of Christ, Assemblies of God, and Presbyterian Church in America, many other evangelicals feel quite at home in independent nondenominational churches where authority resides exclusively at the local level (Jones et al., 2002; Kellstedt, Green, Guth, & Smidt, 1996; Roof & McKinney, 1987; Steensland et al., 2000).

Moreover, since denominational loyalty in the United States is arguably less pronounced than it once was (Gay & Ellison, 1993; Wuthnow, 1988a; see Sherkat, 2001, and Sullins, 1993, for an opposing view), many individuals feel free to search for a church outside of the denomination in which they were raised (Roof, 1989; Roof & McKinney, 1987). Although denominations are still important predictors of political and social values and life-styles (Beatty & Walter, 1984; Gay & Ellison, 1993; Lopatto, 1985), and most religious switchers do not stray far from home (Bibby, 1999; Hadaway & Marler, 1993; Sherkat, 2001; Sullins, 1993), some theologically conservative individuals can be found sprinkled throughout mainline or liberal denominations as well as conservative ones (Hoge & Noll, 2000). This may not mean that individuals with evangelical beliefs are attending liberal churches in great numbers, however, since occasionally one finds entire congregations that are much more conservative or liberal than their parent denomination (Warner, 1988). In keeping with the aforementioned decline in denominational loyalty, evangelicals are not very prone to use denominational labels to describe themselves. Like most Americans, evangelicals define their identities in a variety of ways, sometimes using overlapping combinations of fundamentalist, evangelical, charismatic, and Pentecostal labels, while many others prefer to call themselves "just Christians" (Greenberg Quinlan Rosner Research, 2004; Jelen, 1993; Roof, 1999; Sikkink, 1998; Warner, 1988).

Despite the apparently disjointed nature of conservative Protestantism and the confusion surrounding the use of the term "evangelical," most scholars still believe that there is sufficient internal coherence for the classification to serve as a useful category for societal analysis. While many scholars find evangelicalism easiest to define in terms of theological doctrines, others speak of an "evangelical spirit" apart from any reference to theological boundaries. According to Timothy Weber (1991), though, it is important that the tradition be viewed in both lights, since "evangelicalism is both a set of theological convictions and an ethos" (p. 13).

In the sense that the movement can be captured theologically, evangelical Protestants hold to the gospel of Christ, which, according to Carl Henry (1990), is "the scripturally anticipated-and-fulfilled promise that God's sinless Messiah died in the place of otherwise doomed sinners, and moreover, that the crucified Redeemer arose bodily from the dead to resurrection life as helmsman of the eternal moral and spiritual world" (p. 76). In other words, humankind, estranged from its Creator due to its rebellion, finds itself in need of the intervention of Jesus Christ, whose sacrificial death on the cross and subsequent resurrection promise to redeem and reconcile humans to God both in this present age and for all eternity. This good news is the capstone of historic Christianity. In addition to (and often inseparable from) this gospel, evangelicals hold to other historical beliefs of the Christian Church as well, including:

(a) the eternal preexistence of the Son as the second person of the one God;
(b) the incarnation of God the Son in man as the divine-human person—two natures in one person; (c) the virgin birth, the means by which God the Son

entered into the human race and, without ceasing to be fully God, became also fully man; (d) the sinless life of Christ while sharing the life and experiences of alien men apart from sin; (e) the supernatural miracles of Christ as acts of his compassion and signs of his divine nature; (f) Christ's authoritative teaching as Lord of the church; (g) the substitutionary atonement in which God did all that was needed to redeem man from sin and its consequences; (h) the bodily resurrection of Christ as the consummation of his redemptive work and the sign and seal of its validity; (i) the ascension and heavenly mission of the living Lord; (j) the bodily second coming of Christ at the end of the age; (k) the final righteous judgment of all mankind and the eternal kingdom of God; and (l) the eternal punishment of the impenitent and disbelieving wicked of the world. (Kantzer, 1975, pp. 53–54)

These essential truths are divinely revealed, evangelicals say, not through ecclesiastical tradition, but through the Bible (both Old and New Testaments) as the "Word of God." "As the inspired testimony of a perfect and supreme deity," evangelicals believe, "the Bible is itself perfect, inerrant (which is to say, entirely without error of any kind), and infallible with regard to all spiritual, ethical, and religious matters" (Hunter, 1983, p. 61).

It is obvious, however, that a religious movement consists of more than just the propositions it holds to be true, and evangelicalism is no exception. When one speaks of the ethos of evangelicalism, one must begin with the emphasis on personal conversion. In the evangelical tradition, salvation is an individual, voluntary matter, and many churchgoers (with the exception of those from an Anabaptist or Reformational-Confessional tradition) have experienced a definitive moment of conversion in which they made a conscious choice to "receive Jesus Christ as their personal Lord and Savior" and entered into a "walk with God" (Hunter, 1983, pp. 64–65). This applies to children raised in the tradition as well, who are usually encouraged to consciously "make the faith their own" at some point during their upbringing.

It is a rare occurrence to hear ordinary evangelicals describe their religious experience in sociological terms or to see them look for commonalities between Christianity and other religions. Instead, there is a sense that, although still possessing a fallen human nature, the infusion of God's grace means that Christians no longer think or act in the same way that others do. It is believed that there is something fundamentally different about the Christian, as he or she has become, in the words of Saint Paul in 2 Corinthians 5:17, a participant in the "new creation." Out of duty and gratitude to God and a desire that others experience that same life-changing renewal, evangelicals also place a strong emphasis on evangelization of the "lost," meaning those who have yet to experience a "personal relationship with Jesus Christ."

In the human quest for certainty, this conversion experience can often provide a strong epistemological foundation for belief. In addition, evangelical affirmation of the Bible as God's infallible revelation endows evangelicals with an even greater amount of assurance on religious matters (Wells, 1987). For evangelicals, the Bible is much more than a human creation. In educated circles, one will encounter exegesis of the Biblical text in light of the human author's purpose and the cultural conditions in which he wrote; for other evangelicals, however, the text is almost entirely a divine product free of the taint of time, place, or human touch, "dropped from heaven as a sacred meteor" (Spittler, 1985). This sure, unadulterated provision to evangelicals of specific information and guidance leads to a "certain epistemological style that tends to view the world through one religious truth" (Jelen & Wilcox, 1991, pp. 32–33).

Of course, for the Bible to be understood, it must also be interpreted. Many ordinary evangelicals, however, focus exclusively on the meaning they have acquired from the text, often overlooking the role that they themselves played in arriving at that meaning. For this reason, one will usually hear evangelicals utter the words, "The Bible says. . ." instead of "We understand the Bible to say. . . ." For evangelicals, the ease with which the meaning of a text is ascertained is usually attributed to a combination of the guidance of the Holy Spirit and the self-evident nature of the text itself. That the Bible "means what it says" indicates evangelicals' use of either a literal or selectively literal hermeneutic in which the majority of textual passages are taken at face value, as actual historical events or imperatives, rather than as symbolic or allegorical representations. According to James Davison Hunter (1983),

> Concerning ethical, moral, and historical matters, the Bible is to be understood literally. Only in the poetic imagery (for example, in the Psalms, Proverbs, Song of Solomon, and parts of the Revelation of St. John) is the metaphorical nature of the Bible acknowledged. No part of the Bible is ever regarded as mythical, folkloric, or imaginary. (pp. 61–62)

For evangelicals, interpretation is heavily influenced by pastors and fellow believers in the local church (as an extension of the denomination), and by prominent parachurch leaders, all of whom set the parameters in which viable readings of Scripture fall (Boone, 1989; Ellison & Bartkowski, 1996). Within those guidelines, however, it is seen as each believer's responsibility to make up his or her own mind as to what the Bible means. As Stephen Warner (1988) states,

> Though evangelicals are not unanimous about a six-day creation, they profess to believe in a literal resurrection of Jesus, in Jesus' miracles as facts, and in his active love for them today. Evangelicals do not seek demythologized or

symbolic interpretations of these ideas, and thus there is little need for a
clergy with esoteric learning to provide them. Each person is his or her own
priest, and interpretations of religious experience are as often amazingly creative as they are startlingly naïve. None of this is to deny the role of the clergy
in promoting Biblical knowledge or supplying exegesis of texts, but it is to say
that the community of ordinary believers can speak about their faith with
confidence, because its formulae mean what they say. (p. 291)

Even if evangelicals do not always agree about specific passages or issues,
it is understood that, once the correct interpretation has been determined,
the reader and the community possess ultimate truth. In fact, for evangelicals, the very nature of truth itself is of great significance. In evangelical
educational circles one often hears individuals voicing opposition to relativistic notions of truth prevalent in society at large. Truth is absolute, and
through the Bible (and to a lesser extent, through personal religious experience) the evangelical knows what it is. If there were to exist even one
proven error in the original Biblical manuscripts, the veracity and trustworthiness of the whole of Scripture would be undermined, and the Bible
would no longer serve as pure divine revelation on which one could confi-
dently place one's faith. Thus, devout evangelicals imagine themselves
"either steadfast in absolute truth or whirling in the vortex of nihilism"
(Boone, 1989, p. 24), and without hesitation choose the former.

   With this sense of certitude and emphasis on evangelism, one would
expect to find evangelicals perpetually engaged in sharp disagreement
with those holding opposing truth claims. Although this does occasionally
occur, as evidenced by highly publicized "culture war" clashes, open conflict between individuals is not the norm in American public life. This can
be partially explained by the modern phenomenon of the privatization of
religion, in which faith is pushed to the margins of society, removed from
public discourse and relegated to the private sphere (Berger, 1969; Hunter,
1987; see C. Smith, 1998, for other factors related specifically to evangelicalism). In the public realm, what remains is what sociologist Robert Bellah
(1967) and others have called a "civil religion" devoid of potentially offensive beliefs and infused instead with general moral principles and loyalty to
the American state. One is allowed to believe whatever one wants in private, but in the public sphere there exists a "religion of civility" (Cuddihy,
1978, p. 1) in which individuals are not only expected to be "tolerant of
others" but also "tolerable to others" (Hunter, 1987, p. 152).

   In a multicultural society like the United States, with shameful memo-
ries such as the enslavement of Africans and the destruction and removal
of American Indians so salient in the national psyche, we bear the sober
responsibility not to repeat the past. Thus, the failure to affirm the dignity
of other individuals and cultural subgroups has become one of the greatest
sins our culture can imagine. However, when the merit of an individual's or

group's ideas, beliefs, and practices becomes inextricably equated with that dignity, tolerance can become a form of moral relativism in which one must accept differing views to be just as good as one's own or risk being labeled intolerant (Cromartie, 2001; Taylor, 1994; Woodberry & Smith, 1998). If this is how tolerance is defined, then certainly many evangelicals are highly intolerant people, since they hold their beliefs quite firmly and deem them to be superior to other beliefs they could potentially hold.

On the other hand, if one frames tolerance in terms of supporting the civil liberties of others to believe and worship as they see fit, then a somewhat different picture of evangelicals emerges. Like most of their fellow citizens, the majority of evangelicals see America as a Christian nation due to its Protestant heritage (R. Wuthnow, personal communication, June 6, 2005). Today 9 in 10 evangelicals believe that the United States was founded on Christian principles and owes its past strength to its faith in God, and 4 out of 5 are in favor of symbolically maintaining this through the teaching of the Ten Commandments in public schools (R. Wuthnow, personal communication, June 6, 2005). However, contrary to a popular conception that evangelicals want a "Christian America" in which Christian beliefs are imposed on others, Christian Smith (1998) finds that 67% of self-identified evangelicals also say that they "try hard not to offend people with their Christian views." Additional findings support this, including a survey at evangelical colleges by James Penning and Corwin Smidt (2002) in which 88% of students agree that "people should be free to believe what they want, even if it is very different from what I believe."

Although past research has claimed that both religion and conservativism lead to civil intolerance (Smidt & Penning, 1982; Stouffer, 1955; Sullivan, Piereson, & Marcus, 1982), several methodological limitations should lead researchers to limit the amount of credence they give to some of these findings (Woodberry & Smith, 1998). For example, in certain studies, tolerance scales measure attitudes toward many secular and left-wing target groups such as atheists, feminists, communists, and homosexuals but omit religious and right-wing target groups such as the Religious Right, homeschoolers, fundamentalists, and anti-abortion protestors that might be offensive to those on the liberal end of the spectrum (Busch, 1998; Smidt & Penning, 1982; Sullivan et al., 1982; Woodberry & Smith, 1998). Moreover, these surveys gauge only attitudes, leaving open the possibility that actual behavior of respondents may be quite different than the views they express (Wald, 1997).

With regards to race and ethnicity, it appears that evangelicals are no less tolerant of Jews, blacks, Hispanics, Asians, or immigrants than are other Americans (Davis & Robinson, 1996; T. W. Smith, 1996), although evangelicals are less likely than other Judeo-Christian religious adherents or the general American populace to desire a stronger cultural presence for each of these groups (R. Wuthnow, personal communication, July 22, 2005). As for non-Christian groups, research is mixed on the question of whether evangelicals are any less willing to support the civil liberties of those who believe and act differently than they do (Busch, 1998; Jelen & Wilcox, 1990; T. W. Smith, 1996; Tamney & Johnson, 1997; Wilcox & Jelen, 1990; R. Wuthnow, personal communication, June 6, 2005).

On the whole, it does appear that evangelicals are somewhat less tolerant than the larger American population, although the difference is much less when controls are introduced for age, education level, and region (Karpov, 2002; Reimer & Park, 2001; Tamney & Johnson, 1997; Wilcox & Jelen, 1990; Woodberry & Smith, 1998). It appears that younger cohorts display more tolerance than older ones, although they remain less tolerant than their Catholic and mainline Protestant counterparts (Reimer & Park, 2001). Conservative Protestants also display a greater variance in tolerance attitudes than the general population (Gay & Ellison, 1993), meaning that while many evangelicals are highly tolerant, one does find significantly intolerant attitudes in fundamentalist circles (Corbett, 1991; Green, Guth, Kellstedt, & Smidt, 1994; Kirkpatrick, 1993; Tuntiya, 2005; Wilcox & Jelen, 1990). Additionally, one finds a greater degree of intolerance among those who feel threatened or marginalized by other societal forces and entities (Green et al., 1994; Sullivan et al., 1982; see Marcus, Sullivan, Theiss-Morse, & Wood, 1995, for a discussion of how perceived threat influences civil liberties judgments). When these other societal forces happen to be religious communities of Muslims, Hindus, and Buddhists, one finds that evangelicals are significantly more likely than other Christians and non-Christians to say that these relatively new American groups pose a threat to the country's traditional values (R. Wuthnow, personal communication, July 23, 2005).

It is sometimes held that belief in one absolute truth leads to a dogmatic intolerance of others' points of view (Jelen & Wilcox, 1990). As we have seen, many evangelicals feel called to share their faith with others, even if it means that Christianity is deemed superior to other worldviews from the outset. After all, according to most evangelicals, all ideas are not created equal, and Christian beliefs about ultimate reality are true not just for the person that holds them, but for the rest of the world as well, whether that world accepts them or not. Following this line of thought, Christianity is deemed not just best for evangelicals, but for everyone (R. Wuthnow, personal communication, June 6, 2005). For those conservative Christians who hold theocratic beliefs, this does indeed lead to a greater intolerance of other political views (Karpov, 2002).

For the majority of evangelicals, however, the establishment of an explicitly Christian America is not currently on their agenda (C. Smith, 2000). Since many evangelicals know that all legislation is in some fashion value-laden, and that someone's views must be normative, one finds 60% of self-identified evangelicals and fundamentalists agreeing that "Christian morality should be the law of the land, even though not all Americans are Christians," at the very same time that 61% of the same sample affirm that "People have the right to live by their own moralities, even if they are not Christian moralities" (C. Smith, 1998, p. 128). Thus, evangelicals see Christian values as the best grounding for society, while allowing that not everyone should be compelled to abide by them. In fact, religious beliefs are not something that should ever be forced upon someone, because evangelicals believe very strongly that the Christian faith must be freely chosen if it is to be true faith. Hence, there is something quite civil about evangelical presentations of the gospel today. Partly out of a desire not to put undue pressure on others, evangelicals engage in a "polite" evangelism that "avoids accentuation of the offensiveness of the Gospel" (Marsden, 1975, p. 129) and deemphasizes aspects such as "heresy, sin, immorality, and paganism, and themes of judgment, divine wrath, damnation, and hell" (Hunter, 1987, p. 183). Epitomized in recent history in the crusades of the Reverend Billy Graham, this approach is markedly less doctrinal and confrontational in tone than that found in evangelicalism's early days, as represented by 18th-century theologian Jonathan Edwards's famous sermon *Sinners in the Hands of an Angry God* (Wolfe, 2003).

Whereas evangelicals affirm the right for others to choose their eternal destiny, many suffer internal anguish over the eventual torment they believe non-Christian relatives and friends will experience after death. Although a majority of evangelicals today comply with expected norms of public religious civility and avoid mention of hell as strategically ineffective, "saving the lost" nevertheless remains a central component of evangelical Protestant Christianity. This can be seen in a study conducted by the Princeton Religious Research Center for use by the periodical *Christianity Today* in which 51.3% of evangelicals consider sharing their faith their top priority and 53.1% claim to have done so on at least a monthly basis (Hunter, 1983). Penning and Smidt (2002) find that 21% of evangelical college students say that they share their faith at least weekly. In a study of the wider population, C. Smith (1998) finds that 91% of American self-identified evangelicals and fundamentalists state that converting people to Jesus Christ is "very important" and that 87% of them have shared their faith during a given 2-year period. Corroborating these findings is a recent poll conducted for *Religion & Ethics NewsWeekly* and *U.S. News & World Report* in which 90% of evangelicals agree that it is "important to spread [their] faith" and 80% affirm that it is "important to convert others" (Greenberg Quinlan Rosner Research, 2004). Fully 63% of evangelicals in this poll say that they "talk to others about [their] belief in Jesus Christ" on a weekly basis and 68% have "told teens or adults explicitly about how they could become a Christian" in the previous 2 years.

That evangelism plays such a prominent role in the daily life of parishioners, however, is not indisputable. A recent survey by sociologist Robert Wuthnow finds that although 95% of those affiliated with evangelical churches say that it is important to share their faith with non-Christians, less than half claim more than one or two attempts to persuade a non-Christian to convert to Christianity in the preceding year (personal communication, June 6, 2005). While 80% of evangelical churchgoers say that Christianity is the best way to understand God, a remarkable 43% of this group believe that Christianity is not the best way for everybody, but only for them personally. In two surveys of parishioners from approximately 2,000 predominantly evangelical churches who requested their consultation services, T-NET, an organization dedicated to the reform of the evangelical church, finds that "The average 'evangelical' church in America wins 1.67 persons (less than 2) to Christ and their church each year for every 100 persons who attend that church," not exactly a robust figure considering the centrality of evangelism to the identity of conservative Protestants. In addition, T-Net claims that "Only 11% of [evangelical] church members have shared the gospel even once in the last year, and 33% have never shared the gospel with anyone" (T-NET, 2003; B. Gilliam, personal communication, January 30, 2003).

It must also be noted that the extent to which evangelism is or is not occurring depends on what qualifies as sharing one's faith. "Previously, many American evangelicals believed it was the responsibility of evangelicals to witness verbally to non-Christians at virtually every opportunity; now there is greater emphasis on less verbal and more extended lifestyle evangelism approaches" (Penning & Smidt, 2002, p. 167). This latter method, which C. Smith (2000) calls "strategic relationalism" or a "personal influence strategy," consists of a conscious attempt to influence others in a patient, noncoercive manner through the medium of interpersonal relationships, impressing non-Christians with lives that are good examples. According to Alan Wolfe (2003), this approach "is a good fit for religions that seek to maintain historic commitments to spreading the word but to do so in ways that avoid any direct confrontation with the built-in individualism of contemporary American culture" (p. 192). This assessment is borne out by the statistics, as fully 97% of evangelicals agree that "the best way they can spread [their] faith is by setting a good example for others to follow" (Greenberg Quinlan Rosner Research, 2004). For evangelicals, the components of this model life are twofold: abstention from vice (obscenity, drunkenness, pre- and extra-marital sexual activity, etc.) and manifestation of the "fruit of the Spirit" found in Galatians 5:22 (love, joy, peace, patience, kindness, goodness, faithfulness, gentleness, and self-control).

While it is probably fair to say that while some highly-committed evangelicals are actively involved in public evangelism, many share their faith only when the opportunity falls in their lap and are otherwise "content with living a good life while hoping that others notice" (Wolfe, 2003, p. 254).

To sum up the preceding discussion, according to theologian Allister McGrath (1996), evangelicalism entails:

> (a) a focus, both devotional and theological, on the person of Jesus Christ, especially his death on the cross; (b) the identification of Scripture as the ultimate authority in matters of spirituality, doctrine and ethics; (c) an emphasis upon conversion or a "new birth" as a life-changing religious experience; (d) a concern for sharing the faith, especially through evangelism. (p. 22)

In addition to providing a solid synopsis of the tradition, this definition is later employed to establish the evangelical status of the high school student participants in the case study portion of this work.

CHAPTER 3

AN HISTORICAL OVERVIEW OF THE AMERICAN EVANGELICAL MOVEMENT AND ITS ROLE IN EDUCATION

As seen in the preceding chapter, American evangelicalism is a diverse religious movement with a theology marked by an emphasis on personal conversion and salvation through the atoning death and resurrection of Jesus Christ, a reliance on the divine word of the Bible, and a burden for sharing the gospel with others. Although this theology is derived from historic Christianity, particularly from the European Protestant Reformation, the three subsets of the modern evangelical movement (fundamentalism, neo-evangelicalism, and Pentecostalism) have also been shaped by the American context from which they arose. Their history in American life has been one marked by periods of both social influence and irrelevance, and of alliance and conflict with both secular and religious movements, including the other members within the evangelical movement itself.

A BRIEF HISTORY OF AMERICAN EVANGELICALISM

Evangelical Protestant Christianity has its roots in North America from the inception of the British colonies in the New World. While the term "evan-

American Evangelicals and Religious Diversity, pages 25–39
Copyright © 2006 by Information Age Publishing
All rights of reproduction in any form reserved.

gelical" had been used previously by the German reformer Martin Luther to distinguish the new alternative to Catholicism formed during the Protestant Reformation (Hill, 1989; Kellstedt, Green, Smidt, & Guth, 1996), it first became widely popular in America during religious revivals of the 18th century (T. L. Smith, 1987). Because the great majority of founding settlers were Protestants, the colonies had from its outset a Protestant, though not yet fully evangelical, bent (Noll, 2000a). Prior to 1690, the colonial religious scene was dominated by the Anglican Church (later to become the Episcopal Church), with its heart in Virginia, and the Puritan Congregationalists of New England (Butler, 2003), a group from which the evangelical movement would eventually draw much of its theology.

Although many evangelical Christians today have a highly romanticized view of colonial religiosity, this view needs a bit of nuance. For the founders of Puritan society, religious motivations were indeed central to their settlement in the Americas, but successive generations did not display the same spiritual fervor as their predecessors. Moreover, the high churches of Anglicanism never reached out much to the masses, and with the expansion of settlers into the frontier, much of the population lacked both formal religious instruction and zeal.

This changed considerably in the years following 1690 with a series of developments, the first being a diversification of the American religious scene (Butler, 2003). Before 1690, a full 90% of colonial congregations were either Anglican or Congregationalist. During the next century, Presbyterians, Baptists, Quakers, and Lutherans all emerged as significant actors on the religious stage. Others, such as the Mennonites, Moravians, and a nascent Methodist movement, found their place as well. Whereas the Congregationalists and Anglicans focused primarily on established urban areas, many of the new denominational groups such as the Baptists and Methodists expanded their outreach to include those removed from the regional centers of colonial life.

The second development to impact the colonial religious scene was a series of religious revivals known as the Great Awakening (Butler, 2003). Led by preachers such as George Whitefield, Gilbert Tennent, and Jonathan Edwards, the pietism that had originated in parts of Europe in the 1690s and early 1700s leaped across the Atlantic, surfacing first in Massachussetts, then in New Jersey, and then throughout the middle colonies in the 1730s and 1740s. This brand of religion, which encouraged intense personal introspection and individual spiritual transformation, caught hold of the colonial imagination, aided by a new enthusiastic style of preaching. Whereas previously sermons had been read in a monotone fashion from a set of notes, George Whitefield initiated the use from the pulpit of theatrical techniques to communicate dramatic messages of mankind's sin, separation from God, and subsequent need for repentance and redemption (Stout, 1991).

As the Revolution approached, revivalism waned, only to explode again at the beginning of the 19th century and to last for nearly 70 years in a series of revivals known today as the Second Great Awakening (Wacker, 2003). Although religion became politically disestablished in both national and state constitutions during this period, it found a growing place in the lives of individual Americans. Facilitating this development was a disciplined corps of Methodist circuit riders, led by Francis Asbury, who traversed the Western frontier drawing people to camp meetings and into the swelling ranks of the church by means of intensely fiery sermons. In the Northeast, Presbyterian-Congregationalist preacher Charles Grandison Finney recognized the power, not just of the divine, but of careful planning and orchestration of the revival experience. Breaking from the Puritan heritage, Finney also stressed the free will and ability of individuals to respond on their own to God's mercy, a view that would become predominant in evangelical circles up to the present day. Although not as intellectual as Finney, the Baptists likewise stressed the need for individuals to decide in favor of Christ's offer of salvation. With this precept as a part of their theology, they too flexed their missionary muscles during the period prior to the Civil War, becoming one of the largest American denominations, second at the time only to the Methodists. Overall, church membership grew from no more than 20% in the Revolutionary era to between 30 and 40% by the 1940s (Butler, 2003).

This evangelical revival led not only to the saving of souls and an increase in church membership, but also to the inauguration of social reform movements, particularly in the North (T. L. Smith, 1957). Encouraged by their postmillennial view that Christ would return again and initiate his reign following the establishment of the Kingdom of God on earth, evangelicals set themselves to remedy a number of social ills such as alcoholism, slavery, illiteracy, prostitution, and poverty (T. L. Smith, 1957; Wacker, 2003). By the middle of the 19th century, a confident Protestant establishment wielded great social influence, seeing themselves as the moral custodians of society (Wacker, 1984).

Ironically, this activism was occurring at the very same time that Protestant churches were beginning to lose control over the provision of education in America. Prior to the advent of nonsectarian public schooling in the mid-1800s, education had been a decentralized matter in which educational decision making rested primarily with parents (Rippa, 1992), who often chose to send their children to the local school. In the colonial period, education in the southern and middle colonies was by no means public, but was rather composed of a mixture of private sectarian schools, apprenticeships, and free schools for orphans and paupers' children. In

Puritan New England, however, the ability of individuals to read and understand the Scriptures was deemed so important that the education of every child was mandatory. At the bidding of the Church, the state required New England towns very early in their history to establish primary schools supported by the taxpayers of these communities (Pfeffer & Stokes, 1964). Although these schools were public, they were still sectarian, with religious education provided for pupils emphasizing Puritan doctrine and practice (Rippa, 1992). At the secondary level, colonial education consisted originally of Latin grammar schools, which specialized in instruction in the classics and preparation for colleges such as Harvard, which in turn prepared individuals for leadership in the church. As time passed and middle-class merchants sought a more "practical" education for their children, small private schools and larger academies arose to provide instruction in English and in a number of more vocationally useful subjects. Even so, these schools provided a healthy dose of religious instruction in their courses of study.

Fearing that this religious instruction served to fragment rather than unify the nation, 19th-century educational reformers such as Horace Mann set about to create a common school system. This system, administered by the state, would be open to all children. Its mission would still be religious, but it would be free from sectarian teachings, which the reformers believed led to social conflict (Glenn, 1988). Appointed to the newly created Massachusetts Board of Education in 1837, Mann envisioned a society united under a common moral vision of democracy and progress. For Mann, a Unitarian, humankind was not tainted by original sin as the Puritans held, but was inherently good and improvable if provided the right education. So instead of instructing children on the particular dogma of various Protestant traditions, children were to be thoroughly infused with general moral principles, which Mann saw as the essence of Christianity and the necessary underpinnings of American popular democracy.

Reaction by Protestants to the proposed common school system was mixed (Glenn, 1988). Although not opposed to the education of all students, many protested the stripping of educational decision-making power from parents and its subsequent transfer to the state. Also, since among the "sectarian particulars" to be eliminated from the common school curriculum were the sinful nature of humanity and the death and resurrection of Christ, many orthodox Protestants objected on theological grounds that what would be taught was not "nonsectarian," but rather liberalism and Unitarianism. Strategically, Mann and the other educational reformers were largely able to counter these objections by accentuating those things that orthodox Protestants would find agreeable, chief among them the reading of the Bible in the schools, albeit without denominational interpretation.

Since much of Protestant identity hinged on individual interpretation of Scripture, this served to assuage a portion, but not all, of their concern.

For leaders of some prominent Episcopal, Presbyterian, and Quaker churches, these measures were not enough, and they set out to create their own educational institutions (Curran, 1954). Many of these endeavors were ill-conceived, however, and of those religious schools begun in the 19th century, only those of more insular communities such as the German Missouri Synod Lutherans, the Dutch Reformed, and the Seventh Day Adventists had enough staying power to survive the nationwide sweep toward public schooling (Glenn, 1988; Reese, 1985). For other denominations, particularly the Congregationalists, Baptists, and Methodists, most members believed that the right course of action was to support, often vigorously, the nascent common school movement (Curran, 1954). In the words of T. L. Smith (1967),

> An evangelical consensus of faith and ethics had come so to dominate the national culture that the majority of Protestants were now willing to entrust the state with the task of educating children, confident that education would be "religious" still. The sects identified their common beliefs with those of the nation, their mission with America's mission. (p. 687)

Somewhat earlier in the 1800s, Sunday schools had been established by Protestant churches throughout the nation to evangelize and provide a rudimentary education for poor children, instructing them in the "three R's" and the Christian morality necessary for proper comportment as American citizens (Kennedy, 1966; Lynn & Wright, 1980). Initially intended for the unchurched, soon the children of church members also began attending these weekend schools to avail themselves of the explicitly religious instruction provided there. Convinced that their children were receiving adequate religious training, most evangelicals viewed the side-by-side coexistence of Sunday schools and common schools as a complementary and agreeable arrangement (Carper, 1984; Jorgenson, 1987; Kennedy, 1966; Lynn, 1964; Tyack, 1966).

For those Protestants still undecided, a key factor that compelled many to join the emerging public school movement was their fear of the mass of Roman Catholic immigrants arriving from Europe (Glenn, 1988; Reese, 1982). In the minds of many Protestants, this incursion of people with a primary allegiance to the pontiff of Rome was a threat to democracy and the American way of life. While Protestant church-based Sunday schools had been instrumental in converting many Catholic children, public schooling looked like a much more promising alternative for assimilating Catholics into what many reformers considered a Protestant nation.

Catholics, however, found the "nonsectarian" common schools undesirable. Although the common schools were never subordinate to Protestant churches, they were closely allied with them and practiced Protestant prayers, recited the Protestant version of the Ten Commandments, and, above all, encouraged private interpretation of a Protestant version of Scripture (Curran, 1954; Glenn, 1988). At first, Catholics objected to the schools and their curriculum as too Protestant, but as more and more specific Protestant practices were stripped away, Catholics charged that the common schools were now "godless." Most Catholics wanted to assimilate into American society, but did not want to give up their religious identity to do so. Thus, as they were able financially, Catholics began to create their own parochial school system. As they did so, they were accused of hypocrisy for seeking to make common schools less Protestant while, at the same time, trying to keep their children out of them. When Archbishop John Hughes of New York called upon Catholics in 1952 to demand public funding for parochial education, the reaction of Protestants was strong, with the vast majority of orthodox Protestants rallying behind the common school cause in an effort to maintain a broadly Protestant societal ethos.

This desire on the part of some Protestant leaders to prescribe the spiritual direction of the nation can be seen even more overtly in the 1863 proposal of the National Reform Association, a body composed of 11 Protestant denominations, to amend the preamble to the United States Constitution (W. S. Green, 2003). The proposed amendment read:

> We the people of the United States, humbly acknowledging Almighty God as the source of all authority and power in civil government, and the Lord Jesus Christ as the Ruler among the nations, His revealed will as the supreme law of the land, in order to constitute a Christian government... (Stokes, 1950, pp. 584–585)

The measure, of course, was defeated, and the United States retained the disestablished and voluntary religious nature that has characterized its history as a nation. In fact, events such as the failed amendment and the concessions on the matter of public schools demonstrate that, although they wielded great influence, traditional Protestants were not quite as powerful or as numerous as their leaders sometimes thought they were. Instead of constituting a popular majority, according to historian Robert Handy (1991), "[B]y 1880, the leading Protestant denominations—Baptist, Congregational, Disciples of Christ, Episcopal, Lutheran, Methodist, Presbyterian, Quaker, and Reformed—had an estimated total of close to nine million members, or about 18 percent of the population" (p. 8). Although a significant number, these figures, along with defeats such as those illustrated above, show that even though Protestantism was extremely influential, it could not by itself chart the course of the nation.

As America proceeded through the latter part of the 19th century, evangelical Protestants faced more challenges than just an influx of Catholic immigrants. Along with a growing industrialism and the shift of the U.S. population from rural areas to the cities came some disturbing philosophical and ideological trends (Marsden, 1991). First of all, the revolutionary ideas of Charles Darwin threatened the existing relationship between Protestant Christianity and science. Whereas the prevailing epistemological philosophy of Scottish Common Sense Realism had supported the idea that scientific study confirmed and illuminated God's design of his world, scientists now had a framework in which it became possible to conceive of a world entirely independent of a Creator (Marsden, 1980). Second, a new way of viewing Scripture called *higher criticism* (or *historical-literary criticism*) appeared on the American scene. This approach, which originated among the intelligentsia of Germany, called into question the historicity and truthfulness of many parts of the Biblical text. These developments led to significant changes in American culture. Although evangelical churches continued to grow at a record pace throughout the latter part of the 19th century, they were losing control of the scientific and academic sectors of American society.

Of course, Protestants did not give up their cultural influence willingly, but engaged their enemy in a cultural conflict that came to be known as the *fundamentalist–modernist controversy* (Marsden, 1980). During this time of crisis in the beginning of the 20th century, the Protestant church in America began to split in two. Liberals sought to preserve the faith by making accommodations to the spirit of the modern age (Hutchison, 1976), while conservatives dug trenches and declared an all-out war on the advancing forces of secularization. Between 1910 and 1915, oil magnates Lyman and Milton Stewart bankrolled the production of a series of 12 booklets and their widespread distribution throughout the country (Balmer, 2003; Marsden, 1980). Known collectively as *The Fundamentals*, these booklets attacked modernism and defended the "five points of fundamentalism," conservative doctrines such as biblical inerrancy, the virgin birth of Christ, Christ's substitutionary atonement and bodily resurrection, the authenticity of miracles, and premillenial dispensationalism. This final item referred to the idea that history was divided into a series of distinct eras, each with a different mode of divine interaction with humanity, that culminated with Christ's return to defeat the forces of evil and establish an earthly reign that would last for a thousand years (Carpenter, 1997; Marsden, 1980). Those who held to this compendium of beliefs became known as fundamentalists.

After many battles, replete with sermon slogans and scathing polemics, a highly symbolic blow was struck at the Scopes Monkey Trial of 1925. In this case, a Tennessee high school science teacher named John Scopes was charged with having taught the theory of biological evolution in the public school, in direct violation of a state law that had been passed that spring (Balmer, 2003; Marsden, 1980). In this famous courtroom drama, defense attorney Clarence Darrow succeeded in portraying prosecutor William Jennings Bryan and fundamentalists as intellectually backward and out of touch with life in the modern world. Although the traditional Protestants technically won the case, the aftermath showed that national media opinion had dethroned them as the rulers of culture and had supplanted them with secularism and Charles Darwin.

In what historian Timothy L. Smith has called the "Great Reversal," conservative Protestants, recognizing their defeat, began a retreat from a society now perceived as hostile to everything they held dear (Moberg, 1977). Whereas a century earlier they had been on the forefront of social reform, they now withdrew from the public arena. Having lost control of the northern Protestant denominations, they began to focus their efforts on establishing their own series of congregations, denominations, publishing houses, colleges, seminaries, and Bible institutes (Balmer, 2003; Carpenter, 1980, 1997; Marsden, 1980). During this time, elementary and secondary public schools were not yet deemed sufficiently "godless" to necessitate private alternatives, although it is estimated that between the 1920s and 1940s, around 150 conservative private Christian schools were founded (Carper, 1984).

Undoubtedly this withdrawal from the public square can be characterized as a defensive reaction by fundamentalists against modernism. In the eyes of modernists, this retreat was accompanied by an anti-intellectualism in which "the fundamentalists' loyalty to Jesus Christ often implied an uncritical adherence to their own confessions and a censorious stance toward contemporary intellectual challenges" (Phillips & Okholm, 1996, p. 9). However, according to historian Joel Carpenter (1980), "Fundamentalism bears all the marks of a popular religious movement which drew only part of its identity from opposition to liberal trends in the denominations. The movement [also] had its own ideology and program to pursue" (p. 74). For fundamentalists, this agenda was a continuation of the originally innovative coupling of premillenial dispensationalism with Princeton Theology, a rationalistic, scientific system that asserted the inerrancy of Scripture (Sandeen, 1967).

In the early 1940s there emerged from fundamentalism a group of "neo-evangelicals" led by Harold Ockenga, Charles Fuller, Carl Henry, and shortly thereafter the reverend Billy Graham, who would bring the evangelical tradition of religious revivals back to prominence in the latter half of the 20th century. In conscious opposition to the separatist posture of the fundamentalists, these neo-evangelicals sought to bring their influence to bear on the larger American society. Toward these ends, the National Association of Evangelicals, the periodical *Christianity Today*, Fuller Theological Seminary, Wheaton College, a host of world mission organizations, and the crusades of Billy Graham were launched (Carpenter, 1980, 1997). It is important to note that these neo-evangelicals, with the certainty of divinely revealed truth, emerged to evangelize, not to enter into dialogue. Unlike mainline denominations, which were often associated with the World Council of Churches and saw interreligious communication as part of their mission, evangelicals viewed ecumenical discourse as a suspect activity requiring conservatives to "compromise on truths they believe should not be compromised" (Davidson, 1985, p. 23) and thereby risk the blurring of theological boundaries.

In addition to fundamentalists and neo-evangelicals, the third prominent subset of evangelicalism, Pentacostalism, also finds a significant place in the last hundred years of America's religious history. Rivaling fundamentalists in separatist orientation, Pentacostals derive their moniker from a biblical episode that occurred on the Jewish day of Pentecost. On this day, the Biblical book of Acts records the Holy Spirit descending upon Christ's apostles and bestowing upon them the ability to preach the gospel message in languages comprehensible to those gathered from around the known world. In America, the Pentecostal movement began in the first decade of the 20th century with religious revivals in Kansas and then, most famously, in the Los Angeles Asuza Street revival of 1906 (Wacker, 2001).

Starting with these revivals, Pentecostal believers saw evidence of God's supernatural power manifested in the "baptism of the Holy Spirit," as evidenced by the presence of spiritual gifts such as divine healing, prophecy, ecstatic swooning called "being slain in the Spirit," and especially glossalalia, commonly known as "speaking in tongues" (Anderson, 1987; Wacker, 2001; Wilcox, 1996). Although several Pentecostal denominations were established, such as the Church of God in Christ and the Assemblies of God, in the years following World War II the influence of these "spirit-filled" believers was to spill over from these bodies into Roman Catholic, mainline, and neo-evangelical churches (Anderson, 1987; Wacker, 2001). Stressing an experiential union with God through the gifts of the Holy Spirit, this "charismatic movement" has joined Pentecostalism as one of the fastest growing segments of conservative Protestantism (Jones et al., 2002), further signifying evangelicalism's move away from the Puritan element of its heritage and its corresponding emphasis on doctrine toward the mystical, experiential side of the Christian tradition.

It is important to mention that things are not always rosy within the evangelical coalition. Although from the outside it might have appeared that evangelicalism for many years stood unified behind the figure of Billy Graham, this was a false impression (Noll, 2003), and today it is more obvious than ever that evangelicals are aware not only of their similarities, but of their differences as well. In fact, fraternal infighting between the various subsets of conservative Protestantism can be quite common (Wald, 1997), and religious adherents will at times define their own identity in opposition to the characteristics of other evangelical groups (Sikkink, 1998). For example, fundamentalists find repulsive the Pentecostal practice of speaking in tongues (Marsden, 1980; Wilcox, 1996). In turn, neo-evangelicals, having emerged out of fundamentalism to engage the wider society, do not hold in very high esteem the insular nature of many fundamentalist and Pentecostal communities (Woodberry & Smith, 1998). In the political realm, both fundamentalist Jerry Falwell and Pentecostal Pat Robertson experienced difficulty at various times in the 1970s and 1980s in mobilizing the other's political supporters (Jelen, 1993; Wilcox, 1988). It follows, then, that with regard to schooling we should find a number of different views among conservative Protestants as they wrestle with the vexing issue of how to relate to the wider American culture in their daily lives and in the education of their children.

EVANGELICAL SCHOOLS TODAY

Historically supporters of public schools, many evangelicals still see participation in public schools as a religious calling (Sikkink, 2001). However, in the years since the mid-1960s, it would seem that many evangelicals have reevaluated that stance and chosen new educational alternatives (Carper, 2001). In the last 40 years, America has witnessed a dramatic increase in the founding of Christian day schools (Cooper & Dondero, 1991) in what James Carper (1984) calls the "first *widespread* secession from public schools since the establishment of Catholic schools in the nineteenth century" (p. 111, original emphasis). Although it is difficult to get a precise count of the number of conservative Christian schools and pupils since some schools are not affiliated with accrediting organizations (Carper, 1984; Sikkink, 2001), it would appear that there are currently around 9,000 schools with approximately 1.3 million students (Sikkink, 2001), a number comprising between 20 and 25% of all private school enrollments (Carper, 1999; Sikkink, 2001; Wagner, 1997). In one estimate, private Protestant schools make up nearly 14% of all schools, with total budgets of over $5 billion (Hamilton, 2000). Whereas most Christian day schools are small, with nearly 70% enrolling fewer than 150 students, there do exist some with over 2,000 pupils (Carper & Layman, 2002; Cooper & Dondero, 1991; Lockerbie, 1996; Sikkink, 2001). Nearly two-thirds of these schools offer both elementary and secondary instruction, while one-third teach only at the elementary level, and a mere 3% offer a high school education exclusively (Sikkink, 2001). As for geographical location, these evangelical schools, either founded by individual evangelical churches or local interdenominational associations (Carper, 1984), can be found throughout the various regions of the United States.

Although some of the most prominent studies have dealt with fundamentalist schools (Ammerman, 1987; Peshkin, 1986; Rose, 1988), recent attention has been called to the diversity of conservative Protestant schools (Parsons, 1987; Sikkink, 2001). Whereas fundamentalist schools are often seen as comprising part of a "total world" that includes the church and home (Peshkin, 1986, 1987), neo-evangelical and Pentecostal schools display some theological differences from fundamentalism that affect the character of their institutions. All evangelical schools seek to ground their institutions on the Bible, but the many voices found in Scripture can be used to support a wide variety of educational practices (Sikkink, 2001), even if the financially precarious position of many schools compels them to avoid extreme or controversial positions in order not to offend segments of their tuition-paying clientele (Wagner, 1997). For example, fundamentalist schools tend to use curricula designed specifically for Christian schools in order to promote a Christian worldview, while neo-evangelical schools are more likely to use secular textbooks and engage them critically as part of the learning process. In doing so, neo-evangelicals seek not a retreat from the world, but the "integration of faith and learning" or "active engagement with and critique of modern society and culture from a Christian perspective" (Sikkink, 2001, pp. 4–5). To give another example of the different educational possibilities, some schools are "evangelistic" schools in which non-Christian students are admitted in the hope that they will embrace the faith of those around them, while others are "discipleship" schools that restrict admission to those who have made a profession of faith in Christ and seek to train them up into mature Christian believers (Rose, 1988).

The fact that many of these independent Christian schools initially sprang up in the South in the wake of the 1954 Supreme Court decision *Brown v. Board of Education* that mandated racial integration in public schools has led some scholars to label conservative Christian schools "desegregation academics" (Nevin & Bills, 1976). In the South today it is possible to find counties in which public and private school attendance is divided sharply along racial lines (Menendez, 1998). Likewise, the current lack of racial diversity in most conservative Christian schools has fostered the notion that these schools exist as a means to circumvent educational desegregation policies (Miner, 1998; Nordin & Turner, 1980). While it is possible that some schools have served such a purpose and that current schools may perpetuate the racial divide in certain ways, to attribute these schools' existence solely to matters of race is to miss the primary motivations of those who attend them (Reese, 1985; Skerry, 1980; Turner, 1979).

Although one scholar claims that the lack of growth in private school enrollment during the time periods following the *Brown* decision means that few people were fleeing the public schools due to desegregation (Jeynes, 2003), this assertion is questionable since at this time the Catholic schooling movement was experiencing a steep decline in enrollment, which more than offset the rapidly growing yet relatively tiny conservative Protestant school movement (Cooper & Dondero, 1991; Kraushaar, 1972; Lines, 1988; Nordin & Turner, 1980). Thus, it seems that the number of Catholics entering the public schools at the same time that Protestants were beginning to exit statistically hide the growth of this segment of private education. For this reason, defense against racism on the part of evangelical schools lies not primarily in statistics, but in plentiful qualitative data of Christian day schools that show an absence of racist curriculum and instruction (Skerry, 1980), the sincere efforts of administrators trying to increase the racial diversity of their schools (Sikkink, 2001), and parents giving other reasons for enrolling their children (Ballweg, 1980; Carper, 1984; Evearitt, 1979; Gleason, 1980; Holmes, 1983; Short, 2001; Turner, 1979).

A better explanation for the rise of conservative Protestant schools is found in two other Supreme Court decisions, namely those in 1962 and 1963 that halted mandatory prayer and devotional Bible reading in the public schools (Jeynes, 2003; Parsons, 1987). As long as public schools remained nominally religious and were not undermining the spiritual and moral training provided at home, many parents were content to keep their children enrolled. Although the "de-Protestantization" of American education had been a long and gradual process beginning as early as the 18th century (Dunn, 1958; Nietz, 1952), the elimination of mandatory prayer and Bible reading served for many conservative Christians as unambiguous signs that God had been removed forcibly from the public square. In its place was not neutrality, since evangelicals believe that no education is value-neutral (Sikkink, 2001), but rather the insidious philosophy of "secularism" or "secular humanism" (Carper, 1984; Neuhaus, 1984; Nordin & W. L. Turner, 1980; Volf, 2005). As David Sikkink (2001) has stated, "In the eyes of many Christian schoolers, they have not chosen to withdraw from American society; the culture and society have moved away from them" (p. 38).

Much of the dissatisfaction with public schools present today among evangelicals has to do with a perceived deemphasizing of the "three Rs" and a deteriorating moral climate stemming from the inability of many parents to provide proper moral training to their children (C. Smith, 2000). Nevertheless, all of the major subgroups of churchgoing evangelicals still view the educational philosophies of public schools as hostile to their moral and spiritual values, much more so than do mainline and liberal Protestants, Catholics, and the American population as a whole (Sik-kink, 1999). Since for most evangelical Christians the family is the normative setting where religious views and values are transmitted (Sik-kink, 2003; C. Smith, 2000), the perception that government is overstep-ping its bounds and usurping the parental right and responsibility to direct the content of their children's moral training has motivated many evangel-icals to pursue educational alternatives (Ballweg, 1980). When we also con-sider the rapidly increasing numbers of children who are being instructed at home, surpassing one million, it is obvious that a significant number of conservative Christians are disenchanted with the public educational sys-tem as it currently stands (Carper, 2001).

What one sees in the decision of evangelical parents to forego a public school education for their children in favor of a private alternative depends on the lens through which one views their actions. As we have seen, it is very feasible to see the decision primarily as a fearful reaction against certain cultural developments in American society. However, many parents who have enrolled their children in Christian schools would not frame their actions as fearful, but as proactive measures designed to foster spiritual growth in their daughters and sons. When viewed in light of the numerical growth of conservative Christian churches over the past 40 years, it may be that many of those people are taking their faith more seri-ously, which in this case means sacrificing financially in order to "train up a child in the way he should go." When parents state what they want out of a school, they consistently mention their desire for an academic experience that will form in their children the values, attitudes, beliefs, and practices of their faith (Ballweg, 1980; Carper, 1984; Evearitt, 1979; Gleason, 1980; Holmes, 1983; Short, 2001). As one parent puts it, his school "offers good academics, but the main thing is that it provides a Christian setting with Christian values. It's Christ-centered. It reinforces the Christian life and val-ues that our children get at home" (Gleason, 1980, p. 103). This sentiment also meshes well with the stated goals of conservative Christian school administrators, who say that their primary educational goal is the religious development of pupils (Baker, Han, & Keil, 1996). Although basic literacy and academic rigor are also important, it seems that "Christian schools see their first mission as religious socialization, with moral character as a byproduct of that mission" (Sikkink, 2001, p. 24).

For evangelical parents, the instilling of faith in their children ranks near the very top of life's priorities, and again this phenomenon can be viewed in two ways. For critics, particularly liberal pedagogues, communal religious and moral instruction amounts to indoctrination when only one of many possible alternatives is presented (van der Ven, 2000). In this account, evangelical parents do not want their children to be free, autono-mous moral agents, but rather to be copies of themselves (Balmer, 1989;

van der Ven, 2000). For proponents of religious socialization, however, the above criticisms fall on deaf ears. Most evangelicals believe that their children are autonomous and must exercise that freedom in "owning their own faith" if it is to be true faith. Due to the extreme consequence of eternal damnation for those who do not follow Christ, the effort to transmit a religious identity to the succeeding generation does take on added urgency for many evangelicals (Balmer, 1989). However, if parents have indeed experienced Christ's promise of "life more abundantly," they would be spiritually negligent and utterly heartless if they did not wish their child to experience the same. Thus, to be fair, we must acknowledge intertwined strands of both fearful and affirming concern in the hearts of evangelical parents and view the shift from a public to a Christian schooling alternative as both a reactionary and a proactive move.

At this point, it is important to remember that not all evangelicals are united in support for private Christian schools or opposition to public schools. Due to their "greater tension with the status quo at public schools" and the "much stronger boundary between their faith and 'the world'" (Sikkink, 2001, p. 39), Pentecostals are the most likely of the three primary evangelical subsets to oppose public schools (Sikkink, 1999). Fundamentalists, historically known for separation from the wider American culture, also display an aversion to public schools. Conversely, neo-evangelicals on the whole display support for public schools, believing that "Christians should keep their children in public schools as a witness and as sources of influence on non-Christians, the school, and the nation" (Sikkink, 2001, p. 39). In keeping with their strategy of "engaged orthodoxy," neo-evangelicals maintain their traditional theology yet venture into the public arena as "salt and light," as moral custodians dedicated to the uplift and moral preservation of society (C. Smith, 1998, 2000). Neo-evangelicals have a difficult time articulating exactly how individuals manage to achieve this effect, but they assume that a positive morality will permeate the institutions in which they are present (Sikkink, 2003). Some even believe that the more public schools decline, the more critical is their presence (C. Smith, 2000). Thus, "[neo-]evangelicals usually leave public schools reluctantly, and see Christian schools as a stopgap measure in these 'troubled' times" (Sikkink, 2001, p. 39). The growing legitimacy of Christian schools, however, forces upon neo-evangelical parents some difficult choices (C. Smith, 2000), and it seems that the historic commitment of neo-evangelicals to public schools may be waning.

Although the evangelical school movement is still relatively small when compared to public and Catholic schools, what does their rapid growth mean for the civil life of the nation? In a society drifting away from its Protestant moorings, how much do evangelicals see themselves as Americans? It appears that the relationship between the evangelical subculture and the wider society is an ambivalent one. Three-quarters of evangelicals say that they are part of mainstream American society, but three-quarters also say that they have to fight for their voices to be heard (Greenberg Quinlan Rosner Research, 2004). Two-thirds say that their religious faith has led them to volunteer in their communities, but 48% of evangelical Christians feel looked down upon by most Americans and 72% feel that the mass media is hostile toward their spiritual and moral values. Evangelicals sometimes speak of themselves as a "persecuted minority" (Oldfield, 1996), and yet often live in ways that are nearly indistinguishable from those of their neighbors (Sider, 2005). This dual sense of inclusion and exclusion, of being "in the world but not of the world," is critical to understanding the nature of American evangelicalism and its relation to society as a whole, and will recur periodically throughout the remainder of this work.

CHAPTER 4

RELIGION IN A PLURALISTIC WORLD

Secularization Theory, Religious Vitality, and the Relativization of Tradition

Although this book has thus far dealt specifically with American evangelical Christianity, it will now broaden the scope to examine the larger context of the Western world in which American evangelicalism finds its place. For evangelicalism and other organized religious traditions, the modern world is replete both with opportunities and significant challenges. Maintaining a hold on the religious imaginations of people is something to which religious communities must devote considerable efforts, and it is not at all clear whether their job is getting easier or growing more difficult as the world around them becomes more interconnected and religiously pluralistic.

SECULARIZATION THEORY

One of the hallmarks of modernized Western societies such as the United States is a fascination with cultural diversity. One can now peruse the religion section of any sizable American bookstore and find an abundance of literature on Buddhism, Islam, Judaism, Christianity, Hinduism, and New Age spiritualism. Although cultural diversity has existed in the United States from its earliest days (Butler, 1990; Butler, Wacker, & Balmer, 2003;

American Evangelicals and Religious Diversity, pages 41–66
Copyright © 2006 by Information Age Publishing
All rights of reproduction in any form reserved.

Eck, 2001, 2005; Hutchison, 2003), the range of religious options available to the average American today is both extensive and no longer restricted primarily to different shades of Christianity. Even if the number of non-Christian religious adherents is still a very small percentage of the total population (Kosmin, Mayer, & Keysar, 2001) and is commonly exaggerated (T. W. Smith, 2002), non-Christian religious groups do seem to have reached enough of a critical mass to make their presence felt in the architecture and civic life of many communities throughout the nation (Eck, 2001, 2002, 2005). In fact, it is claimed that the United States is now home to a greater number of religious groups than any other country in the world (Adherents.com, 2005; Eck, 2001). If this is true, what does it mean for the religious life of the country? Does this mean that religion in the United States is flourishing, albeit in a wider range of forms than two or three centuries ago? Or does it mean that religion is being diluted and losing its power as our society moves further and further from a common enframing of the world?

For many sociologists of the latter part of the 20th and early part of the 21st century, the dominant paradigm for explaining the relationship between religion and modernity has been that of *secularization theory.* In short, classical secularization theory holds that the modern world is not a friendly place for religion. There are many versions of the theory that explain why this is so, with each linking different aspects of modernity such as industrialization, urbanization, and scientific rationalism with purported religious declines at the levels of society, organizations, and individuals. According to one very influential version, since the continuance of one's belief system is dependent on *plausibility structures,* or social reinforcement from one's surroundings, as society becomes more culturally pluralistic, the traditional sacred canopy that has shielded religious believers will collapse, leading inevitably to a decline of faith in individuals and the weakening of their religious institutions (Berger, 1969). For proponents of this framework, the only hope of survival for traditional religious communities is to isolate themselves from the larger, pluralistic society in a desperate attempt to hold off the corrosive effects of modernity. It is in this light that the current proliferation of conservative private Christian schools is seen as an attempt to escape from the dangers of a world that is hostile to religious faith.

Very few secularization theorists are brash enough to predict religion's ultimate demise, such as anthropologist Anthony Wallace (1966) does when he states that the "evolutionary future of religion is extinction" (p. 264). Nearly all those currently favorable to the theory of secularization allow that religion will continue as part of modern societies and the lives of individuals, although all believe religion's grip to be weakening in one way or another. In recent years, however, a growing number of scholars have challenged the secularization paradigm, alleging that it is mistaken (1) in its empirical claims, (2) in its causal explanations for changes that have occurred, and (3) in its predictions for the future of traditional religion.

Secularization at the Macro Level

On a macro level, it is difficult to dispute that religion in the West no longer plays the role that it did in pre-Reformation Europe, the preferred point of comparison for most secularization theorists. For modern European, American, and Australian societies, the church–state relationship is markedly different than that which existed in Europe during the medieval period, when the Christian church was much more tightly bound to the state. According to Steve Bruce (2002), as long as societies were authoritarian, hierarchical, and shared a common worldview, there was little reason why Christianity could not be privileged at the societal level. However, as societies have become more democratic, egalitarian, and culturally diverse, they have "had to place social harmony before the endorsement of religious orthodoxy" (p. 17). This desire to avoid religious conflict has resulted in both the formal diminution of Christian authority and the development of increasingly nonreligious states.

In the United States, the passage of the Bill of Rights in 1789 ensured that there would be no national establishment of religion. How this clause from the First Amendment is to be interpreted is still a matter of fervent debate, as individuals and communities form alliances and utilize available resources in the historic struggle to determine how secular or religious the state will be (Monsma & Soper, 1997; C. Smith, 2003a). Proponents of the *strict separationism* enforced by the courts since the middle of the 20th century see the removal of any governmental support for religious organizations as the best way to maintain neutrality. This effectively relegates religious organizations to the private sphere, at least when it comes to issues such as funding and display of religious symbols in public spaces. Those in favor of *structural pluralism* counter that barring religious organizations per se from receiving governmental support is anything but neutral and instead privileges nontheistic points of view in matters of public policy (Monsma & Soper, 1997). Structural pluralists lobby for allowing religious organizations access to governmental funds on equal footing with nonreligious organizations. A third option, *religious accomodationism*, pictures a society in which either a particular religion or religion in general is given preference over nonreligious interests. Although some conservative Christians still see themselves as the moral custodians of society, the fact that only a minority now lobbies for exclusive Christian privilege in governmental affairs (C. Smith, 2000) shows how far the United States has moved away from the idealized picture of a Christian nation envisioned by the Protestant cultural superintendents of the 19th century.

Indeed, the political realm is not the only area to have largely shed the influence of religion. In the modern era, religion has become "progressively differentiated from other domains of social life, eventually emerging as a very specific institutional domain within a new type of social structure made up of several such institutions" (Tschannen, 1991, p. 400). As Bryan Wilson (1976) puts it,

> The presidency that the Church once exercised over social life has gone, as other agencies have assumed the functions that it once fulfilled. Instead of being the local center of community life, the Church has become more narrowly and specifically a religious centre, segregated and encapsulated. Whereas once the clergyman, if he was a diligent incumbent, was also the educator, the guardian of community morals, the social worker, at times even the magistrate, the sick visitor (when not actually a medical adviser), [sic] today, these roles have been taken over by others. (p. 16)

Thus, religion finds itself moved to the margins, in "retreat to a private world where religions have authority only over their followers and not over any other section of the polity or society" (Bell, 1980, p. 332). These "privatized religious institutions do not make larger-than-individual claims upon the world, that is, they tend not to speak out on, or be involved with wider moral, economic or political issues on the social agenda" (Dowdy, 1991, pp. 92–93).

Although treated by some scholars as a nearly inevitable occurrence spanning all spheres of society, more nuanced formulations have acknowledged the variable nature of differentiation and privatization, recognizing the unique circumstances present in different geographical locations and societal sectors (Alexander, 1990; Martin, 1978) as political and social actors struggle to either enlarge or diminish the public role of religion (Beyer, 1994; Chaves, 1994; C. Smith, 2003a). In this conception, religious organizations and individuals are not always on the defensive, but can actually bring about significant reversals, even in the modernized West. José Casanova (1994) documents several cases of religions either effectively renegotiating a public role or moving from the private to the public sphere. Based on these cases, he concludes that "an indiscriminate position against all forms of public religion is unfounded, and that there are some forms of deprivatization of religion which may be justifiable and even desirable from a modern normative perspective" (pp. 220–221), since "there are public religions in the modern world which do not need to endanger either modern individual freedoms or modern differentiated structures" (p. 215).

Secularization at the Micro Level: The European Experience

The extent to which the structural developments of societal differentiation and privatization affect the religiosity of the individual is a matter of debate. Some scholars, such as Frank Lechner (1991), hold that secularization theory applies only at the macro level, thus deeming individual religiosity irrelevant apart from any support it provides for the notion of societal differentiation. Although it is possible to conceptualize secularization only as the weakening of traditional religion's authority (Chaves, 1994; Yamane, 1997), other scholars explicitly or implicitly claim that the decline in religious prominence at the societal level holds ramifications at the level of individual belief, namely a decline in personal religious piety and the certainty with which individuals hold to religious worldviews (Acquaviva, 1966/1979; Berger, 1969, 1998; Bruce, 2002; Dobbelaere, 1981). In this model, when the state establishes religious belief, it leads to a heightened presence of religious ritual, symbols, and rhetoric in the cultural realm and, consequently, in the lives of its citizens. Absent this endorsement of religion at the macro level, individuals purportedly find religion less a part of their daily lives as plausibility structures disappear. With religious symbols no longer as prominent in their surroundings, individuals lose their connections to the supernatural, and end up either consciously embracing atheism or, more often, becoming merely indifferent to matters of religion in daily affairs.

In the regions of western and central Europe it would indeed appear that there is much truth in this, as fewer and fewer people are finding traditional religious participation desirous. In Britain, church membership has declined from 31% in 1930 to only 12% in the year 2000 (Brierley, 1999). Church attendance has dropped as well, from approximately 12% in 1979 to less than 8% in 1998, with pews increasingly filled by those in older age brackets (Brierley, 2000). At first glance, these numbers would seem to support the secularization thesis. Grace Davie (1994) has argued, however, that these numbers do not mean that British citizens have become irreligious, but rather that they have given up associating with one another in religious settings. This phenomenon, which Davie calls "believing without belonging," is growing in other European countries as well, "as if it were becoming a permanent feature of Western society" (Lambert, 2004). Instead of abandoning religious beliefs, many Europeans' beliefs are now subjective and individualized rather than traditional and institutionalized—characteristics of what Thomas Luckmann (1967) has termed "invisible religion." These religious individuals, in a sense, slip beneath the civic radar because they tend not to participate in formal religious activities. Instead, many have taken up New Age and other metaphysical practices in place of traditional Christian ones (Heelas, 1996; Houtman & Mascini,

2002). According to some analysts, the diffuse nature of these beliefs and lack of strong social networks to sustain them makes it unlikely that this form of religiosity will endure (Bruce, 2002). Until that prediction comes to pass, however, this religious transformation in itself does not entail secularization, unless these "spiritual phenomena" are deemed too nebulous to properly qualify as "religious" (Riesebrodt, 2001). It may be that personal association with small groups of like-minded friends and an overriding cultural ethos that encourages individual autonomy provides enough of a plausibility structure for these individuals to continue to hold their customized sets of metaphysical beliefs.

Thus, European popular religious life as it now stands is not particularly Christian, although it should be noted that there are recent signs that the youngest generation of adults in many European countries may have a greater faith in the Christian church to provide answers to spiritual needs and may believe more in a personal God, in life after death, and in heaven and hell than did their parents' generation (Lambert, 2004). Some European Christians viewing these recent developments may hold out hope for the future of their faith in Europe. Whether this is just a hiccup or constitutes a turning point in European religiosity remains to be seen, but at this point, popular participation in traditional Christianity is undoubtedly low in much of western and central Europe.

Although most scholars would concede the decline in European religiosity over the last century or so, claims for a long-term decline in European religiosity have not gone unchallenged. One of the sharpest critiques of secularization theory in recent years has come from sociologist Rodney Stark (1999), who argues that scholars have been misled by the "myth of past piety" as they look back on a medieval world covered by the sacred canopy of Christianity. According to Stark, "The evidence is clear that claims about a major decline in religious participation in Europe are based in part on very exaggerated perceptions of past religiousness. Participation may be low today in many nations, but not because of modernization" (p. 260). For decline to have occurred in Europe, religious observance had to be robust to begin with in the medieval and Renaissance periods, a claim that Stark strongly disputes. As evidence, he quotes a number of bishops from these earlier eras bemoaning the ignorance of the clergy, and a number of frustrated clergymen bemoaning the apathy of the laity. He also claims that individuals were as interested in magic and animism as they were in the orthodox doctrines and practices of the Christian church. Bruce (2002) counters that these beliefs were largely connected with Christian objects such as holy water and shrines of saints and still constituted a belief in the supernatural that was greater than that found in Europe today. Bruce also points out that religion during this era was not a particularly personal matter. . . . The notion that the church's professionals could glorify God independent of the laity's involvement seems foreign to our very individualistic culture. It rested on the implicit assumption that religious merit could be transferred from the religiously observant to those who were less so. . . . [T]his does not mean that our ancestors were not religious; it just means that most were not evangelical Protestants. (1999, p. 62)

Secularization at the Micro Level: The American Experience

The greatest difficulty secularization theorists face in trying to establish a causal relationship between a macro-level differentiation and a micro-level lack of religiosity is the case of the United States. Over the long term, American religiosity has not displayed the decline expected of it. When compared to the 17th, 18th, and 19th centuries, church membership and attendance today seems to have either increased or remained steady (Brauer, 1953; Finke & Stark, 1992; Garrison, 1948; Herberg, 1956; Holifield, 1994; Schneider, 1952), although it should be mentioned that official church membership is a somewhat problematic measure due to the greater ease with which membership can be obtained today as compared to the country's early years (Chaves & Stephens, 2003). In the short term, there are some good reasons to believe that religious participation is not what it was in the 1950s, the decade that many sociologists would consider the peak of American religious activity (Putnam, 2000; Warner, 1988). According to most studies, recent decades have shown a modest decline in religious participation. Although the number of adherents (adult members and children) reported by Christian denominations from 1990 to 2000 grew nearly 9%, this number is 4% less than the national population growth during that period (Jones et al., 2002). Another comparison shows that the number of adults who identify themselves as Christians grew 5% from 1990 to 2001. When adjusted for U.S. population growth, however, this represents nearly a 10% decline in relation to other religious and non-religious belief systems (Kosmin & Lachman, 1991; Kosmin et al., 2001).

Unlike its forebear across the Atlantic, self-reported participation in traditional religious services has remained steady in America in recent decades (Hout & Greeley, 1987; Wuthnow, 2003). A series of four Gallup polls conducted every 10 years from 1970 through 2000 finds the number of those who claim to have attended church in the past 7 days hovering around 40% of the American population (Wuthnow, 2003). As some scholars have recently shown, these numbers may be misleading, since self-reported attendance numbers seem to be inflated due to the way survey respondents interpret questions and the tendency they have to respond to pollsters in socially desirable ways (Hadaway & Marler, 2005; Hadaway, Marler, & Chaves, 1993; Marcum, 1999; Marler & Hadaway, 1999; T. W. Smith, 1998). When alternative measurement techniques such as time-series journaling are employed, respondents do not report having attended church as often (Hofferth & Sandberg, 2001; Presser & Stinson, 1998). This finding, along with the fact that every generation since the one born between 1920 and 1925 has gone to church less than the one before it (Chaves, 1989), problematizes any claims to absolute stability in American religious attendance.

Even so, the rate of religious service turnout is still higher in the United States than in most of the industrialized West (Bibby, 1993; Davie, 2002; Iannaccone, 1991; Inglehart & Baker, 2000; Inglehart, Basañez, & Moreno, 1998). Moreover, religious association has fared much better within the United States than almost any other form of civic association (Warner, 1988), and, according to Robert Putnam (2000), produces fully half of the nation's *social capital,* defined as "connections among individuals—social networks and the norms of reciprocity and trustworthiness that arise from them" (p. 19). In light of the noted decline in civic associational activity in nearly all sectors of American life during recent decades, for church attendance to have remained fairly prevalent means that at least some factors must be working in favor of institutionalized religion (Wuthnow, 2003).

Of the slack left in recent years by the modest decline of Christianity, a small portion has been picked up by other religions such as Islam, Hinduism, and Buddhism. Adherents of these faiths have arrived in greater numbers since quotas on non-European immigration were dropped in 1965, leading to a vast diversification of the American religious scene (Ebaugh & Chafetz, 2000; Eck, 2001, 2002; Warner, 1991; Warner & Wittner, 1998). In terms of sheer numbers, however, it has not brought as much pluralism as is sometimes thought (T. W. Smith, 2002), since about half of those who choose the "other" option on the General Social Survey (GSS) are actually Christians (Sherkat, 1999) and the majority of immigrants to the United States are at least nominally Christian as well (Casanova, 2005; C. Smith, Denton, Faris, & Regnerus, 2002; C. Smith & Woodberry, 2001; Warner, 1998, 2004). It would be interesting to explore how the adherents of each of the aforementioned world faiths negotiate the tensions induced by modernity, but since each of them comprises less than 1% of the total population (Kosmin et al., 2001) and are therefore not numerous enough to appear in many national quantitative studies (e.g., Beyerlein, 2004), they do not appear more prominently in this chapter on the alleged secularization of the United States as a whole. Likewise, Judaism, long a part of the American religious landscape, is today relatively small. It has not picked up any of the territory recently ceded by Christianity, instead losing ground as the number of adherents has fallen to barely over 1% of United States residents (Kosmin et al., 2001).

The group that has experienced the greatest statistical growth in recent years is those who call themselves "nonreligious." When asked to self-identify, the 2001 American Religious Identification Survey found that 14% of respondents chose "none" or "no religion" (Kosmin et al., 2001). GSS data expand on this, showing that the number of American adults who claimed no religious preference doubled from 7 to 14% between 1990–1991 and 1998–2000 after 17 years of no significant change (Hout & Fischer, 2002). Moreover, since 1950 the largest numbers of nonreligious have become increasingly concentrated in the younger age brackets (Glenn, 1987; Hout & Fischer, 2002), although the current cohort of adolescents do not appear more antagonistic toward organized religion than the general American public (C. Smith, Faris, & Denton, 2004). It is a normal part of the life cycle for young adults to go through an uncommitted phase of life before settling down at about age 30 (Greeley, 1989; Greeley & Hout, 1988; Hoge & Roozen, 1979; Wilson & Sherkat, 1994), so a portion of the recent growth of "nones," as sociologists call them, may be temporary.

So why do we see such growth in the number of people calling themselves nonreligious? One reason that does not explain the increase is that individuals have consciously deemed naturalistic or epistemologically skeptical worldviews superior to supernatural ones. Although research has measured a very slight upturn in the number of atheists, agnostics, and "secularists" in recent years (Kohut, Green, Keeter, & Toth, 2000; Marler & Hadaway, 2002; Sherkat, 2004), upon further examination Hout and Fischer (2002) attribute the rise in Americans identifying themselves as nonreligious more to political and demographic factors and an avoidance of churches than to religious skepticism.

Mirroring that which has occurred in much of western and central Europe, it would seem that since the 1950s there has been a significant rise in America of those practicing a privatized, invisible religion (Wuthnow, 1998). For the vast majority of these people, some of whom feel more comfortable describing themselves as "spiritual" rather than "religious" (Hout & Fischer, 2002; Roof, 1999; Wuthnow, 1998; see Marler & Hadaway, 2002, for an explanation of how these terms are not always incompatible), the term "nonreligious" means that they have disassociated themselves from organized religion in favor of more individualized, subjective forms of religious belief, and not that they have given up belief altogether. Although this spiritual/religious dichotomy has yet to find expression in the lives of America's youth (C. Smith, 2005), a number of "seeking" individuals from the Baby Boom and subsequent adult generations display forms of religiosity in which the salient vision is not that of dwelling in a religious "home," but of embarking on a "journey" (Wuthnow, 1998). In many instances, this takes the shape of what has been called "religion a la carte," as the individual becomes the locus of religious authority, assembling various items from the world's traditional and nontraditional religions into his or her own personal set of beliefs (Bibby, 1987). Other labels given by critics, such as "dabbling" or "spirituality lite," imply that these individuals do not take religion seriously, but rather as "useful for some personal or social end rather than as an expression of devotion to God alone" (Carroll, 1979, p. 36). If the permanence of beliefs is the measure of seriousness, this appears to be true, since the items are often pragmatically discarded when they no longer serve their purpose in favor of other newfound beliefs (Wuthnow, 1998). However, this does not mean that these "spiritual" individuals do not invest significant resources in choosing what to put on their plate. As William Swatos and Kevin Christiano (1999) have noted,

> That people are more likely to want their religion a la carte does not necessarily mean that they are "less religious." The metaphor is helpful: first, people who order meals a la carte often actually spend more than they would have if they bought a prix fixe meal. Of course, choosing a la carte does mean that people do not simply take whatever is dished out to them. However, it should not be assumed that as a result they will eat irresponsibly. (p. 221)

As a modern cultural phenomenon, this "massive subjective turn" (Taylor, 1991, p. 26) does not exist solely outside of churches. A 1978 Gallup Poll finds that 8 out of 10 Americans agree with the statement, "An individual should arrive at his or her own religious beliefs independent of any churches or synagogues" (Princeton Religion Research Center, 1978, p. 32). Some churches, such as those of an evangelical stripe, have been able to use this to their advantage. With the historical emphasis on making a "personal decision for Christ," evangelicalism "is proving the most vital response to the modern situation, . . . even in the developed world. It takes individualism or self-expression and contains and incorporates them" (Martin, 1997, p. 242).

Although a heavy dose of subjectivism can be found within many Christian churches, as evidenced by the rise of psychological and therapeutic forms of Christian spirituality (Roof, 2003), the communal component of Christianity problematizes any full embrace of individualism. In fact, statistics show that it is the regions in the United States in which Christian practice is the weakest that display the greatest measure of individualistic, posttraditional religion (Stark & Bainbridge, 1985). Although there have probably always been in America a significant number of nominal Christians who rarely darken the door of a church and occasionally partake in non-Christian practices (Butler, 1990), it does appear, in these regions particularly, that younger generations now feel somewhat less compelled to join religious (or other) organizations or to identify themselves specifically as Christians.

As mentioned earlier, these nonreligious individuals are not particularly agnostic or atheistic. Many modern scholars have assumed that the rationality of scientific thought would displace supposedly irrational religious worldviews. Hence we have Wilson's (1968) statement that "Christianity, with the impact of scientific and social scientific hindsights, has lost general theological plausibility" (p. 86). Recent developments in philosophy have compellingly argued, however, that scientific worldviews are inherently no more or less rational than theistic ones, but that all worldviews are based on foundations that are not empirically or rationally verifiable (Wolterstorff, 1976). That there has not been a mass abandonment of supernatural worldviews due to a triumph of scientific rationalism has also led many to reexamine the relationship between science and religion, with the conclusion that the two have been mutually relevant in so many ways throughout history as to make a simplistic science versus religion generalization impossible (Brooke, 1991). It has been argued by others, however, that since science offers "this-worldly" explanations for the events of our lives, our need to explain things in "other-worldly" terms is diminished. Since technology has allowed us to increasingly manipulate the natural world, we also feel a sense of mastery over fate and have less reason to plead for divine intervention (Bruce, 2002; Dobbelaere, 1993, as cited in Houtman & Mascini, 2002; Martin, 1969). If doctors, using scientific technology, can cure diseases, then there is less reason to ask God to do so. Nevertheless, a great many modern individuals do not view the world in these reductionistic terms. The continued persistence of belief in the supernatural seems to indicate that many modern religious believers see the matter as *both/and*, not *either/or.* They both thank God for the technology and ask him to grant the attending physician wisdom and skill in treating their infirmities as well.

The fact that there is less conflict between science and religion than is often thought also can be seen in the religious participation of scientists themselves in comparison to other Americans and scholars in other disciplines (Iannacone, Stark, & Finke, 1998; Wuthnow, 1985). According to Stark (1999),

> [T]he conflict between religion and science is largely fictional and . . . scientists are not notably irreligious, being as likely to attend church as is the general public. Even more revealing is the fact that among American academics, the proportion who regard themselves as religious is higher the more scientific their field. For example, physical and natural scientists, including mathematicians, are more than twice as likely to identify themselves as "a religious person" as are anthropologists and psychologists. . . . Possibly even more

important is the fact that theologians and professors of religious studies are a
far more prolific source of popular works of atheism. (pp. 264–265)

While it is clear that the general population of the United States has not
greatly secularized, and it is debatable whether they are headed in that
direction or not, it is clear over the last century and a half that one sector
of American society has indeed secularized. Specifically, it consists of "a
thin but very influential stratum of intellectuals... with Western-style
higher education, especially in the humanities and social sciences"
(Berger, 2001, p. 445). America's intellectual class, which exercises power
through its ability to control the social definition of knowledge, is markedly secular. This instantiation of the "substantial difference between the
belief systems of mass publics and those of elites" (Jelen, 1989, p. 427) has
elicited the famous quote attributed to Berger that "if India is the most religious country in the world, and Sweden the least religious, then America is
a nation of Indians ruled by Swedes" (Johnson, 1993).

So what is it specifically about these scholars that make them more likely
to hold a worldview incompatible with traditional religion? According to
Wuthnow (1985), academicians are drawn disproportionately from irreligious parts of the American population to begin with. C. Smith (2003a)
claims that Western intellectuals tend to be more secular for a number of
other reasons as well. Because of a mixture of detachment and skepticism,
high social ideals, a tendency toward a superior self-concept, and the frustration that stems from having to rely on others for funding, they tend to
be critical of mass opinions and of the established social order. Since the
life of common people is often religious, academics find themselves in
opposition to a religious status quo. Moreover, scholars of the modern
period owe their cultural ascendancy directly to the decline in the authority of the Western religious establishment, which many intellectuals have
historically seen as restricting their path toward greater autonomy, status,
authority, and income.

THE RELATIVIZATION OF TRADITION

Obviously, awareness of other people with differing beliefs and values is
not something exclusively reserved for the intellectual class, but something that affects all members of pluralistic societies unless they have consciously decided to segregate themselves (Berger, 1979). As a result of a
confrontation with previously alien cultures, at least some people do seem
to experience what is termed a "relativization" of tradition (Berger, 1979;
Beyer, 1994; Robertson & Chirico, 1985). George Van Pelt Campbell
(1999) states,

Described simply, the "relativization" of tradition is seeing one's tradition "relative to" another tradition. It is the confrontation with an alien tradition which results in seeing one's original tradition in a new light, the light of a hitherto unrecognized option. Relativization is the recognition that one's taken-for-granted viewpoint is but one option among a plurality of options; this results in the process of rethinking one's own tradition because of that recognition. In other words, relativization is awakening to the fact that what one previously perceived as "reality," or "the truth," may only be a "view-point." (pp. 1–2)

For many individuals, this newfound awareness of alternative explanatory frameworks can be cognitively and existentially disconcerting. As Campbell describes,

Relativization is the generation, in confrontation with an alien tradition, of a sense of threat and of insecurity about the assumptions people use to make sense of the world and of the self, calling into question such things as the definitions, boundaries, categories, and conclusions through which they have understood the world and established their identity; this insecurity, in turn, generates secondary effects such as intellectual disorientation, bewilderment, doubt, and fear. (p. 72)

According to Berger (1998), socialization processes in the modern world are not as uniform as they were in premodern societies where cultures were more homogeneous and religious monopolies were more common. Hence, instead of adopting the taken-for-granted worldview prevalent in one's social surroundings, the truth claims of one's upbringing become relativized, requiring modern individuals to choose from a variety of options. Because individuals are aware that faith is now based on a relative (and therefore, subjective) personal choice, Berger contends that convictions are held with less certainty than if they were the only option, evident to all. As Bruce (1992) puts it,

[P]luralism threatens the plausibility of religious belief systems by exposing their human origins. By forcing people to do religion as a matter of personal choice rather than as fate, pluralism universalizes "heresy." A chosen religion is weaker than a religion of fate because we are aware that we choose the gods rather than the gods choosing us. (p. 170)

C. Smith (1998), however, views the necessity of choice much differently. He asserts that since the manner in which individuals have legitimized their identity is historically variable, "modern religious believers can establish stronger religious identities and commitments on the basis of individual choice than through ascription" (p. 102). To authenticate one's choice, it must be one's own, and to simply adopt the view of one's family without question is seen in modern society as artificial and shallow. "It is only through the observance of individual choice . . . that it becomes 'real' and meaningful" (p. 103). In modern America, with individualism as its cardinal virtue (Bellah, Madsen, Sullivan, Swidler, & Tipton, 1985), a person often "leaves home" and "finds him- or herself," in order to solidify his or her identity by means of personal choice. Empirical studies have confirmed that this "emancipation of the self" often serves "to 'tighten up' or clarify commitments to [religious] institutions" (Marler & Roozen, 1993, p. 265). Interestingly, once the decision is made, what was originally an individualistic, voluntary act can quickly become a deeply community-oriented act in which one chooses to devote oneself to the welfare of one's religious community.

Whether modern individuals actually have more choices than their predecessors is, like many other comparisons with the past, debatable. Bruce (1999), for example, states that "never before have so many people been free to choose or had such a range [of religions] to choose from" (p. 3). Anthropologist Mary Douglas (1982), however, counters that although "moderns certainly like to tell one another that they have free choice," in reality

> It is difficult to turn the idea of increased choice into anything that can be closely compared. There could be a wider range of trivial choices and a smaller range of weighty ones, or the other way around. If the choices we have are mostly of the bazaar kind, small, similar items purveyed at similar prices—like the difference between numerous highly standardized programs on cable television—the case for our enjoying increased options is not made. Quite the contrary, it has to be reconciled with a daily lament against the dull uniformity of our lives—the same menus, the same clothes, the same sports, and the same homes. Where is free choice? Our Viking ancestors had much more of it, free to spend a few years in Greenland, nip back to Scandinavia to help a political ally, or join a raid on Britain. (p. 11)

Enlightenment visions of progress and of throwing off the strictures of tradition and religious authority have led many modern religious scholars to overestimate the autonomy of individuals in the present age, and to underestimate the autonomy of those in the past. Thus, Douglas claims that, in the debates over modernity and religious change,

> Everything is wrong because the stereotype of premoderns is wrong. It has been constructed to flatter prejudged ideas. Some premoderns are indeed organized according to the stereotype, in highly ascriptive social institutions. But some of them are as mobile, footloose, and uncommitted as any modern academic. Some have been gripped in the throngs of bureaucracy; some have been ruthlessly competitive individualists. In none of these variations do religious beliefs float free of social and moral pressures. (p. 18)

Even if one concedes that there exists in the United States and the rest of the modernized world an unprecedented level of cultural diversity, does it truly make any difference? Theologian John Hick (2001) has noted that the opportunity to study a full range of religions has been limited to a relative few in the West, meaning that most people's choice is not fully free. But how much does it really matter whether one must choose between three religious or nonreligious options and 300? In both the premodern and modern worlds one finds variation in belief not just between different societies, but within particular societies as well (Douglas, 1973). So premodern individuals also had at least some options and were presumably forced to deal with the relative nature of their worldviews. Thus, even if one grants that diversity in the modern world exists in greater degree than ever before, it may have been just as likely to have one's beliefs relativized in the Hellenistic world or medieval Spain as in 21st-century America. One's opinion on the matter depends on whether individuals need plausibility structures as extensive as the sacred canopy of an entire society to legitimize their views or whether they can get by with merely the "sacred umbrella" of their particular subcultures (C. Smith, 1998).

Community-based studies from the early 20th century such as the famous depiction of Muncie, Indiana, by Robert and Helen Lynd (1929) suggest that, during this time period, religion reflected vague social and community obligations and individuals had little social contact with those from divergent religious backgrounds (Gay & Ellison, 1993). As Wolfe (2003) writes,

> Throughout the first half of the twentieth century, religion possessed what sociologists called an "ascribed" rather than an "achieved" status. Certain aspects of an individual's identity were determined by circumstances of birth and others were the result of what one chose to do with one's life. Race, region, class, and religion were generally held to belong to the former category, while luck, income, and career could belong to the latter. This tendency to treat religion as an ascribed aspect of individual identity existed for the simple reason that it had roots in reality; a Gallup Poll taken in 1955 found that only 4 percent of Americans—one in twenty-five—did not adhere to the religion of their childhood. (p. 41)

Although Americans have always had choices, and much of today's religious life is still shaped by powerful ascriptive forces (Ammerman, 1997a), the difference between present-day America and that of 50 or 100 years ago may be that "within a longstanding context of multiple [religious] options and against the backdrop of growing conviction about [religious] voluntarism, Americans are increasingly acting on the options as choices" (Marler & Roozen, 1993, p. 275) as they "become more aware of the role they themselves [are] playing in shaping their religious lives" (Roof, 2003, p. 139).

Another factor to consider is the possibility that, although individuals in the modern world share awareness of other worldviews with their predecessors, the degree of that awareness may be different. After all, simply knowing about the existence of religions called Buddhism, Hinduism, and Islam is much different than developing a relationship with an adherent of one of these religions or seriously reflecting on the tenets and practices of their faith. It has been shown that the urbanization of the modern world increases individuals' ability to choose their associates, since cities bring together large numbers of disparate individuals and provide a wider range of relational options than existed in premodern times (Fischer, 1982). However, since people generally like and choose to affiliate with those who share their views and values (Homans, 1961), social networks in modern times may in fact be *more* homogeneous than those of the past. For this reason, if pluralistic settings are large enough, modernity may mean shallower, not deeper, interreligious contact. On the other hand, if a greater number of those who define the character of America consider diversity to be part of its national identity, and members of subcultures do not entirely shut out their voices, does this not make ordinary individuals more conscious of those who are not like them?

For most ordinary believers, the abstract concept of diversity itself is a nonissue. As Wuthnow (2004) explains,

> To speak of diversity is, of necessity, to adopt at least momentarily the perspective of the outsider, the dispassionate observer who views religious traditions from on high rather than from within any single tradition. Thus, it must be granted that for most people, at least those who live and practice their faith from within a religious tradition, the question of diversity is not one that is most immediately on their minds. Those who adhere faithfully to their own religious tradition may be aware of others who follow different religions, but from the perspective of such insiders, these followers of other religions are indeed "others," usually specific others, rather than instances of diversity itself. (p. 161)

Although most people do not approach the subject as do sociologists of religion, the increasing number of non-European immigrants and non-Christian houses of worship and the general cultural awareness fostered by higher education, mass communications, international travel, and the national integration into world markets (Wuthnow, 2004, 2005a) may still make 21st-century Americans "more aware of pluralism as a next-door reality and not just an abstract possibility than were previous generations" (Stroup, 1998, p. 167). Although very few Americans claim to have had a "great deal" of contact with those such as Muslims, Buddhists, or Hindus, between one-third and one-half of the general public claim to have had at least "a little" contact with individuals from each of these world religions

(Wuthnow, 2005a). This contact seems to take place primarily within the workplace or through commercial activity, and not within Americans' neighborhoods or religious settings. When it does occur, most Americans characterize their contact as pleasant, although it seldom appears to include discussions of religious matters.

As for familiarity with the teachings of religions such as Islam, Buddhism, and Hinduism, between 22 and 33% of Americans claim to be at least "somewhat familiar" with the content of these traditions, a number that leads Wuthnow (2005a) to characterize religious diversity as a larger issue than one might initially surmise given the small numbers of Muslims, Buddhists, and Hindus in America. Of course, this must be taken with a grain of salt, since many Americans claim to be familiar with Christianity as well, yet have difficulty naming things such as the birthplace of Jesus or the four gospels that begin the New Testament (C. Smith, 2005; Wuthnow, 2005a).

RESPONSES TO THE RELATIVIZATION OF TRADITION

Before moving on, a caveat is in order. It should be made clear that relativization is not the same thing as *relativism*, which denies the existence of universal standards of truth and moral behavior.

> [Relativization] refers only to the process of seeing one's tradition "relative to" an alternative. The process of relativization implies no necessary conclusions at the moral or ethical level, as relativism, popularly understood, does. It entails people becoming aware of alternatives. . . . Relativization as the recognition that there are alternatives to one's viewpoint does not mean, depend upon, or necessarily lead to relativism. (Campbell, 1999, pp. 4–5)

In fact, relativization as a result of cultural pluralism does not produce any particular predictable reaction. Numerous responses to relativization are possible, including, among others, (1) summarily rejecting the alien traditions in an attempt to defend one's original tradition, (2) redefining or rediscovering something that had been forgotten in one's own tradition in order to neutralize the challenge from outside, (3) moving to other traditions of faith, and (4) abandoning religion outright. In all but the most closed reactions, some aspect of conscious self-reflection and change is present (Campbell, 1999).

Of all of the potential responses to life in a diverse society, it would appear that belief implausibility is a relatively uncommon one. Only 16% of the total U.S. adult population report that they have switched their religious preference or identification at some time during their lives, meaning that they have moved beyond the various expressions of their original religion to an entirely different religious or nonreligious belief system

(Kosmin et al., 2001). C. Smith (1998) addresses the issue of belief implausibility in American Christianity by interviewing those from major Christian traditions that he labels as "doubters" and "defectors." In a survey of Catholics and churchgoing Protestants (a significantly biased sample, Smith admits, since it eliminates nominal Protestants whose doubts may have resulted in abandonment of the church and their tradition of belief), Smith reports that, of the 2,591 practicing American Christians, only 5.3% "often" have doubts about their religious faith. When they do, these doubts prove to be largely nonthreatening to their faith and mostly unrelated to issues of modernization, cultural pluralism, or the secularization of society. Of the 35 in Smith's sample who can legitimately be called doubters, most have only minor doubts that do not much affect the plausibility of their belief. Four express moderate doubts, while four others express intense doubts about their religious faith. Even these doubts, however, appear "to spring not from anything distinctively modern, but from timeless and universal human difficulties, such as tragedy, suffering and moral hypocrisy" (C. Smith, 1998, p. 165).

For those defectors from institutional Christianity, the story is similar to that of the doubters. Out of the same sample of 2,591 respondents, only 76 individuals who were raised in Christian homes have become nonreligious as adults. Of those from other Christian traditions who have become nonreligious, only 6 out of the 34 persons reflect "clear cases of sacred canopies collapsing under the weight of cultural pluralism, scientific authority, and rationalization" (C. Smith, 1998, p. 170). As in the case of the doubters, the majority of the defections from organized religion occur for reasons seemingly unrelated to modernity, such as "choosing to live a lifestyle incompatible with church ethics, moving to a new city and failing to become integrated into a new congregation, or just losing interest and 'drifting away' from church" (C. Smith, 1998, p. 170). Thus, Smith demonstrates that the faith of Christians, including evangelicals, is not nearly as fragile as proponents of secularization theory had once supposed.

So why do so few nonelites deeply experience the challenges of modernity? The reason, according to C. Smith (1998),

is that because the mainstream American cultural tradition is strongly pragmatic and activist—rather than doctrinal and contemplative—first-hand spiritual experiences that "work" for people can provide for them stronger epistemological foundations for personal religious faith than can the narrative elegance or intellectually [sic] defensibility of theological systems.... Few ordinary people, religious or otherwise, are theoreticians. And few ordinary religious believers begin or proceed in their beliefs with a "hermeneutic of suspicion." People do not generally adhere to their religious faiths because as cognitive frameworks they are intellectually nonproblematic. They adhere to them because they provide identity, solidarity, meaning, order, and purpose—very fundamental human requisites. Whatever cognitive quandaries modernity imposes on ordinary religious believers, most seem capable of disregarding, defusing, or somehow resolving them in a way that does not seriously undermine their faith. (p. 177)

So it can be said, then, that many versions of secularization theory fall short because they fail to take into account the way in which belief systems are constructed on the popular levels of American culture. Wuthnow (1988b) lends support to this in his description of the tenets of popular religion in America as "relatively discrete elements with few systematic relations with one another, thus permitting them to adapt with relative flexibility to diverse and changing circumstances" (p. 483). Thus, when one of these beliefs is challenged, it does not call into question the validity of the entire system.

This does not mean, however, that there are no logical connections between the substantive elements of religious belief structures, particularly traditional ones. As David Martin (1997) explains,

[The] basic grammar or structure of perspectives and pictures is quite tightly organized. This is not to say that it yields a single logical line, but it does give rise to a group of logical lines, expanding organically from the basic root. One line or another will come into view in the course of history as possessing special relevance, according to the thrust of varying circumstances. (p. 173)

That being said, Martin acknowledges in religious signs a "fantastic scope for variant readings" (p. 173), and expounds further,

There are always coronation psalms to crown Kings and Magnificats to console the lowly. Notoriously proverbs come in twos to allow you either to look before you leap or else to act immediately because he who hesitates is lost. The religious sign is both A and not A, so that the cross stands simultaneously for the non-violent martyr and the Christian crusader. Indeed, the religious sign, like the political sign, is often most powerful when alive with dynamic contradiction. (p. 174)

Since the rich array of symbols, texts, and other "polysemous resources" (Sewell, 1992) of traditional religions can hold a wide variety of both complementary and contradictory meanings, they can be adapted to meet many of the challenges that believers encounter in a changing world (Regnerus & Smith, 1998). This adaptation, however, is not always immediate. There is often an unsettled period, which Pierre Bourdieu (1972/1977) calls the "hysteresis of habitus," in which the old ways of responding to the rest of the social field do not seem to work as well as they once did. This inability to assimilate changes in the environment using existing patterns of thought and perception can bring on considerable discomfort, although the longevity of major world religions is testimony to their ability to deal with troubled times.

Another reason that worldviews with supernatural components are not as fragile as scholars sometimes suppose is their ability to counter empirical challenges with superempirical answers (Billig, 1996; Dein, 2001; Melton, 1985; Snow & Machalek, 1982; Tumminia, 1998). For example, if following prayer one gets a different outcome than one expected, it does not necessarily mean that God did not answer the request. Perhaps God either said "no" or that the desired outcome would occur at a future date. Of course, neither of these explanations is subject to empirical scrutiny. And neither are they necessarily false. They are just not testable or refutable. They become false only when they are ruled out of bounds a priori by the supposition that the only beliefs one can rightly affirm are those subject to empirical verification. This demand of logical positivism is routinely ignored by many residents of the modern world, and justifiably so by positivism's own criteria, since positivism itself, like all epistemological systems, is based on assumptions that must be taken on faith and are not empirically verifiable (see Alston, 1993; Wolterstorff, 1976).

That is not to say, however, that belief in the supernatural cannot be shaken. It is thought that belief systems that have more tightly interconnected components are more susceptible to outside pressures than are loosely integrated ones, since the undermining of one element will affect the entire structure (Borhek & Curtis, 1975). Moreover, supernatural religions of both types become more vulnerable when individuals employ posivitist empirical standards as the arbiter of veracity. When this happens, the lack of fit between belief and experience can lead to severe "cognitive dissonance" (Festinger, Riecken, & Schachter, 1956) and the potential abandonment of the faith. It would seem that this describes fairly accurately the psychological experiences of some of the aforementioned scholars working in the humanities and social sciences. For these scholars, the traditional Christian sources of epistemological certainty

> have been considerably weakened by the modern human sciences—the certainty of the institution [the Christian church] by historical scholarship and the social sciences, the certainty of the text by the findings of biblical criticism, and the certainty of inner experience by psychology and the sociology of knowledge. (Berger, 1998, p. 792)

Therefore, secularization theories based on the model of a collapsing sacred canopy and the pressures resulting from religious pluralism have considerable merit in narrating "the psychological experience of intellectuals who emerge from religiously conservative families to the religiously indifferent world of the academy, where they learn that religion is socially

constructed and that theirs is only one of many systems of meaning"
(Warner, 1993). For most modern individuals and their religious organizations, though, it is far from a given that modern society encourages movement only in the direction from faith to a loss of faith. In the words of
Berger (2001), who has recently recanted some of his early work, the existence of shortcomings in the secularization theory "does not mean that
there is no such thing as secularization; it only means that this phenomenon is by no means the direct and inevitable result of modernity" (p. 445).

ALTERNATIVE EXPLANATIONS OF RELIGIOUS VITALITY

For those scholars who find secularization theory limited in its ability to
describe the modern religious milieu, alternative explanatory models are
necessary. In recent decades, the competing theory that has received the
most attention is that of Rodney Stark, Roger Finke, and Laurence Iannaccone, among others, who have sought to apply economic models to the
field of religion (see Stark & Finke, 2000, for the most comprehensive presentation of the theory). This model is derived not from the European
experience, but from the United States, whose religion "has typically
expressed not the culture of the society as a whole, but the subcultures of its
many constituents" (Warner, 1993, p. 1047). As R. Stephen Warner (1993)
states, "Very few of the hundreds of religious organizations flourishing in
the United States today... have had to adjust to a pluralistic situation. Most
of them were born into it" (p. 1054). More attuned to the voluntary, democ-
ratized nature of American religion (Ammerman, 1997b; Hatch, 1984; Roof
& McKinney, 1987; Warner, 1988, 1993), this *supply-side* or *religious economies*
model holds that cultural pluralism, rather than being detrimental, may
instead create market conditions that serve to bolster religious participation
(Finke & Stark, 1988).

Instead of rooting fluctuations in the changing demand of religious
consumers, these scholars claim that religious demand remains fairly constant in that people always ask questions of deeper meaning and purpose.
How many people end up participating in religious communities depend
on how well religious producers succeed in convincing people that the religious answers they provide are able to meet their perceived needs. In this
view, the process of secularization is self-limiting, since humans will continue to desire things such as assurance of eternal justice and life after
death that cannot be satisfied by purely naturalistic belief systems (Stark &
Bainbridge, 1985). For this reason, religion is said to possess a competitive
advantage. In America, unlike in "monopolistic" religious settings, this
edge does not lead to complacency. Rather, the removal of religion from
the public arena increases religion's presence in the private sphere. Since

there exist currently in the "deregulated" market setting of the United States such large numbers of competing Christian and non-Christian religious groups, each trying to convince individuals of the benefits of their product, it follows that each religious group will work harder to market that product and succeed in drawing more people to join them.

This theoretical approach is often subsumed under the larger rational choice paradigm that assumes human actors rationally choose their actions so as to maximize personal benefit, even if these benefits look different for different individuals (Stark, 1997). Although derived from the American experience, this supply-side explanation purports to be applicable at all times and in all places (Stark, Finke, & Iannaccone, 1995). Whether it works as well in cultures in which the free market is not a salient icon remains to be seen. The model has come under criticism from scholars who believe that human actors make decisions based fundamentally on underlying moral orders and not solely from calculated self-interest (Etzioni, 1988; C. Smith, 2003b). As Nancy Ammerman says,

> [R]eligious life is about a relationship between human beings and a divinity, and relationships have other dimensions besides exchange. They're about persons, emotions, shared experiences—a whole range of things that aren't captured inside an explanatory scheme that says what we're about is "I'm after things I can't otherwise get and that you can give me." (Miller, 2004, p. 31)

The religious economies model has also been critiqued by scholars who dispute its empirical fit even in America. It has been around for nearly two decades and tested more than any other alternative to the secularization paradigm (see Chaves & Gorski, 2001, for an overview of both positive and negative assessments of the theory). Unfortunately, nearly all of the results of research, both in favor and unsupportive, have recently been invalidated due to flaws of methodology (Voas, Olson, & Crockett, 2002). One study since then has found a negative relationship between pluralism and religious participation (Montgomery, 2003), but the jury is undoubtedly still out.

Up to this point, our focus has been on religion in society as a whole. However, within a religiously diverse society, it is also important to ask why particular religious groups, congregations, and denominations fare better than others. In America, the dominant religion, Christianity, may have ceded ground in the last 45 years or so, but not all of its subsets have followed the same gentle, downward curve. Some, such as Pentecostal/Holiness denominations, have done exceedingly well while moderate and liberal Protestants have floundered (Roozen, 1993). Others, such as Catholics, have experienced a bit of both trends (Greeley, 1989, 2003; Roozen, 1993). As would be expected, several approaches to religious growth and decline have been developed to account for this disparity.

The earliest of these is a much-debated theory presented by Dean Kelley (1972) that many conservative churches are stricter, requiring more commitment of their members than liberal churches, thus giving conservatives a greater sense of personal investment in the churches than their liberal counterparts have. Religious beliefs, such as those held by conservative Christians, that are supposedly more at odds with the larger culture are socially more costly to hold. This screens out the "free riders" whose complacent modus operandi of consuming resources without contributing many in return is a drain on the organization (Iannaccone, 1994). When the resources that they have been consuming are reallocated, it enhances the functioning of the organization as a whole.

Another recent explanation of the difference between growing and shrinking denominations and churches significantly qualifies Kelly's approach. According to C. Smith's (1998) *subcultural identity theory,* what is needed for a subculture to thrive in modern society is not strictness per se, but rather a combination of engagement with and distinction from the larger society. Arising from his study of American evangelical Christianity, Smith draws upon a key insight of social psychology in which cohesion within a societal subgroup can be enhanced through perceived or actual conflict with other subgroups in society (Coser, 1956; Simmel, 1923/1955; Sumner, 1906). A limited amount support for this theory has since been found in theologically liberal denominations such as the Presbyterian Church (USA) as well (Evans, 2003).

Of course, growth and decline could conceivably have little or nothing to do with these theories at all. David Roozen and Jackson Carroll (1979) have elaborated a framework comprised of multiple factors running along local/national and institutional/contextual axes. Although the framework has some minor flaws (see Warner, 1988), they have drawn attention to the fact that there are many factors affecting church and denominational growth and decline that are both inside and outside of the control of religious leaders. Without attempting to distinguish between local/national and institutional/contextual factors, a partial list of explanations for the disparity between growing and shrinking religious organizations is as follows: (1) a difference in fertility rates of parishioners (Bibby, 1978; Bouma, 1979; Hout, Greeley, & Wilde, 2001; Roof & McKinney, 1987); (2) the effective expenditure of resources on evangelism and establishing new churches (Compton, 2003; Greer, 1993; Hadaway, 1993; Marler & Hadaway, 1993); (3) the willingness of congregations to try innovative programs or forms of outreach to adapt to changing local environments (Ammerman, 1997a; Hadaway, 1982); (4) the religious proclivities of immigrants new to the United States (Bouma, 1979; Mathisen, 2004); (5) the presence in congregations of a friendly atmosphere and quality Christian education programs (Donahue & Benson, 1993); (6) the willingness of individuals to actively participate in the religious socialization of their children (Bibby, 1978; Bibby & Brinkerhoff, 1973; Hadaway & Marler, 1993; Roof, 1999; C. Smith & Sikkink, 2003; Sullins, 1993; Wuthnow, 1999); (7) the ability to counter the skepticism and individualism of philosophical liberalism (Fowler, 1989); (8) congregational location or denominational concentration in geographical regions experiencing population growth or decline (Marler & Hadaway, 1993; Stump, 1998; Thompson, Carroll, & Hoge, 1993); (9) the number of years since the founding of the congregation (Donahue & Benson, 1993); (10) the ability to attract and retain younger cohorts by catering specifically to people in those age brackets (Schaller, 1995); (11) lower levels of secularism that provide distinction between the religious community and other voluntary, communal institutions (Hadaway & Roozen, 1993); (12) the migration of religious Southerners into less religious parts of the United States (Shibley, 1996); (13) the ability to create a sense of belonging through member participation in the workings of the church (Dougherty, 2004); and (14) the willingness to tailor religious messages to meet the public's search for spirituality and ultimate meaning (Bibby, 1993; Hoge, Johnson, & Luidens, 1994).

According to Carroll (1979), church analysts are mistaken when they limit their focus to only one of the above items.

> Single cause explanations of the [religious] trends...attract attention. But to explain them by any one factor alone oversimplifies an exceedingly complex set of relationships. Thus, we look not to single factor explanations, but to the impact of multiple factors whose interrelationships we cannot trace out or understand. (p. 37)

Roozen and Carroll (1979) concur that "There is no single cause or simple pattern of causes related to church growth or decline. Rather, growth or decline involves a complex pattern of multiple and often interacting factors" (p. 39).

With certain exceptions, the primary measures in this chapter of the strength of religion in the United States have been church membership and attendance. There are, however, many other ways in which religious vitality can be measured. As C. Smith (1998) has noted, attendance in itself is not necessarily a sign of true spirituality since "a church's pews could be completely filled with regular attenders who are exceptionally uncommitted, uninformed and apathetic religiously" (p. 20). Indeed, one can see a similar dynamic at work in Gordon Allport's (1966) examination of the difference between parishioners whose motivation for religious participation is *intrinsic*, an end in itself, and those whose motivation is *extrinsic*, meaning that they attend as a means to gain some other unspiritual end such as business contacts, social connections, and so on. Nevertheless, in light of the alleged cultural decline in voluntary association, church membership and attendance remain important indicators of religious dedication. As historian Martin Marty puts it, "[W]hile church growth and decline are far from being the only ways of measuring religious health, they give at least some indication of how citizens are voting with their bodies" (1979, p. 10).

Compared to many other industrialized nations, the United States may be highly religious, yet many Americans who claim to be religious often display little understanding of even the most rudimentary tenets of their religious traditions (C. Smith, 2005; Wuthnow, 2005a), a finding that should surprise no one due to the large statistical gap between the number of people who identify themselves as Christians and the number who attend church on a regular basis. Although Mormon and conservative Protestant churches seem to do a better job than most of instilling in their congregants a sense of religious identity that informs and influences their thoughts and actions (C. Smith, 2005), for many other Americans religion seems to operate in the background, as "part of the furniture of their lives" (p. 122). For these individuals, religious faith only becomes salient in rare occasions, primarily when needed as a tool to gain comfort, peace, or some other form of therapeutic self-satisfaction (C. Smith, 2005).

At any rate, when instruments such as national public opinion polls are employed to capture other measures of American religiosity, the results are similar to those seen earlier in this chapter. For example, the Gallup Religious Index, in addition to church membership and church attendance, measures items such as belief in God, having a religious preference, believing that religion can answer today's problems, confidence in organized religion, feeling that clergy are honest, and viewing religion as very important in one's life. This composite of polls demonstrates a creeping decline slightly greater than the drop in church membership and attendance since the 1950s (Roozen, 1993), although a jump in 2004 has brought the index back up from its record low to levels resembling those of 1990 (Gallup, 2004; Roozen, 1993). Using similar measures such as religious affiliation, belief, salience, ritual observance, and private devotionalism, Lyman Kellstedt, John Green, James Guth, and Corwin Smidt (1996) summarize the ambiguous nature of religion in the United States in this way:

> On the one hand, a very large portion of the adult population has more than a minimal commitment to their religion, making the United States a highly "religious" society, particularly compared to Europe. On the other hand, many of these same people do not have especially high levels of commitment, and a large portion of the population scores very low, making the United States a "secular" society, particularly compared to some points in the past. (p. 184)

Which of the models presented in this chapter best explains the current state of religion in the United States and the rest of the world is still very much up for debate. Ironically, with all the ink spilled on the subject, it may turn out that cultural diversity neither favors nor undermines religiosity (see Voas et al., 2002). It also may be that the rise and fall of religious participation in specific regions of the West indicates no trajectory at all, but rather cyclical fluctuations brought about by cultural crises, shifts of resources available to different societal groups, and the influential actions of key historical figures. To use the metaphor of a weather map (Todd, 2003), much of Europe may be experiencing a religious cold front while the United States experiences temperate weather and parts of what used to be called the third world find themselves in the midst of a heat wave (Inglehart & Baker, 2000). Whether temporary upturns and downturns in the religious temperature are part of a general trend toward global warming or an ice age, or neither, only time will tell.

CHAPTER 5

THE STATE OF AMERICAN EVANGELICAL CHRISTIANITY

SHIFTING EVANGELICAL THEOLOGICAL BOUNDARIES

In keeping with the debates of the preceding chapter regarding American religion (and nonreligion) as a whole, it is not surprising that the current state and future prospects of the evangelical Protestant subculture can be viewed in a number of different lights. If one views evangelicalism in terms of secularization theory, such as James Davison Hunter (1983, 1987) does in two very influential books, then the movement is in trouble. According to Hunter, although evangelicalism has held out thus far, it is in the process of succumbing to secularization. As evangelicals find their beliefs ever more implausible, they are now engaging in cognitive bargaining and changing their views to accommodate those of modern society. If, on the other hand, one believes that the internal resources found in the evangelical Christian "cultural toolkit" (Swidler, 1986) are sufficient to meet the challenges of modernity, then one can view change not as a weakening or bargaining away of the faith, but as a series of creative developments serving to both reinvigorate the church and to relate the gospel of Christ to a changing world (see Webber, 2002). As historian Mark Noll puts it, in reverse order, "When a religious tradition adjusts to new conditions, there is always the chance of having a great appeal for that religious tradition, but there is also a chance that what had defined that religious tradition can be given away" (*Religion & Ethics NewsWeekly*, 2004b).

American Evangelicals and Religious Diversity, pages 67–87
Copyright © 2006 by Information Age Publishing
All rights of reproduction in any form reserved.

Like any subculture, evangelical Protestant Christianity has boundaries that distinguish it from the larger society and contribute heavily to members' individual and collective identities. Although there are also moral boundaries between evangelicals and the wider world, the issues explored in this chapter and the rest of the book are primarily theological. As was stated earlier, some analysts believe that the boundaries of evangelicalism show signs of shifting (Campbell, 1999; Hunter, 1987). Whether these changes are a weakening or merely a pragmatic realignment depends on how essential to evangelical identity one perceives the particular elements in question to be. It also depends heavily on one's prior theoretical commitments. For example, in the conceptualization of Talcott Parsons (1966), fundamentalism is by definition a defensive reaction, an attempt to maintain the boundaries of an older paradigm in the face of a newer, more generalized alternative (Ethridge & Feagin, 1979; Hood & Morris, 1985; Hood, Morris, & Watson, 1986).

According to Hunter (1987), what one now finds in the evangelical church is "a brand of theology that for generations had been considered 'modernistic' being advocated by theologians who vigorously defend their right to use the name of evangelical" (p. 32). Although more truly aligned with postmodern thought, members of this "small and diverse movement," labeled "postconservative evangelicals" by Roger Olsen (1995) and Millard Erickson (1997), "insist on wearing the label 'evangelical'" but "are shedding theological conservatism" (Olsen, 1995, p. 480). Olsen identifies the defining characteristics of these postconservative evangelicals, including (1) a rejection of triumphalism and epistemological certainty regarding theological truth-claims due to the "perspectival and paradigm-dependent" nature of human knowing; (2) an eagerness to engage in dialogue with nonevangelicals; (3) a reliance on a broader variety of theological sources than just the Bible; (4) a theological shift from Reformed Calvinism (an outgrowth of the Protestant Revolution with a strong emphasis on predestination and propositional truth) toward Arminianism (which emphasizes human free will) and Pentecostalism (with its emphasis on the experiential working of the Holy Spirit); (5) an affirmation of God's grace permeating nature and every human culture; and (6) an abandonment of the traditional exclusive view of conservative Protestants on salvation for a more inclusive view in which it is possible for many of those who have never heard the message of Christ to be saved. Since three of these very issues surfaced when high school student participants in the case study portion of this book investigated Islam, Roman Catholicism, and the indigenous cultures of the Mayas, Aztecs, and Incas, these items will be explored now in greater detail: (1) the willingness to learn from other religious traditions, (2) Scripture and other divine revelation, and (3) the scope of salvation.

Willingness to Learn from Other Religious Traditions

One alleged effect of the relativization of the evangelical tradition is an increased willingness on the part of evangelicals to learn from other religious traditions (Campbell, 1999). Particularly noteworthy is the shifting relationship between Protestants and Catholics. Some scholars see in the historical record an anti-Catholic sentiment in America up until the 1960s, with events such as the election of Catholic John F. Kennedy to the U.S. presidency and the reforms of the Catholic ecumenical council known as Vatican II turning the tide of overall Protestant opinion in a more favorable direction (Wuthnow, 1988a). As common as this view is, however, there are indications that social relations between American Protestants and Catholics had begun to improve several decades earlier (Kalmijn, 1991).

For evangelicals specifically, the 1960s does seem to be the decade in which at least some of their members began to jump on the ecumenical bandwagon (Noll, 1995). Certainly not all did, as evidenced by those present-day evangelicals who still do not consider Catholics to be fellow Christians. However, as evangelicals and Catholics have joined together in pursuit of common social goals in recent years, several prominent evangelical leaders and scholars have become more involved in significant dialogue on matters of faith with Roman Catholics as well (see Colson & Neuhaus, 1995; Rausch, 2002). This new ecumenical discussion has not been limited only to evangelicals and Catholics, but also has been occurring between evangelicals and Eastern Orthodox Christians (see Cutsinger, 1997), liberal Christians (see Brown & Pinnock, 1990), Jews (see Rudin & Wilson, 1987), Unitarians (see Quebedeaux & Sawatsky, 1979), and Mormons (see Blomberg & Robinson, 1997).

As has been shown earlier, evangelicals are, when compared to other Americans, probably only slightly more intolerant of adherents of other religious traditions. C. Smith (2000) finds that "for every one evangelical opposed to pluralism, there [are] about five other evangelicals who [voice] a strong commitment to freedom of choice and toleration of diversity" (p. 64). Allowing others to hold divergent views, however, is not the same as approving of those views. When it comes to evaluating the merits of other religions, the majority of evangelicals do claim superiority for the Christian faith; otherwise, in a culture of religious voluntarism, they would presumably choose something else. Nevertheless, according to C. Smith (2000),

> Ordinary evangelicals exhibit a broad diversity of viewpoints when it comes to the issue of evaluating other religions. Some evangelicals are hard-line exclusivists, and others are virtual universalists. Most fall somewhere in the middle, working to retain both their belief that Christianity is the true religion and their belief in mutual respect and religious freedom of choice. (p. 73)

With regard to Catholicism, a Gallup Poll finds that "contrary to widespread opinion that anti-Catholic bias exists disproportionately among evangelical or born-again Protestants, the survey [finds] that only 29% of that group—compared to 30% of Protestants generally—[describe] Catholicism as 'unfavorable'" (Reese, 2000). A survey by the Barna Research Group (1996) finds that 69% of Baptists and evangelicals support "more extensive unity in ministry between Protestants and Catholics" (p. 2). In a more recent poll, evangelicals give the late Pope John Paul II a 59% approval rating (Greenberg Quinlan Rosner Research, 2004), a finding that would have been unthinkable 50 years ago.

As for the religion of Islam, evangelical evaluations are not nearly as positive. A mere 7% of evangelicals say that Muslim teachings or practices have had an important influence on their thinking about religion or spirituality, and few can claim more than a minimal amount of personal contact with Muslims (R. Wuthnow, personal communication, June 6, 2005). Although a majority of evangelicals characterize the interactions they do have as "mostly positive," they still consistently gravitate toward negative labels to describe Islam more often than do their fellow American citizens (Wuthnow, 2005a; R. Wuthnow, personal communication, June 6, 2005). For example, the percentage of evangelicals who believe the terms "strange," "fanatical," and "violent" apply to the Muslim religion are 55, 51, and 48%, respectively, compared to 44, 47, and 40% in the general American public. Only 11% of evangelicals find Islam "appealing," a number 5% less than Americans as a whole. For those aligned with the Religious Right, a political movement "made up primarily of evangelical Protestants that seeks to infuse 'traditional values' into public policy " (Green, 1996, p. 4), Muslims are seen as more distant and less patriotic than other Americans, and less deserving of political support should a Muslim run for president (T. W. Smith, 1996). A recent survey of evangelical leaders finds that 77% have an unfavorable view of Islam, although 79% say that it is "very important" to "protect the rights of Muslims" (Ethics and Public Policy Center, 2003). Although evangelical views of Islam are often harsher than their views of Muslim Americans themselves, the negativism on the part of evangelicals toward Islam has grown increasingly severe since the September 11, 2001 attacks on the Pentagon and World Trade Center (Pew Forum on Religion and Public Life, 2002, 2005), although it must be stated that evangelical hostility toward Islam already ran fairly deep prior to the infamous bombings, as will be seen later in the ethnographic portion of this work (see Casanova, 2005, for some of the sources of this antagonism).

As for the third religious entity to be addressed in this book's case study, namely the indigenous religion of the Americas, there is little data. Unsurprisingly, few pollsters have bothered to ask evangelicals what they think of the Mayas, Aztecs, and Incas, although it has been found that 18% of evangelicals say that Native American Indian teachings or practices have had an important influence on their thinking about religion or spirituality (R. Wuthnow, personal communication, June 6, 2005).

Fully three-quarters of American evangelicals are of the opinion that people should learn more about religions other than their own, although currently only one-fifth to one-third of evangelical Christians claim to be very or somewhat familiar with Islam, Hinduism, and Buddhism (R. Wuthnow, personal communication, June 6, 2005). Additionally, most evangelical and other Christian churches have yet to make interreligious education or cooperative ventures with those of other religions a high priority (Wuthnow, 2005a).

For those who do take the step from abstract notions regarding the desirability of learning more about other religious traditions to concrete engagement with those of other faiths, motivation for doing so generally falls into one of three categories. For some, interfaith dialogue and study is a strategic method to improve one's ability to proselytize. This is actually a unilateral attempt to gather information on the person of the other religious tradition in order to tailor one's message in the hope that he or she will convert. For others, the purpose of exchange is to draw something from the other tradition to enhance one's own set of beliefs. Finally, it is possible to engage in dialogue for the sole purpose of gaining a clearer understanding of the Other, with no change intended for the belief systems of either party of the discussion.

Scripture and Other Divine Revelation

It has historically been the view of evangelicals (and many other Christians) that God has revealed himself in human history in a number of ways, including the creation of the world and the incarnation of Jesus Christ. Whereas all humankind can understand the *general revelation* of God's existence by reflecting on the created order or heeding one's conscience, there is needed for salvation a *special revelation* to impart the gospel of Christ, which the vast majority of evangelical Protestants have found almost exclusively in the infallible testimony of the Bible.

According to Hunter (1987), evangelicals have traditionally posited that "the primary purpose of the Bible is not to be a historical or scientific text. Nevertheless, when it makes statements of historical or scientific fact, it does not err" (p. 25). However, Hunter's survey of college and seminary students finds that a slim majority instead chooses the alternative statement that "the Bible is the inspired Word of God, is not mistaken in its teachings, but is not always to be taken literally in its statements concerning matters of science and historical reporting, etc." (p. 25). This subtle hermeneutic shift from "does not err" to "is not always to be taken literally" is significant, Campbell (1999) claims, in that it "indicates a concern to be freed from the necessity of defending the Biblical statements as they stand in some cases" (p. 171).

Before proceeding, it is important to note that under the banner of a broad evangelicalism are found Pentecostals, fundamentalists, and neo-evangelicals, all of whom take a somewhat different approach to biblical interpretation. For example, the neo-evangelical parameters for interpreting Scripture are a bit broader than those of their fundamentalist cousins (*Religion & Ethics NewsWeekly*, 2004b). One can see this in the ongoing debates of the scholarly community, as some neo-evangelical theologians have shied away from describing the Bible as *inerrant* in favor of the term *infallible*. To give another illustration, in a study that includes fundamentalists with neo-evangelicals, researchers find that 66% of evangelicals believe that the Bible is "the actual word of God and is to be taken literally, word for word" and 29% prefer to say that the Bible is "the word of God, but not everything in it should be taken literally, word for word" (Greenberg Quinlan Rosner Research, 2004). In a study that places fundamentalists in a separate category, only 52% of self-identified evangelicals view the Bible as "literally true" and 45% see it as "true, not always literally." Only 3% view the Bible as "true, but with errors" (C. Smith, 1998).

While data such as that found in the preceding paragraph confirm to some scholars that literal Bible interpretation is no longer a mark of evangelicalism (Ammerman, 1982; Hunter, 1987; Regnerus & Smith, 1998), it should be mentioned that there is a problem with the questions used in nearly every study to measure the hermeneutical views of survey respondents. Although they work well to measure whether individuals perceive themselves as "literal" or "figurative" Bible believers, few of the questions are able to measure what respondents actually read as literal and what they read as metaphorical. For example, the response "true, not always literally" can be chosen in good conscience by the most ardent fundamentalist as well as the most permissive liberal. This is because all Christians, to some extent, read the Bible figuratively. As Bruce (2002) provocatively puts it,

> No fundamentalist thinks that the "Lamb of God" would be good with mint sauce. Conservatives understand metaphor and allegory. The difference is that the conservative asserts that the text itself tells us what is metaphorical; the liberal supposes that all texts are in some senses metaphorical. (p. 113)

Therefore, if researchers truly want to measure how evangelicals interpret Scripture, they need to ask respondents to specify which things in the Bible are to be taken either literally or metaphorically (parables, creation narratives, events in the lives of specific Biblical figures, etc.). Otherwise, they only end up measuring respondents' self-perception or hermeneutical awareness. It may be that the way evangelicals read the Bible has remained constant, but how they see themselves as reading may have shifted.

One thing that has undoubtedly changed regarding evangelical views of the Bible is how it relates to other sources of authority. In 1978/1979, for example, the Princeton Religious Research Center found that nearly 68% of evangelicals claimed the Bible as their primary religious authority, with the Holy Spirit second at 25% (Hunter, 1983). The date of this study is located near the chronological midpoint in an evangelical shift from the "theological to the relational," from "knowledge about God toward the experience of God" (Hatch, 1995, p. 402). Just as the postconservative evangelicals depicted by Olsen (1995) are open to a broadening of theological sources beyond the Bible, a number of evangelicals are moving beyond a tightly controlled propositional conception of revelation (represented by the Bible and the Reformed tradition) to more subjective experiential forms of divine communication (represented by the Holy Spirit and Pentecostalism). As such, individual evangelicals are now more than twice as likely to say that God's truth is "revealed in many ways, such as history, culture, nature, and tradition" than they are to say that it is "fully revealed only in the Bible" (R. Wuthnow, personal communication, June 6, 2005). For a sizable minority, divine revelation extends to other religious traditions as well, as demonstrated by the 29% of evangelical churchgoers who think God's word is revealed in writings such as the sacred texts used by Muslims or Hindus.

Moreover, the use of the Bible as a propositional text may be diminishing as some parishioners come to identify more with the Bible's narrative quality. Instead of embodying a divine constitution, the Bible is valued as the source of, as theologian Stanley Hauerwas says with an unevangelical brusqueness, "the best damn story in the world" (Clapp, 2001, p. 25). In this sense, truth is not centered primarily in the text itself, but rather, as Robert Webber (2002) has written, the Bible "infallibly takes us to Jesus, the living embodiment of truth" (p. 106).

The Scope of Salvation

A third change in evangelical beliefs is said to be occurring with regard to the doctrine of salvation. To use a famous analytical framework (see Hick, 1984), the views of religious adherents on the scope of salvation (or whatever else the goal of different religions may be) can be divided into three categories: (1) exclusivism, which sees one's own religion as the sole repository of truth and salvation; (2) inclusivism, which acknowledges that although one's own religion is superior, there may exist true revelation and salvation outside of this tradition; and (3) pluralism, in which all religions are equally true and salvific.

Traditionally, according to Hunter (1987), evangelicals have believed that "all other religious faiths and world views are either misdirected or else patently false and, therefore, potential instruments of satanic delusion. There is only one absolutely true faith" (p. 34), and it is through this one true faith in Jesus Christ that salvation comes. In support of this, C. Smith (1998) finds that 94% of self-identified evangelicals and fundamentalists affirm that faith in Christ is the only hope for salvation. In the survey employed by Hunter, the majority of evangelical college and seminary students agree with the statement, "The only hope for heaven is through faith in Jesus Christ." Nearly a third, however, choose an option not presented in C. Smith's study, that "the only hope for Heaven is through personal faith in Jesus Christ *except* for those who have not had the opportunity to hear of Jesus Christ." When asked about the eternal destiny of Gandhi, an eminently moral man who was not a Christian but rather a devout Hindu, "many students were absolutely certain he was saved, a few were certain he was not, but most were unsure of either" (Hunter, 1987, p. 38). "The existence," Hunter says, "of such a sizable minority of evangelicals maintaining this stance represents a noteworthy shift away from the historical interpretations" (p. 38).

As Hunter suggests, there does appear to be a significant minority of evangelicals who hold relatively inclusive positions regarding the saving work of God in the world's religions. According to Penning and Smidt (2002), this should surprise no one, since "[w]hile there may be core evangelical beliefs, their existence does not mean that all evangelicals necessarily agree on each and every one" (p. 51). Still, considering the exclusive claims to truth and salvation for which evangelicals are well known, it is difficult not to be taken aback by the details of some recent studies. First of all, Wuthnow (personal communication, June 6, 2005) finds that of those affiliated with evangelical churches, nearly 3 in 10 disagree to some extent with the statement, "Christianity is the only way to have a true personal relationship with God." Additionally, one-third agree that all major religions are equally good ways of knowing about God and nearly two-thirds agree that all major religions contain some truth about God. Wuthnow does not address whether these individuals see the knowledge of God present in other traditions as sufficient for eternal salvation, but another recent study finds that while a full 84% of evangelicals affirm that "the only hope for salvation is through personal faith in Jesus Christ," only 48% of the same sample believe that "only born-again Christians go to heaven" (Greenberg Quinlan Rosner Research, 2004). Unfortunately, in this latter study there is no follow-up question to determine the makeup of the "non-born-again Christians" that the remaining 52% have in mind, so it is unclear the extent to which this group includes Christians of the non-born-again variety and how much it applies to those of other faith traditions who have or have not heard of Jesus Christ.

While recent empirical results appear to further substantiate some of Hunter's claims, it should be noted that his statements purporting an evangelical drift toward inclusivism and away from rigid notions of Biblical authority have been called into question on the grounds that he does not adequately verify the extent to which previous generations of evangelicals actually held to his summary of the "historical interpretations." As such, Penning and Smidt (2002) charge that Hunter's lack of historical data allow him to present a distorted, idealized picture of the past by presuming a theological unity that never existed. Although there exists some data showing that the percentage of Americans as a whole that believes the Bible to be inerrant has dropped sharply since 1965 (Princeton Religion Research Center, 1996), there is little available data specific to the views of evangelicals in the 1950s and 1960s. Thus, whether the present state of evangelical thought is a result of change or merely a continuation of past inclinations is up for debate. Nevertheless, as a purely descriptive statement, Hunter's (1987) claim "that there is a measurable degree of uneasiness within this generation of evangelicals with the notion of an eternal damnation" (p. 38) may hold some merit for evangelicals living at the outset of the 21st century.

EVANGELICALISM: DISTINCT, ENGAGED, AND THRIVING?

At this point, it should be noted that many of the purported changes in evangelical theology, including the rise of postconservative evangelicalism documented by Olsen and Erickson, have taken place within the realm of academia. The extent to which theological developments at the scholarly level impact the average Sunday morning church attender is debatable since, like other segments of American society, evangelical elite culture varies considerably from that of its masses (J. C. Green, 2003; Green et al., 1994).

With this in mind, C. Smith's (1998) influential book *American Evangelicalism: Embattled and Thriving*, which takes a "bottom-up" approach to measuring the strength of the movement, purports that, instead of weakening evangelicalism's hold on the ordinary believer, modernity and cultural pluralism actually serve to strengthen it. Whereas many studies measure a single component of religious vitality such as church attendance or membership, Smith employs 34 different religious indicators, which fall under the following domains: adherence to beliefs, salience of faith, robustness of faith, group participation, commitment to mission, and retention and recruitment of members. These indicators are used to compare American fundamentalist, evangelical, liberal, mainline, and Roman Catholic traditions.[1]

Although it has been charged that many of the 34 measures demonstrating evangelical vitality are more stylistically indicative of being "evangelical" than being "vital" (Chaves, 1999), Smith nevertheless deems evangelicalism the strongest Christian tradition in America today. In seeking to explain these findings, Smith rebuts Hunter's (1983, 1987) claim that the success of evangelicalism is a result of the construction of a *sheltered enclave* (Smith's term, not Hunter's) that maintains social or geographical distance from the corrosive effects of modernity.

To explain evangelicalism's vigor, C. Smith (1998) advances his subcultural identity theory, in which active engagement with the larger culture is a requisite for maintaining religious vitality. However, in Smith's model, active engagement alone does not suffice to make a movement strong. Liberal Christianity, with its lack of separatist orientation, has been and is currently experiencing a marked decline in strength (Johnson, Picard, & Quinn, 1974; Jones et al., 2002). This is due to the fact that, unlike evangelicalism, it does not erect or maintain clear boundaries between itself and modern culture. What is needed, according to Smith, is an emphasis on defining one's social and theological identity using those encountered in the wider world as negative reference groups, since perceived (or real) conflict with outgroups can enhance religious cohesion and vitality within one's own tradition. In this model, it must be noted, merely to define one's boundaries is not sufficient either. Self-identified fundamentalists, with a greater separatist orientation, do not experience as vividly the threat of modern culture and thus have grown lax and fallen slightly behind self-

---

1.   It is difficult to compare the results of Smith's studies based on religious self-identification directly with other studies because the Protestant labels available to survey respondents did not include a Pentecostal option, the third historical subcategory of evangelicalism. This omission makes any comparison of Smith's self-identified "evangelicals" with the historical "neo-evangelicals" problematic, since Pentecostals are potentially included as well in Smith's "evangelical" sample. For comparative purposes, the best course of action is probably to identify Pentecostals based on respondents' denominational affiliation, as at least one study that makes use of Smith's data has done (see Sikkink, 1999), or conflate Smith's "fundamentalist" and "evangelical" samples to arrive at a sample of the broader evangelical movement. So as to avoid confusion during the remainder of this chapter, it should be mentioned here that Smith distinguishes between evangelicals and fundamentalists, whereas in the rest of this book we have considered fundamentalism as one of the three subsets of conservative Protestantism and used the term "evangelical" to refer to the wider conservative Protestant movement.

identified evangelicals on almost all measures of religious strength. What is needed to thrive in modern society, Smith claims, is both active engagement and active distinction, both qualities possessed by evangelical Protestant Christianity.

What Smith means by distinction is obvious enough, since the evangelical practice of defining oneself in opposition to others is rather commonplace (Sikkink, 1998). But if distinction means emphasizing the boundaries between one's own group and outgroups, what does "engagement" mean? On this point, Smith's theory has come under criticism for being somewhat imprecise (Hill, 2004). In the case of liberal Christians, engagement begins as the opposite of distinction, namely as a lack of cognitive boundaries with the wider American society (C. Smith, 1998). In the case of evangelicals, however, the engagement that Smith describes is not a matter of boundaries or mere categorical self-identification. In contrast to the fundamentalist strain of conservative Protestantism, which is seen as restricting social contact with others in the public square by retreating into a world of its own creation, self-identified evangelicals are engaged in the sense that they are more present and involved in the affairs of the wider American society. As Smith states, the historical modus operandi of neo-evangelicals is that of "engaged orthodoxy," or taking a stand for conservative Christian values in the public square. This interaction with others who do not share evangelical values leads to a heightened sense of threat, which in turn strengthens evangelical boundaries and increases subcultural cohesion.

So how truly engaged are evangelicals with the wider culture? One study finds that conservative Protestants, in addition to having more distinctive beliefs, also have a greater number of intragroup social relations than do moderate and liberal Protestants (Olson, 1993). Compared to social ties generated in other settings such as work, neighborhood, extended family, and voluntary organizations, conservative Protestants are more likely than moderates or liberals to name fellow church attenders as "friends, persons with whom respondents socialize, share personal matters, and persons whose opinions respondents value" (p. 42). Wuthnow (1999) similarly finds that "evangelicals are much more likely than mainline Protestants... [and] Catholics... to belong to *small* congregations, and they are the most likely to say their close friends belong to the same congregation" (p. 341, original emphasis).

According to C. Smith (1998), two-thirds of self-identified evangelicals say that most or almost all of their important family, friends, and work colleagues are Christians. Although this seems like a substantial number, Smith takes this as evidence that self-identified evangelicals are no more isolated within "micro-level enclaves of relational groups" (p. 82) than those of other principal Christian traditions (fundamentalist, mainline, liberal, and Roman Catholic). Although the numbers are similar for all of the aforementioned groups, the problem with this reasoning is that it does not take into account the differing criteria that the traditions use to determine who does and does not qualify as a fellow Christian. In the eyes of most evangelicals (including fundamentalists), in order to be considered a "true" Christian, one must be an evangelical with a conversion experience, adhere to orthodox beliefs about Christ and the Bible, and live a godly life-style to validate one's commitment (Reimer, 1996). Therefore, this more restrictive definition leads one to believe that the within-group social net-works of evangelicals are denser than those of mainline or liberal Protes-tants. When taken together with evangelicals' greater penchant for participating in church activities (J. C. Green, 2003), the evidence for this is fairly strong. It may be that societal "engagement" for most evangelicals consists not of significant day-to-day conflict with non-evangelicals, but is instead primarily a product of social comparison *within* evangelical social circles in which the speech of evangelical leaders and laypeople alike serves to reinforce the boundaries between evangelicals and the rest of the world (Hill, 2004).

Nevertheless, it does seem that evangelicalism is a very different crea-ture than the "socially encapsulated" (Stark & Bainbridge, 1985) one envi-sioned by many secularization theorists. The fundamentalist wing of conservative Protestantism has often been characterized as living in a tightly knit web of church, home, and school, and Pentecostals also display some of the same separatist tendencies. On the other hand, when taken as a whole, evangelicals are much more likely to dwell in two worlds simulta-neously. There is a sense that mass media is hostile to evangelical values (Greenberg Quinlan Rosner Research, 2004), which has led to the devel-opment of a "multimillion-dollar Christian alternaculture" (Kirn, 2002), a series of radio stations, publishing houses, and music recording labels intended to more adequately reflect those values (Bandow, 1995; Hunter, 1983). This fits Fisher's (1982) description of the institutional component of subcultures. The further the values of a subculture are from society at large, the more likely subcultural members are to create their own institu-tions to sustain their way of life (Olson, 1993). For these industries to be so profitable means that a sizable number of evangelicals consume their prod-ucts. However, for most evangelicals this does not comprise a "total world," since they still consume secular culture at about the same rate, albeit with-out allowing their children to partake of some of the products they find most offensive (Greenberg Quinlan Rosner Research, 2004; *Religion & Eth-ics NewsWeekly*, 2004a).

That evangelicals form relatively strong communities does not mean that they stay cloistered within them. Just as neo-evangelicalism emerged out of fundamentalism in the mid-20th century to bring its influence to mainstream society, evangelicals today, when distinguished from fundamentalists, are the most deprivatized religious Americans (Regnerus & Smith, 1998). Fully two-thirds of them say that religion should speak to political and social issues. Even with fundamentalists included, evangelicals' level of civic involvement is nearly as high as other religious traditions such as mainline Protestants and Catholics (J. C. Green, 2003). Although their faith does not always translate into political activism such as participating in a political protest or an election campaign, the majority of evangelicals say that they are likely to vote and that their faith has led them to engage in volunteerism (Greenberg Quinlan Rosner Research, 2004; Sherkat & Blocker, 1997; Wuthnow, 1999).

While it is unclear whether evangelicals vote more or less often than non-evangelicals (see J. C. Green, 2003; Greenberg Quinlan Rosner Research, 2004; Manza & Brooks, 1997; Wuthnow, 1999), they have been instrumental in electing evangelicals Jimmy Carter and George W. Bush to the presidency and numerous Republican party candidates at the national and local levels in recent years (Green, 2004; Green, Rozell, & Wilcox, 2003; Manza & Brooks, 1997; Woodberry & Smith, 1998). Identifying moral decline as the source of many of America's ills (T. W. Smith, 1996), evangelicals have entered the political arena in response to perceived intrusion of the state into the personal lifeworld (Regnerus & Smith, 1998), as evidenced in recent elections by efforts to maintain traditional "family values." For those whose desire to apply their faith to public policy leads them to seek public office (e.g., Deckman, 2001), the goal is not usually to maintain, create, or recreate a Christian America, but merely to make society a hospitable place for the practice of their faith and the raising of their children according to Biblical standards.

It should be noted that when conservative Protestants do enter the political arena, they sometimes do so with reservations. In what C. Smith (1997) calls the "pluralism-versus-Christendom dilemma," many evangelicals hold two conflicting and compartmentalized views regarding the legislation of morality. On the one hand, they believe that the principles found in the Bible and mandated by their faith are the best possible standard for the regulation of society. On the other hand, their commitment to individualism and free will encourages them not to force these views on people who do not wish to live by them. One can imagine how this internal tension presents difficulties for leaders wishing to mobilize the evangelical electorate in the effort to transform society.

Voting and participation in the political process is one important aspect of civic life, but another that deserves attention is volunteering in one's local community. Religion is often a predictor of whether an individual is likely to engage in volunteerism (Becker & Dhingra, 2001; Greeley, 1997; Lam, 2002; Wilson & Janoski, 1995; Wilson & Musick, 1997; Wuthnow,

1991), and evangelicals seem to volunteer at about the same rate as those of other Christian traditions (Becker & Dhingra, 2001; J. C. Green, 2003; R. Wuthnow, personal communication, July 22, 2005, finds evangelicals slightly less likely to volunteer). There are differences between evangelicals and other Christians regarding the values that inspire volunteerism, what this activism means (Becker & Dhingra, 2001), and the venues in which the activity occurs. Indeed, this final item is representative of the larger debate about multiculturalism, assimilation, social capital, and the health of America's civic order. When evangelicals volunteer, do they expend their time and financial resources only for the benefit of their own group, or do they serve the larger good as well? To use Putnam's (2000) terms, do evangelical communities form "bonding capital" with those who share core identity components but no "bridging capital" with those who do not?

Christian congregations of any stripe "exist primarily as places of worship and fellowship, where building up the spiritual and moral lives of their own members is at the heart of what they do" (Ammerman, 2002, p. 131). While it is true that evangelical churches have an even greater percentage of activities geared toward community maintenance and growth than do other Christian traditions (Wilson & Janoski, 1995), it is debatable whether this is a good or bad thing. For some scholars, this buildup of bonding capital is detrimental to the health of American society in that it creates an insular setting that, when coupled with a theology that stresses the depravity of human nature, fosters prejudice and distrust of those who are not part of the ingroup (Apple, 2001; Welch, Sikkink, Sartain, & Bond, 2004; Wilson, 2000). This view is supported by some studies that have found that evangelicals (or at least certain strains of them) display a somewhat lower level of generalized trust in others (Smidt, 1999; Welch, Sikkink, Sartain, & Bond, 2004; Wilson, 2000).

Other scholars see strong subcultures as a prerequisite for participation in the wider American society. It has been shown that membership in voluntary religious organizations increases the number of one's associates *without* diminishing the number of acquaintances in other settings (Fischer, 1982; Olson, 1993). In this view, individuals who have a network of friendship bonds within a shared moral culture will display a greater amount of trust in these specific people, which may then result in a willingness to deal openly and generously with those beyond subcultural circles (Veenstra, 2002; Wilson, 2000). Moreover, since most people volunteer because of personal connections (Becker & Dhingra, 2001), the social contacts made in church can lead to increased political activism and community service (Brown & Brown, 2003; Wilson & Janoski, 1995). Finally, leadership and other organizational skills necessary for participation in civic life, which are often learned and honed in the activities of the local church, can be transferred for use in secular organizations, including those that work for the betterment of the local community (Ammerman, 1997a, 1997b; Verba, Schlozman, & Brady, 1995). Support for this view can be found not only in churches, but also in studies of Christian educational settings, which find parents of private- and home-schooled students more engaged in certain civic activities than public school parents (C. Smith & Sikkink, 1999). Moreover, the ability of private schools to provide a secure, respectful environment with a moral consensus and collective identity is said to constitute a "hidden curriculum" in which students learn to curb self-interest in favor of contribution to the common good (Sikkink, 2004).

The problem with this second view, critics reply, is that although civic skills and other-centeredness may be developed, they are rarely transferred because church members' time and financial resources are limited (Wuthnow, 1999). Thus, a competition ensues between the congregation and other societal organizations for the services of individuals (Becker & Dhingra, 2001; Lam, 2002). Since evangelical churches expect a higher level of internal commitment (Iannaccone, 1994), this leaves little time for church members to get involved in the wider context of American civic life, which only serves to exacerbate the cultural fragmentation threatening our multicultural nation. As Wuthnow (1999) writes,

> To the extent that social capital is a way of creating the volunteer labor to get important tasks done, evangelical churches may be growing because they do a better job of guarding their own social capital. But to the extent that they grow, they may also contribute to the depletion of the society's wider stock of social capital. (p. 346)

So does the broadly defined evangelicalism of today more closely resemble the activist evangelicalism of the Second Great Awakening era or the insular fundamentalism of the 1930s and 1940s? In response to this question, the answer appears to be *neither.* More than 9 in 10 evangelicals say that, instead of "separat[ing] from the world to avoid evil," they should "engage in the world to fight evil" (J. C. Green, 2003). Yet evangelicals still have a greater number of congregational maintenance activities than outward-reaching ones (Becker & Dhingra, 2001; Putnam, 2000; Wuthnow, 1999). When individuals expend their resources for the benefit of the larger society, they do so primarily through social service agencies instead of their congregations (Chaves, 2001). For self-identified evangelicals, the majority of these agencies are religious (Park & Smith, 2000), but for individuals measured by affiliation with evangelical denominations, these organizations are more likely to be nonreligious (R. Wuthnow, personal communication, July 22, 2005). Overall, evangelicals do seem to participate in fewer activities with secular agencies than do mainline Protestants and Catholics (Ammerman, 2002; Chaves, 2001; J. C. Green, 2003; Putnam, 2000; Wuthnow, 1999), but the difference appears to be slight (R. Wuthnow, personal communication, July 22, 2005).

Moreover, although many evangelicals feel called to engage the wider society, there remains within the evangelical camp a disagreement about how best to focus their efforts. Most evangelicals see eternal salvation and reconciliation with God as humankind's most basic need. They also believe that once people surrender their lives to their Maker, their priorities will be realigned in such a way that they will live in harmony with and care for others. Thus, almost three-quarters of evangelicals agree that "if enough people are brought to Christ, social ills will take care of themselves" (J. C. Green, 2003). Consequently, much of the outreach done by individuals and their churches is evangelistic in nature as opposed to meeting individuals' temporal needs (Wilson & Janoski, 1995).

Within the last generation, however, this picture has shown signs of change. Although the conversionist impulse in itself serves to prevent isolationism (Ammerman, 1997a), it has been claimed that within the last generation evangelical churches have increased their participation in a wide range of activities designed to benefit their local community (J. C. Green, 2003). A national study finds that about a third of evangelicals now say that religious people should "help other individuals solve their own problems" (J. C. Green, 2003). Although still lagging behind mainliners in community service through congregations and secular organizations (Ammerman, 2002; Chaves, Giesel, & Tsitsos, 2002), there may be a growing number of evangelicals intent on meeting the needs of the wider public. In the case of evangelical Protestantism, therefore, it appears that "religious engagement can be both a source of, and a substitute for, secular engagement" (J. C. Green, 2003, p. 28).

BELIEF PLAUSIBILITY, MULTICULTURALISM, AND THE LIFE OF THE MIND

So does the contact with the wider American society, minimal though it may be at times, relativize and shake the beliefs of evangelicals? On an individual level, C. Smith (1998) finds that ordinary evangelicals who experience belief implausibility due to life within a pluralistic society are relatively few. Of those who identify themselves using the labels "evangelical" and "fundamentalist," only 15% admit to sometimes or often having doubts about their own faith, a number equal to mainline Protestants and less than both liberal Protestants and Catholics. With the exception of Roman Catholicism, evangelicalism (when separated from fundamentalism) also has the highest rate of intergenerational member retention, with 78% of those raised in evangelical families remaining in the tradition as they grow older. In fact, of those self-identified evangelicals surveyed who have abandoned the evangelicalism of their childhood, all have done so by moving to another of the Christian traditions, and not by abandoning their faith altogether. For those raised in fundamentalist homes, retention is admittedly a bit more difficult, with only 57% remaining within the fold, and 11% abandoning religion altogether.

As for the possibility of a younger generation of evangelicals possessing a strikingly different worldview or a lesser amount of certainty than previous generations due to the purported increase in cultural pluralism during recent decades, Penning and Smidt (2002) found that those younger than age 35 are just as orthodox and certain of their beliefs as those in older age brackets. In fact, it is those over 54 years of age who exhibit the least certainty. This statistical claim does not seem to match up with Americans as a whole, who display more certainty in God as they age (Sherkat, 2004). Nevertheless, Penning and Smidt take this distribution as evidence contradicting Hunter's (1983, 1987) secularization claims, although one could possibly counter that the older generation, due to more time in an already sufficiently pluralized and secularized environment, has been given greater opportunity to make concessions to modern society. To test Hunter's claims directly, Penning and Smidt in 1996 measured potential cohort effects by replicating Hunter's 1982 survey of evangelical college students and using Hunter's data as a baseline to determine whether a shift in boundaries had occurred as the subsequent cohort reached an equivalent point in their lives. They found that on issues such as life after death and Biblical authority, there was no indication that a significant shift had occurred during the 14-year interval.

Do these findings mean that secularization theory does not apply at all to evangelicalism? The best case could be made, again, for that small segment of the American populace, such as academics in the humanities and social sciences, for whom critical inquiry and the intellectual cohesion of beliefs is of primary importance. Possibly for this reason, Olsen and Erickson can document a shift in the beliefs of certain evangelical scholars, but C. Smith can find the masses almost entirely unaffected. For evangelicals, their own academic elites have been neither numerous nor influential. In a book titled *The Scandal of the Evangelical Mind*, which raised eyebrows in evangelical circles when it was first published in 1994, Mark Noll scolded evangelicals for not making the intellect a greater priority. He noted that although there had been some recent gains by a limited number of evangelical scholars, most of their innovation was due to the influence of nonevangelical Christians. The reason for this, Noll wrote, was that for many within the evangelical world there remained a deep-seated mistrust of scholarship, often derived from Biblical passages contrasting the "wisdom of God" with the "foolishness of men." As for those evangelicals striving at the time to use their minds in the academic world, Noll saw little hope that the larger evangelical world would pay much attention to their endeavors.

In subsequent years, however, Noll (2000b) has seen some encouraging signs, such as the launching of the journal *Books & Culture*, which provides a forum for what another observer calls a "small cadre of evangelicals" to struggle "explicitly against... anti-intellectual isolationism" (Turner, 1999, p. 12). To be sure, in some disciplines it is now inaccurate to describe either the number or the influence of evangelicals as small. For example, the Society of Christian Philosophers currently has over 1,000 members on its rolls, many of them evangelical. Additionally, the millions of dollars in research grants provided by the Lilly Endowment and the Pew Charitable Trusts in recent years have enabled a network of evangelical scholars in other disciplines to find their voices (Wolfe, 2000). In this mobilization one can see "a growing willingness among at least some evangelical Christians to consider seriously—as part of their Christian vocation—the domains of science, art, psychology, history, world affairs, social forces, literature, politics, and more" (Noll, 2000b, p. 5).

If, hypothetically, an even greater number of evangelicals were to suddenly value the life of the mind, would it serve to strengthen the evangelical movement as a whole or to weaken it? It has been said that "to the degree that it is *not* indoctrination, education liberalizes" (Hammond & Hunter, 1984, p. 233, original emphasis). Additionally, education has been shown to make people more tolerant of difference (Hyman & Wright, 1979; Jelen & Wilcox, 1990; Reimer & Park, 2001; Wilcox & Jelen, 1990), morally individualistic (Houtman & Mascini, 2002), more likely to switch religious denominations (Wuthnow, 1988a), and less certain of their beliefs (Johnson, 1997; Sherkat, 2004), including belief in an inerrant Bible (Sherkat, 1998). Consequently, evangelical parents may be justified in fearing that their children will "lose their faith" when they leave for college.

To account for evangelicalism's continued vitality, Hunter proposed in 1983 that evangelicals' lack of education served as a barrier shielding evangelicalism from the effects of modernization. In the years since Hunter's study, however, evangelicals as a whole have become considerably more educated, and currently exhibit levels of education that rival those of other religious and nonreligious subsets of American society (Greenberg Quinlan Rosner Research, 2004; Guth, 1996; C. Smith, 1998; Wuthnow, 1999; see Reimer & Park, 2001, for a differing conclusion). While fundamentalism and Pentecostalism still tend to inhibit educational attainment (Beyerlein, 2004; Darnell & Sherkat, 1997; Green et al., 1994; Keysar & Kosmin, 1995; Kosmin, Keysar, & Lerer, 1992; Lehrer, 1999; Sherkat & Darnell, 1999), neo-evangelicals are now more likely than all other religious and nonreligious groups except Jews to be college educated (Beyerlein, 2004).

Moreover, these educated neo-evangelicals are more likely to say that their faith should speak to public issues (Regnerus & Smith, 1998) and less likely to abandon the faith of their childhood (C. Smith & Sikkink, 2003). Penning and Smidt (2002) find that evangelicals with some amount of college experience are *more* orthodox and *more* certain of their beliefs than those with no postsecondary education. If the very nature of the educational process is detrimental to religion, why does it serve to strengthen the commitment of many evangelicals?

First of all, some studies have presented evidence that education per se does not lead to a decline in religious beliefs (e.g. Merrill, Lyon, & Jensen, 2003); rather, "it is much more likely that the content of education and the environment in which it is experienced shape education's effects" (Penning & Smidt, 2002, p. 68). If this were indeed true, one would expect that education at secular institutions would undermine evangelical beliefs due to the predominately humanistic and scientific nature of the instruction provided there, while education provided at evangelical postsecondary institutions by committed Christian professors would serve to strengthen orthodox beliefs (Darnell & Sherkat, 1997). Hammond and Hunter (1984), however, claim the opposite. They state that education does indeed have a destabilizing influence on the worldview of individual evangelicals, and that it occurs not primarily on the secular campus, but on the more highly insular evangelical college campus. While in "enemy territory," the evangelical student is vigilant, keeping the boundaries of his or her faith in the forefront of his or her mind in the face of the "ever-present external threat to [his or her] view of reality" (p. 233). When behind allied lines, the evangelical student, fearing no one, may let down his or her guard and open him- or herself up to influences that undermine faith.

Second, I would posit that another critical factor to be considered is the amount of true exposure to the Other experienced in different educational settings. Hammond and Hunter (1984) write of "insular" educational settings, but the term must be clarified. One can be insular in the sense that one is so culturally isolated from the Other that there is no perceived threat. However, one can also be insular by creating what I will call a *selectively sheltered enclave,* in which outgroups are acknowledged as real threats but are still kept at arms' length by the manner in which they are portrayed to ingroup members. In this method, students in a selectively sheltered enclave are only minimally exposed to negative reference groups. Because the goal is not true understanding but community maintenance, leaders portray outgroups in unflattering ways that serve to maintain and fortify subcultural boundaries. Commonalities between others' faiths and one's own are ignored and differences are stressed, creating a caricature of the Other that leaves the student with little option but to maintain the boundaries between the groups. In fact, rhetoric is sometimes strongest when religious leaders sense a need to reign in those followers who may be straying from the party line (Riesebrodt, 2003).

This is not to say, of course, that all religious information is mediated in this way and that gatekeepers such as teachers, pastors, and parents are the only limiting determinant in what is presented or received. No modern subculture is a "total world," as evidenced by the fact that even Amish children sometimes leave the setting in which they have been raised. Those in subordinate roles have access to a wide range of voices in the national and local news media, television, motion pictures, music industry, and so on, and likely derive only some of their views from pastors and other religious leaders. However, followers too have an interest in boundary maintenance, and it is often the students, parishioners, and children themselves who restrict the influx of information by choosing to listen or give credence only to those messages that will reinforce their view of the world. With these things in mind, the case study found later in this work was specifically designed in order to measure how students responded when a gatekeeper within the selectively sheltered enclave of an evangelical high school allowed more information than usual to slip through the selectively permeable membrane surrounding the educational cell by portraying outgroups in a more balanced fashion in which both differences and commonalities were given expression.

We have seen earlier in this chapter that post-conservative evangelical scholars display openness to learning from other religious traditions. Historically, however, evangelical attitudes toward the study of other cultures and other religions have been ambivalent. On the one hand, if one already knows the truth, there is no need to look for truth in the religions of others. Instead of investigating other religious traditions, it is immeasurably more profitable to spend one's time studying the Bible and the theological riches of the Christian tradition. On the other hand, 67% of Christian school parents think that "a top educational priority is teaching children about diverse cultures, races, and religions" (Sikkink, 2001, p. 37). Why would this be so if one already knows the whole truth, and nothing but the truth?

Before seeking to answer this question, it must be noted that evangelicals do not see all aspects of culture in the same light. For example, you would certainly get a more favorable reaction from parents if you encouraged students to don Indian garb than if you tried to get them to participate in Hindu religious rituals. Many elements of culture such as architecture, vestments, and cuisine are viewed as nonthreatening and even enriching by many evangelicals. Although not verified by empirical studies, American evangelicals do seem to like falafel and chicken teriyaki as much as their fellow citizens. When one moves into the area of alternative religious beliefs, however, things change considerably since the eternal consequences of misplaced religious belief are so severe. Most evangelicals handle this facet of culture very cautiously, both because conversion to another faith would be catastrophic and because of the potentially "corrosive insight into the relativity of beliefs and values" (Berger, 2001, p. 445). Therefore, it is not surprising that those strains of multicultural education that promote relativism and appreciation for religious difference are often met with resistance by many evangelicals (Sikkink & Mihut, 2000).

In contrast, evangelicals are much more congenial to strains of multicultural education whose goals include understanding, but not promoting, other systems of religious thought (Sikkink & Mihut, 2000). After all, even if one is convinced of the truthfulness of one's vision of the world, there still exist reasons for learning about others' views, even if they are deemed less meritorious from the outset. This is obvious from the prevalence of courses in evangelical Christian high schools dealing with the different worldviews found in human societies around the globe. As we have seen throughout this work, one of the things evangelicals see as a core element of their purpose in life is evangelism (Warren, 2002). Consequently, in order to spread one's faith, one must be able to relate the gospel in terms that are comprehensible to one's listeners, and to do so requires understanding of their cultural and religious backgrounds. Additionally, should others in society choose not to accept Christianity, but rather to go on the offensive, it is important to know what they believe in order to effectively refute their accusations.

Ironically, when viewed from a national civic perspective, evangelicals and proponents of diversity, traditionally wary of or antagonistic toward one another, share in common an opposition to the strict liberal agenda of assimilation (Wilson, 2003). If multicultural activists and educators envision American Christianity as holding a culturally privileged position from which it silences dissenting voices, then the two are bound to be enemies. On the other hand, if Christianity is seen as no longer possessing a central, custodial role in society, then evangelicalism and other Christian subcultures fall under their purview as entities in need of appreciation and support. In the same way, evangelicals who still harbor dreams of a Christian America find little room in the nation for those who are not of their faith. But for those who have abandoned those dreams, the future may find them banding together with advocates of diversity in an effort to maintain a place for the distinctive identities that give meaning and purpose to their lives.

CHAPTER 6

A SUBCULTURAL EDUCATION CASE STUDY

Setting, Participants, and Methodology

PURPOSE OF THE STUDY

With diversity posing such a challenge both for our civic life as a nation and for the foundational beliefs of some individuals, many have called for further study of the diverse religious communities of the United States, and the ways in which they relate to both the wider society and to its specific subgroups. For example, Wuthnow (2004) describes the challenge as

> more than simply engaging in reconnaissance work to find out what may be going on in religious communities that have not been part of the landscape earlier in our nation's history. Although each religious community deserves to be studied for what it can tell us about our common life together, these communities also co-exist in dynamic, often conflictive, but also sometimes cooperative, relationships with one another. Foremost are questions about how these communities view one another, what perceptions are communicated, and what the potential for misunderstanding may be, especially when the majority partner in many of these encounters remains, as perhaps it should be expected to, committed to the exclusive truth of its own teachings. (p. 168)

The primary purpose of this book is to explore how evangelical Christians, who comprise a subgroup that is both a majority partner (when

American Evangelicals and Religious Diversity, pages 89–103

viewed as part of the Christian whole) and decidedly committed to the exclusive truth of its own teachings, demarcate the boundaries between themselves and the religious Other. Specifically, this case study portion contributes an illustration of how students at a private evangelical high school viewed their identity within their own religious tradition and in relation to those who did not share their faith commitment.

SETTING AND PARTICIPANTS

The participants in this study, which was conducted in the Spring of 2001, were 14 students enrolled in a third-year Spanish course at an evangelical high school, which I will call Midwest Christian Academy.[1] In a typical year, this class would be composed mostly of juniors, and the 2000–2001 school year was no exception. Of the 6 males and 8 females, there were 12 juniors in the class, accompanied by 1 sophomore and 1 senior.

In existence since 1994, Midwest Christian was a private, college-preparatory high school. The school was not the extension of a particular church, but was started and sustained by three businessmen who wanted to provide a Christian education for their children and the surrounding community. Unlike most Christian schools, which begin with the elementary grades and later add middle and high schools as the children age, Midwest Christian Academy was composed only of grades 9 through 12. During its first 7 years, the school had seen rapid growth, and at the time when this study took place, the student body was made up of around 220 young people. After spending its startup phase on the upper floor of a large local church, the school now enjoyed a new building on a 70-acre campus on the outskirts of a city.

As a school, the life of the Spirit and the life of the mind were Midwest Christian's top priorities. According to the school's policy manual and promotional materials, the school's mission statement was, "Midwest Christian Academy is dedicated to providing a Christ-centered college preparatory education for parents and students committed to spiritual growth and academic excellence." Moreover, it was explicitly stated that "The purpose of Midwest Christian Academy is to train students to know, honor, and love Jesus Christ by imparting truth, faith, and character."

As a college-preparatory school, Midwest Christian had seen over 95% of its graduates continue their studies after high school. Few of these alums sought admission to Ivy League schools or other elite postsecondary insti-

---

1.   In addition to the institution, all names referring to participants and other persons related to the research setting have been coded for confidentiality.

tutions; rather, most selected state universities in the Midwest, while a significant minority attended Christian and other private colleges. In order to gain admission to Midwest Christian in 2000–2001, it was required that a student score in at least the 6th stanine (out of a possible 9) on the Otis–Lennon School Ability Test (OLSAT). By the time the average student graduated, he or she would have taken the ACT test and received a score of approximately 25, a number nearly 4 points higher than the state norm. For most students, academic achievement was deemed a priority in the home. In fact, for the great majority of the students at Midwest Christian, these home lives were relatively stable; very few came from divorced or single-parent families. Most of these students' parents could be characterized as well-educated and located in the middle and upper socioeconomic classes. Among their number were both millionaires and those who made significant sacrifices in order to pay the yearly $5,450 tuition. It has been said that

> [M]iddle class and more educated parents tend to shape Christian schools toward less tension with the outside world, greater emphasis on academic excellence, less rigid social control of students and greater room for individual creativity and expression, and less denominationally distinctive ways of integrating religion into school life. (Sikkink, 2001, p. 9)

In many respects this description fit Midwest Christian quite well. In a survey administered in 2004, the top reason parents gave for choosing to enroll their children at Midwest Christian Academy was the school's spiritual emphasis, with academic quality only slightly behind. Like many schools, there existed a tension between student expression and social control. Students were required to wear uniforms, although the dress code was only sporadically enforced. Some teachers were more concerned with student appearance than others, and efforts made on the part of administration to crack down elicited occasional parental protest that the school was becoming too "legalistic." Students were able to express themselves to various extents in classes such as journalism and creative writing, in theatrical and musical productions, and through varsity and junior varsity sports, all of which were at different levels of proficiency due to the relative newness of the school and its programs.

Regarding the religious nature of Midwest Christian Academy, the school was squarely evangelical, yet shied away from any sort of specific denominational instruction. As we have seen, market realities typically encourage private Christian schools to move toward broader, less sectarian, religious instruction (Wagner, 1997). Although in racial terms the school was composed predominately of white students, in religious terms it was not entirely homogeneous. Although the students at Midwest Christian came primarily from three feeder middle schools that were associated with nondenominational Christian, Lutheran Missouri Synod, and Assembly of God churches, the number of congregations represented by the student body surpassed 50. For that reason, employees were instructed that whenever controversial issues that were known to cause division within the evangelical community arose they were to refer students to their parents and the pastor of their local church for answers. As a private school, Midwest Christian was not accountable to the views of the general public, but rather to its tuition-paying constituents, who held a variety of doctrinal positions. It should be noted, however, that this diversity still existed within the parameters of conservative Protestant Christianity. Therefore, although parents and students may have had different theological views stemming from divergent interpretations of the Bible, it was still the Bible that was appealed to as the source and authority for those views.

Although not directly accountable to the general American public, it would be false to say that Midwest Christian was not influenced by the wider American culture. It has been shown that nearly all private Christian subcultural schools make a number of accommodations to both contemporary popular culture and the professional education culture (Wagner, 1990), and in a single day at Midwest Christian one could find an abundance of practices that had been drawn originally from the public school system and exuded the style and content of popular culture. In many other ways, however, life at Midwest Christian was much different than that found in a public high school. For starters, students were required to take a course in the Bible each year, to attend a weekly chapel service, and to respectfully participate during prayer and a devotional reading that preceded many classes. In addition, the majority of students either led or participated in weekly small group times designed to foster spiritual accountability and encouragement among peers.

In some sense, Midwest Christian Academy could be considered an enclave, but in other ways it could not. The school was a discipleship, not an evangelistic school, meaning that all those who entered were expected to share the values of a generalized evangelical Christianity. Therefore, alternative enframings of reality were generally not provided to students by other students. There were certainly some students who were not saints and did not practice a devout lifestyle, but these students were not likely to be able to articulate alternative worldviews; rather, they were just "uncommitted" Christians (although other students sometimes doubted whether these students were truly Christians since they did not show much evidence of a transformed, virtuous life). In the area of curriculum, Midwest Christian did expose students to some alternative worldviews. Very few of the courses used textbooks designed specifically for Christian schools; most teachers preferred to use secular textbooks and provide a conservative

Christian critique when necessary. For example, the school's biology instructors taught creationism and intelligent design to explain the origins of life, but used secular texts in order to equip students to refute the evolutionary theories found within. In English classes, students read Christian authors such as C. S. Lewis, but also explored the classics of Western civilization, from Beowulf to Shakespeare to Oscar Wilde. In this way, students could be physically removed from modern society (as represented by the public schools) between the hours of 8:00 A.M. and 3:00 P.M., and yet could still intellectually engage its ideas and philosophies during this time by holding them up to the light of conservative Protestant Christianity.

Concerning other world religions, however, it must be admitted that the amount of exposure at Midwest Christian was minimal. Although one of the required Bible courses was named *Worldviews*, the curriculum of this class was centered on a commonly used text in Christian high schools named *Understanding the Times*, which in its first edition dealt extensively and exclusively with New Age, Marxist, and secularist worldviews and completely ignored world religions such as Islam, Buddhism, and Hinduism. The lone exception to this pattern of omission occurred one year when an individual teacher, Mr. Weaver, took it upon himself to expose students in this class to various world religions. Apart from Mr. Weaver's class, whenever non-Christian religions were addressed in other settings, such as informal talk between teachers or between students, the tone expressed toward other faith traditions was usually negative.

In one notorious instance, a misunderstanding led to a certain Lakota Sioux man giving the message at a chapel service, with a rather telling response on the part of the school administration. Initially, the chapel coordinator thought that the speaker was a Christian involved in an evangelistic ministry to the Lakota, but he instead turned out to be an active practitioner of Lakota ways who in his presentation sought to show how many Lakota beliefs were commensurate with the Christian faith. The speaker was less than successful in making his case and before the session was over the administration had already begun to think in terms of parental perceptions and damage control. In short order a letter was sent home explaining the misunderstanding, apologizing, and assuring parents that the school would make every effort to see that future religious instruction was done from a Christian perspective.

Although the religious instruction provided by the school was presented from a conservative Protestant perspective, the students themselves were far from isolated in a "total world" when they left Midwest Christian following the school day. Students had available to them the Christian alternaculture with its music, websites, and books, yet they did not limit their cultural intake to these items. For example, students were just as likely to listen to secular musicians such as the Dave Matthews Band as to

Christian groups such as Third Day or Jars of Clay. Although the range of explicitly Christian entertainment available to students was extensive in the area of music, there were (and still are) very few conservative Christians involved in the production of television shows and motion pictures (Woodberry & Smith, 1998), two other favorite pastimes of American youth. Some students at Midwest Christian consciously refrained from indulging in certain cultural products such as R-rated movies or music with explicit lyrics. Even so, the values present within the wider culture were sure to have made an impression on their minds, not least the constant and considerable appeal of mass-consumer capitalism and its normative moral agenda (C. Smith, 2005). Although generally not news junkies, many students were at least minimally exposed to local, national, and international affairs through local and national news media, which influenced the way they viewed other subcultures. For instance, on the one hand they heard calls for religious tolerance and, on the other, saw Muslims portrayed primarily as fanatical zealots.

The extent to which parents played a role in determining their children's accessibility to the surrounding culture was variable. For some, the protective barriers surrounding their children were highly porous, while others attempted to restrict access to those things they found most potentially harmful. Yet even those parents who were highly involved in their children's lives realized that they had to choose which battles to fight, and most allowed their children a moderate amount of leeway when it came to cultural consumption. However, when it came to explicit religious instruction of their children, most parents saw the home and family context as the proper place for the religious narrative to be spun. As a result, some parents spent time daily with their children, inquiring into their experiences and encouraging them with religious insights. Other parents did less of this, and instead trusted that their children would receive what they needed from the youth programs at their church and from Midwest Christian, whose philosophy of "in loco parentis" meant that the school's role was as an extension of those values that evangelical Protestant families would typically promote in the home.

To establish that Midwest Christian Academy was indeed evangelical, one can use all three of the measurement methods presented in Chapter 2. Theologically, although the school did not take a strong stance on many potentially divisive issues, it did have a list of non-negotiable beliefs found in its statement of faith. This statement was drawn from Christian schooling's largest accrediting body, the Association of Christian Schools International (ACSI), a ministry "with the goal of being an 'enabler' for the evangelical Christian community of preschools, elementary and secondary schools, and post-secondary schools" (Council for American Private Education, 2005; see Appendix A for a copy of this statement of faith). In terms of denominational affiliation, the school was not associated with a particular denomination, yet the overwhelming majority of students came from churches that would be classified as evangelical. To use self-identification, the evangelical nature of Midwest Christian can be established through the school's self-identification with ACSI, along with occasional mention of the term in the speech of school administrators and in the faculty employment manual.

As for classifying the student participants in the study as evangelical, it can be noted that two requirements of the admissions process were that each student sign a form affirming that he or she had "accepted Jesus Christ as their Lord and Savior" and that he or she express agreement with the school's statement of faith, which included theological affirmations of the inspiration and inerrancy of the Bible, the saving power of Jesus Christ through his death on the cross, and the mandate to proclaim the gospel to all the world. These items correlate perfectly with McGrath's (1996) definition of evangelicalism (see Chapter 2). Denominationally, the students' evangelical identity can be established through the specific churches they attended.

As for self-identification, students did not use the term "evangelical" to describe themselves during our investigation, though they sometimes used other identifiers such as "Bible-believing." That they did not use the specific term is not surprising, however, for a number of reasons. First, they were never asked specifically whether they identified with the term. Second, as Sikkink (1998) has shown, religious individuals use multiple monikers to describe themselves. The term "evangelical" is not always a primary label, and when people use the term, they do not always mean what researchers have in mind. Studies that distinguish evangelicals by self-identification (e.g., C. Smith, 1998) usually find smaller numbers of evangelicals than studies employing the other two methods, which may mean that the label, when used in the manner in which researchers intend, is significant only for the highly committed or more theologically sophisticated. In the case of youth, the latter of these makes self-identification somewhat less useful for classification purposes. At any rate, I believe that the combination of evangelical church attendance and doctrinal assent with the principal tenets of evangelical Christianity are sufficient to establish that the students were professing evangelicals when they enrolled at Midwest Christian.

RESEARCH METHODOLOGY

Guiding Research Questions

This study was not fully emergent in design, but rather began with some guiding questions that evolved into a fuller analysis of student perspectives.

Specifically targeted were those areas in which the theological boundaries of the evangelical movement are purported to have been shifting due to the pressures of the wider American culture and its various religious sub-cultures (see Chapter 5). In the context of a class investigation of Latin American and Spanish religious and cultural history, this meant analyzing student views on (1) the specific religious traditions of Islam, Roman Catholicism, and the worldviews of the Mayas, Aztecs, and Incas; (2) divine revelation and the Protestant canon of Scripture; (3) the presence of God in other faith traditions and the scope of salvation; and (4) the relative importance or unimportance of evangelism and interreligious dialogue. In addition to these four areas, I also sought to analyze anything else that indi-cated that a relativization of tradition was taking place (or had already occurred) on an individual level in the lives of any of the students, and to examine their subsequent responses to that relativization.

Research Instrument and Methodological Approach

This study was teacher-based research from a qualitative paradigm, and I, the teacher-researcher, was the research instrument. As Maykut and Morehouse (1994) explain, the aim of the qualitative researcher is *indwell-ing*, a process in which the researcher, instead of standing apart from the subjects as an objective observer, purposefully interacts with the partici-pants in the research process and, in doing so, gathers data from the inside. It means "being at one with the persons under investigation, walk-ing in the other person's shoes, or understanding a person's point of view from an empathetic rather than a sympathetic position" (p. 25).

As a Christian who had been raised in the evangelical subculture but had since begun to explore issues pertaining to the wider religious world, I believe that I had some advantages in this study that another researcher might not have had. First of all, as a "pilgrim with one leg still stuck in the tent," as Grant Wacker (2001, p. x) describes it, I knew immanently the world of the evangelical faith tradition, yet had the distance necessary both (a) to present religious material in a more multivalent fashion than was normally done at Midwest Christian and (b) to step outside of the tradition to gain another vantage point from which to view the data during analysis. Second, I believe that my insider status at the school allowed me access to the setting. As Alan Peshkin (1986) found in his study of a fundamentalist school, access is not easy to obtain from the gatekeepers of Christian schools who are concerned about protecting their constituents from the influences of "the world." Although Midwest Christian Academy did not have nearly the same degree of separatist orientation as the fundamentalist school of Peshkin's study, it is highly doubtful that an outsider would be allowed to teach or facilitate discussion on matters of religion. Admittance might have been granted to someone from within the wider Christian tradition, since the school did have on staff at the time a history teacher who was a member of the Eastern Orthodox Church and a member of the maintenance staff who was Roman Catholic, but teaching responsibilities certainly would not have been given to someone from outside of the Christian tradition.

From the outset, the approach I strove to take toward the various religions we explored was one of balance. During the 4 previous years that I had spent at Midwest Christian Academy, I had seen a positive treatment of other faith traditions only once, in Mr. Weaver's class. As a selectively sheltered enclave, teachers generally accentuated differences with outgroups and focused on "what's wrong with what they believe" and "how you can refute or evangelize them." In my study, however, I attempted to implement a more multivalent curriculum, dealing with genuine differences when they arose, but also acknowledging commonalities between the different faith traditions and evangelical Protestant Christianity.

Of course, complete impartiality on the part of a researcher is impossible in qualitative research. What is meant here by the term "balance" is that, in exploring with students how other religious traditions relate to Christianity, neither difference nor commonality was portrayed as the orthodox position. I do not claim to have presented an equal number of commonalities and differences, but can say that I presented enough of each for students to have to deal with both, whether they chose to acknowledge difference, similarity, or a combination of the two.

As any researcher knows, refraining from premature judgment is a necessary measure if you want to encourage forthrightness and full disclosure on the part of one's participants. I had promised to tell the students some of my personal opinions at the end of the study, but up until that time no point of view was ruled out of bounds. Although I previously had not heard many positive assessments of other faiths at the school, I wondered if there were students who did hold more favorable views but remained silent because they knew they were in the minority. To find out, my classroom had to be a safe place to express divergent opinions, and this meant trying to eliminate social desirability effects as much as possible. Of course, the attempt to be nonjudgmental may have seemed a bit odd in itself, since this was not the normal approach to other religions taken by most teachers. However, I believe that refraining from judgment allowed the more unorthodox students the freedom to speak, while the more conservative students still felt comfortable expressing themselves due to the overall position of the school.

On a pedagogical note, I must state here that withholding my views during the data-gathering process did not amount to implicitly teaching that there were no answers to the questions we were asking or that any one answer was as good as another, since I had pledged to reveal later what I thought on some of the issues we had discussed. Had I been at the point where I had more solid opinions on the subjects we had been studying, I might have encouraged students to adopt my viewpoint. However, when I eventually did reveal my positions, I prefaced my talk with the disclaimer that the contents were a matter of personal opinion and that the students were free to take, leave, or modify them as they saw fit.

I was also aware at the outset of the study that, even though I had a solid base of knowledge in religion and other disciplines of the humanities, I was not an expert on the religions we were to investigate. Although familiar with the general historical outline of Spain and Latin America, the majority of my formal training had been in education and the Spanish language. For this reason, to compensate for any lack of understanding on my part, the curriculum I compiled relied heavily on primary texts, videos, and a guest speaker on Catholicism in addition to my survey lectures (see Appendix B and Appendix C for a list of the texts and videos). I had first become familiar with a number of the texts during a 2000 summer institute for teachers at Arizona State University underwritten by the National Endowment for Humanities. The speaker I had come to know personally from his employment on the maintenance staff at Midwest Christian. If it were possible, I would have invited guest speakers from the other religions as well, but it was likely that visits by Muslims or those practicing Native American religion would have been seen by at least some of the school gatekeepers as suspect.

At the beginning of the study I had planned to profile the entire class, but with over 200 essays, collages, surveys, etc., not including the numerous transcribed pages of class discussions, it soon became evident that this would be entirely unmanageable. For this reason, through the method of purposive sampling (see Maykut & Morehouse, 1994), three key informants were selected who best represented the different perspectives within the class as a whole. This sample included students at different points along a continuum: (1) the student most interested in defending orthodoxy, (2) the student with the greatest desire to explore unconventional ideas, and (3) the student in the middle, wrestling with the issues that arose during this encounter with different traditions of faith. Analysis was limited primarily to these individuals. Admittedly, the above continuum measures actively involved students, and not the religiously apathetic. I do not think, however, that lack of interest in religious matters was much of an issue, since each of the 14 students participated frequently in our discussions and other class activities.

Data Collection and Analysis

The data in this study were collected in a variety of ways. A survey (see Appendix D) was given at the outset to collect demographic data and information regarding each student's level of previous experience with other cultures in general, and specifically with Islam, Roman Catholicism, and the worldviews of the Mayas, Aztecs, and Incas.

Following this, the class began a series of instructional units on these religions as historically and currently practiced by the peoples of Spain and Latin America. At the beginning of each of the first three units, students were instructed to create a montage of at least six images displaying their initial impressions of the religion we were about to study. Students were also required to write reflective essays (see Appendix E) dealing with issues raised during classroom lectures, videos, and primary documents written by historical and contemporary adherents of the aforementioned religions. In addition, I occasionally collected other writings, such as the students' definitions of salvation and notes that they took as they read the Koran.[2]

As the studied topics provoked class discussion, I took field notes of student comments and reflected on what had been said in class. Class discussion was taped and meaningful sections were transcribed verbatim, minus nonmeaningful utterances (e.g., um, like, you know). Also taped was the dialogue between students and our Catholic guest speaker.

After our investigation of the various cultures drew to a close, students did three things. First of all, they filled out a questionnaire (see Appendix F) asking them to choose, from a list of options, the statement that best fit their point of view on items related to the essential questions guiding the study. Some of these questions were adapted from Hunter's (1983) study *American Evangelicalism*. Second, each student participated in two focus group interviews to discuss these issues as encountered during the study (see Appendix G for interview schedules). Finally, nearly a year later, after almost all of the initial data had been analyzed, longitudinal member checking was done with the three principal informants to clear up some of the remaining questions I had regarding the information they had provided.

---

2.   As the reader may have noticed, the titles of sacred texts are not italicized in this book. Although this is customary nowadays in the cases of the Bible and Koran, this practice will be extended to other sacred texts such as the Apocrypha and the Popol Vuh of the Quiche Maya as well. Additionally, although the transliteration Qur'an is currently more prevalent in scholarly circles, the version of the sacred Islamic text that we used during our investigation was an older translation that still used the spelling Koran. Since the students chose to use this spelling as well, it will be found throughout this work.

All of the data in this study were collected in such a way as to ensure proper data and methodological triangulation (Denzin, 1978). Data triangulation, or multiplicity in the data-gathering process with regard to the components of (a) person, (b) space, and (c) time, was achieved as students expressed themselves (1) both independently and in my presence; (2) in the classroom and as homework; and (3) over a period of 3 months, with a longitudinal member check occurring a year after the end of the study. Methodological triangulation was achieved by the use of a variety of data collection instruments and forms, including a survey, questionnaire, essays, group interviews, individual interviews, class discussion, and montages, thereby incorporating verbal, written, and aesthetic expression.

Although the researcher in a qualitative study "is a part of the investigation as a participant observer, in-depth interviewer, or a leader of a focus group," he or she "also removes him/herself from the situation to rethink the meaning of the experience" (Maykut & Morehouse, 1994, p. 25). It was my responsibility as the teacher-researcher to step back after gathering the data and assess and report the significance of what had been experienced in the classroom setting.

In analyzing the data, my purpose was twofold: to measure the *static* (which I defined as the students' current status as a result of previous experience, or lack thereof, with religious diversity) and the *dynamic* (which I defined as any noticeable change due to contact with the particular traditions during our investigation in class). If measuring the static had been my sole objective, it may have sufficed simply to administer a questionnaire or two and to conduct an interview. However, I also wanted to see the guiding questions answered in the context of an actual encounter with other religious traditions. As such, the study was composed of a series of five curricular units. The first four dealt specifically with (1) Islam; (2) Roman Catholicism; (3) the indigenous worlds of the Mayas, Aztecs, and Incas; and (4) the Spanish conquest and mission endeavor in the New World. The fifth and final unit sought to address the primary research questions without limiting discussion to any particular religion. Broadening the scope in this final stage allowed students to explore the key issues by drawing from any and all of the traditions we had studied and from other previous life experiences as well.

Once the data were collected, I set out to analyze what I had gathered. Using a modified constant comparative method (see Lincoln & Guba, 1985), I separated the student data into individual *units of meaning.* For each of the three primary informants, I then placed these units in preestablished categories corresponding to each of the five essential issues/questions guiding research detailed earlier in this chapter. Relations within each of these categories then led to a structure for reporting the data.

During analysis, the original casing of informants was maintained, even if it varied from accepted usage (e.g., God, Virgin Mary, Catholic, Pope, Indian, Indians), since divergence from accepted norms could be meaningful. Parallel to the issue of inappropriate casing, students made many statements that were either factually incorrect or potentially offensive to some people. As a researcher, I made no attempt to standardize or otherwise subjectively correct them, although as a teacher I certainly would have liked to reteach those concepts that students had misunderstood.[3] Additionally, although Midwest Christian was a college-preparatory high school, students still made numerous grammatical and punctuation errors in writing samples and often spoke in a stream-of-consciousness fashion with enough twists, turns, and run-on sentences to make one's head spin. In reporting incoherent data, clarifications of meaning were often provided in brackets, but no attempt was made to correct student language mistakes or to waste valuable paper and ink on [sic] notations.

Although the Bible does contain feminine as well as masculine metaphors for God, nearly all English translations use masculine pronouns and possessive adjectives to refer to God. In keeping with this convention and common evangelical usage, this study did the same. With regards to people, however, all direct Biblical quotations (which were provided in brackets whenever student participants cited verses but did not provide their own quotation) were taken from *Today's New International Version* (TNIV), a recent gender-inclusive revision of the *New International Version* (NIV), a translation commonly used by the students at Midwest Christian. In at least two cases in this study, use of this version lent clarity to passages that have been traditionally translated using masculine terms when the intent of the original author was to refer generally to all of humanity, both men and women.

---

3.   As a nonexpert in world religions, I am certain that I made a few errors myself in presenting the different religious traditions, yet as a disclaimer I must say that there are many things expressed by the primary informants that are in direct contrast to what I taught. For example, one of the primary informants held that the Koran was written by Mohammed, even though I explicitly mentioned that he is traditionally held to have been illiterate. This same student called the Incas "Meso-americans," despite the fact that I taught that the term applied only to those indigenous groups living in modern-day Mexico and Central America. To give a final example, another of the primary informants believed the Mayas to be peace-loving, even though I described how warfare between various Mayan kingdoms is seen by many scholars as the best explanation for the collapse of Classical Mayan civilization.

Provisions for Trustworthiness

In a study like this one on religious convictions, in which the topic is of a sensitive and personal nature, a researcher runs the risk that informants will not tell the entire truth or will be hesitant to express their opinions, especially in a selectively sheltered enclave where unorthodox views are not usually affirmed. In my case, however, I believe that the students were more honest than would normally have been expected. At Midwest Christian, the third-year Spanish class was not a required course, so those students enrolled in the class were there voluntarily. Since I was the only Spanish teacher at the school, all of the students except the lone sophomore had been in my class for 3 years, and I believe that they felt safe discussing these issues with me due to the rapport we had built during that time.

It is also possible in a qualitative study that, since the researcher is so heavily involved, the study may be skewed due to researcher bias. I realized that my biases were a factor in how I introduced subject material and interpreted the resulting data. Regarding the traditions we were to be investigating, I had grown up with mostly positive experiences with Catholicism, but had few significant relationships apart from a couple of neighbors and, more recently, with the guest speaker who visited the class during our investigation. My early years were also colored by my grandfather's involvement with an organization whose goal was to reach Muslims with the Christian gospel. In college, I became friends with a Muslim, although due to a language barrier and a lack of curiosity on my part, we did not dialogue very deeply on matters of faith. As for indigenous American religion, I spent 2 years prior to accepting a position at Midwest Christian Academy teaching at a Christian private school in Quetzaltenango, Guatemala, and was able during various excursions to observe a few instances of indigenous religious practice.

Although I would describe myself at the time we began the study as having been fairly open to new understandings of the theological issues we explored (salvation, the nature of Scripture and revelation, etc.), I was in the process of thinking through many of these issues myself. For this reason, I believe it was truly an ideal time to conduct the study. Obviously, the fact that I had begun to explore the wider religious world indicates a measure of dissatisfaction with some of the answers I had originally been given, but since I had yet to make up my own mind on several of the issues at hand, I do not think that I would have encouraged students too strongly toward any particular view. Because some of my students were people-pleasers who might have told me what they thought I wanted to hear, I withheld my opinions from those who asked for them, promising that I would tell them after the study was completed. For those issues on which I did hold a particular view, I routinely checked myself, mentally reviewing previous field notes and upcoming lecture outlines to ensure that I did not stray from my intended position of balance.

As for the ethical considerations in this study, all students and their parents were informed prior to the start of the study that they were to be involved in a project to document how they responded during the investigation of the aforementioned cultures. The students were assured that their privacy would be respected and their real names would not be used in the final report. A letter was also mailed to parents, which they returned, giving consent for their child to participate in the study.

CHAPTER 7

MIDWEST CHRISTIAN ACADEMY ENCOUNTERS ISLAM, ROMAN CATHOLICISM, AND THE WORLDVIEWS OF THE MAYAS, AZTECS, AND INCAS

In the previous chapter readers got their first glimpse of Midwest Christian Academy, an evangelical high school "dedicated to providing a Christ-centered college preparatory education for parents and students committed to spiritual growth and academic excellence." While the last chapter introduced the methodological approach and many of the details of the study, this chapter will narrate the course of events and curricular implementation of the historical and religious investigation that I undertook with the students in my class. The point of this chapter is not to present the data, although there may be a minimal amount reported, but rather to give an overall sense of what we did together as a class. The vast majority of the data will be presented in the upcoming chapters reserved for the views of the three primary informants: Amy, Caleb, and Nathan.

American Evangelicals and Religious Diversity, pages 105–116
Copyright © 2006 by Information Age Publishing
All rights of reproduction in any form reserved.

A BRIEF TIMELINE OF EVENTS

Introducing the Study

The investigation with the third-year Spanish class was initiated on the afternoon of February 14, 2001, the end of the sixth week of the spring semester. I explained to the students that they would be participating in a project to document their opinions on some of the cultures we would encounter during a historical exploration of medieval Spain and the beginning of its relations with the Americas. Prior to this, I had mailed consent forms to each of the students' parents. I had also prepared a short explanation to assuage any concerns that parents may have had. Concerns about the content of the study never materialized, however. In fact, the only feedback I got from parents was from two mothers who commented to me that their children had truly enjoyed and learned a great deal from their experiences during our investigation.

On day 1, after receiving signed consent forms from each of the students, the first set of data was collected with the administration of the demographic survey. The purpose of this instrument was to gauge the breadth of each participant's exposure to the world—through different places they had lived or visited, different churches and schools they had attended, and previous exposure to religious traditions other than evangelical Protestant Christianity. As a whole, the class expressed an eagerness to learn about other cultures, with a mean score of just over 7 on a scale of 1 to 10, with all students rating their desire somewhere between 5 and 9. The average rating given by students for the importance of the Christian faith in their daily lives was an 8, with eight of the students choosing the maximum score of 10. Over two-thirds of the students had lived in the Midwest City metro area for their entire lives, and over four-fifths of them had traveled outside of the United States, with Mexico the most frequent destination. Nine of the 14 students had attended only private Christian schools during their educational years, while the remaining five had attended a mixture of both public and private schools. Two of the 14 had some experience with home schooling as well. The number of churches in their backgrounds was great, although the majority had attended churches classified as nondenominational Christian, Evangelical Free Church, or Presbyterian.

Regarding exposure to other religious traditions, all but two of the students declared that they had watched a television show or read about one of the traditions that we were to encounter during our investigation. Over half of the students reported having attended one of these traditions' religious services. With only a few exceptions, this meant having been present at a Catholic mass. All students checked that they had an acquaintance, friend, or family member of at least one of the faiths listed. Specifically, all students had a relationship with a Catholic, and four had a relationship with a Muslim, with two of them categorizing him or her as a friend.

The First Unit: Islam

After completing the demographic survey, we began our historical exploration with a video introduction of Spain, beginning in its prehistoric days and culminating with a cursory explanation of medieval Spain's tricultural composition of Christianity, Judaism, and Islam. Before delving very deeply into the substance of Islam, however, I wanted to ascertain what students' initial impressions of the religion were.

In my original conception of the study, a glimpse of the perceptions on each of the religions was to be captured by asking each student to come up with a list of word associations upon hearing the title of each religion mentioned. However, I later decided that, in order to get away from sole reliance on the spoken and written word, an arts-based component would be added to better triangulate the data. Although initially skeptical of how much information I could obtain from the montages, I believe that the pictures, symbols, and words yielded greater insight than a list of words alone would have. By employing the montage, I found out whether students actually had in mind the correct religion, which, in some instances, they did not. For example, on the montage characterizing Islam, one student, Amanda, labeled her display "Induism," and several others included Hindu images. If I had relied solely on words, I might have incorrectly assumed that the students had a better conception of the various traditions than they actually did. To facilitate my analysis of this data, each student was also asked, just before they turned in their montage, to write a sentence or two describing why he or she had chosen each of the images on the montage. This served to minimize conjecture on my part during the analysis process.

We continued the same video from the previous day during class 2, and students turned in their montage of Islam. Day 3 began with a brief lecture on the background of the prophet Mohammed and the revelation of the Koran.[1] At this point, I gave students a seven-page handout with selections from the Koran and approximately 10 minutes at the end of class to begin

---

1.   As was mentioned in Chapter 6, the spelling *Koran* came to be the preferred by the students, even though I also presented the transliteration *Qur'an*, which is preferred today by many scholars. Looking back on the lecture, I do recall presenting the spelling *Koran* first since the translation we were to be using was an older one that employed that transliteration. It may be for this reason that it stuck in the minds of the students.

reading. I asked them to keep a running list as they read of anything that they found noteworthy.

On day 4 I attempted to initiate a discussion on the readings, but quickly realized that the majority of students had not read the entire Koran hand-out. Unfortunately, even in a school such as Midwest Christian, with its rel-atively high academic standards, I found that students did not always complete assigned readings outside of class, no matter what the subject was. In fact, one occasionally heard students boasting to each other that they had managed to pass literature tests in English class without having read the books; instead of reading, their strategy was to pay attention dur-ing discussions, use summary notes, or watch a movie version of the literary work. Thus, the fact that students did not complete the handout of excerpts from the Koran should have come as no surprise. Adjusting my plans to account for this, I decided to give them the last 10 minutes before the lunch break to read further and told them to continue reading at lunch if they had not finished before then. Due to block scheduling at Mid-west Christian, I usually met with the students three times a week. On Mon-days and Wednesdays we met for half an hour, went to lunch, and then returned to class for another hour; on Fridays we met in the morning for 50 minutes. When the students returned from lunch, I passed around a sheet asking them to write the letter corresponding to the last selection that they had completed reading. Only one student had read the entire handout, but since the majority had read at least half, I decided to con-tinue with my lesson plans. I asked students to tell the class some of what they found of interest, and used student comments as a springboard for a lecture on Islam. After the ice was broken, almost all students had either questions or comments at some point during the discussion.

As the study progressed, I found that, although it necessitated wading through hours of audio tapes, some of the best data was gathered from stu-dent questions and comments during lecture portions of the class. My goal, of course, during each of the lessons and the resulting discussions was to maintain a nonjudgmental position so as not to limit what students felt comfortable sharing. In fact, one student, Lisa, wrote to me near the end of the study stating that she liked "how you allowed us to have our own opin-ion instead of forcing certain aspects on us." On this particular day, due to the large number of questions and comments, we made our way through only the first four pages of the handout, so I instructed the students that we would finish our exploration of Islam during the next class period and that they were to read the last three pages of selections from the Koran if they had not done so already.

During the conversation over these final three pages on day 5, I realized that I could get a very useful piece of information based on one of our dis-cussion topics. I was somewhat uncomfortable with the way I had explained the Islamic conception of salvation the previous class period, so, in order to reteach it, I asked the students to write a paragraph or two describing how they as Christians would define salvation and how one is saved. We then went on to compare and contrast the Islamic conception with what they had just written. Since the students' view of the scope of salvation was one of the guiding research questions of this study, it was important to know exactly how the students saw that salvation, and this provided a perfect opportunity to gather that information. At the end of class I picked up these paragraphs along with the running list of notes they had taken on the readings from the Koran.

At this point, I also assigned the first of the eight reflective essays that the students were to complete during the course of the study. I informed the students that the essays were to be typed. This was done to encourage students to take them seriously and also to aid me in unitizing data for analysis, as it would be much easier to scan them into a computer with Object Character Recognition (OCR) software than to type them all in myself. Students were also told that there was no length requirement, but that they were to write until they had nothing important left to say. This sometimes yielded only a couple of paragraphs, but often the essays ran longer, approaching or slightly exceeding a full page in length.

On both days 5 and 6 students were given opportunities to pick up non-required supplemental readings from the Koran if they were curious about some of the stories that were present in both the Bible and the Koran. Five of the 14 students chose to do so. After collecting essay #1 and lecturing briefly on day 6 about life in medieval Spain and the relations among coexisting Jews, Christians, and Muslims, I handed out readings on Christopher Columbus and reflective essay question #2, telling students that their response would be due the following period. In addition, I assigned the montage of initial impressions of Catholicism, informing them that this assignment would be due at a later date.

The Second Unit: Roman Catholicism

After collecting essay #2 on day 7, we began our study of Catholicism with a review of the Christian reconquest of the Iberian Peninsula and a brief lecture and video over the life of Columbus. On day 8, the montages of Roman Catholicism were collected and students were given time in class to begin reading a handout of selected chapters from the Apocrypha (books that are included in the Catholic, but not the Protestant, version of the Old Testament), which 9 of the 14 students claimed to have read in its entirety when I checked later in the week. They were also given time on day 8 to peruse selected sections from the *Catechism of the Catholic Church* that they were to summarize and present to the class during my upcoming lecture on Catholicism. I spent the last 10 minutes of class answering the many questions students had about what they were reading. The rationale behind this activity was to see how the students would frame a section of Catholic doctrine and practice that was different than their own, listening to tone of voice and any value judgments they might make as they presented their synopses. The activity, however, turned out to be only moderately successful. On day 9, when students presented their summaries during the course of my lecture, I realized that in my attempt to use a primary document, I had given my Protestant high school students an overly difficult text. Since they were uninitiated in Catholic doctrine, most had at least some trouble comprehending what they had read, and their reactions were often of confusion rather than reactions to something they fully understood.

As the presentations and my lecture continued, many students had questions about Catholicism. Some of these I answered, while others I instructed the students to save for Mr. Mandel, the guest speaker who would be visiting us toward the end of class. Since Mr. Mandel was employed in a nonteaching role at the school, the students had seen him before, although it is doubtful that more than one or two of them had engaged in extensive personal contact with him prior to his visit. Unfortunately, my lecture and the student summaries ran long, so our guest did not get into much discussion of the practice of Catholicism, but rather spent the majority of his limited time introducing himself and talking about his family. At the end of this brief talk, he opened the floor for questions. No one raised their hand immediately, so I told the class to ask some of the questions that I had requested that they hold for his visit. They did so, although there was rarely more than one hand in the air at a time, and once I was forced to ask a question because there was a dead pause. Later, though, I heard Amanda comment on how nice Mr. Mandel was and Erin describe how everyone had been listening with rapt attention. At the end of class, after Mr. Mandel had finished speaking, reflective essay #3 was assigned, and the students were dismissed.

I began day 10, the day before spring break, by asking Nathan to give the synopsis of his catechism excerpt, since he had been absent the day before. Following this, while playing the role of a television talk show host and moving about the room with a dry erase marker as a microphone, I solicited student comments on Catholicism and the events of the previous class. Since Nathan and Travis had been absent on day 9, they were disappointed that they had missed our guest speaker's visit and asked if he could come back and talk some more. I thought about it briefly and decided, since he had not been able to delve very deeply into the substance of Catholic life and faith during the previous class period, to ask Travis to see if he could find him and request that he make another visit. After about 5 minutes, Mr. Mandel appeared, and this time there was a more visible inquisitiveness on the part of the students. Questions were continuous, with several hands raised simultaneously for the remainder of the class period, which was about 30 minutes. This time our guest was able to discuss much more extensively his experiences as an adherent of the Catholic faith. After he finished speaking, I collected essay #3. Because there had been a significant amount of new information on Catholicism presented since the previous class, I told students that if their views had changed or if they wanted to add anything based on what had been discussed, they had the option to rewrite their essay and I would accept it after spring break.

Although the majority of our class time had been spent recently on our historical investigation, I did continue to teach an occasional lesson on the Spanish language in order to keep students' language skills fresh. Although day 11 was one of those days, I did ask for any remaining essays that had not been turned in before the break. No one had chosen to rewrite essay #3, but I did get two essays from students who had been absent the day it had been originally assigned. In addition to this, I spent about 5 minutes at the beginning of class observing student responses as they viewed a photo of the Virgin of Scottsdale lent to me by Mr. Mandel, who said it had been taken by a friend of his father. The photo was of a priest giving a homily. In the photo, however, the priest was offset to the left, leaving a space to the right in which there appeared the faint but distinguishable image of the Virgin Mary. I let the students come three at a time to view the photo. After the first set of students approached my desk, I remembered that the tape recorder was situated on the stool in the front center of the room, so I moved over to that area as subsequent groups came up to take a look. All of the students looked at the photo in a very attentive manner, with mixed reactions. Some thought it was "cool." Others used the word "weird." After this, I gave students the opportunity to pick up supplemental readings from the Apocrypha, explaining that it was not required reading and that the page contained selections from the Letter of Jeremiah and the story of Susana, an addition to the book of Daniel. Two students raised their hands to request a copy.

The Third Unit: The Mayas, Aztecs, and Incas

After completing the segment on Catholicism, I told students that for the next class I wanted them to create a montage that illustrated their initial impressions of the Mayas, Aztecs, and Incas. I reminded them that they could use more than just physical images of the cultures, but that images could be feelings, metaphorical images, or things from their own culture that they felt described the three civilizations. I then began to speak in Spanish and we moved into studying Spanish vocabulary and grammar for the remainder of the period.

On day 12 I collected the montages on the Mayas, Aztecs, and Incas, which several students had obviously not finished before class, since they spent the first part of class hastily looking for ways to affix images to their backing paper. After giving the students a chance to write a sentence or two about their images, we began our exploration of Meso-American indigenous worldviews. We started by reading a modern account of a Mayan legend named *El arco de Balam-Acab*. This took the majority of the hour following lunch, during which several students showed noticeable signs of sleepiness.

The following class, day 13, was rather chaotic, as there were students visiting from another school who sat in on the class, which consisted of an overview lecture of Meso-American religion. After completing the lecture, I handed out a copy of the Quiche Mayan creation account found in the Popol Vuh to each student and we began to read it in class, with each student taking a turn. We finished it on days 14 and 15, although as we began a couple of students expressed displeasure at having to continue reading. Several students also asked questions that expressed confusion about the content of the text. After we finished, I handed out reflective essay question #4 and told them that they had two class periods to read the first 11 chapters of Genesis from the Bible and write a comparison of the Biblical creation account and that of the Popol Vuh.

On day 16 I completed the lecture on the Mayas. Students seemed particularly attentive to the video we watched on the daily life of a Mayan girl in Santiago Chimaltenango, Guatemala, and to the pictures I took during the 2 years I lived in Guatemala. On day 17 we finished our coverage of the Mayas with the collection and a brief discussion of essay #4, although I wrote in my journal at the time that some of the students seemed more interested in talking to their neighbors about other matters than discussing the topic of the essay.

For the remainder of day 17 and all of day 18 we explored the world of the Aztecs through (1) two written Aztec creation narratives, (2) a teacher lecture, and (3) a video on the historical Aztec practice of human sacrifice. All of these provoked a great deal of student comment, including discussion on the origin of sacred indigenous stories and how much God would hold the indigenous peoples accountable for their beliefs since they did not have access to the Bible.

We began our exploration of Incan civilization on day 19, the day following Easter break. I had given students a set of readings on the Incas at the end of the previous session, but found that only 4 of the 14 had read them. When asked why they hadn't done so, most said that they had forgotten about them or hadn't taken them along as they traveled over the extended weekend. During the lecture, I did my best to lead students through selected portions of the readings, and, with just over half an hour remaining, I played a video on Peru, during which several students fell asleep. When asked why they had been so sleepy, David attributed his weariness to the fact that the class met right after lunch and Shannon and Kimberly to the drone of the Andean flute music. Although this was the most pronounced example, it was not uncommon during lectures (to a limited extent) and videos (to a greater extent) to see an occasional student exhibit signs of sleepiness or nod off from time to time, especially during the hour following lunch on Mondays and Wednesdays. On this particular day I wrapped up the lecture and assigned them reflective essay #5, explaining that in describing their impressions of the New World indigenous cultures they should feel free to discuss the Mayas, Aztecs, and Incas not only collectively, due to their similarities, but also individually, since we had noted many differences between the three. Voluntary supplemental readings were not offered during this unit.

The Fourth Unit: The Spanish Conquest and Mission Endeavor

The next class, day 20, we introduced the topic of the Spanish conquest and missionary ventures among the indigenous peoples. After collecting essay #5, we began class with a video, and then a reading about the fall of Tenochtitlan, the Aztec capital. After the lunch break, Stephanie asked a question about the eternal destiny of those that had not heard the gospel or had a less-than-perfect understanding of what the gospel was. Not about to lose this opportunity, I let the students talk about it for a while. They discussed it quite fervently, incorporating various arguments with regard to divine predestination and human free will, before I drew it to a close near the end of the class period.

On day 21 students read a selection in class about the sending to the New World of the first 12 Franciscan friars and I began a lecture focusing specifically on the Spanish mission endeavor. In addition to the subject of disease brought by the Spaniards, one of the topics we covered was the way in which missionaries saw the presence of the devil in the rites and beliefs of the indigenous peoples. Although not the same as the presence of God, I thought I could use this to get at the students' perceptions of other spiritual forces at work in these religious traditions. My original plan had been to ask each student to write a paragraph in class, but, since the discussion had been so substantial the day before, I thought I would try that approach again. When I asked, though, if the students agreed that those things in the other traditions that conflicted with what they believed were the result of satanic influence, I got a few seconds of bewildered stares, followed by Nathan's comment "Well, [pause] yeah" [laugh, as if saying "Of course I do"]. Although this brief, awkward exchange was somewhat telling, I wish I had stuck with my original idea of a written paragraph so that, in addition to seeing the students' affirmation of the devil's role, I might have been able to analyze some of the subtleties of their views. The only additional event on this day was the assigning of reflective essay #6.

After collecting essay #6 on day 22, I continued the lecture on the encounter between the American indigenous peoples and the Spanish missionaries, including several examples of past and present-day religious syncretism (which I defined as the intermixing of cultural religious symbols and their significance) and parallelism (which I defined as the practice of one religion in one's public life and another religion in one's private life). At the end of this class I assigned reflective essay #7.

We began day 23 with the collection of essay #7 and an opportunity for students to express their opinions on the questions raised in essays #6 and #7. This resulted in a moderate amount of comment. Most of the responses were made directly to my questions, however, and students did not play off of one another as they had during some previous discussions. After this wound down, I informed the students that they were to complete in class the final writing assignment, reflective essay #8. I gave them an excerpted passage from a chapter in *A Thomas Merton Reader* titled "Conquistador, Tourist, and Indian" and ample time to read and write their response. Before collecting their writings near the end of class, I began a brief discussion, only to realize that several students had misunderstood one of Merton's key points and the specific point on which I wanted comments, namely that the conquistadors should have seen Christ already potentially present in the Indians of the New World. After explaining what Merton meant, I asked those students who had previously misunderstood the statement to briefly add any new reactions onto the end of what they had already written before I collected them.

On day 24 we watched the remaining minutes of a video on the Spanish colonization of the New World.

The Fifth Unit: Approaching the Issues Directly

On day 25 I began class by thanking students for their participation in the study and, as a token of my appreciation, I extended an invitation for the students to join my wife and I at our house for lunch after the semester was finished. Most of the students were noticeably excited about coming, and I told them that I would have more details for them later. As we were about to begin the day's activities, Erin and Nathan asked when I was going to tell them what my opinions on these topics were. Since I had been asking them to share their beliefs with me, I thought it only fair that I return the favor, so I agreed to tell them once the study was completed. At this point, I handed out the questionnaire, reading the directions aloud to encourage students to expound on their answers. We spent the remainder of the time before lunch, about 20 minutes, quietly filling out the questionnaire.

When we returned from lunch, I divided the class into two groups of seven students each for focus group interviews. I tried to structure each group so that it was composed of students who, up to that point, had expressed a diversity of opinions. I also split up students who I thought might distract one another from the topic at hand. I placed seven chairs in a semi-circle with the opening facing me. This shape was chosen in order to allow the students to see one another without feeling the discomfort of people staring directly at them. During the lunch break I had placed a half-sheet of paper on each of the desks with a name on it. I told the students that if they found their name on one of the desks they were to be seated; if not, they were to make their way to another classroom and work on a Spanish language assignment that was awaiting them there. For those students who remained in my room, I asked them to turn over the paper in front of them and begin answering the questions that they found on it. As soon as this was completed, I explained that the purpose of the approximately 45-minute interview was to get their views on some of the topics we had been discussing. I informed them, since the interview was being taped, that they needed to speak one at a time and in an audible voice. I assured them that I would be the only person listening to the tapes and that their real names would not be used when the data were reported. We then proceeded to conduct the interview. The same procedure was followed the next class, day 26, with the remaining students participating in the interview while the first group went to another room to complete the Spanish language assignment.

I had planned to conduct the second round of interviews in much the same way the following week, with each group participating on a separate day, but due to a death in the family I was forced to conduct both interviews on day 27 before leaving for the funeral. I got permission from the school administration to move the students' lunch period to the first part of class, giving us an uninterrupted hour and a half to conduct both interviews. As had been done the previous week, those students who were being interviewed remained in my classroom as the other group went to another room, and then, halfway through the class, the groups switched locations. After completing the final interview, I told students that, except for letting them know my views, we were finished with the study, and I thanked them for their participation.

On my return, I spent the first part of class 28 reading an essay that I had prepared beforehand expressing my thoughts on many of the pertinent topics. Students listened attentively, and then we broke for lunch. Due to the hectic nature of the previous week, I had been unable to include the essay comments on all of the issues we had discussed, so I gave the students the opportunity following the break to ask any questions they had. There were a number of questions at this time, but not quite as many as I had expected. I answered the questions as best I could, made a few other points, and brought our class investigation to a close.

After the passage of a year, following the coding and categorization of data, I also asked my three primary informants if I could ask them a few questions to clarify some of the issues I had encountered during data analysis. They responded affirmatively, and I spent from 10 to 20 minutes with each of them. With this, the data-gathering process was complete.

CHAPTER 8

AMY

The following three chapters will illustrate how the primary informants in this study viewed those areas in which the theological boundaries of the evangelical movement are said to be shifting due to the pressures of the wider American culture and its various religious subcultures. To reiterate, these are (1) willingness to learn from other religious traditions—in this case the specific religious traditions of Islam, Roman Catholicism, and the worldviews of the Mayas, Aztecs, and Incas; (2) divine revelation and the Protestant canon of Scripture; (3) the presence of God in other faith traditions and the scope of salvation; and (4) the relative importance or unimportance of evangelism and interreligious dialogue. In addition to these four areas, data will also be presented to illustrate student responses to the relativization of tradition.

Unlike some books of ethnographic research that limit data reporting to only the pithiest or most polished of informant responses, I have made the decision to present in the following three chapters all of the data provided by the primary informants on these five topics. Because of this, and because youth speech patterns are often free-flowing and disjointed, the data are not all extremely refined or easy to read. However, nearly all of it is meaningful and illustrative of the differing perspectives of the primary informants. To see all the data on this topic will give the reader the chance to view the data without my interpretation, which will be given in Chapter 11.

As a reminder, the three primary informants were representative of different theological positions regarding the various guiding research ques-

American Evangelicals and Religious Diversity, pages 117–136
Copyright © 2006 by Information Age Publishing
All rights of reproduction in any form reserved.

tions. Amy, the subject of this chapter, was the student most interested in maintaining orthodoxy. Caleb, the subject of the next chapter, was the student most eager to explore what his fellow students saw as unorthodox positions. Finally, Nathan, to be profiled in Chapter 10, was the student in the middle trying to make up his mind on many of the issues he encountered during our investigation.

The first participant, Amy, a 16-year-old female, was born and had lived in Midwest City her entire life, attending two Presbyterian churches and two different Christian private schools during that time. The owner of a cheerful disposition and a ready smile, Amy maintained a perfect 4.0 grade point average and played an active part in the student life of Midwest Christian Academy, participating in athletics and serving in student government. Although strongest in mathematics, as evidenced by her representation of the school at various competitions, Amy was not afraid to try her hand at writing, penning an ongoing inspirational column in the school newspaper on selected Biblical texts. She also served as leader of a student spiritual growth group and on the demographic survey she assessed the importance of the Christian faith in her daily life as a 10 on a scale of 10, with 10 being the most important.

IMPRESSIONS OF OTHER FAITH TRADITIONS

Islam

For Amy, previous exposure to Islam included (1) the reading of a book or magazine article about the religion; (2) seeing "a religious service in action" during a tour of the Blue Mosque in Istanbul, which she characterized as "weird" because the Muslim Turks "pray in Arabic, but they don't know any Arabic"; and (3) having a Muslim foreign exchange student live with her family for a period of time. These prior experiences led her to rate her amount of exposure to Islam as a 7 on a scale of 10. Although aware of the existence of the Koran, Amy had not read any of it. When she encountered it for the first time, while reading the excerpts provided in class, Amy noted almost exclusively those aspects that she found "strange" and different from her own faith. In the following quotations, transcribed verbatim from Amy's notes, passages taken directly from the various excerpts of the Koran are indicated by quotation marks.

> "Nor of those who have gone astray." This statement is strange because Christ came to seek and save the lost, but Muslims seem to curse the lost.

> The last two sentences are strange because they seem to delight in others' suffering.

The part about an infant girl committing a crime makes no sense. They also try to swear by the "turning planets and the stars that rise and set."

"Did we not spread the earth. . . ." They seem to think they have something to do with creation. They seem to keep track of others' wrongdoings.

Allah forced angels to bow down to man. Satan says he'll torture all but who serve Allah.

It swears by this city. The Bible, however, forbids swearing.

It mentions that if you do good works you will return to Allah.

The Koran tries to use examples such as Moses and Noah.

The concept of "good works" is mentioned again.

The Koran tries to say Abraham served Allah.

It says "They" revealed the will to Jesus.

It says "Allah loves the righteous." It says something about Allah punishing us for our sins.

It doesn't seem to be against divorce.

It says you can't take more wives, but that slave girls are okay to abuse. It also talks about veils on "believing" women.

Muslims are forbidden to eat a few foods including swine.

For Amy, this focus on differences was not restricted to a personal reading of the Koran, but carried over into her interaction with other students. When a classmate pointed out a perceived similarity between the two faiths, she was quick to stress that the traditions were, in reality, quite different. Following class on day 3, Nathan, after reading the initial excerpts from the Koran handout, approached me, with Amy standing nearby.

> Nathan: It's really similar to things that are said in our Bible.
> Teacher: Like what?
> Nathan: Like the terminology about praising the Lord, King of Creation, stuff like that. Sounded very similar, I thought. I put that [in my notes] too. There are things where if you would switch Allah for God, it would sound just like you were reading the Bible.
> Amy: Yeah, but there are also parts where they're saying what will happen and stuff.

Amy described the relationship between Islam and Christianity as an adversarial one. On her Islam montage (see Figure 1), Amy selected a photo of the Hagia Sophia, a Christian church that was noteworthy

Figure 1.   Montage representing Amy's initial impressions of Islam.

because "the Muslims took over and turned it into a mosque by destroying all the pictures of Christ inside." When describing her final image, Amy wrote that the Mediterranean Sea "reminds me of Muslims also because the Muslim stronghold is around the Mediterranean Sea." On day 5, students were instructed to get out some paper on which to take notes as we continued our discussion of Islam. Amy did so, and titled her notes for the day as "Muslims—Feb. 26, '01." After learning that we would be comparing the conceptions of salvation in the two traditions, Amy wrote, beneath "Muslims," the words "vs. Salvation." Later, following a brief discussion on the shift in Muslim thought regarding compulsory conversion during the early centuries of Islam, Amy agreed when Stephanie stated, "See, Christianity never changes."

In only one instance during our study of Islam did Amy draw attention to the similarities of Islam and Christianity, and she did so in a negative manner. When asked to give a summary of her impressions following our brief study of Islam, Amy wrote,

> After studying the Koran, I think Islam is really weird. It seems that they delight in torturing the unbelievers. The religion seems based on good works. Allah will only let you in to heaven if you believe in him and have good works to back it up. The religion seems to be only for men because men can beat their wives and divorce them at any time. The Koran seems to take some parts from the Bible and twist it to say what it wants. They say that Jesus is a prophet, not the Son of God. They have a deep respect for Muhammad and lift him above all other men. They have five pillars of faith that they have to accomplish. The strange thing about the second one, prayer, is they don't even understand what they are saying! When I was in Turkey I heard the Muslim prayer over the speaker every day. The Turks didn't even understand it! In closing, I think the Muslim faith is very dangerous. It closely resembles the Bible in a couple ways in order to "trap" people into believing it. The major difference is the hope we can find in Jesus that the Muslims have no way of finding.

Interestingly enough, Amy's picture of Islam as antagonistic to her Christian faith did not adversely affect her willingness to learn about the religion. In fact, Amy read further into the packet of excerpts from the Koran than all but one of her classmates. Although her final one-word summary of Islam was "confusing" and an off-the-cuff synopsis of the Koran was "They like to kill people and torture them in hell," on the questionnaire she still checked the box labeled "slightly negative" when describing her impressions of Islam as a whole, curiously avoiding the more extreme "mostly negative" and "entirely negative" options.

Roman Catholicism

At the outset of our class investigation, Amy claimed more familiarity with the Catholic tradition than she did with either Islam or the indigenous cultures of the New World. On the demographic survey, Amy indicated that she (1) had read a book or magazine about the religion, (2) had attended a religious service, (3) had an acquaintance who was of the religion, and (4) had a friend who was of the religion. Amy also said that she had read part of the Apocrypha.

Amy's initial impressions of Roman Catholicism represented on her montage (see Figure 2) were symbols of both local and international scope, with images devoted to a Midwest City high school and hospital, and two photos related to the Vatican. To supplement these images, Amy

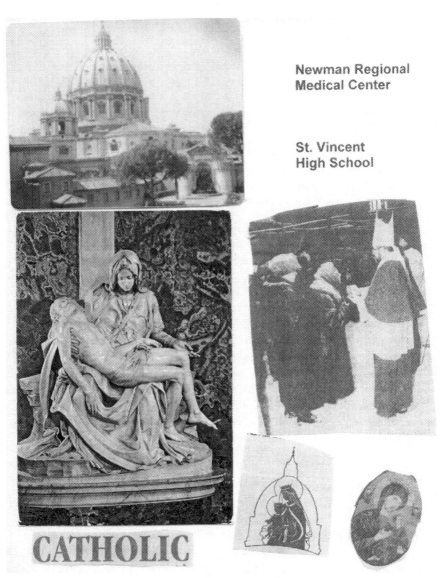

Newman Regional
Medical Center

St. Vincent
High School

CATHOLIC

Figure 2.   Montage representing Amy's initial impressions of Roman Catholicism.

selected a pair that she labeled, in curious language for a Protestant, "Holy Mother Mary and her child."

Although these prior experiences resulted in some knowledge of Catholic practice, Amy's understanding was very fragmentary. When describing her attendance at the Catholic religious service, Amy stated that she "went to a Roman Catholic wedding service that was more like mass," not understanding that what she witnessed was, in essence, a mass. Additionally, she was under the impression that bishops were the pastors of individual churches. During our guest speaker's initial visit, Amy was the first student to ask a question.

> Amy: I have a friend that's Catholic and she wears this thing, I don't know what it is, but it's like a necklace, kind of, with pictures or something that she has to wear in case she dies or something like that.
> Mr. Mandel: Are you talking about a cloth? A scapular?
> Amy: I think so, but I'm not sure what it's made of.

During Mr. Mandel's second visit, Amy asked, "I have a friend that's Catholic and she goes to church on certain days, like Holy Days of Obligation and stuff. What do you guys believe happens if you don't go to it?" and "Do you [Catholics] think of us as brothers and sisters in Christ?" At the end of our time together, Amy claimed to have increased her knowledge of Catholicism, saying that the investigation "helped me understand."

At one point Amy noted that the order in which baptism and profession of faith usually take place in the Catholic Church and her Protestant denomination was reversed. Although this was one instance in which Amy saw a difference between the Catholic faith and her own, on the reflective essay detailing her impressions of the Catholic faith following the visit of our guest speaker and the class lecture and readings, Amy stressed similarities and differences almost equally. She wrote:

I think there are many similarities and differences between Catholicism and Protestantism. Both religions believe in Christ and that He is God's Son. Both religions believe in the Bible and try to live by it. Both religions baptize their followers in the name of the Father, the Son, and the Holy Spirit. Both religions use communion in their services. However, there are many differences as well. The Catholics also believe Mary to be sinless and they pray to God through her and other saints. They also have extra books in their Bible. Their communion is thought to actually be Christ's blood and body, but we think of it to symbolize His sacrifice.

When asked to select from a range of options, Amy chose the response "mostly positive" to describe her impressions of Roman Catholicism as a whole, explaining that, in her eyes, "Roman Catholicism is mostly positive because they believe in Christ and salvation. However, they also have many other 'requirements' that seem like works."

The Mayas, Aztecs, and Incas

Amy checked none of the boxes on the demographic survey indicating previous experience with the worldviews of the Mayas, Aztecs, and Incas. When she did experience them, she found them, from the outset of the presentation until the final group interview, to be "strange." Although Amy was absent for the first two days of our investigation of the three American indigenous cultures, she handed in her montage (see Figure 3) when she returned.

Ignoring the Mayas, Amy selected six computer-generated images of the Aztecs and the Incas. In her brief explanations of the images, items of religious note were:

The dancer on the upper left looks strange and something the ancient Aztecs would do.

The temple on the upper right is an Aztec temple and reminds me of all the gods the Aztecs have.

The statue (center right) looks strange and may be a statue to an Aztec god.

The statue (bottom left) I found on an Inca website and reminds me of their strange beliefs.

Amy continued to use the word "strange" in her writing, in this case as an overarching statement introducing the worldviews of the Mayas, Aztecs, and Incas in her fifth essay. She wrote:

After studying the Meso-American religions, I think they are very strange. There seems to be little hope in any of the religions. The only way to get to heaven is through works and constant reverence to the gods. Often, it came down to human sacrifice to get into heaven. All the gods in the Inca, Mayan, and Aztec culture seem to be distant. Our God came down to earth to save us and does not demand anything back. In fact, he even offered us eternal life because he is so merciful. However, in the Aztec culture the gods demanded that the people worship them and if not they had them destroyed. All three thought that different plants and things on earth have sacred powers and made up stories as to why they are there. They all seem to think that we too can be gods someday. They value different parts of the body and hold them sacred. The Incas do not even seem sure about what they believe. They would mix up their beliefs with Christianity and say they may be true. One thing I

Figure 3.   Montage representing Amy's initial impressions of the Mayas, Aztecs, and Incas.

do admire about these people is their architecture. They accomplished amazing feats through mathematics. Sadly, not much is known about these people because the Spanish wiped them out in the sixteenth century.

In the fourth essay, in which students were asked to compare and contrast the creation account of the Quiche Mayan Popol Vuh with the first 11 chapters of Genesis, Amy did note similarities, but chose to focus primarily on the differences between the two texts.

> There are only a couple similarities but many differences between the Popol Vuh and the book of Genesis. One similarity is that man is the only creature that communicates with God (or the gods). Another similarity is that man was created and didn't just happen. A third similarity is the flood that wiped out evil things. But that is where the similarities end. The Popol Vuh accounts for four creations where the Bible only has one. The Mother and Father in the Popol Vuh weren't satisfied with their first three creations because they had imperfections. However, the Bible says that God saw "that it was good." Another difference is the purpose of the flood. The Popol Vuh wipes out all of mankind to start over. The Bible wiped out mankind as well, but Noah, his family, and two of every kind of animal were saved.

When asked to sum up her impressions of the Popol Vuh, Amy characterized it too as "really strange." Although she later stated that she thought almost everything about the class presentations was interesting, Amy "didn't like the readings because they were really strange," although she admitted they were "necessary for a better understanding of the people."

Not only did Amy consistently label the indigenous worldviews as strange, but during the first group interview she exhibited notable discomfort when polytheism was presented as a sensible way to view the natural world. This particular exchange between students resulted from discussion of whether the created order alone was sufficiently explicit to reveal the existence of God to those who had not heard the gospel.

> Caleb: I don't see how you could see God in creation unless you knew God already. Like, if I didn't know God I wouldn't look at creation and think how creative God is. I believe we can see God through creation. I just know how creative and, just, ingenious he was in all the ways he created things, but I don't think you could look at that without already knowing God and seeing him in that.
>
> Amy: Probably because we take it for granted. If we looked at it as closely, you'd see how complex everything is. You'd realize that it didn't just happen by chance.
>
> Nathan: Yeah. I was laying in Colorado one time at a camp and we were laying, I was just laying down, looking up and it was

night and, all the stars. I was thinking, even if I didn't know who God was, you would *have* to question that. There's no way. There's just too many stars. [*laughs*] You know?

Teacher: That everything would happen by chance?

Nathan: Yeah. You'd have to question something. You know? You'd have to.

Stephanie: And that everything works together.

Teacher: Okay. Amy, were you going to say something?

Amy: Yeah, just how we might take it for granted and I think if you studied it more, like how he's saying, when you went out and just observed it, you'd realize it more.

Lisa: But [*pausing for dramatic effect*] if you never had religious stuff, it's kind of weird, but, okay, if you had no religious background at all, and you're looking at creation, how would you know, why would you automatically think there was *one* God? Why wouldn't you think there was a wind god, a branches god, a flower [god], what would make you think there must be one big god?

Amy: (*interrupting*) But they all work together.

Lisa: Yeah. Like a bunch of little gods that work together.

Amy: (*taken aback, speaking slowly*) I don't think that.

Lisa: (*playfully*) I don't know.

Amy: I don't know. 'Cause there's always so much trouble with humans, at least, when more than one person works together, you know.

Erin: But there could be a head god.

Amy: (*hesitantly*) Yeah.

[*Several students make uncomfortable, one-word comments.*]

Nathan: 'Cause the problem with having a whole bunch of gods is, first of all, do they all think the same? Or are they all different? They all think the same, so they all know when to act at the exact same time?

Caleb: I think that would be kind of part of the complexity of, like that's what we think of God and—

Nathan: (*interjecting*) Yeah, but it makes more sense for one person.

Amy: Yeah.

Caleb: Yeah, but if you believed in a bunch of gods—

[*Lisa tries to interject.*]

Teacher: One at a time, one at a time.

Caleb: If you believed in a bunch of gods, that would be part of your belief of how amazing those gods are, 'cause they can all work together.

[*Amy and Nathan laugh nervously.*]

In the second group interview, when asked if the manner in which the other traditions saw the world made sense, Amy replied, "Parts of it do, except for all of a sudden somebody [in the Popol Vuh] became a monkey or whatever." In the end, Amy chose the questionnaire's "mostly negative" option to summarize her impressions of the worldviews of the Mayas, Aztecs, and Incas.

VIEWS ON SCRIPTURE AND OTHER DIVINE REVELATION

The Bible, in Amy's view, was the "Word of God." In choosing the option that best described her conception of Scripture, Amy selected the option "The Bible is without error in everything it says on matters of faith, but is not always to be read literally on matters such as history and science." To expound on this, Amy wrote, "I think there are things in the Bible that paint pictures (parables) rather than offer facts." When asked later to clarify which Biblical texts were parables and which were to be read literally, we had the following exchange:

> Teacher: It [your questionnaire] says, "The Bible is without error in everything it says on matters of faith, but is not always to be read literally on matters such as history and science." You said, "I think there are some things in the Bible that paint pictures, like parables, rather than offer facts." My question was, the painting pictures and the parables, are you talking about [something] like the parables that Jesus told in the Sermon on the Mount?
>
> Amy: Yeah.
>
> Teacher: ...Some people would say [that] a story in [the Old Testament book of First] Kings of King David was a parable, that you don't have to take it literally.[1]
>
> Amy: ...Oh, no. I wouldn't, I would probably say that's literal. Maybe I was just confused when I answered that. I would say, just like, parables... [*unintelligible*]
>
> Teacher: And then the science stuff, too, in creation stories?
>
> Amy: Would be literal, yeah.

During a class discussion in which Caleb voiced his perception of a great difference between the portrayals of God in the Old and New Testaments,

---

1.   Although King David does appear briefly in 1 Kings, most of his life is narrated in the books of 1 and 2 Samuel.

Amy expressed agreement with Amanda, who had said, "I don't think God changed. I think it's just a different portrait that's been painted." Shortly thereafter, Amy asserted that "the Bible doesn't contradict itself."

During our study of the other religions, Amy saw the Bible, in its Protestant form, as the standard by which other sacred texts were to be measured. When reading the Koran, she found it notable that "It swears by this city. The Bible, however, forbids swearing." She characterized the Apocrypha as "extra books" and when asked if the text of *Bel and the Dragon* belonged in the Bible, Amy responded, "No. . . . Sounds like a fairy tale, kind of. Dragons and stuff." Regarding the origin of an Incan story we had been reading, Amy said "they made it up." As for the proper stance of Christian missionaries toward the "[American] Indians' ancient literature," Amy stated that, once converted, "they should be encouraged to get rid of offensive books . . . missionaries should encourage that the books be destroyed because they may not mirror the Bible." After reading the creation story in the Quiche Mayan Popol Vuh, Amy posited that differences from the creation story of Genesis "come from the Mayan fables that eventually became the truth where the Bible has always been the truth."

During the first group interview, when asked whether she believed that God was speaking through the similarities in the other sacred texts that did "mirror the Bible," Amy at first answered, "I don't know if I do or not." As the discussion continued, she arrived at the conclusion that the similarities were not a result of even a limited divine inspiration of these other texts.

> Nathan: I guess the whole problem I have with it is that if we believe the Bible to be inspired by God, or God-breathed, or any of those other terms, then are the other ones, 'cause—
> Amy: Could they contradict themselves?
> Nathan: Yeah.
> Amy: And the Bible doesn't contradict itself.
> Lisa: Ooh, that's a point.
> Amy: That's why I don't agree with it, yeah.
> Nathan: That's the only thing I was thinking.
> Amy: 'Cause if they are, like, God is speaking through them, and if they do contradict in other ways, I don't think He would be talking through them.
> Nathan: Then what would that mean for the Bible?
> Teacher: Okay. Think about that for just a second. I'm going to turn off the AC because I think that it's messing up my tape here, but—
> *[I get up and make my way to the thermostat. The students continue speaking.]*

> Nathan: And if the other one were God-inspired, why would He say
> different things?
> Amy: Kind of like the Apocrypha.
> Stephanie: Yeah, I was going to say—
> Amy: It wasn't God-breathed, but they think it was.
> Nathan: Right, right, and—
> Amy: And there might be attributes about it that you can see
> through it, such as love, but—
> Nathan: But you wouldn't say different things either.
> Amy: Yeah.

Although in her eyes a lack of internal consistency denied non-Biblical texts "God-breathed" status, Amy later agreed with Caleb when he said that lack of divine inspiration did not mean that one could not see God in them.

When the topic of alternative means of revelation arose, Amy asserted that "God can reveal himself in any way he wants." The primary nonscriptural method that Amy affirmed was "through creation," stating that "man can know God by creation" and that "man is without excuse because God has revealed himself by nature."

Another way in which Amy saw God communicating was through people, although in a more limited fashion, since God could "use us to reveal his scripture to other people." Referring to papal teaching authority, however, Amy wrote "I don't think the Church should be able to speak on the same level as the Bible because the Bible is God-breathed and humans can't work on the same level as God." She reiterated this later, declaring that "He [God] can speak to us through creation, others, etc., but humans are sinful and are often in error, so the Bible is the most authoritative." Believing Mohammed to be the writer of the Koran, Amy applied this principle of human fallibility in her evaluation of Islam's sacred text, asking, "Why would they [Muslims] think that their scripture is perfect, though, if it was a man that wrote it?"

Later, when Caleb raised the issue of human involvement in the Bible, not in the writing of the text itself, but in the establishment of criteria for the compilation of the canon, Amy played a prominent role in the ensuing discussion.

> Caleb: I think that, I just thought it's just kind of weird 'cause we
> believe the whole Bible to be completely inspired of God,
> but the Apocrypha isn't because it isn't part of the Bible,
> but some of the credentials that the Bible, the first Bible
> had to be to be inspired of God were just made up by man.
> Like, one of them was, like, people who wrote the Bible,
> like for the books to be in the Bible they decided that they

had to have some kind of encounter with Christ. You had to know him like the disciples did, or Paul, who had the Damascus thing. You had to have some kind of encounter with Christ, so they're, like, if the Apocrypha is inspired it's because, I don't know, it's kind of weird, 'cause it's like the credentials are made up by man.

Nathan: That's like a really good point. I've thought of that point before.

Stephanie: But...

Nathan: I've thought about that, too, but I think, at the same time, it would have to be God's will what books went in there. I think if something was wrong, then it wouldn't [*pause*], I don't think it would be wrong.

Amy: I think it [*hesitant pause*]

Nathan: Yeah. The way it happened was the way it, obviously, he wanted it to go together.

Amy: Yeah, that's true.

Nathan: But, yeah. Yeah. That's what I ultimately concluded when I have thought about that, you know.

Teacher: Would you say then, that God was just as involved with the early church fathers who decided what was going to be in the thing as he was with the people who wrote the books?

Amy: Yeah, probably.

Nathan: Well yeah, he had to have been, I mean, they had to have been past his will in subject matter and—

Stephanie: But see, if God inspired the people to write the books, you know, 'cause it was written through them, couldn't he just as well inspire, like, us to talk?

Amy: But the Bible's complete, so—

Teacher: So the age in which he speaks with that authority is over with, [to speak] through people?

Amy: I think he still can speak through people, but the Bible's completely just [*brief pause*] I don't think there's anything new necessarily, but [*pause*] the things that they say are already in the Bible.

VIEWS ON THE PRESENCE OF GOD IN OTHER TRADITIONS AND THE SCOPE OF SALVATION

As one of only two students in the class with a theological disposition toward predestination, Amy repeatedly made it clear that salvation was achieved solely by a sovereign God, apart from any human efforts. "It's not on your own that you get into heaven," Amy stated, "It's only by God that we get into heaven." In her definition of salvation, she expounded:

> Salvation is God's free gift through his Son's death (and then victory over) on the cross to take away our sins.

> I believe one obtains salvation by being chosen by God. God is all-knowing and all-powerful so he alone can give us salvation. He touches our hearts in such a way (or reveals himself) that we can't turn him down. After all, man's sin separates us from God, how then could we choose him instead of Him choosing us. It's by grace that we are even saved. Our salvation brings glory to him alone. I believe we have nothing to do with our salvation, only God does.

In response to Stephanie's question of how a forced devotion would bring God glory, Amy answered, "We're only human. We can't understand everything, though. There are a lot of things about God that we can't understand."

After reading the article in which Thomas Merton proposed that Europeans should have seen Christ already present in the Indians of the New World, Amy wrote:

> There is a possibility that the Indians could know who Christ is. However, it was obvious that many of them were wrong in many areas. But that doesn't mean that there weren't any "saved" Indians. I think he was right that we can hear and see God anywhere whether it be a Christian friend or a stranger.

Although Amy seemed at first to have left the door open for those of other traditions to enter paradise, she soon made it clear that "Christ is the only way into heaven." On the questionnaire, she chose the option "The only hope for heaven is for those who profess and demonstrate faith in Christ" rather than the option "In addition to Christians, there is hope for heaven for those who have never heard the gospel of Christ." When asked about the eternal destination of "people that have not heard the gospel or have a less-than-perfect understanding of what the gospel is," Amy stated that she thought such people would end up in hell. If they were to have been saved, she said, "God would have revealed himself to them."

In explaining her questionnaire choice that "God is present and at work in all religious traditions," Amy wrote that "God has control of everything and can use other religions to fulfill his plan. However, even if he is at work, the people may not be saved. They, too, can only be saved through Christ." "If the Islam, Catholics, and Meso-Americans are left to their own accord," Amy stated, "they wouldn't accept Christ. However, if God reveals himself and predestines them to be Christians, then they will be saved."

Apart from Christ, Amy saw little hope for those within other religious traditions. She saw Islam as a religion that was "based on good works" and characterized the Koran as "without hope." Muslims, according to Amy, "would need Christ to be saved," presumably because "the major difference [between Christianity and Islam] is the hope we can find in Jesus that the Muslims have no way of finding."

As for Catholics, Amy allowed the possibility that they may be "saved," but that not all were. Amy wrote that, like Protestants, "[T]hey too have to have a personal relationship with Christ. It seems to me that Catholics think they are saved if they are part of the Catholic Church and obey everything they have to."

Although Amy allowed the possibility that someday she might see some of the Mayas, Aztecs, and Incas in heaven "if God revealed himself to them," the belief system itself contained "little hope." In the view of these three indigenous cultures, "The only way to get to heaven is through works and constant reverence to the gods. Often, it came down to human sacrifice to get into heaven." Whereas "All the gods in the Incan, Mayan, and Aztec culture seem to be distant," Amy wrote, "Our God came down to earth to save us and does not demand anything back. In fact, he even offered us eternal life because he is so merciful." Due to this difference, "It could only help them to have a society that has the influence of Christ rather than idols."

VIEWS ON EVANGELISM
AND INTERRELIGIOUS DIALOGUE

Amy did not list evangelism as the highest priority in her Christian walk, instead choosing "spiritual growth" because "if one grows spiritually, they might feel led to get more involved in other things in their life." Nevertheless, evangelism, for Amy, was still extremely important. Quoting from Acts 1:8, she affirmed that "God calls us to be his 'witnesses in Jerusalem, and in all Judea and Samaria, and to the ends of the earth.' I believe this means we are to take the gospel everywhere."

The primary reason Amy gave for learning about other religious traditions was "so you can evangelize to them better." She asked, "How can we share the gospel if we don't know where others are coming from?" and stated, "If you don't understand where they're coming from, then you can't really show them what you believe."

In learning about the other faith traditions, however, Amy did place limits on how far one should go. When asked whether she would attend a Muslim or Native American ceremony if invited, Amy agreed with Erin, who had said, "I think it would be kind of interesting to watch. I don't know if I would, like, actually like being in it." Since conversions from Christianity to other faiths do take place, learning about another tradition could constitute a danger because "if you're not strong in your faith . . . and you do end up switching over, obviously, it would be bad for you." Therefore, the appropriate thing to do for Amy was to "listen to them and learn it, but you probably shouldn't try and change your beliefs."

Amy estimated that between 30 and 50% of her friends (most of them met through her athletic events) were non-Christians. She also estimated that she shared the gospel with people who did not already profess faith in Christ a "couple times a week." What this meant for Amy, though, was more than just words, because "even if you don't verbally express the gospel, your actions can express it." She claimed that "Through example, like [sports] and stuff...people will know that I'm different just by the way I act." When asked specifically whether the phrase "couple times a week" referred to verbal or exemplary expression of her faith, Amy said, "It's probably both."

In the case of a hypothetical Muslim neighbor, Amy found a nonverbal witness more comfortable than explicit verbalization of the gospel message.

> If I had new neighbors move in that were Muslim, I would try to get to know them first. I think I would be comfortable interacting with them, but I don't know if I'd share Christ until I was even more comfortable. I know that they would need Christ to be saved and would try to show them that through example. When my family had a Muslim foreign exchange student stay with us, he wasn't very open to Christianity. We had to make him go to church with us. He was rude to us and never took baths. I think because of this experience I would be most hesitant to share my faith with other Muslims. I think I would be in constant prayer over what to say and how to act. Even though I would be hesitant, I think it would be interesting to see how they viewed different areas of life and share my faith with them.

For Amy, the manner in which this evangelism by example occurred was a matter of great concern. For example, compulsive conversion in the case of Christians with the indigenous peoples of the Americas was ruled to be inappropriate. "Instead of being forceful," Amy wrote, "we are supposed to show Christ through love." With regard to the sacred items of the indigenous peoples, Amy didn't "think it is right to destroy their sacred items because some may have historical value." In addition, she wrote:

> Destroying sacred objects might scare the people away from Christianity. However, once the people are converted, they should be encouraged to get rid of offensive books....The missionaries should be examples of what is right through their lives. If they come in and love the Indians, the people may be more willing to take the advice to destroy the books.

For Amy it was unloving to let converts continue in their previous ways, for "even if something is comfortable, it is not always right." "I think we are called to take the gospel to groups of people," Amy said, "even if it means it will change their way of life." As justification for this, Amy cited the example of Christ.

> Christ never worried about how he affected the culture of the people. He cared about the people themselves, and I think if a missionary cares about the people he will witness to them no matter what. If Christ had worried about hurting the culture, he would have given in to the Pharisees' complaints. Then he would not have died on the cross for our sins and we would be without hope.... Everyone who becomes a Christian has to go through changes when they become Christians. Historically, God has blessed the groups of people who follow him (not always immediately or in the ways we may desire), so a change for the better can never be bad.

If there existed the possibility that contact between missionaries and their target populations would cause adverse physical effects, such as the Spaniards introducing disease into the New World, Amy still affirmed the evangelistic endeavor when she wrote:

> I think that spiritual peril outweighs the physical. If we can even win one person to God, it is worth the effort. Of course, we would not want to inflict the pain ourselves, like the Spanish did when they killed the natives. We would be called to look after their physical needs as well as their spiritual. Christ valued each human's spiritual life above his own. After all, physical pain on earth does not equal the pain the victims would go through in hell.

RELATIVIZATION AND CHANGE

Although the majority of data that will be used in Chapter 11 to discuss any change in Amy's thinking has already been presented, there are a few noteworthy items that do not fit in any of the previous sections. First of all, when asked directly whether the study had caused her to think about her own faith in a new way, Amy explained, "I didn't see much in a new way, but reaffirmed my belief in predestination." Second, Amy asked me what my opinions were on the issues we had been discussing. Finally, near the end of the study, Amy stated that adherents of other faiths could also be having a discussion similar to the focus group interview in which she was participating.

> Stephanie: It's like the other religions, they strongly believe that they're right and we're wrong, so...
> Nathan: Right. Exactly. So they could just, everything we say they could be having a discussion . . .
> Amy: (*faintly*) Just like this.

Apart from this one utterance, nearly all of the data presented in this chapter display Amy's concern for staying within the boundaries of ortho-doxy as defined by her tradition, which she did by denying any substantial connection between her own faith and the traditions of the various groups we were studying. Also notable were Amy's literal reading and trust in the Bible as the final word on all things necessary for the proper Christian life, which included sharing the gospel with all who were not Christians and were therefore without hope of eternal salvation. As we will see, all of these things were called into question by Caleb, the subject of our next chapter.

CHAPTER 9

CALEB

If Amy represents the student most attracted to the orthodoxy of her tradition, Caleb represents the other extreme within the class, the student drawn to notions that many evangelicals would consider unorthodox. In the this study, Caleb approached (1) the specific religious traditions of Islam, Roman Catholicism, and the worldviews of the Mayas, Aztecs, and Incas; (2) divine revelation and the Protestant canon of Scripture; (3) the presence of God in other faith traditions and the scope of salvation; and (4) the relative importance or unimportance of evangelism and interreligious dialogue from a different perspective than many of his classmates. In addition, Caleb's comments and writing indicate that he had done a fair amount of thinking on these issues due to the relativization of tradition that he had already experienced.

Caleb, a 16-year-old male, was born in Midwest City and, apart from a 5-year stint in another city while very young, had lived there his entire life. During his school-age years, he had attended two Christian private schools and two nondenominational churches, at least one of which his father had served as pastor. Popular with his classmates, he was very involved in the student social life of the school, although not in a formal leadership capacity. Gifted with a keen sense of humor, Caleb enjoyed entertaining his classmates and occasionally got into trouble for talking in class or disregarding the uniform policy by neglecting to tuck in his shirttails. A somewhat disorganized student who occasionally nodded off in class during the reading and video segments of our investigation and whose grades suffered at times

American Evangelicals and Religious Diversity, pages 137–155
Copyright © 2006 by Information Age Publishing
All rights of reproduction in any form reserved.

from missing homework, Caleb showed particular interest in those assignments on which he was able to use his computer in a creative manner. On the demographic survey, Caleb rated the importance of the Christian faith in his daily life as a 2 on a scale of 10.

IMPRESSIONS OF OTHER FAITH TRADITIONS

Islam

Caleb quantified his previous exposure to Islam as a 6 on a scale of 10. This included having owned and read at least part of the Koran and having read or watched more than two books, articles, or television programs about the religion.

The initial impressions of Islam expressed by Caleb on his Islam montage (see Figure 4) included the text "war" in capital letters and "Jews vs. Arabs" accompanied by computer photos of a soldier carrying an assault rifle and a group of people carrying a bloodied victim away from the scene of a violent incident.

In a very brief description of these images, Caleb wrote that he "chose the image of WAR because of the continuing war in the Middle East" and that "both of the pictures represent the violence and attitude of war in the people." In addition, on day 2 of our investigation, when Travis exclaimed that he had the impression that Muslims were passive people, Caleb let him know that that was definitely not the case. Apart from this, Caleb's only other "negative" reaction to Islam was that he found the selections from the Koran "kind of boring," evidenced by the fact that he read only 13 of the 33 assigned sections and left class on day 5 without turning in a list of noteworthy items encountered during his reading.

Caleb's remaining impressions of Islam were positive. At parent–teacher conferences, Caleb's mother mentioned that he had learned a great deal and had been enjoying our investigation of Islam, an impression supported by the fact that he asked several questions during the days we studied Islam.

As we covered the material, Caleb made comparisons three times between Islam and the Christian faith. During the second group interview, he agreed with an assessment by Nathan that Islam was "so close to Christianity." He also spoke of an experience in a previous class.

> Caleb: I took Apologetics freshman year with Mr. Weaver and he had a really, really good friend that was Muslim, and he came in one class and talked to our whole class about it and, I don't know, it was kind of weird. It was kind of like Christianity but, I don't know, it wasn't. They couldn't ever

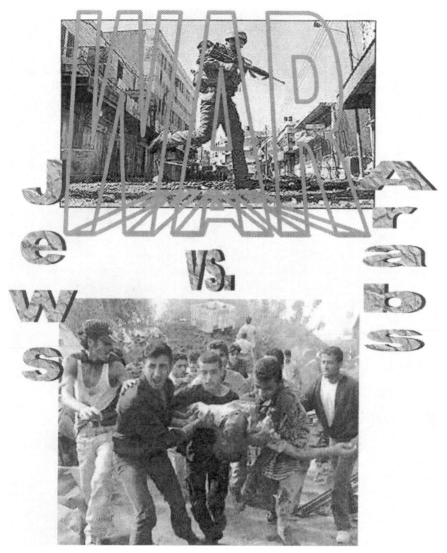

Figure 4.   Montage representing Caleb's initial impressions of Islam.

judge anyone. He told us that they would never say that a
Christian wasn't going to heaven because he wasn't Muslim. He said that they don't judge anyone.

Teacher: Because it's God who judges, he would say?

Caleb: Yeah.

He also wondered if Islam was monolithic, or if it was like

older religions, like Christianity, that have had so many different split-offs and sects. Like Christianity, there's Roman Catholicism and then there's a bunch of Protestants and then we have tons of denominations. Were there any, like, David Koreshes in Islam? I just kind of thought that would be really interesting if there were any of those kind of things, or if they've always...just had one idea and kind of stick with it.

When asked to give an assessment of Islam following our investigation, Caleb wrote,

> When I think of what I knew before we studied Islam in class, and what I know now, my outlook on them is basically the same. I think they are a truly dedicated and passionate people. Their religion has standards, and they do their best to live up to them. They don't seem to me to be a people that are easily swayed in their thinking, and would not be likely to convert to any other religion.

Twice during our exploration of Islam, Caleb joked about converting to Islam, such as on day 4 when he stated, "I'm going Islam" after reading that paradise in the Koran included "high-bosomed maidens." Later in the class period, after Lisa asked whether the phrase "Do not kill except for a just cause" in the Koran meant it was okay to kill every once in a while, he quipped, "Another reason to join the Muslims." In addition to these things, Caleb also characterized Islam as "kind o' cool" and described his overall impression of Islam as "mostly positive."

Roman Catholicism

Caleb rated the amount of his previous exposure to Catholicism as a 4 out of a possible 10. For him, this included (1) having read or watched more than two books, articles, or television programs about the religion; (2) having attended a religious service; and (3) having an acquaintance who was Catholic. Although unfamiliar with some common terminology such as "Eucharist," Caleb had previous exposure to at least a portion of the Apocrypha, which he described as containing "cool stories." Regarding the selections we read in class, Caleb stated, "I thought they were really interesting. I liked reading most of the stories like *Bel and the Dragon.* The stories were really kind of cool to read, I thought." When asked to characterize our investigation of Catholicism as a whole, though, Caleb chose the words "lil' boring," a somewhat unexpected response since he had asked three questions during my lecture on Catholicism and one more to our guest speaker during his initial visit.

On his montage of preliminary impressions of Roman Catholicism (see Figure 5), Caleb focused mostly on aesthetic matters. In describing the images he chose, he wrote,

The picture in the background I chose to show the almost palace-like designs of the Catholic Churches. The other pictures I chose because they have a Catholic look to them. Some represent the holiness and righteousness of Mary. There are the usual halos, and very elegant style of painting.

Figure 5.   Montage representing Caleb's initial impressions of Roman Catholicism.

In addition to the images of Mary, three of the images included were of Christ.

When asked to give his synopsis of the catechism segment detailing the order of events in the Catholic baptismal ceremony, Caleb was unprepared to do so, having misplaced the excerpt and any notes he may have taken. Thus, he improvised:

> Um, I lost my paper, so I don't know, but I can tell you what I remember. It was basically, uh, the thing was that it was a lot different than our baptism was. We don't usually have much of a ceremony. We just, the only thing that we always do is the name of the Father, Son, and Holy Spirit, but other than that there isn't really a certain order too much for things, but they have about 12 different steps that they have to do every time, like the priest has to do it. The priest has to say an already memorized prayer and then they have to do the, the whatever thing [Caleb crosses himself]....Then they have to, uh, there's, I didn't understand it, really, but whoever gets baptized has to take communion after they get baptized, and they said they usually take it right after, but then, if they didn't take it right after, they had to take it at some weird third quarter. I don't know. It was really weird.

As for the perceived relationship between Catholicism and his own tradition, Caleb wrote,

> I think that Catholics have a lot in common with Christians. They have many more traditions and ceremonies that they must perform. But their base beliefs are very similar to ours. They believe in God the Father, the Son, and the Holy Spirit. They believe that God became flesh as Christ and died for our sins.

Finally, on the questionnaire at the end of our investigation, Caleb checked the box "mostly positive" to describe his impressions of Roman Catholicism.

The Mayas, Aztecs, and Incas

On the demographic survey, Caleb checked that he had seen a television show and read a book or magazine article about each of the Mayas, Aztecs, and Incas. However, he later claimed to have had almost no knowledge of the three traditions at the outset of our study, quantifying his prior experience as a 1 out of a possible 10.

On his montage of initial impressions of the Mayas, Aztecs, and Incas (see Figure 6), Caleb once again chose pictures because they had the right "look," guessing as to their function. His comment on the only image of

Figure 6. Montage representing Caleb's initial impressions of the Mayas, Aztecs, and Incas.

religious significance demonstrated at least an awareness of the practice of polytheism when he stated, "The picture of the statue of a distorted face is a representation of one of the gods they worshipped."

When he read the Popol Vuh, he found it to be "weird." For other similar texts that followed, though, Caleb commented, "These are kind of fun to read." When comparing the Popol Vuh to the first 11 chapters of Genesis, Caleb neglected to answer why he thought similarities existed, but noted a plethora of both differences and similarities between the two texts. In the following text, quotations taken directly from Genesis are indicated by quotation marks.

> "In the beginning God created the heaven and the earth" (Genesis 1:1). In Maya tradition there was one like God. A supreme being who always was and always had been, and who created the world as it is.

"And the earth was without form, and void; and darkness was upon the face of the deep. And the Spirit of God moved upon the face of the waters" (Genesis 1:2). When God created the earth there was nothing. In Maya tradition, their creator made the earth from nothing also.

In Genesis, chapter one, we are told of the creation of the world. In our belief there was only one. God created everything in a period of 6 days. The Mayan god tried four different times before he created an acceptable being. One of his attempts to create man was out of clay. This is similar to God creating man out of dust and clay. However, in Mayan tradition, the man of clay was not successful.

In Mayan tradition woman was created the same way she was in Genesis 2. "And the LORD God caused a deep sleep to fall upon Adam, and he slept: and he took one of his ribs, and closed up the flesh instead thereof; And the rib, which the LORD God had taken from man, made he a woman, and brought her unto the man." (Genesis 2:21–22)

In Genesis, chapter 9, we read the story of the great flood. God looked at his creation and no longer saw that it was good. In all the world, there was only one righteous man. He told Noah to build an Ark and him and his family would be spared while the rest of the world would be destroyed by the flood. In the third creation of the Mayan tradition, the beings that are created are once again unacceptable. The Mayan god sends a great flood to destroy all of them. The difference is that not one of them was spared. They were all destroyed and the fourth creation began.

Other associations that Caleb perceived between the indigenous American belief systems and his own included the myriad of names for the Creator in the Popol Vuh and the many Hebrew names for God in the Old Testament, as well as the common notion of sacrifice as repayment for what had been done on behalf of humankind. As he stated:

> Caleb: I was going to add to what Nathan was saying how there was a common thing. I think it was the Aztecs. I think it was them and that's the reason they had so many human sacrifices because they thought that their gods died for them, or whatever. They sacrificed themselves. That was just kind of a common thing or something.
>
> Nathan: That's true.
>
> Teacher: They sacrificed themselves to create the (*pause*) life in the fifth world.
>
> Caleb: Yeah.
>
> Nathan: Almost like Christ coming.
>
> Teacher: The fifth cycle.
>
> Nathan: Yeah. That's good. Like they knew there was something they had to try to make up for or something. Yeah.

Teacher: A debt payment to the gods is what it was.

Nathan: Yeah, but Jesus was, yeah.

Caleb: (*jokingly*) They just got a little confused between lambs and humans [as sacrificial offerings].

Caleb used "interesting" to describe the creation of the Earth, a word that he would use several more times during our exploration of the three indigenous American cultures. In the fifth reflective essay, Caleb wrote,

> I thought the study we did on the Aztecs, Incas, and Mayans was very interesting....It wasn't a scientific age, and yet they were extremely advanced in reading the sky and devising calendars and keeping track of the time by means we would definitely consider scientific.

During the lessons on the Mayas, Aztecs, and Incas, Caleb asked several questions, including one regarding native Meso-American cosmology. He asked, "Like most civilizations of, in history, they always think of, they do have a world underneath theirs of some sort of a hell or underworld thing. Do they think that or is it just another regular place?" At other times during the lessons, Caleb jokingly identified himself with the indigenous peoples of the Americas. While viewing a flyer that I had picked up on the campus of Arizona State University from a pseudo-Mayan, New Age organization devoted to "creating energy synergistically," "preserving the four root races," and "establishing galactic communication," Caleb remarked, "That's personally what I believe, too" [*class laughs*].

After Travis commented that without divine intervention people would invariably follow the prevailing beliefs of the culture in which they were born, Caleb and I had the following exchange:

Teacher: What if we were living in the year 750 A.D.?

Caleb: In Central America?

Teacher: In Central America.

Caleb: I think I'd choose Aztec.

[*Other students laugh.*]

Teacher: Not a choice. Aztecs do not exist [yet]. You are a Quiche, a person that has been born a Quiche Maya.

Caleb: (*tone of voice somewhat serious, but also looking for a laugh*) I'd be Mayan and I'd believe in Mayan gods.

Teacher: How much do you think we would, you would have gone along with the crowd?

Caleb: All the way.

Caleb summed up our study of the Mayan, Aztec, and Incan cultures as "*very* interesting." On the final questionnaire, he stated that although he "liked about all" of our investigation of Spain and Latin America, he "thought the Incas, Mayas, and Aztecs were the most interesting" and that "it was cool to learn about their ancient civilization and how they viewed the world."

This evident interest led to some teasing by a fellow student. During our reading of the Popol Vuh, Caleb's friend Jason asked, "Did you write this, Caleb?" to which Caleb responded "No, my dad did." Later, when Nathan expressed bewilderment over a part of the Popol Vuh, Caleb joked, "You can call my dad if you want, Nathan."

As we concluded our coverage of the Mayas, Aztecs, and Incas, Caleb once again expressed his affinity for the three cultures.

> Teacher: I think today we're going to be finishing up the last of our three indigenous peoples.
> Caleb: Yes!
> Teacher: Yes? Ready to be done with it?
> Caleb: No, I actually like it. I said "yes" 'cause I like indigenous peoples. [*Other students laugh.*]

In fact, Caleb liked them enough to choose the option "mostly positive" in describing his overall impressions of the Mayan, Aztec, and Incan belief systems.

VIEWS ON SCRIPTURE AND OTHER DIVINE REVELATION

On the item of the questionnaire related to how he viewed the Bible, Caleb was the only student to choose the option "I'm not sure." He gave no further explanation on the questionnaire, but expressed many musings on the matter over the course of the study.

As previously quoted in the section on Amy's view of Scripture, Caleb raised the issue of human participation in establishing criteria for including books in the scriptural canon. At other times, Caleb focused on both the humanity of the Biblical authors and the Bible's similarity with other sacred texts. For example, Caleb stated, "There are, uh, the Koran, anyways, and in the Bible and the Apocrypha, it's like, the Catholic part of the Bible, but they were written by a person that thought they were inspired by God, or Allah, or whatever." When asked for some clarification on this disjointed statement, Caleb nodded affirmatively when I asked whether he meant that "the people that wrote those [other sacred texts] were similar to the people that wrote the different parts of the Bible in that they claimed divine inspiration."

Later, Caleb continued his comparison of the Bible and the Popol Vuh.

Caleb: I think the Popol Vuh is like, I don't know, everybody may disagree with me, but I think it's just as believable to those people as the Bible is to us.

[*Several students interject comments.*]

Teacher: (to Caleb) Why? Expound just a bit. What, why do you say that?

Caleb: Well, the Bible, it has a bunch of unbelievable stuff in it too, but we all believe it.

[*Other students comment.*]

Caleb: I'm not saying I believe in the Popol Vuh. I'm just saying that the stuff, the stuff that we read in the Bible is just as unbelievable to somebody else as the Popol Vuh is for them, but it just isn't weird to us.

Teacher: ...You're saying there are things in both that have to be taken on faith?

Caleb: Yeah. I mean, unless you have faith, you don't really believe that someone just raises from the dead. You believe on faith. It's like that in the Popol Vuh.

During discussion of the origin of the sacred stories of the indigenous civilizations, Caleb stated, "I think they made up their own creation stories" and, "they did look at creation, they did make up their own creation stories, but it's not based on our Christianity or our God or anything." Notwithstanding the "made-up" nature of the stories, Caleb later agreed with Lisa that "even though [other sacred texts are] not, like, correct completely, I think he [God] was still speaking." This echoed the statement quoted earlier in which Caleb felt that "the books like the Popol Vuh and the Apocrypha, they weren't inspired by God, but that doesn't mean that we can't see God in them." Caleb went on to explain further:

It's kind of like the Indians, like the Native Americans up here. They worship some of the stuff in the land, like they may look at a tree and see it as some kind of spirit, but we can look at that same tree and not see it as holy or divine, but still see God in the tree and in nature. But it's not necessarily inspired by God to be something holy. It's just that we can see God through it.

Caleb wrote during our study of the three American indigenous cultures that he "thought it was intriguing how the fact that not all of their stories lined up or remained the same didn't bother them." This incongruity of stories was a feature also seen by Caleb as present in the Bible, as expressed by the following excerpts from class discussion:

Caleb: There's a huge difference between the Old and New Testament, like, the Old Testament God was almost evil and

> wanted to kill all of these people, and then in the New Testament, like, love.

Teacher: So there's a big difference between God as he's portrayed in the Old Testament and the New Testament?

Caleb: Yeah. It's just like, all of a sudden changed. I mean, in the Old Testament, people who believe in God went in and destroyed everybody else. In the New Testament, everyone who believes in Jesus goes to prison for speaking and takes it. It's really weird.

Later in the same class, Caleb added:

In the New Testament, people believed in Jesus 'cause it was something to believe in, but if it would have been like the Old Testament, a lot more people would have believed in him 'cause they all thought he was going to be a king and a conqueror person like the God of the Old Testament.

Despite these inconsistencies, Caleb did affirm the role of the Bible in God's revelation.

Caleb: Yeah, I kind of agree with Nathan that there could be stuff that God can kind of guide you and ... at my church I go to, people every once in a while, they'll go up to the front and they'll say something over the mic and some people, they'll bring up their Bible with them and it's just something they found, like they were reading or something, and read something in the Bible, and they just feel that they should share that or something. But then other people go up there and they don't have anything that they found in the Bible. They just go on this 5-minute spiel of "Thus saith the Lord" kind of thing. So, I think those are kind of weird, because [*pauses*]

Teacher: So you would question that that actually was the Lord saying that?

Caleb: Yeah. And when you have something like you find in the Bible already to just kind of share that with people, I think that can be kind of, like, kind of led by God. [*voice trails off*]

When asked to describe the relation of the Bible to other forms of divine revelation, Caleb said that he agreed that "God speaks to us in other ways that are just as authoritative as the Bible," but qualified this statement with "I think a lot of times a message that God has for us can be misinterpretcd because of people's emotions." In the first group interview, Caleb gave an example of what he meant by this.

> In the sort of things that aren't exactly right, God's still speaking but it's kind of like...what they think what God might be saying to them is messed up, but...it happens to Christians sometimes, too. Have any of you ever been to a church where people are prophesying? I've gone to a church like that before and people get up and they have a word that they think is from God. So you could say, "Oh, well, God's trying to speak to us," but then when people and their emotions, they can mix that up and get that all confused. So you actually don't get what God really might want to tell us, or if he's even trying to tell us anything and they just think he is. So it just can get messed up easily.

On the question of God speaking through the Pope, Caleb responded to David's assessment of the idea as "pretty stupid" by saying, "It's no more stupid than when we believe our pastors when they talk to us in church [*continues his sentence, but mumbles and his voice trails off*]."

With regard to divine revelation manifest in the created order, Caleb found the general revelation of the natural world insufficient in itself to reveal the existence of the Christian God.

> I don't see how you could see God in creation unless you knew God already. Like, if I didn't know God I wouldn't look at creation and think how creative God is. I believe we can see God through creation. I just know how creative and ingenious he was in all the ways he created things, but I don't think you could look at that without already knowing God and seeing him in that.

As for the revelation of specific Christian doctrine through nature, Caleb found this notion equally preposterous when he asked Amy, "How do you know through creation? [Do] you look at it and go, 'Jesus died for my sins'?"

VIEWS ON THE PRESENCE OF GOD IN OTHER TRADITIONS AND THE SCOPE OF SALVATION

In response to Thomas Merton's statement that the conquistadors should have seen Christ already present in the Indian, Caleb wrote, "I don't believe that Christ would have already been in them as Christ is in us [Christians], but God's influence can be seen in all his creations, even people who are non-Christians."

In his definition of salvation, written on day 24 because he neglected to turn it in on day 5, Caleb wrote the following:

In the Christian tradition, there is only one widely accepted way of gaining salvation: Romans 10:9–10 [If you confess with your mouth, "Jesus is Lord," and believe in your heart that God raised him from the dead, you will be saved. For it is with your heart that you believe and are justified, and it is with your mouth that you profess your faith and are saved.]. However, I believe that Christ came for everyone, even those who die not believing in him. I don't think there is any way to know who or what makes someone able to go to heaven without believing in Christ. But I think that God knows, and he has a sense of justice that we could never begin to understand with our finite minds.

In the specific instance of the hypothetical Muslim neighbor, Caleb stated,

> I don't think it is my place to judge whether or not he will go to heaven if he is a Muslim. Some Christians wouldn't hesitate to say that he's going to hell, because he isn't saved. I don't think anyone has any right to say who [will] and who will [not] go to heaven.

When asked what he believed would happen after death to those people who had not heard or had a less-than-perfect understanding of the gospel, Caleb said, "I vote heaven."

On the questionnaire, Caleb selected "God is present and at work in all religious traditions" and "In addition to Christians, there is hope for heaven both for (a) those who have never heard the gospel of Christ and (b) those who live a moral and spiritual life but do not profess faith in Christ, although they have heard of him." This final selection he made after scratching out his first answer, "In addition to Christians, there is hope for heaven for those who have never heard the gospel of Christ."

On the question of non-divine spiritual forces at work in other religious traditions, Caleb several times on day 17 used Jason's propensity to equate indigenous barbarity with demonic influence to get back at his friend, who had teased him earlier. As we read from a set of Aztec creation stories, the two students had the following exchanges:

> Jason: Did they, like, worship the devil or something?
> Teacher: I don't know. Did they?
> Jason: I don't know. They've got all these weird things.
> Caleb: (*mockingly*) Worship the devil.
>   [*Several minutes pass.*]
> Jason: Oh, I love those things [ocelots]! They're smaller [than tigers].
> Caleb: They're of the devil.
>   [*Later in the same class period.*]
> Jason: What kind of people were these, Señor?

Caleb: (*teasing*) They must have been demons or something, Jason.

Nevertheless, when asked directly whether he thought that the devil made the Aztecs commit human sacrifices or influenced what they were doing, Caleb responded affirmatively.

Satanic influence notwithstanding, Caleb stated that "all these religions, or people involved in them, had their flaws, as do Christians. But for the most part I felt positive about them. They are all in search of something higher and greater than themselves."

VIEWS ON EVANGELISM
AND INTERRELIGIOUS DIALOGUE

Instead of evangelism, Caleb stated that "My highest priority is how I interact with other people. Being kind and loyal and understanding, etc." In fact, evangelism was an activity in which Caleb never participated. Of his friends, he estimated that less than 10% were non-Christians. For those of other faiths, Caleb did not feel compelled to share the gospel with them, as seen in the second reflective essay in which he encountered a hypothetical Muslim neighbor.

If I were to get a new neighbor that was a Muslim, I wouldn't treat [him] any differently than I would anyone. I am not a judgmental person at all. The thought that I need to get him saved in order for him to go to heaven probably wouldn't even cross my mind. In my thinking, it's not my place to try to convert him. Just like Christians don't like to answer their doors when the Mormons or Jehovah's Witnesses come calling, I'm sure a Muslim wouldn't want his new neighbor trying to convert him. If we became close friends, I would share with him what I believe, and in turn listen to his beliefs. But I would never try to convert him unless he told me he wanted to become a Christian.

With Catholicism, Caleb expressed a similar notion:

If I had a Catholic neighbor I wouldn't feel like I needed to witness to them about Christianity or convince them that my religion was better or that they needed to give up the Catholic traditions to be truly saved.

Caleb expressed his desire to learn about other cultures as a 7 and 8 out of 10, respectively, on both the demographic survey and the questionnaire. On the questionnaire, Caleb selected the option "I am interested in learning about other religious traditions so that I can understand people better, but not necessarily so I can share the Gospel with them." During the second group interview, Caleb stated, "I agree that it's important to know about other religions and other people's beliefs." When asked to explain why, he said, "I just think it's important to know that about people, just kind of like history. I think it's important to know where you came from and where other people came from." For the same reason, referring to the Spanish destruction of indigenous sacred objects and texts, he said, "I thought that they shouldn't burn their things or destroy them because I think that tradition is really important" and also for "our benefit, so we can know about them and what they believed and who they were, like, a thousand years later."

When asked whether evangelical Christians should seek to learn anything from those of other religions, Caleb replied,

> I think so. I think you can learn something from anyone. I talked to a Buddhist guy once for, like, 45 minutes on the street in Kansas City because he wanted me to buy some book. I didn't buy it, but I talked to him for a while. It's just interesting to learn what other people think, so you can compare it to what you believe, and that either can help you get a better understanding of it or completely confuse you, but it helps.

The idea of attending a Native American ceremony "sounded good, like, really interesting." Caleb went on to explain in an extremely disjointed fashion,

> I haven't gone to really very many Native American [ceremonies], but I went to a Buddhist temple once and sat through one of their, it was, like, 2 hours, I think, but it was, like, some of the priests that were, like, it was like a Buddhist, it was like we have Catholics [that] have monasteries, you know, where monks go. It's where Buddhist monks go, so that's where they live, and have to do a certain number of ceremonies and things every morning, and it was really weird, but it was really cool and interesting. It made you feel kind of weird 'cause they'll have a whole thing that they pray for and they say all these different thankfulness prayers for locusts and all this stuff, but it's kind of interesting just to see what they do.

When asked whether there were any dangers implicit in learning about other religions, Caleb said there probably were, because "people do convert." He also said,

> There would be a danger for us to learn other religions because you can learn them, but still, when we preach Christianity, people convert to Christianity. So if we learn about other religions, then it's possible for us to convert to another religion.

Despite the possibility of conversion to another faith, he agreed with Lisa when she claimed that "the benefits [of learning about other religions] outweigh the dangers," and later expounded further:

> I think the benefits outweigh the dangers and I think there can be a lot of benefits if you're a Christian or a Muslim, either way, because you grew up Christian or Muslim, I think it's a really good thing to learn about other religions. I mean, maybe you don't want to spend most of your life as a Christian or a Muslim. If it's a Christian, it's a bad thing [to convert to another faith], but still, you have a choice and still get to learn a lot of things to find out for yourself what you think is right. I mean, not just Muslims. Yeah. Some people are Muslims 'cause they were born in a country where Islam is the religion. I just think that for those people it's a really good thing to learn other religions and other beliefs.

When describing the mission endeavor of the Spaniards in the New World, Caleb affirmed the rightness of their enterprise, but disapproved of their approach and method. He wrote,

> I thought he [Thomas Merton] had a very good point. The Spaniards would have surely disagreed with his point that they should have already seen Christ in the Indians. But the fact is that the Spanish didn't try to see Him in them. As he said, they effectively and rightly brought Christ to the Natives, but they failed in helping the Indians *encounter* Christ. They did not listen to what the Indians had to say. They simply preached their message and did not stop to think that the Indians would maybe have something useful to say.

Earlier, during our study of the friars and their evangelization of the New World, Caleb wrote,

> Every person deserves to hear the Word of God in their lifetime. In the Bible we are called by God to go into all the world and preach the Gospel.... Although I do not believe that someone who has no knowledge of the Word of God is automatically doomed to hell, it would be wrong for a Christian not to try to reach them with the Word, if they knew that that people group existed.

When I later asked him, during longitudinal member checking, why, if he believed each person deserved to hear the Word of God, he personally did not engage in evangelism, we had the following conversation:

> Caleb: [Are you] saying that if I said everyone should know the Word of God, but yet I don't see myself needing to go?
> Teacher: Right. Right. How did that work for you?
> Caleb: Um, I don't know. I think that with missions and stuff like that, people are, people need to be called to missions

wherever you are. I think wherever you are, you're going to display what you believe to people no matter where you are, even if you're still in America. But as far as foreign missions, I think that you'd have to be called to foreign missions because if I went over to Africa and tried to be a missionary there just because I wanted to or thought I needed to do it, it probably wouldn't do any good, because I don't have really any feeling or desire or conviction to do that, necessarily, you know?

Teacher: What about with your friends? You only said that less than 10% of your friends are non-Christians anyway. Is that just because you know they're Christians or 'cause you don't really think it's your business to know?

Caleb: No, most of them it's 'cause I know they are, then, I don't know, probably, I probably have a *lot* more friends now that are non-Christians now than I did then.

Teacher: Okay. But with the less than 10% that you did have, would you have felt a call to [*pause*] I mean, you didn't seem like you really felt a call to be the one doing that [evangelizing the 10%] either.

Caleb: [*Laughs.*] Yeah, I know. I don't know. I don't know. I wouldn't, like, my friends that aren't Christians, I probably wouldn't go up to them and try to witness to them or try to present the gospel to them just because, I don't know.... It's not that I think that I shouldn't or that I have no right to or something. I don't know. I don't know how to explain it.

Teacher: Okay. It's just kind of a gut feeling?

Caleb: Yeah. Just kind of what I would or wouldn't do. I don't know.

RELATIVIZATION AND CHANGE

Although relativization will be discussed in greater detail in a later chapter, it is important to note at this point that Caleb claimed to have had a similar experience in a previous class. On the questionnaire, when asked to explain if the investigation of the different religious traditions had caused him to think about his own faith in a new way, Caleb explained, "I took a class similar to this unit. It was Apologetics and Worldviews with Mr. Weaver. That class and this one bring to mind many questions about the Christian faith and its validity and fairness." Later, during our second group interview, Caleb said,

It can be really confusing, like that. Like I remember taking *Apologetics and Worldviews* from Mr. Weaver and I came out of that class really confused. I loved that class. It was really cool to learn about it, but it can make you wonder a lot of things and ask a lot of questions and you learn a lot of... new material and you have questions, but you don't really ever get answers to the questions any more to, you know, but I don't think it's a bad thing, but I think it can be really confusing if you're inquisitive.

About a week and a half after he said this, I asked Caleb to tell me a bit more about this sense of confusion. He said he had been "just a little bit" confused, that he didn't know how he lost his sense of confusion, and that the conclusions he arrived at just came to him. He also realized that some people would see the things he had expressed as negative.

Finally, I asked Caleb during longitudinal member checking why, on the demographic survey, he had rated the importance of the Christian faith in his daily life as only a 2 on a scale of 10. We had the following exchange:

> Teacher: You said that your highest priority was how you interacted with people and being kind and loyal and understanding, and then up here [on the questionnaire] it said that on a scale of 1 to 10, the Christian faith is just a 2. Is that because you don't see these things [I point to where he has written "kind and loyal and understanding"] as being exclusively Christian? Is that what you were meaning?
>
> Caleb: Right. Yeah. I mean, you can be all of those things, and be a person with all of those characteristics without being, without having Christianity as a main factor in your life, or what's most important in your life.

Obviously, comments such as these never would have proceeded from the mouth of Caleb's classmate Amy. In fact, Caleb was aware that many of the students in the class disagreed with his willingness to see positive elements in other faith traditions and negative ones in his own. He also knew that not everyone agreed with his questioning of the Bible, his inclusive vision regarding eternal salvation, or his lack of evangelistic zeal. However, among his classmates there were those who were dealing with some of the very same issues with which he had previously dealt. And it is to Nathan, the student who most vividly displayed this intellectual struggle, that we will turn in the next chapter.

CHAPTER 10

NATHAN

In the previous two chapters, all of the relevant data were provided for Amy, the student most committed to maintaining religious boundaries where they stood, and Caleb, who showed the greatest inclination to traverse those boundaries. In this chapter, the data are presented for Nathan, the "in-between" student dealing most overtly with the intellectual effects of relativization as he tried to decide in which direction to move. Since the objective in this chapter is to present all of the data relevant to Nathan's approach to the five guiding research questions, this chapter will be longer than those of the two other primary informants. This is due in part to Nathan's enthusiasm and verbosity, but also to the urgency with which he approached the subject as he tried to sort out how to best fit his newfound knowledge with what he already believed to be true.

A 17-year-old male, Nathan was born in Midwest City and had lived in the metropolitan area his entire life. During his school-age years he had attended both public and private schools and three different churches, one Baptist, one Evangelical Free Church, and one nondenominational Christian. An inquisitive, occasionally absent-minded, but above-average student, Nathan was active in athletics and as a leader of a student spiritual growth group. For Nathan, though, the greatest joy seemed to be found in serving the student body as a worship leader during Midwest Christian Academy's weekly chapel service. To rate the importance of the Christian faith in his daily life on a scale from 1 to 10, he circled the number 10 on the demographic survey and added a plus sign to the right of his answer.

American Evangelicals and Religious Diversity, pages 157–191
Copyright © 2006 by Information Age Publishing
157

IMPRESSIONS OF OTHER FAITH TRADITIONS

Islam

Nathan quantified his previous exposure to Islam as a 4 out of a possible 10. For him, this meant he (1) had read a portion of the Koran; (2) had read or watched more than two books, articles, or television programs about the religion; and (3) had an acquaintance and a friend of the Islamic faith.

Nathan's montage of initial impressions of Islam (see Figure 7), which I saw him hurriedly completing during the break before class using pictures from a magazine that Travis had brought, demonstrated a mixture of prior knowledge and misconception. Nathan wrote,

> I chose these pictures because I see islamic people as dark-skinned [and] often wearing robe-type clothes. In picture #1 this man represents the typical islamic man that I envision, dark with facial hair, skinny, and wearing a robe. As does the man in #2. He even has the headdress and has his knees crossed on the carpet (#3) they use to pray on. [Picture] #4 I think isn't as much of a resemblance to the others, but is a good depiction of a muslim/Islamic woman. [Picture] #5 is the wailing wall in which all Islamics have to travel to in part of the pillars of Islam, the pilgrimage to Mecca (#6) being that trip. And #7 is just a common animal that I think of them using.

In addition, Nathan labeled picture #1 "my uncle" and picture #2 "my cousin."

As previously mentioned during the chapter on Amy, Nathan approached me following the reading of the first excerpts from the Koran and said,

> Nathan: It's really similar to things that are said in our Bible.
>
> Teacher: Like what?
>
> Nathan: Like the terminology about praising the Lord, King of Creation, stuff like that. Sounded very similar, I thought. I put that [in my notes] too. There are things where if you would switch Allah for God, it would sound just like you were reading the Bible.
>
> Amy: Yeah, but there are also parts where they're saying what will happen and stuff.
>
> Nathan: (*jumping in, talking over the last part of what Amy says*) No, there are, uh [*pause*] Oh no, there *are* [differences].

The next day, when Matthew mentioned that in the Koran "they intertwine a lot of Biblical concepts into the thing," Nathan replied, "Yeah, it's real similar." In response to various excerpts from the Koran, of which he

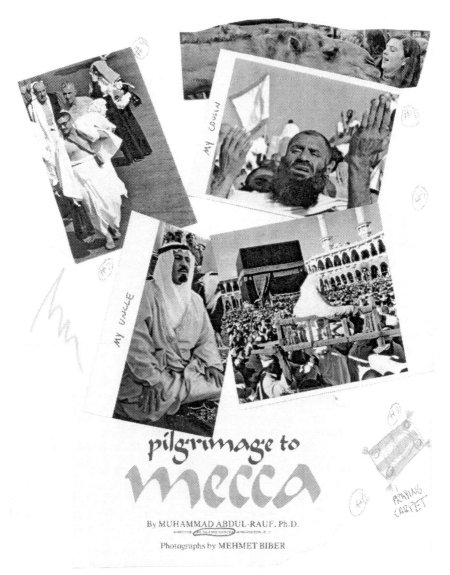

Figure 7.   Montage representing Nathan's initial impressions of Islam.

claimed to have read 18 of a possible 33, Nathan listed several things that he considered noteworthy:

It seems like Allah is scared of earth.

Sounds very similar to our God.

Admittance is given through good works.

If you do bad, it is all held against you!

Seems Satan is outwardly afraid of Allah.

We?

No praising, just silence.

Said Satan was created as Satan.

Talks about what specific good works to do.

Change bad actions to good through repentance?

Weird heaven.

Dead—living, living—dead?

Are you good enough for Allah?

Unsure of salvation?

You don't necessarily know if your heart is pure enough, or you can just repent and have it continually erased?

During our discussion the following class period, Nathan explained some of the items he had written in his notes. First of all, he said,

> Nathan: I've got to read mine here. I put "It seems like Allah is scared of earth" [*chuckles*].
> Teacher: Allah is scared of earth?
> Nathan: Yep. 'Cause when it was talking about him in the beginning here somewhere, when he was talking about him being revealed and everything, you know,
> Teacher: Mm, hmm.
> Nathan: And then it's like "but Allah" [*pause as he looks for the exact quotation*]. Here it is. "Nothing prevents men from having faith when guidance is revealed to them but the excuse: 'Could Allah have sent a human being as an apostle?' Say: 'Had the earth been a safe place for angels to dwell in, We would have sent forth to them an angel from heaven as an apostle.'" It's like earth is too bad for Allah. It's like he's too special and so he can't be down on a personal level.

On the question of gaining entrance to paradise, Nathan said, "Admittance [in Islam] is given through good works, and if you do bad it's held against you. If you do anything bad, then at the end that's put against you, and not, and not taken away" and, "They keep score and then you've got to outweigh the bad."

In addition to these statements, Nathan made several lighthearted comments during class. Referring to the vocal style of the Muslim call to prayer, Nathan exclaimed, "Don't they kind of yell it, sing it, like [vocal imitation of the call to prayer]? We don't do that. It's a lot more fun." In reference to those women who were required to wear veils, Nathan joked, "I think they're protecting them [*pauses*] from dust [*laughs*]." On day 6, he excitedly explained,

I saw an *Up Close* on ESPN the other day [*pause*], which is like an interview on ESPN with a boxer named Prince Nahim Kadesh,[1] or something like that, and he was like, the whole time he was talking about how if it's Allah's will that he loses the next fight, then it's okay if he got defeated and he kind of talked about his Islamic beliefs a little bit. It was kind of interesting, 'cause it's exactly what we were talking about.

Although Nathan had earlier made the comment that "It seems like all the terrorists all the time are always Islamic," he wrote in his first essay that the violent stereotype did not represent the average Muslim.

Many times in American society, other religions or religious groups are looked at with certain preconceived ideas. Islam is one of the more heavily criticized of them. American society often labels Islamic people as being terrorists or violent people. But these people are only the radicals, representing only a few Islamic groups.

I believe Islam's basic ideas are good, and have good ideas of moral standards. Some of the Koran even relates closely to the Bible in its sayings. The idea of a single God in control and in charge of creation is good, but they are off in their understanding of Jesus Christ and their prophet Mohammed.

Islamic people are very disciplined, and follow Allah closely. They hold up their instructions from Allah probably better and more accurately than Christians, or at least most Christians. At the same time, however, I believe that Islam is the hardest religion to convert its followers to Christianity, largely because of family tradition and fear of punishment for converting.

Overall, I perceive Islam as good for a person as far as morality is considered, but, [due to] its inconsistencies with Christianity, [it] isn't acceptable to me as a religion. And I don't think all Islamic people are violent, but if you think about it, all major religions have radical groups within themselves that take the words of their religion and misconstrue them.

In the first group interview, Nathan used the word "understandable" as his primary description of the Koran because it "made sense" and he "understood what they were saying." In the second group interview, Nathan characterized the whole of our investigation of Islam as "helpful" in that it "helped me realize a whole lot more of what they [Muslims] meant." On the questionnaire he chose the option "mostly negative" to describe his overall impressions of Islam.

---

1.   The boxer's real name is "Prince" Naseem Hamed.

Roman Catholicism

Nathan chose the number 7 on a scale from 1 to 10 to describe his amount of prior experience with Catholicism. For him, this meant he (1) had read more than two items about Catholicism, including part of the Apocrypha; (2) had attended a religious service; (3) had met the acquaintance of Catholics; and (4) had a Catholic friend. He explained further, "I have been to a service. Many acquaintances of mine are of the religion. None of them, however, seem to follow the same path as far as their belief system [is concerned]."

Nathan's montage of initial impressions of Catholicism (see Figure 8) consisted of six pencil sketches on notebook paper.

Although it could not be reproduced perfectly in this format, beneath image #6 was an outline of a group of animals jumping from a cliff, which Nathan erased and replaced with a drawing of the "non-standard Bible," although the written text that he provided still described his initial sketch. The description of each of these six images was as follows:

> The pope is a symbol to me of Roman Catholicism because it seems like he rules almost as God since he is the primary messenger.
>
> I always think of a glass of their "holy water" or whatever it is they sprinkle.
>
> The image of the cross seems to mean they are saved. They always wear one.
>
> Seems as if the grandeur of the cathedral is as important as the religion.
>
> I always think of Mary, because she is the central point of Roman Catholicism.
>
> They seem to change rules and go according to whatever the pope says. Like animals following each other off of a cliff, they just do whatever.

When asked a year later why he had erased the sixth image, Nathan surmised, "I probably just made a bad drawing." He then went on to explain that by the erased picture he meant that the Pope "changes things...just randomly, he'll come up with some new law that they have to follow," and asked, "How can it just change all the time and be always correct? According to them it can, but I'm saying it's just like making up the rules in some kind of pick-up game."

Although he described the Apocrypha as "more similar to what I know and easier [to understand]," Nathan expressed frustration at his inability to comprehend the section of the catechism assigned for him to present to the class. When he did present the section, titled "The Communion of the Church of Heaven and Earth," he included statements such as "It's like they [the saints] have direct communication with God, but we don't so we have to talk to them to have them ask God questions and stuff" and "I put

Figure 8.   Montage representing Nathan's initial impressions of Roman Catholicism.

'[the saints are] like Obi-Wan Kenobi' [*class laughs*]. In *Star Wars*, you know how he's kind of, after he dies he's that little guy, and he goes around and you can talk to him." After finishing his synopsis, he remarked to a student sitting nearby that "It was really confusing."

In addition to this confusion, Nathan described an instance where not knowing how to act led to what he perceived as an awkward social situation.

> Nathan: I was over at a friend's house and they were Catholic, and they said their prayer and they were all saying stuff and I was, I didn't know what [to do].
> Teacher: You mean they were saying what?
> Nathan: I don't know, just however they were praying.
> [*Another student speaks.*]
> Nathan: And then when they were done they did that [*crosses himself*] and I was like [*brief pause*] I didn't know how to do it.

Nathan also speculated that it would be more comfortable for a Catholic to visit an evangelical Protestant church than the other way around, since in evangelical churches "they're [Catholics] are not forced to do it [make the sign of the cross]," although he later agreed with Erin that Catholics "might feel bad not doing it."

Twice during class discussion, Nathan badgered me for an answer to a question regarding Catholicism. The first came as I was describing a visit to a mass.

> Nathan: So did you drink blood?
> Teacher: No, I didn't. I didn't take communion.
> Nathan: (*somewhat argumentative*) But did they drink blood?
> Jason: (*astonished by Nathan's persistence*) Nathan.
> Teacher: They would say that Christ was present there. In a laboratory they would—
> Nathan: (*as I speak*) So—
> [*As Nathan is about to ask again, several students turn to him. One says "gosh."*]
> Nathan: What? I just want to know.
> Teacher: In a laboratory they would say that it would still look like bread, still look like grape juice [wine], but that Christ was present there.
> Nathan: (*in a "know-it-all" sort of voice*) Oh, oh.

The second instance of badgering occurred following my expression of my opinions on the issues we had studied. After I had finished reading the piece I had written, Nathan asked me four times whether I thought the Virgin Mary was sinless or divine. He then commented that the sinlessness of Mary was "impossible" and that if she were free of sin it "would take away everything Jesus did."

On his third reflective essay, after completion of the unit on Catholicism, Nathan summed up his impressions of the tradition as a whole:

From what I have already known about Roman Catholicism to what I have heard recently from Mr. Mandel, I have found that Catholicism has many faults from Christianity. I think that the main fault is in salvation. Mr. Mandel expressed the idea that living a "good" life will get a catholic to heaven, and not simply accepting Christ into your life. I also see Catholicism as being unnecessarily complicated with many strange rules. However, I also feel like the rules aren't constant. They are changed when the pope decides to believe something new or different. I don't understand the whole thing with the saints either. I think it is weird that they believe these saints are so holy. Even farther out than that though is the catholic outlook on the virgin Mary. I think Mr. Mandel called her by a special name. He also expressed to me that Mary is believed to be sinless and [that she] comes down to earth frequently to help people out. I thought that was inconsistent as well. The last thing I noticed from him was how easily and quickly he believed in strange phenomena. Such as stigmata and bleeding Mary statues. I guess my outlook on Catholicism is basically inconsistency all around. What I mean by that is that it seems inconsistent with the Bible, with its leadership, its members, and its own self!

In the second group interview, Nathan used the words "confusing" and "lost" to describe Catholicism, explaining that "There's no definite thing. It's just kind of a wandering." On the questionnaire, he chose the option "mostly negative" to express his overall impressions of Roman Catholicism.

The Mayas, Aztecs, and Incas

Nathan quantified his previous experience with the Mayan, Aztec, and Incan religions as a 1 out of 10 and checked no boxes on the demographic survey indicating prior exposure, although he later related to me that he had seen videos on the Discovery Channel about the Meso-American temples and that he had always wanted to climb them.

On the montage of initial impressions of the three American indigenous civilizations (see Figure 9), Nathan included seven images, about which he wrote:

To me, pictures #1 and #2 remind me very much of the ancient indian culture. It seems like they had many gods for many different purposes and so they made lots and lots of statues or heads in gold in order to worship them or to be shown favor from them. Also, the heads were extravagantly decorated and made from their finest resources.

Pictures #3 and #4 also represent their belief system. Gods were placed in stone in their buildings and picture #4 looks more like a doll. But all of these types of statues kind of all have the same look. A triangular-shaped head or face with a round, more plump body. I don't know why, but these always remind me of that culture.

[Picture] #5 . . . is neat because it is more detailed. It seemingly shows two indians working. I think they were very disciplined workers.

[Pictures] #6 and #7 . . . are Indian buildings. They were very well made and geometrically sound. I always think of the long staircases and they seem to always be high at the top of a hill.

As our investigation progressed, Nathan exhibited a variety of responses to Mayan, Aztec, and Incan culture and religious practice. He remarked, "Oh, cool!" when he saw pictures of Chichen Itza that another student had brought and expressed curiosity about the materials used to construct the tops of the Meso-American temples. He also suggested on day 16 that the class have a Mayan dress day. After seeing a picture two class periods later of a victim being sacrificed by the Aztecs, he initiated the following exchange:

> Nathan: So they're alive every time?
> Teacher: Yeah.
> Nathan: Auhh [revulsion].
> Stephanie: Don't you die when they cut your heart open?
> Nathan: Yeah, but you're alive while they're cutting into your chest.

Referring specifically to the sacrifice that took place during the Aztec New Fire Ceremony, Nathan said, "That's so horrible." Later, after hearing that the Inca's [the king's] wife was also his sister, he exclaimed, "Okay [that's weird]."

When he first saw the thickness of the Popol Vuh reading packet, Nathan exclaimed, "Oh, man. Are we going to read this?" At one point while we read, however, he laughed as he attempted and then succeeded in pronouncing the divine names Xpiacoc and Xmucane, which he then went on to repeat several times. Finally, he began the last day of our readings by exclaiming, "Let's Popol Vuh it up!"

According to Nathan, the creation account of the Popol Vuh was "hard to understand" and full of "crazy ideas." Referring to the many-named dual Creator, and Quetzalcoatl, the plumed serpent, Nathan exclaimed, "This is talking about the god, the dual god-type thing, making man, and then there's some little thing flying around and this, has nothing, has nothing [*stops*]. It's weird." After reading a section in the Popol Vuh about the deities' destruction of their first creation, Nathan commented, "Pretty good. Pretty good creator [*laughs*]. Doh! [the sound Homer Simpson of the television show *The Simpsons* blurts out when he makes a mistake]."

Figure 9.   Montage representing Nathan's initial impressions of the Mayas, Aztecs, and Incas.

As we read the section of the Popol Vuh describing the destruction of the third creation, which includes the destruction of wooden people by a deluge, Nathan asked in a funny voice, "They flooded out wood people? Can't they float?" In the same section, after the domesticated animals and tools have verbally and physically attacked their human masters, Nathan asked, "How does a groundstone talk [laughs]?" Finally, after the surviving wooden people have been banished to the woods and have become monkeys, Nathan laughed and asked, "How are they [the monkeys] wood?" Later on day 15, the following exchange occurred:

> Lisa: If there are four creations, how can there be four destructions? 'Cause they just now created them and they haven't destroyed them yet so there are only three destructions.
> [*Other students speak. I then comment about how the account is not a scientific treatise and that the Mayas might not have required that their stories line up in the way that we in the West would.*]
> Nathan: So they just hope that no one asks questions like that?
> Teacher: What's that?
> Nathan: I guess they just hope no one asks too many questions like that.

In comparing the Popol Vuh and the Bible, Nathan saw two similarities. The first was that in both sacred texts, "In a very, very broad way of creation... something was created." Second, Nathan came during class discussion to see the many names of the Mayan creator as analogous to the many names of the Christian deity.

> Nathan: Which name was the one for the supreme god? Which one was that?
> Teacher: (*jokingly*) Yes [all of them].
> Caleb: Aren't they all?
> Nathan: What? [*makes a noise like a child who doesn't get what he or she wants*]. So Xpiacoc and... Hunter Coyote and Q'aholom and all them are the same one?
> Caleb: It's like all the different Hebrew names for God, kind of.
> Nathan: No it's not.
> Teacher: You think so?
> Nathan: No. That's not right.
> Matthew: It's along the same lines.
> Nathan: Because if—
> Teacher: Like if you were to refer to God as Father and Lord?
> Caleb: Yeah. It's the same thing. It's a bunch of different names.
> Nathan: Is that what it is then? 'Cause I was wondering.

As seen in the fourth essay, however, these were the only two similarities Nathan acknowledged.

> One of the most prominent similarities between the Popul Vuh and the Bible is the fact that they both give an account of at least some type of creation. In the Popul Vuh, however, there are seemingly multiple creators and even another creation already present, when in the Bible there is only one creator God. In the Bible, God created the earth in 7 days perfectly, totally in order, and without messing up. But, in the Popul Vuh, the creator gods seem to mess up the creation, or at least they don't do it correctly the first three times. This seems weird to me because you would think that an almighty creator wouldn't be messing up because that wouldn't give you very much faith as a believer to be sure that your god isn't messing up other things too. The creator or creators in the Popul Vuh have several names that they are called, just like we call God by several different names as well. So, the fact that both had a creation and both have multiple names is pretty much the only similarities. Other than that, the stories are very different because of the faultiness of the gods in the Popul Vuh and the strangeness of the creations and even the world.

Nathan, however, did not always see indigenous conceptions as "strange." At one point, when I spoke of how the Aztecs perceived mountains as being vessels of water, some students said, "This stuff is weird." Nathan disagreed.

> Nathan: I don't think so. It's not really that far-fetched.
> [*Travis makes a comment.*]
> Teacher: (*to Nathan*) Are you being serious?
> Nathan: Yeah.
> Teacher: Why?
> Nathan: Because it makes sense that if the mountains could have water in them they could fill up the earth. I understand that.

When I asked him later during longitudinal member checking to explain what he had meant by this, we had the following conversation:

> Teacher: We were talking about how the Indians of the New World kind of saw the world as floating on a layer of water.
> Nathan: Yeah.
> Teacher: And that the mountains contained the water, were like these bowls of water.
> [*I play the tape.*]
> Teacher: Were you kidding there?
> Nathan: What?

Teacher: ...a lot of people were saying, "It's weird." You said, "I don't think so. It's not really that far-fetched that the mountains could have water in them, that they could fill up the earth." You said, "I understand that." And, if you can remember way back when

Nathan: Oh. Just what you'd surmise if you didn't know anything? I think I was saying, probably, if you're trying to figure it out by yourself, anything could be possible. You know, water could come out of the trees. I guess. I don't remember everything about that. I'm guessing it was because I figured that if they didn't have any, if no one had anything [*pause*]...You know, people say "That's crazy." That's 'cause we know. That's why.

Teacher: Right.

Nathan: It's like on a movie, when the person on the horror movie doesn't know what's going on, but you do.

Teacher: Okay, kind of behind the scenes?...You already know

Nathan: So it's not as crazy, yeah. People don't think that, though. They don't think about that. They're, like, "Well, that's ridiculous." They're like, well, [*laughs*] you've got to put 2 and 2 together.

On the fifth reflective essay, Nathan described his impression of the three indigenous civilizations following our exploration in class.

At first, I didn't know anything about the Maya, Aztecs, or the Incas. I knew that they had all disappeared one way or another, and I had seen a few videos on them on the Discovery Channel, but I didn't know anything of the ancient culture. I think that the Maya seemed to be a more peaceful tribe than the others. They worked more on culture than they did on conquering or fighting. But my favorite are the Aztecs. They were a warrior tribe. They worked on conquering other tribes and ended up with a vast empire, but also with lots of enemies. The Aztecs also had a cool empire. They were situated on an island and pretty much controlled everything around them. The Inca tribe is probably the most interesting, however. Maybe because we don't know as much about them, or maybe just because they are farther away. It's interesting how at one time the Inca could have an empire stretching 2,500 miles and then just disappear at the hands of a conqueror. I also think that it is neat how each of the tribes settled. The Incas were in a tough region, but found their own ways to cultivate land on the side of the mountains. It is really neat also how their construction could be so perfectly put together. Each stone was placed perfectly together.

In the second group interview, Nathan used the word "enlightening" to summarize our investigation of the Mayas, Aztecs, and Incas, and on the questionnaire he wrote, "The indian cultures were VERY interesting. Also it was cool to learn about some facts, like how their buildings mysteriously fit perfectly with no mortar. Stuff like that." However, Nathan chose the option "mostly negative" to describe the beliefs of the Mayas, Aztecs, and Incas.

VIEWS ON SCRIPTURE AND OTHER DIVINE REVELATION

According to Nathan, the church denomination to which he currently belonged was made up of "Bible-believing Christians." On the questionnaire, when asked to choose from the list of options on how he viewed the Bible, he did not circle any of the answers, but wrote in the comment section, "I believe the Bible is inerrant and inspired. Yes, it is to be taken word for word, but not always literally in the sense that some of the stories are parables." During longitudinal member checking, Nathan explained what he meant by this:

Teacher: Let me see, on [question] number 7. I think it was number 7. Which one most accurately describes your view of the Bible? . . . You didn't pick one of the choices here. . . .

Nathan: Looks like it probably would have been A, maybe, [*pause*] but I kind of fixed it.

Teacher: . . . This one said it was to be taken literally, right?

Nathan: (*reading*) "The Bible is without error in everything it says on matters of faith." Yes. Okay. And it is to be taken literally, word for word. Yeah, except for parables.

Teacher: Except for parables?

Nathan: There's a lot of that type of stuff, symbolism. If you were reading it literally, you'd have no clue what was going on. You know?

Teacher: Okay. So B, then, wasn't accurate either?

Nathan: (*reading*) "The Bible is without error in everything it says on matters of faith, but is not always to be read literally on matters such as history and science." Well, yeah. See, I would agree with that, because it should be read literally with matters of history and science.

Teacher: But not parables, meaning specifically the stories that Jesus told?

Nathan: Right. Or symbolism and stuff. Yeah. Or [the Biblical book of] Revelation [*laughs*]. I mean, if you took that literally, you're like "What?" [*confused*]. It wouldn't make any sense. You know what I mean?

Teacher: What about things like—

> Nathan: (*interrupting*) So I guess I didn't really, none of them were quite exactly what I thought.
>
> Teacher: Okay, but history, for example. A story of King David or something like that would be taken literally, as an actual historical event?
>
> Nathan: Mm, hmm. 'Cause it happened. Yeah, right. Exactly.
>
> Teacher: And science, I guess I was thinking creation maybe, the creation in Genesis.
>
> Nathan: Perhaps maybe 7 days wasn't 7 days, but other than that, the way it was done, yeah.
>
> Teacher: Okay, and the order is right and all that stuff?
>
> Nathan: Sure. Yeah. I mean, there's always that argument about 7 days, whether it was 7 days to us or to Him [God] if that means 7 years to us in time, you know? It's, that's, I've heard that before, but yeah.

During the second group interview, Nathan said,

> It [the Bible] never contradicts itself, ever. Everything that they wrote and inspired by, it all came through, and everything happened just like they said it would happen, and all the principles hold or held intact, you know, nothing [*pause*] There's no discrepancy.

At one point, when Caleb said that the credentials used in the compilation of the Biblical canon "were made up by man," he said that the idea had occurred to him as well.

> Nathan: That's a really good point. I've thought of that point before.
>
> [*Another student tries to interject.*]
>
> Nathan: 'Cause you can only go [so far]. I've thought about that, too, but I think, at the same time, it would have to be God's will what books went in there, you know, I think if something was wrong, then it wouldn't [*pause*], I don't think it would be wrong.
>
> [*Amy tries to interject.*]
>
> Nathan: Yeah. The way it happened was the way it, obviously, he [God] wanted it to go together.

Later, during the discussion in which I told the students my own opinions, Nathan wanted to know if I agreed with him that "the Bible turned out the way God wanted it to."

As for the sacred texts of other traditions, Nathan made a range of evaluative statements. He referred to the Catholic scriptural canon as the "non-standard Bible." As for the Koran, he noted a correlation with the Bible when he said, "Some of the Koran even relates closely to the Bible in its sayings." For the texts of the American Indians, however, the opposite was the case, as seen in his comments while reading the Popol Vuh and coming across a series of unfamiliar names for the Mayan creator deity.

Nathan: Oh no, Blue Rain! No! [*Turns and addresses me.*] This is the strangest story I've ever heard in my entire life.

Teacher: Really?

Nathan: Yeah. [*laughs*] Especially for something as big of a deal as that [the foundational account of the creation of the world]. It's kind of weird. So it's like, some of these people sitting down going "Uh, yeah, and then there's, uh, Rain Blue, uh, I'd better write that down."

Shortly after this, Nathan attributed the origin of Aztec creation stories to human invention. After Jason said, "Some crazy guy made it [the account we were reading] up," Nathan laughed and remarked, "I was going to say that."

Nevertheless, Nathan acknowledged many similarities between the different sacred texts and his own, as he expressed on day 20.

Nathan: It's interesting how, how diverse the belief systems can be, but yet how they all have this really similar, really close almost in a way, you know, they all have this concept of creation just about all those things. They were weird, but they had an idea of, that something was created, even though the one [the creator god in the Popol Vuh], you know, he screwed up and stuff, or whatever. But like, they [*I begin to speak, but Nathan keeps talking*] knew that something made these trees and made the, you know, so I think that's interesting how there's a common thread, even though it's pretty weird and stuff. But I thought that just, that really did kind of poke out to me.

[*Caleb tries to interject, but Nathan doesn't let him.*]

Nathan: They're not necessarily that far off, just coming up with it by themselves.

Teacher: And where did that come from? Do you think they came up with it just on their own?

Nathan: Well, no, [*befuddled pause*] I don't know.

Later, during the first group interview, I asked the students if they believed that God could be speaking in the places where these texts coincided with Christianity. After Lisa and Caleb answered affirmatively, Amy said, " I don't know if I do or not," after which Nathan said "I don't [know] either."

During the ensuing discussion, Nathan said, "I guess the whole problem I have with it is that if we believe the Bible to be inspired by God, or God-breathed, or any of those other terms, then are the other ones [sacred texts] [inspired]? Seconds later he asked, "If the other one [some other sacred text] were God-inspired, why would He [God] say different things?" After Amy stated, "There might be attributes about it that you can see through it, such as love," Nathan remarked, "But you wouldn't say different things either." He then said,

> Nathan: Following those same lines. That you, God wouldn't say different things to people. If they were inspired, they wouldn't contradict themselves or the Bible. It would be the same. So obviously, he didn't, if he was part of it at the beginning, then he never revealed everything to them later. You know what I mean?
>
> Teacher: Okay.
>
> Nathan: As far as the Bible [is concerned].
>
> Teacher: So if something has any sort of mistakes or anything in it, then it, then it's not at all inspired?
>
> Nathan: Well, they're not even close, though, to being similar. Like the Popol Vuh, how could that be inspired?
>
> Amy: There's a couple of [similarities], *sort of* [*her tone insinuating that they are not even close enough to be worth considering*].
>
> Nathan: Yeah. That's not even, like, a little bit.

In fact, when he later thought that Lisa was claiming "partial inspiration" for the other texts, he pressed her for an answer to how that was possible.

> Lisa: I think that there could be a little bit of God based in everybody.... The Indians created the Popol Vuh ... but they ... had a little bit of God in it. They made the book themself, and they might have mixed in a little bit [*She and others laugh and comment on her simulated "mixing" gestures*], mixed in a little bit of God, but it's still [*pause*] mixed a little bit of what the truth is, but it's not completely inspired by God unless God inspired it 100%.
>
> Teacher: Okay. So it's a possibility then, you would say, to be partially, kind of partially inspired?
>
> Lisa: Yeah, that's what I was saying. That's what I think in the first place. They're partially inspired.
> [*Several students speak.*]
>
> Amy: Why would God partially inspire?

Nathan: Which parts? You got your Bible?

Lisa: No, God didn't inspire the books!

[*Amy and Nathan speak.*]

Teacher: One at a time. One at a time.

Lisa: God didn't inspire the books. There's some truth in, I think, in everyone's religion. But they, the people created the books. I know the disciples created these books, the Bible.

Nathan: (*slightly confrontational*) But did he inspire them? Which part?

Lisa: He inspired those [the books of the Bible].

Nathan: Inspired what? No, for them [the indigenous Americans], what did he inspire? [*I glance at Nathan, instructing him to let up a bit in order that other students might still feel comfortable to express their opinions.*] Well, I just was wondering.

As we moved on to another topic during our first group interview, I asked whether as a group we had said that God spoke through "some of these other texts, but in a very limited way." Nathan said "Yeah" to indicate that what I had said was accurate.

As we continued, Nathan indicated that another way in which God spoke was through "objects" and "material things,... creations and stuff." He agreed with Stephanie when she said, "You can see him in the sunset, just his power and creativity and everything through the sunset." Then Nathan gave his own illustration.

Nathan: I was laying in Colorado one time at a camp and we were laying, I was just laying down, looking up and it was night and, all the stars. I was thinking, even if I didn't know who God was, you would *have* to question that. There's no way. There's just too many stars. [*laughs*] You know?

Teacher: That everything would happen by chance?

Nathan: Yeah. You'd have to question something. You know, you'd have to.

Although he affirmed its validity, Nathan viewed the natural world as insufficient to reveal the specifics of the Christian message, as seen when he asked, "How would you know [through nature] to 'accept Christ'?"

When Nathan used the word "objects" to describe how God communicated, he apparently did not mean the photo lent to me by Mr. Mandel of the apparition of the Virgin Mary in Scottsdale, Arizona. His comments while viewing the photo that day were:

They drew it. Yep, they drew it [*laughs*]. That's what I was thinking. It's hard to take pictures, any picture seriously any more because, seriously, you can put anything on a picture with a computer. I always wonder, like *anything*. 'Cause they can. Anybody can put anything they want on there.

In his third reflective essay, Nathan also noted "how easily and quickly he [Mr. Mandel] believed in strange phenomena. Such as stigmata and bleeding Mary statues." Later he stated,

The one problem I have is that, with those Mary instances. I have a hard time with it because God doesn't want us to be drawn to Mary. Mary didn't do anything. She's not, you don't get to heaven through Mary. She was just the one who was chosen to have Jesus.

In addition to the natural world, Nathan allowed for the possibility that God could reveal himself through other people. During the first group interview, Stephanie introduced a scenario of a person having a problem during the day, saying that God could reveal something in the Bible to address that particular situation. When I asked if he could do the same through another person, Nathan replied, "He could be using them." On the question of God employing the Pope as his messenger, however, Nathan balked, saying, "I think the Pope, the whole deal with the Pope is strange because I don't see how one guy is the only one who can do that [speak infallibly]." For the average Christian, however, Nathan stated,

I believe God can, if you're going to teach a message or something, I believe that God can move you and move your heart in places to help you say what needs to be communicated and stuff like that, but I don't literally believe that he speaks through anyone like "mmm" [as if someone were in a trance or channeling a spirit].

Nathan repeatedly made it clear that God didn't communicate "in an audible voice." Although he did speak to humans, according to Nathan, "He doesn't say, 'Kimberly, tell Caleb . . .' [*laughs*]." He later explained on the questionnaire the reason for this belief. He wrote, "I don't believe in any audible voice of God. I have heard of experiences, but I don't understand how only a select few can experience them. The Bible can be experienced by everyone." This corresponded with the option Nathan chose that most accurately described how he thought God spoke, which was "God speaks to us in ways other than through the Bible, but the Bible is more authoritative than any of these other ways."

VIEWS ON THE PRESENCE OF GOD IN OTHER TRADITIONS AND THE SCOPE OF SALVATION

When asked to define salvation and explain how one obtains it, Nathan wrote,

> Salvation is confessing with your mouth and believing in your heart that Jesus is Lord. You accept God's free gift into heaven, receive Him in your heart, and he reigns inside of you.

> You are saved by confessing to God you are a sinner, then you ask Him to come into your life, into your heart, mind, and soul, and accept His free gifts. You have to do this or else you are like everyone else. The Bible says that even the demons believe in God, but to be saved, you take the extra step and invite Christ into your heart.

On the question of divine presence within Islam, Nathan acknowledged that Allah as presented in the Koran "sounds very similar to our God" and that the Koran "looked at Allah a lot like we look at God, only just with a different name. In a lot of ways, actually." However, Nathan viewed the Koran's depiction of salvation as problematic for two reasons, the first of which was seen in an exchange on day 4:

> Nathan: Admittance [to paradise] is given through good works, and if you do bad it's held against you. If you do anything bad, then at the end that's put against you, and not, not taken away. Apparently.
>
> Teacher: ... That's partially true. There is [however] the idea of repentance and of God being forgiving.
>
> Nathan: But they have to do more good than bad. Apparently.

Second, Nathan wrote on his Koran notes the phrases: (1) "Unsure of salvation?" (2) "Are you good enough for Allah?" and (3) "You don't necessarily know if your heart is pure enough, or you can just repent and have it continually erased?" When I attempted to explain the Muslim conception of salvation, we had the following dialogue on day 5:

> Nathan: So their salvation is gradual? They never attain, um
>
> Teacher: You don't necessarily have to achieve perfection.
>
> Nathan: But you're never just *saved*. You're always working on it.
>
> Teacher: (*after thinking for a few seconds*) I think it's a little bit different picture of salvation. It's a thing that a Muslim is supposed to continually be working on,..., but they would say that really only Allah knows who is and who is not saved.
>
> Nathan: Whoa. That stinks.

Later during the same class, Nathan commented that "It [the Muslim conception of salvation] seems a little more unsure than ours."

If he were to have a Muslim neighbor, Nathan affirmed that "they would need to hear the gospel," because "even though they are strictly different, God can move anybody to accept Christ.... Muslims, even with their strict adherence to their faith, can be accepted into God's kingdom just as well as any other race."

For Catholics, Nathan wrote on his montage, "The image of the cross seems to mean they are saved." During the visit of our guest speaker, Nathan asked specifically about the Catholic conception of salvation.

> Nathan: Well, I have, kind of, two questions that kind of go together, but, um, okay. Do you believe that you will go to heaven as a Christian once you have gone through confirmation, so, 'cause like what if something happens to you before you reach that, can you, will you not go to heaven?
>
> Mr. Mandel: No, you'd, you'd still.
>
> Nathan: But, then how do you get there?
>
> Teacher: God's grace begins with the baptismal sacrament.
>
> Nathan: So like, when you're baptized as an infant, that starts everything, or something, kind of, and then...
>
> Mr. Mandel: Basically. And at that point, you know. You're born in original sin.
>
> Nathan: Right.
>
> Mr. Mandel: [That] is the teaching, so the baptism basically washes that from you and gives you the chance to start anew.
>
> Nathan: So you don't think works, you don't believe that you're saved by works?
>
> Mr. Mandel: No. Not saved by works alone.
>
> Nathan: But saved by what?
>
> Mr. Mandel: There is a place for, for those works because what does God tell us in the great commandment?
>
> Nathan: (*as Mr. Mandel continues speaking*) Right. Yeah. I hear you.
>
> Mr. Mandel: Do unto others.
>
> Nathan: Yeah. [*pause*] So then what is it that saves you then?
>
> Mr. Mandel: The grace of the Lord. If you're living the way the Lord asks you to live, and you're baptized, then there's really nothing holding you back from salvation.
>
> Nathan: Okay. That's all.
>
> Mr. Mandel: If you're not living in the Lord and you're out there stealing from people and, you know, taking your neighbor's wife and that kind of thing, you're not in the Lord even if you're baptized [pause]. But, as I was saying the first time

I came to talk to you, we don't believe there's any sin that ever is unforgivable.

Nathan: Uh, huh. Yeah.

Mr. Mandel: You can always turn your life around. You're given the opportunity to do that right up 'til you leave your death-bed and somebody carries you out.

Nathan: So you need to be living your life the correct way.

Mr. Mandel: Right. I would believe so. I'm not the judge.

Nathan: No. I'm just saying—

Mr. Mandel: We know who the judge is.

Nathan: Right. Right.

Following our guest speaker's visit, Nathan wrote, "The main fault [of Catholicism] is in salvation. Mr. Mandel expressed the idea that living a 'good' life will get a catholic into heaven, and not simply accepting Christ into your life." He said, "When I asked him [Mr. Mandel] about salvation, it wasn't any, anywhere like the same thing, at all. It wasn't even close. Remember? His view of salvation, getting saved." Later, Nathan expressed that it was the Catholicism of the Spaniards who brought the gospel to the New World that contributed to the indigenous peoples' distortion of the concept of salvation. In the sixth essay, Nathan declared:

> It also isn't good if the people who are trying to tell their religious beliefs aren't even telling the truth. If their beliefs aren't correct, and they bring physical harm, then all they are doing is sending people to hell. So, if they are true Christians and are speaking the true way to heaven, the people are benefiting, but if they are wrong, then the people are dead wrong. I think in the case of the indians, the people coming across were wrong.

When I asked him directly during longitudinal member checking about whether Catholics were or were not saved, Nathan replied, "Some are. It depends on how they feel about Christ, whether he's the focus or whether Mary is the focus, or which they believe. Some of them are. There are Christian Catholics, you know."

When asked whether Satan was deceiving the indigenous people of the Americas during the worship of what the Spanish friars called "idols," Nathan responded, "Well, [*pause*] yeah [*laughs in an incredulous manner as if saying, "Of course I do"*]." On the question of salvation for the Mayas, Aztecs, and Incas, however, Nathan said, "I guess I don't understand. How did, if we know everything, everything through the Bible, then how could, how are they to know those things? I still don't understand that. They did not have the Bible, right?" After I confirmed that they did not, he continued, "They didn't have access to it [*brief pause*], so wouldn't you kind of make up some stuff too? I mean, how are they accountable? I don't understand that." Later he said, "If you set me where they were and I had no access to anything, I was just looking at it, I'd be like 'okay.' I'd come up with something too." On day 20 Nathan commented,

> I don't know how it works, but it just seems that if it was before the time of Christ or if it was before the time that the Bible was written, there must have been some way for people . . . to reach heaven other than through the Bible. I mean, [if] it does not exist, then you cannot use it. Therefore, there has to be a means of going to heaven, right?

On the questionnaire, Nathan chose the option "In addition to Christians, there is hope for heaven for those who have never heard the gospel of Christ." In the comment section below, he added, "There has to be. All men have seen. Maybe we don't understand, but God does." When I asked him a year later to explain what he meant by "have seen," Nathan expounded:

> Teacher: When you said, "There has to be. All men have seen," what did you mean by "have seen"? What have they seen?
>
> Nathan: Oh. I think that was in reference to that verse, uh, what is it, "the truth has been revealed to all men who have seen the, nature," what is it?
>
> Teacher: The Romans verse about creation and God's divine power?
>
> Nathan: (*cutting me off, quoting*) All things have been seen [*pause*]. It's a verse. Through what has been made, all men have seen through what has been made or whatever. Do you know what I'm talking about?
>
> Teacher: Okay, so in seeing creation then, they would know, at least, that—
>
> Nathan: Well, it says that all men know. I think what it means is that it's like one way or another, like I put "Maybe we don't understand, but God does." There may be a way that they see through nature and they realize, and therefore they accept that and then they're, to them, to God, you know. They'll go to heaven. You know what I mean? Like, 'cause if there's no gospel presented to them exactly, I don't think that would mean that there's no way you could go to heaven, because it [the Bible] doesn't say you have to have heard the gospel to go to heaven. It says you have to believe in Jesus, and if they can get to that point one way or another, or maybe not even, or close to that point, then God would have a way for them to go to heaven.

Teacher: So, God might have a different standard knowing that people had not heard the name Jesus or had not—

Nathan: (*hesitantly*) Yeah. I don't know, a different standard, but kind of, sort of like that, yeah. Because if it were an actual gospel presentation, yeah, 'cause that's obviously not possible, by any means.

Teacher: And a lot of people may have died never hearing the name of Jesus?

Nathan: Exactly. Which, and then you're like, "Well, is that fair?" or whatever, but I think there's ways for them to figure it out and to accept it. I'm not sure how 'cause I've never been in that situation.

Teacher: But that's why you would say that God does and that God would understand?

Nathan: That's what I would think 'cause that would be an awful [*pause*], and then you get into the elect and all that. You do.

Teacher: We had some fun discussions on that [*laugh*].

Nathan: You do. 'Cause then you're like, "Well, then, were some of those random tribal people elect?" and then, I mean, that's a whole other discussion. So, I do, I do think there's ways.

Nathan disagreed three times on day 20 that if the Mayas, Aztecs, and Incas were to be saved, they would have been members of the "elect," a term used by Calvinists to describe those God has predestined for heaven. When Amanda quoted from Ephesians 1:14, saying "For he [God] chose us in him before the creation of the world to be holy and blameless in his sight," Nathan responded, "Yeah? To be holy and blameless. What does that have to do with it?" If God merely predestined people, he asked, "Why did he give us a mind?" Finally, Nathan affirmed that free will "has to be part of it."

On the questionnaire, Nathan chose the option "God is present and at work in all religious traditions," though he commented,

Although it may not be seen, or not seen as we always think, I believe God is always at work. He desires relationships. However, if He is continually blocked out of a particular religion, then how can He help them? So it goes both ways.

When asked a year later for specifics, Nathan and I had the following conversation:

Teacher: Do you remember if you were thinking of any... particular ones [religions] that had blocked him out?

> Nathan: Well, anyone whose theology is other than his [God's]. What I think I really meant is when, like if you project God and the Bible as being the truth and you have something completely different, then it's hard for him to work through it because, you know, consciously you're... [*laughs*]
> Teacher: So the stuff that's... completely different?
> Nathan: Yeah. Completely, that has no—
> Teacher: What about the stuff that's a little bit more similar?
> Nathan: I think he could, I mean, I think he's at work no matter what, with the whole world, but I think with the more similar ones they have a better chance of figuring out the actual truth, because they're closer. You know? The closer you are to getting it right, you know, they have a better chance of someone going "Hey, what if...?"
> Teacher: And then, as a springboard from that, to learn about—
> Nathan: Yeah, 'cause even Catholicism. They can believe, they can be Christians if they get past their, I mean they can believe all that stuff with the saints and Mary and everything, but if they still believe Christ as being the savior and all that, then they can still be Christians 'cause they at least know he exists, as opposed to someone who thinks mountains are God, or whatever.

On the questionnaire, Nathan wrote, "These religions aren't getting people anywhere because they are ultimately wrong. However, I didn't check entirely negative because each also has its own way of being close to Christianity." In his final statement on the subject prior to the longitudinal member check, Nathan said that he didn't know "where God fits into everything on different religions. Where does He come in? Somewhere. I don't know. I can't figure it out."

VIEWS ON EVANGELISM
AND INTERRELIGIOUS DIALOGUE

For Nathan, it was difficult to single out the highest priority in his life as a Christian. He did not circle any of the responses provided on the questionnaire, but instead wrote,

> It's hard to pick one because each part is needed to have a Christian walk. For example, I need spiritual growth to be better at evangelism, but I also need my local church to help with spiritual growth. They are all intertwined.

Nathan estimated that 10–30% of his friends were non-Christians, although he added that you "can't know for sure [who is and isn't a Christian]!" He also figured that he shared the gospel with people who did not already profess faith in Christ "once a month," adding the comment, "Maybe a little less, but close to that. I would like more."

Although he neglected to answer the part of the question on the third reflective essay concerning whether evangelical Christians should share the gospel with Catholics, he did make several declarations regarding evangelization of Muslims. He wrote, "I believe that Islam is the hardest religion to convert its followers to Christianity, largely because of family tradition and fear of punishment for converting." Nathan had experienced this firsthand with a former classmate. He wrote, "[I] had a friend at Birch and Washington [public schools] whom I led to know Christ. His family was all Islamic and he felt pressure to not change, or at least not to tell anyone in his family that he did." Nathan also stayed after class on day 4 to further describe this experience.

> Nathan: It was actually middle school, sixth grade. Yeah, it was really interesting. It was such a family thing, but, [*The classroom door slams, making two or three words unintelligible on the tape*] type of deal, but it was more of just getting him to understand it as much as he just knew that that's the way I had to be. But it was really weird talking to him. They just kind of like, he was open. He just didn't 'cause we were young then, you know, and every time I would tell him something he would agree that it all made sense and everything, and I let him read stuff and he just said, he just, he was scared of what his parents would think of him. He was real scared of what the family would do. He was like, "You don't understand. I can't just do that, 'cause, like, 'cause my parents won't accept" and then I was like, "Well, you can do this, just keep it to yourself."
>
> Teacher: How faithful were his parents [as] Muslims?
>
> Nathan: Pretty faithful.
>
> Teacher: They were pretty, pretty much into—
>
> Nathan: Well, yeah. I mean, they, for him to be that scared of mentioning Christ.
>
> [*I make a comment regarding how I had heard of instances in which Muslims had been cut off from their families for converting.*]
>
> Nathan: Right. So that's why I think he was just going to kind of keep it to himself, but at the same time we prayed together, so I know he at least said something that I told him that he had to mean it, and I think he did, but it was,

it was an experience, something that I may never experience again. You never [*pause*] It's just, like you said, the
ties are just so deep.

Teacher: Right.

Nathan: In tradition and everything. It's weird. It's almost kind of
scary. He was scared.

When presented with the scenario of how to act around a hypothetical
Muslim neighbor, Nathan wrote,

I'm sure if my new neighbor was a Muslim, I would not treat them any differently than I would treat any neighbor. I think that the best thing for someone
like that would be for them to get a good first impression, and then to see
how you live out your daily life. Usually people get ideas from you by how you
live and act. If I eventually wanted to reach out to this person religiously, they
would have to see some backup by watching me first.

Yes, I think they would need to hear the Gospel. I think everyone should, and
I feel that in being their neighbor, it would be my job to reach them with the
good news. I think also that even though they are strictly different, God can
move anybody to accept Christ.

I would definitely try to encourage them to accept Christ, and like I said, I
think it would best be done through example first, and then easily leading
them. In fact, I have already had this opportunity once in life and would definitely pursue it again.

For Nathan, the importance of employing the correct method of evangelism arose when he was asked whether spiritual well-being was more
important than physical well-being for the indigenous peoples of the New
World. He responded,

Spiritual matters are always more important than physical because they get
you to heaven. However, the way in which they [evangelistic efforts] are done
matters too. For example, if a group of people come in and force another
group of people to follow their ways and don't show compassion . . . and they
are being mean, it isn't very effective.

During our investigation of the conquest of Peru and the capture, baptism, and execution of the Incan emperor Atahualpa, Nathan sarcastically
remarked, "I think that's a really great demonstration of a Christian, to
have him be a Christian and then strangle him." Later, in the seventh essay,
he wrote concerning Spanish destruction of indigenous religious objects,

First of all, I think it is a very bad idea to destroy the other people's treasures
and books, etc., because it gets things off to a bad start. I think it makes it
harder to evangelize right off the bat because you have already made a bad

impression and the people you are trying to save will be much less likely to listen to what you have to say. Second, it makes it harder also because you could have potentially destroyed all means of communication with the tribe. If you have burned their books and belongings, you might as well have burned their language and then you are stuck completely. People aren't as willing to conform to something that they cannot relate with. I believe there would have to be a medium for the two parties to work with. I understand the argument that you would have to rid the indians of all the things they are wrong about, but I don't think you can get very far unless you are at the same level. Another problem with getting rid of their customs is for history's sake. Like for instance, now we can't learn very much about the Incas, Mayas, or Aztecs because the conquistadors destroyed them, and another thing we can take from that is the fact that the indians weren't willing to change to Christianity because of the force and brutality. How well does that show Christianity or even how a Christian should act? To conclude, it is my opinion that a compromise must be found in order to be effective in sharing Christ with others.

Nathan mentioned this final idea several times, including once during the final essay. In response to Thomas Merton's statement concerning the Spaniards' inability to see Christ already potentially present in the Indians [of the New World], Nathan wrote,

> I think what it means by "should the conquistadors have seen Christ in the indians" is more along the lines of should they have made an attempt to look for Christ in the indians. If there is no trying to put God in their lives with what they already know, then the effort is in vain.

Nathan echoed this statement during the second group interview as well, when he said,

> If you're a Christian but you don't get into the things that other people [*pause*], not get in, but you're not familiar with the way other people act or what they do within the world, not to be in the world, but to know of it, then you're not as effective 'cause you're not coming to them on their level. You have to, or they're not going to be interested.

On the questionnaire, Nathan explained his interest in learning about other religious traditions by choosing the option "I am interested in learning about other religious traditions so that I can more effectively share the Gospel." He added, "[That option] is perfect. That's exactly what I want."

Learning for the sake of more effective evangelism was not the only reason given by Nathan to study other religious traditions. As seen earlier, he bemoaned the cultural loss of indigenous peoples in the New World "for history's sake" since "now we can't learn very much about the Incas, Mayas, or Aztecs because the conquistadors destroyed them." In another instance, Nathan went so far as to say,

> I think you can learn things [from other religions], like disciplines. I think that the Islamic people are really disciplined in their faith and the fact that they pray consistently and stuff, sometimes they're a little sharper than we are. I don't think you should believe what they believe at all, not by any means, but I think you can learn certain things like, praying, doing things that you need to be doing, just out of the, however they do it. [*pause*] What am I trying to think of? [*pause*] besides *discipline*. I don't know. Anyway. You know what I mean?

At first, Nathan said that he saw no dangers in learning about other religions, but later agreed with Caleb when he said "there probably is a danger in it, 'cause...people do convert." Nathan then speculated that "there must be a line somewhere where that [conversion] happens." He then theorized where that line existed when he said, "Instead of depending necessarily on the group of people, I think it depends on the individual more." When asked whether he would attend an Islamic or Native American ceremony, Nathan stated that "As long as there are no sacrifices, I would come [*laughs*]."

RELATIVIZATION AND CHANGE

The majority of the data that will be used in the next chapter's discussion of Nathan and relativization has yet to be presented. Most of it surfaced in the fifth unit in which we attempted to address the issues apart from any one particular cultural context. Before these are presented, however, a few noteworthy items from the first four units must be introduced. First of all, on the second essay Nathan wrote,

> Honestly, sometimes I think we in America we see Christians as predominately the people we see in our community. I hope that through these studies, I can see how diverse the world is and how God can inhabit anybody for His glory!

During class on day 18, after explaining that he understood how the Aztecs could believe that the mountains contained water that filled the earth, Nathan became slightly antagonistic:

> Amanda:　Well, okay, *that* [the mountains full of water], but try other
> 　　　　　things like—
> Nathan:　(*with a disputatious voice*) Like what?

Amanda: Like, all that other stuff.

[*Several other students speak at the same time, then Amanda and Caleb speak.*]

Matthew: All you have to do is find a kid who has an overactive imagination.

Nathan: (*interrupting with the same tone*) How do you know? How do we know? How do we know?

At the outset of the fifth unit, when asked whether our investigation had caused him to think about his own faith in a new way, Nathan wrote, "I see how other religions can sound completely absurd, but at the same time, those people could see mine the same way." During the first group interview, after asking for the second time when I was going to tell the students my opinions, Nathan and other students expressed the following:

Nathan: Um, it made me start thinking a lot more now. Like, no, I don't know, now I can really see how easy it is for someone to just think up something. Like now that Popol Vuh thing doesn't seem so weird, because after, like they were saying, the wind god and all this stuff—

Lisa: Branches—

Nathan: (*continuing*) I could see a lot easier how something could be conjured up. 'Cause when you get, even just us, we could have so many different ideas about one thing. You know? So it's, everyone could think so differently. It's kind of crazy to think that's what they thought and I could see how they could write something like that.

Stephanie: But then, did they just totally make it up from what they thought?

Nathan: (*laughing*) I know. I don't know. I don't know.

[*Three other students make comments.*]

Nathan: I don't know. I'd just, I'd be real interested to hear someone, either you [the teacher] or someone, I don't know, I'd want to know more. I don't feel like I know enough to be able to make any real judgments.

Teacher: On what, specifically?

Nathan: Well, on if God, where God fits into everything on different religions. Where does He come in?

Teacher: Okay.

Nathan: Somewhere. I don't know. I can't figure it out.

Teacher: Yeah. I'll let you know what I think on May 11.

Nathan: Okay.

Teacher: (*continuing*) Um.

Nathan: I'm going to have to go to seminary now.

[*A brief discussion ensues about whether Nathan should be a pastor.*]

Teacher: (*interrupting*) Anything else about our topic today?

Nathan: (*semi-sarcastically joking*) Yeah. Now I'm really confused. Thanks.

[*I give a mock sheepish look. Everyone laughs.*]

Lisa: (*in a chirpy voice*) Thanks.

[*More laughter.*]

Nathan: No, but, uh—

Caleb: All my core beliefs just [*makes a "splat" sound with his mouth*].

[*More laughter, including Nathan.*]

Nathan: I still believe what I believe, but it's just that now I wonder about, about everybody else. I never really thought about everybody else as much.

Teacher: You mean that you can at least see how some people might tend to believe what they did?

Nathan: Yeah, who was it that said, someone in class said something about, "You can believe something with all your heart, but if you're wrong, you're dead wrong."

Teacher: Yeah. That was Jason.

Stephanie: Right.

Nathan: Yeah, I think it was Jason. And he's right. I mean, and that bugs me now, when you think about it.

Stephanie: It's like the other religions, they strongly believe that they're right and we're wrong, so—

Nathan: Right. Exactly. So they could just, everything we say they could be having a discussion in—

Amy: Just like this.

Nathan: Wherever their country, you know.

Lisa: Aztec Villa High School.

[*Laughter.*]

Nathan: You know what I'm saying, yeah. Okay, there's this one god and they pray to [*pause*], you know? [*pause*] They'd be saying the exact same thing.

Lisa: (*mimicking a cheerleader*) Go sacrifices!

[*Laughter.*]

Lisa: Oh, sorry.

Nathan: So [*sighs*], I don't know.

Nathan continued to have difficulty speculating about how adherents of other traditions would think during the second group interview.

Nathan: You just asked us that [if there are any dangers in learning about other religions] and she [Lisa] said if you're strong enough in your faith [you won't convert].

Teacher: Mm, hmm.

Nathan: Well, how do these people feel about us?

[*Stephanie tries to interject.*]

Nathan: Wouldn't they feel the same way? You know what I mean? Wouldn't, okay, like, we're in a class of Islamic people and they're like, and you ask the same question. Is there any dangers in learning about Christianity? Well, not if we're into Islam enough. So then that would mean no one would ever convert to anything.

Teacher: Do you think that—

Nathan: (*cutting me off*) So, now I'm thinking, "I wonder what makes them think theirs is wrong then and we're right?" Does that make sense to anybody?

[*Everyone responds, trying to talk at once. Amy says, "But it's not just us evangelizing to them." Several people say "Yeah." Lisa says, "Who's right?"*]

Nathan: Now that you think about it? Wait a second. If we're right, then how can we impress it on them, and they're not going to believe it, or, what makes them believe it? I don't know. Sorry. I didn't mean to do that [*broach such a perplexing subject*]. I was just thinking.

Teacher: So they're saying the same things that we're saying right here?

Nathan: Yeah.

Following a statement by Stephanie, who said that the Bible makes it evident that Christianity is the one true religion with the one true God, Nathan continued,

Nathan: Maybe I think the Koran is right and it makes sense.

[*Awkward silence.*]

Stephanie: (*hesitantly*) Well [*pauses*]

[*Laughter.*]

Nathan: See that's what I'm thinking, like, kind of playing the devil's advocate a little bit.

Teacher: You're trying to say maybe what somebody else [of another faith] would be saying at the same time [as us]?

Nathan: What if I'm Islamic and you're like, "Well I see the Bible shows the truth" and I'm like, "Well, I think the Koran shows the truth."

Stephanie: But, have they changed and everything because of, can you see God in them, or their gods in them?

Nathan: Sure. [*chuckles*]

Teacher: You think so?

Nathan: Well, I mean, I'm just, if I was [*leaving his devil's advocate persona*] Yeah. Why not? I mean, they have the same—

Stephanie: (*trying to interject*) Yeah, but they don't —

Nathan: (*cutting Stephanie off*) They're so close to Christianity, right? I mean, they really are, in a lot of, in a sense. The Koran—

Lisa: Mmm. ["Not so fast."]

Nathan: There's one God, right? Allah. Isn't there?
[*Several students speak at once.*]

Caleb: I agree with Nathan.

Lisa: Yeah, but—

Amy: I think they see it as the same.

Lisa: Nobody's the same, unless it's God.

Nathan: No. I'm not saying they're the same, but they're, it's very, [*brief pause*] it parallels, in a lot of ways.

Later in the interview, while the students discussed whether conversion was to be seen as a benefit or danger, Nathan said,

Nathan: So you're saying the only benefit is Christianity, though? Right?

Erin: Yeah. For *us*. [*small laugh*]

Nathan: Or for them, if they convert to Christianity.

Erin: Well, that's our point of view.

Nathan: Right. Exactly.

Shortly thereafter, Nathan added,

Well, it's just hard, because everyone thinks, kind of like in the Old Testament or whatever, when they were just, like, everyone did what was right in their own eyes. I mean, it's just like, it's still true. To them it's one thing, to us it's one thing, and everyone thinks they're right. Ultimately, I mean, individuals can change, but, so it's hard to kind of discuss that 'cause you're kind of coming from a biased view, almost.

At the conclusion of the second group interview, when given a final opportunity to express anything he had been pondering during the course of our investigation, Nathan said, "I now wonder many things," and began the following exchange:

Nathan: I guess I just wish I could understand more what *they* [Muslims] think. I don't think I know enough. Yeah.

Erin: Yeah.

Teacher: Do you think that you're just kind of assuming that they're doing the same things that [*brief pause*], saying some of the same things that we are and you really would like to know a little bit more whether they actually are?

Erin: Yeah.

Nathan: Yeah.

Teacher: Seeing evangelism [*pause*]

Nathan: Yeah. What do they think about it? I don't [*pause*], we don't know. We're just guessing. We're like, "Well they probably think this or they think that." Do all Christians believe the exact same thing even within our own Bible and stuff? No. . . . One person could think something completely different about the Koran or something, and they have their own thing. I mean, who knows? I don't think we have enough exposure to the actual people around us to know enough. I don't think so. Maybe somebody does, but [*pause*] . . . so I think that makes it harder to know exactly how they feel about things.

Teacher: Or whether it's just a uniform belief, or whether there is variety of—

Nathan: Yeah, 'cause the ones who have a certain variety might see Christianity better, you know. I'm sure. There's got to be different ways of thinking with them.

CHAPTER 11

INTERPRETING THE PRIMARY INFORMANTS

Although Amy, Caleb, and Nathan were selected for detailed portrayal in the preceeding chapters, each of the students in my Spanish 3 class could have served as unique and interesting subjects for depiction. Jason, for example, fell in love with Catholicism but found the devil lurking behind every rock when it came to the religious practices of indigenous Americans. Travis generally displayed a fairly orthodox outlook, but would occasionally express sentiments that were wildly heretical by conservative Protestant standards. Erin often reacted as though it were the first time she had ever given any consideration to the relations between her Christian faith and other religions.

These and other pupils notwithstanding, Amy, Caleb, and Nathan were chosen because they most clearly illustrated the various ways in which students reacted to their encounter with other religious traditions. Again, these were (1) the student most interested in maintaining the boundaries of orthodoxy, (2) the student most inclined to traverse those boundaries, and (3) the student in the middle, wrestling with the issues that arose during this encounter with different traditions of faith.

I will now attempt to draw some meaningful conclusions with regard to the way they approached and were affected by knowledge of the other religions, identifying what I believe to be the key theological issues that influenced their responses. In doing so, a few of the conclusions may seem somewhat speculative, particularly to those unfamiliar with the inner work-

American Evangelicals and Religious Diversity, pages 193–220
Copyright © 2006 by Information Age Publishing
193

ings of the evangelical subculture. In these instances I note that the interpretations I give are possibilities, not certainties. However, as an insider who intuitively understands much of the lingo, thought patterns, and concerns of evangelicals due to my years within the tradition, and as a teacher with three years of class time spent with each of the primary informants, I firmly believe that they are more likely on the mark than not.

AMY

Boundaries

For Amy and the other students, a limited amount of relativization, if defined as "seeing one's tradition in relation to another," was inevitable due to the very nature of some of the activities in which they were involved. For example, analysis of the creation narratives of the Bible and the Popol Vuh required students to place the different traditions side-by-side in order to compare and contrast them. At other points in the study, however, Amy herself chose to make comparisons without explicitly being asked to do so. In an overwhelming majority of these cases, as we have seen, Amy specialized in contrasts.

From the outset, Amy was intent on drawing sharp boundary lines between the non-Christian religions and her own faith. Beginning with her first assignment, the Islam montage, she used violent and militaristic phrases such as "the Muslims *took over* [the Hagia Sophia] and turned it into a mosque by *destroying* all the pictures of Christ inside" and "[The Mediterranean Sea] reminds me of Muslims also because the Muslim *stronghold* is around the Mediterranean Sea" [emphasis added]. This language, reminiscent of the medieval age of crusade and conquest, demonstrates that there existed, in Amy's mind at least, the sense of threat that C. Smith (1998) claims in his subcultural identity theory to be an integral component of reinforcing boundaries and maintaining the vitality of an embattled evangelicalism. Tellingly, the fact that our study (minus the one member checking session) concluded 4 months prior to the events of September 11, 2001, illustrates that for Amy the threat of Islam was about more than airplanes and exploding buildings, the prevalent reason used in recent years to explain Americans' antagonism toward Islam and Muslims.

Throughout the first unit, Amy's constant focus on the distinctions between Islam and Christianity served to place Muslims definitively within the category of Other. In fact, in the only instance in which she acknowledged similarities, she did so in order to question the ulterior motives of Islam when she wrote, "I think the Muslim faith is very dangerous. It closely resembles the Bible in a couple ways in order to 'trap' people into believing it." While investigating the Mayan worldview during the third unit, she continued this trend of differentiation when she asserted that the Popol Vuh contained only "a couple of [similarities], *sort of [her tone insinuating that they were not even close enough to be worth considering]*."

Amy's recurring use of the words "strange" and "weird" to describe the beliefs of the non-Christian religions is noteworthy for several reasons. One gets a clear sense that, coming from Amy, these were not positive or neutral words, such as the word "exotic" might be, but rather implied a negative evaluation of beliefs with which she was unaccustomed. For Amy, unfamiliar religious matters were suspect, most likely since all religious truth was already known through the previous revelation of the Bible. Also, by labeling them as weird or strange, Amy minimized the seriousness with which she was required to consider the claims made by the other faiths. As has already been seen, Amy repeatedly resisted attempts to place non-Christian worldviews on the same plane as Christianity. Comparison was acceptable, as long as the other religions were denied the veracity or sensibility of her faith. When asked if the way the other traditions viewed the world made sense, Amy replied "Parts of it do," but quickly added, "except for all of a sudden somebody [in the Popol Vuh] became a monkey or whatever." She also laughed uncomfortably when fellow students presented polytheism as a sensible way to view the natural world.

Even though she found the non-Christian traditions sorely lacking, Amy still found "almost everything" about our study to be "interesting," including the prospect of being an onlooker at a Native American religious ceremony and observing how a hypothetical Muslim neighbor viewed different areas of life. At first glance, it might appear odd that one would pay close attention to something one had already judged as inferior, but the reason became clear when Amy stated that the end result was the opportunity to "evangelize to them better," and not for any merit intrinsic in the traditions themselves.

At only two points during our investigation of non-Christian religions did Amy seem to deviate from her modus operandi of disapproval and differentiation. The first occurred on the questionnaire when she checked the box labeled "slightly negative" to describe her impressions of Islam as a whole, and the "mostly negative" box for her impressions of the worldviews of the Mayas, Aztecs, and Incas, ignoring altogether the option "entirely negative." It is unclear why, when she had been at least as outspoken in opposition to the Muslim faith as she had been regarding the indigenous American worldviews, she would rate Islam as the more favorable of the two. It may have been due to the greater amount of time that had elapsed since we had studied Islam and that the perceived threat was not as immediate. If she had been asked the question directly following our investigation of Islam, she may have selected a different option.

As for the avoidance of the "entirely negative" option in both cases, it may be that the phrasing of the question biased Amy's responses. Despite the persistent negative evaluations of the other religious systems, I doubt that Amy would have seen herself as a "negative" person in daily life. Although somewhat serious, she exhibited a cheerful demeanor, and may not have felt comfortable identifying herself with the term "negative." This interpretation is supported by the structure of Amy's fifth essay. After a full 13 sentences describing the shortcomings of the indigenous American worldviews, it seems that she realized that the orientation of her essay was critical and tacked on two lines in admiration of the indigenous civilizations' architectural and mathematical accomplishments. If, on the questionnaire, an alternative term to describe the faith traditions such as "unfavorable" had been used instead of "negative," it may have solicited a different response, or it may be that she would have avoided the most extreme column no matter what the wording was.

The second potential anomaly exhibited by Amy occurred during the first group interview. After Stephanie stated that the other religions "strongly believe that they're right and we're wrong," Nathan commented that "everything we say, they could be having a discussion . . ." At this point, Amy can be faintly heard on the tape voicing the words "just like this." To allow that those of other religions could share with her something in common seemed so out of character for Amy that I revisited the tape more than once to verify that she had indeed said it. Since the comment truly was hers, we must acknowledge the possibility that, near the end of our investigation, even the class's most ardent defender of evangelical orthodoxy had experienced a paradigm shift in her views of the Other.

However, I believe that to see this utterance as evidence for a radical change in Amy's thinking would be overreaching, for three reasons. First, it is important to note that what Amy saw the other religions holding in common with her own, in this instance, was the exclusivity with which they held truth claims, and not the content of these truth claims themselves. Therefore, Amy could allow that adherents of other religions claimed to be right (as she did) and still be mistaken (as she was not) in all that they held to be true. Second, just as nowhere else in the study prior to that articulation could there be seen a willingness to equate her beliefs with those of non-Christians, nothing afterward exhibited it either. Although there remained only the final group interview (not including the member check a year later), Amy vocalized nothing during that session to indicate that she now saw others in a significantly different manner than she had before, and reverted instead to use of the words "weird" and "strange" yet again. Finally, in an entirely unexpected and unsolicited turn of events, a younger sibling of Amy, who was a part of my Spanish 3 class 2 years later, volunteered some very interesting information during the course of a normal class discussion on the history of Muslims in Spain. She related that after graduation from Midwest Christian Academy, Amy had been required as part of her university's summer reading program for incoming students to read a portion of the Koran, but had instead written an essay explaining why she objected to reading the text. For these reasons, I believe Amy's comment "just like us" is best seen, not as an epiphany leading to monumental or lasting change in the way she viewed Islam and the worldviews of indigenous Americans, but as a minor incident, if anything at all.

When we studied Roman Catholicism, however, Amy's tone was strikingly different from the way she responded to the non-Christian traditions. On her third essay, Amy noted a nearly equal number of similarities and differences between the Catholic and Protestant faiths, and did so in a very dispassionate manner, without any antagonistic rhetoric. She chose the option "mostly positive" to describe her impressions of Catholicism. She also described a Catholic that she knew as her "friend" and asked Mr. Mandel, "Do you [Catholics] think of us as brothers and sisters in Christ?" These things indicate that Amy perceived little or no threat from Catholicism and was not invested in actively distinguishing between the Catholic faith and her own.

This is not to say, however, that Amy had no qualms with Catholic practice. On her montage of initial impressions, she included two images of the Virgin Mary, which she labeled "Holy Mother Mary and her child." In this title, which I had never before heard an evangelical use, Christ was not mentioned by name, but only in relation to his mother. This may indicate that Amy saw Catholicism as focused more on Mary than on Christ. Even if this is true, however, it does not mean that Amy saw Christ as excluded from the Catholic faith, since she wrote clearly that "both religions [Catholicism and Protestantism] believe in Christ and that He is God's Son."

Later, Amy opined, "It seems to me that Catholics think they are saved if they are part of the Catholic Church and obey everything they have to." However, she then qualified the statement with "I know there are people just like that in Protestant churches who don't realize just belonging to a church doesn't assure salvation." This addendum, I believe, indicates two things. Although a weak one, it amounted to a sort of defense of these individual Catholics. Misguided as they were, it was not is if they were the only ones foolish enough to believe such a thing. Second, this statement was a critique of some people associated with Amy's own tradition. This mode of self-reflection was never evidenced during the Islam and indigenous American units. Since she perceived no threat from Catholicism, however, Amy felt the freedom during the second unit to critique individuals in her own tradition, without the need to maintain a unified front in the presence of a perceived adversary.

Key Issues for Amy

Heaven, Salvation, and Predestination

As one of two students in the class with a Calvinistic view of salvation, heaven was of major concern for Amy. In fact, the primary issue with which she had seemed to be wrestling during the study was how the Christian God was at work among members of other religions and how the doctrine of predestination applied to these people. As noted earlier, the conclusion she finally reached was "If the Islam, Catholics, and Meso-Americans are left on their own accord, they wouldn't accept Christ. However, if God reveals himself and predestines them to be Christians, then they will be saved." On the questionnaire, she chose the option "The only hope for heaven is for those who profess and demonstrate faith in Christ." In doing so, she avoided the option "In addition to Christians, there is hope for heaven for those who have never heard the gospel of Christ," presumably since such a category of people could not exist, as a God who was loving as well as sovereign would have revealed himself to them. Amy asserted that God could do this "in any way He wants," whether it be through the natural order as described in Romans 1:20 ["For since the creation of the world God's invisible qualities—his eternal power and divine nature—have been clearly seen, being understood from what has been made, so that people are without excuse"] or through some other method.

This willingness to leave God's options open regarding how and to whom he revealed himself led to a tension between two strains of thought for Amy. Whereas she had previously framed her responses to the non-Christian religions in terms of "us" (Christians) versus "them" (non-Christians), she now acknowledged that God was "present and at work in all religions" and that one could "see God anywhere." The possibility that a sovereign God, if He so chose, could be somehow present in "them" caused Amy pause.

Amy was not a know-it-all, as indicated by her willingness to ask questions and her occasional use of the hedge "seems to" when characterizing the other religions (see Lakoff, 1973, for an introduction to the linguistic function of hedges). At another point during the study she stated that there are "a lot of things about God that we can't understand." For Amy, however, God's method of salvation was not one of these incomprehensible things. On the questionnaire near the end of the study, Amy wrote, "God has control of everything and can use other religions to fulfill his plan. However, even if he is at work, the people may not be saved. They, too, can only be saved through Christ."

At several points during her writing Amy made use of the word "hope" to describe Christianity or the other religious traditions. When she used the term in reference to the salvation of Christians, it implied no uncertainty, but rather assurance of life with God after death, a matter for Amy (and for many other evangelical Christians as well) whose importance could scarcely be exaggerated. For those, like Amy, who believed in the doctrine of predestination, this salvation was even more assured, and would not be withdrawn since the elect had been chosen by God before the creation of the world.

Non-Christian faith traditions, on the other hand, were entirely bereft of this hope because the saving presence of God resided exclusively within Christians. By affirming this, however, Amy was faced with a dilemma, namely that non-Christians sometimes exhibited noble or admirable behavior. How was one to account for this apparent goodness if those of other religions had not accepted Christ and received the Holy Spirit? To deal with this issue, Amy employed *solo fide*, the tenet of the Protestant Revolution that declares that human effort and good works avail nothing in the eyes of God, but that salvation comes solely through faith in the grace of God bestowed on humankind through the atoning death of Christ. Amy made mention of these useless human "works" when describing Catholics as having many "'requirements' that seem like works." However, she extended the application of this principle to those outside of the Christian fold as well. Amy saw Islam as a religion that seemed to be "based on good works," and in Meso-American belief, "the only way to get to heaven is through works and constant reverence to the gods." In this way, Amy dismissed the admirable actions of non-Christians as a futile attempt to earn God's favor and personal salvation, and not as a result of God's influential presence in their lives. Therefore, what initially appeared to be good, Amy painted as yet another instance of misguided belief and behavior.

Scripture

Amy was aware that all humans, including she herself, could at times be misguided. For that reason, if one were to speak with certainty on how and whom God saved, one needed something much more certain than tradition or human speculation. For Amy, this certainty was found in the Bible, as evidenced by statements such as "Humans are sinful and are often in error, so the Bible is the most authoritative [means of revelation]" and "I don't think the Church should be able to speak on the same level as the Bible because the Bible is God-breathed and humans can't work on the same level as God." In fact, it was this viewing of the world through the one epistemological truth of the Bible that led her to make the definitive statement that God was salvifically present only in those who had "accepted Christ," a conclusion most likely drawn from verses such as John 14:6 ["Jesus answered, 'I am the way and the truth and the life. No one comes to the Father except through me'"].

As a book written by God, Amy generally regarded the Bible as a univocal, internally consistent unit. In fact, divine "inspiration" was predicated on a sacred text's complete freedom from contradictions. Although Amy acknowledged the human component in the writing of the Bible once when it suited her argument that differences between the Old and New Testaments were just "different portraits" of God instead of incongruities, this was by no means the norm. In nearly every other case, Amy's view of Scripture displayed an almost total lack of acknowledgment of the human component in Biblical revelation. She saw the Koran as written by a man, and, for that reason, as imperfect. The Bible, however, was different in that there existed only a divine component. If asked directly, Amy would probably have admitted that human hands scribed the individual books, but at no point other than the one instance mentioned earlier did she ever apply this piece of information to the issues we were discussing. To acknowledge human complicity would have weakened the authority of the text, and the certainty of the guidance that it provided.

As for the canonization process, Amy allowed that God was "probably" just as involved with the compilers of the Bible as with the authors of the books themselves. Logically, this was imperative, since to allow for the possibility of human error in the compilation phase of the Protestant Scriptures would likewise have led to diminished trustworthiness, as the collection of texts could be incorrect or incomplete. The Bible, however, was complete, and contained everything necessary for salvation and for correct living. For this reason, Amy found that any new revelation from God was merely a restating of what had previously been disclosed in Scripture, such as when she claimed that the things God communicates through other Christians are "already in the Bible." The historical revelation of the Bible was fixed. At the end of the second group interview, when she affirmed that "Christianity never changes," she reiterated that truth was not relative, changing from person to person or from age to age, but absolute and immutable. This denial of historical change in order to solidify the grounding of belief did not originate with Amy, but appears often throughout the annals of Christian apologetics. As historian Jaroslav Pelikan (1971) writes,

> It seems that theologians have been willing to trace the history of doctrines and doctrinal systems which they found to be in error, but... the normative tradition had to be protected from the relativity of having a history or of being, in any decisive sense, the product of a history. (p. 8)

If human involvement in the production of the Biblical text was ignored, what was Amy's view on interpretation? Did there not exist the possibility for the introduction of error during this human process? The extent to which Amy believed that the Holy Spirit superintended the interpretation process or that meaning of Scripture was self-evident is unknown and would require further research, although both would fit well with her desire to limit the possibility of corruption due to human involvement. What she did display, however, was the use of a nearly literal hermeneutic in which the creation narrative(s) in the book of Genesis and events such as those in the life of King David were to be read as literal, chronological, historical occurrences. The only exception she made was the parables told by Christ, which were not narratives of actual people, but stories meant to illustrate a spiritual lesson. Although other stories in the Bible also taught spiritual lessons, they were to be taken literally, meaning that the people truly existed and that events transpired exactly as stated in the text.

Evangelism

Since Amy's interpretation of Scripture led to a clear division between the "saved" and the "unsaved," it was readily evident who needed to be evangelized, namely those who did not have a "personal relationship with Christ." Quoting from Acts 1:8, Amy wrote, "God calls us to be his 'witnesses in Jerusalem, and in all Judea and Samaria, and to the ends of the earth'." By using this quote, Amy applied a command originally given by Christ to his apostles as her own scriptural call from God. However, having received this divine mandate to spread the gospel did not mean that she always felt comfortable doing so. She related her hesitance to share her faith with hypothetical Muslim neighbors because of an unpleasant personal experience with a Muslim foreign exchange student who had lived with her family. For this reason, she would be cautious at first, although she wrote that she eventually would share the gospel with these neighbors.

This discomfort that Amy felt regarding evangelism may provide a possible explanation for how evangelicals can claim evangelism as something in which they are actively involved (see C. Smith, 1998) and yet see fewer converts than some might expect (see T-NET, 2003). To begin with, Amy was probably aware that exclusive truth claims were not always well received in the public sphere, and that to be outspoken would violate the ethic of civility (see Cuddihy, 1978) and risk personal rejection from others, including from those with whom she had established relationships. Not relishing this prospect, Amy preferred to demonstrate her faith with her actions. In keeping with C. Smith's (2000) personal influence strategy, this distinctive and virtuous lifestyle, necessary proof of God's presence in her life, was to serve the purpose of drawing others to question what it was about Amy that made her different. At this point, once there was a better chance that the message would be well received, she would feel more comfortable to verbally share the gospel. As illustrated here, this lifestyle evangelism approach seems to be only partially efficacious. On the one hand, it serves to eliminate the excuse of those who would reject the claims of Christianity based on the hypocrisy of some of its members. However, it can also potentially hinder the evangelistic cause if it also allows individuals who fear rejection to remain silent and still feel like they are being faithful witnesses for Christ.

Although she did not always issue proclamations from the rooftops or pursue public debate, evangelism was still of great importance in Amy's eyes. After all, one's decision whether or not to heed the call of God had eternal consequences. Because of the gravity of the matter, Amy was able to say that temporary human physical concerns, although important, were secondary to everlasting spiritual ones. At this point, Amy was faced with a difficult question. If a non-Christian's eternal soul hung in the balance between heaven and hell, was it possible to go too far in trying to get him or her to convert? Did the ends justify the means?

On this issue, it appears that Amy held a set of interesting and somewhat contradictory opinions. In one instance she wrote, "I think that spiritual peril outweighs the physical. If we can even win one person to God, it is worth the effort." Although she also stated that present-day Christians would be called to look after both physical and spiritual needs of the "natives" and would not want to inflict pain on them as the Spanish did when they brought disease to the New World, it is implied that the Spanish were nevertheless justified in their evangelistic efforts because "physical pain on earth does not equal the pain the victims would go through in hell."

Although she saw the modification of a target group's culture as an integral component of their conversion, the manner in which those cultural changes were effected was a matter of importance for Amy. At first she denounced the destruction of the "[American] Indians' ancient literature" and "their sacred items" because they may have held historical value. Interestingly, however, she did not feel the same about holy objects used by non-Christian groups today. Taking no account of the potential historical value that someone living in the future might find in artifacts from the 21st century, she instead stated that missionaries should encourage their destruction. Most likely this is because Amy saw the religious value of Mayan, Aztec, and Incan sacred items as having ended with the historical conquest of their civilizations, and no longer holding the potential to mislead people. Her tone might have changed if she had seen them as possessing religious significance for people in the modern world.

This destruction of idolatric objects, according to Amy, was a way of following Christ. It was important, however, that missionaries only *encourage* the destruction of items that did not "mirror the Bible," and not *compel* it like some of the Spaniards did. In fact, Amy decried the use of force by the Spanish primarily for strategic reasons, since a potential convert would be more willing to accept something that was not forced upon him or her.

However, in a glaring discrepancy, Amy did not apply this to her own family when she wrote, "When my family had a Muslim foreign exchange student stay with us, he wasn't very open to Christianity. We had to make him go to church with us."

In reality, it should not take us aback that Amy exhibited a variety of somewhat incompatible positions on this subject. Amy's positions on other matters during the course of the investigation were fairly consistent, but, like most evangelicals (and nonevangelicals, for that matter), she was not a theoretician (see C. Smith, 1998). In fact, ethicists have wrestled with whether ends justify means for centuries, so the inability of a high school student such as Amy to state a cogent position on the matter should not come as much of a surprise.

Amy's Response to Relativization

Amy was selected as one of the three primary informants because she best represented the student most interested in defending evangelical orthodoxy. As with any typology, no one individual in all of his or her complexity exactly fits the mold. In this case, Amy's Reformed background and resultant belief in predestination was a minority position in a class that leaned toward Arminian free will. In addition, some other students may have given more weight to nonscriptural divine communication than did Amy. Nevertheless, Amy's views can be called fairly typical of conservative evangelical Protestants.

Throughout the study, Amy enjoyed our class discussions, although the same can not be said for the readings, which were "really strange, but... necessary for a better understanding of the people." She was never aghast that difficult questions were being raised or that I did not jump in to try to answer them all. At the end of our investigation, she wanted to know my opinions on the pertinent issues, but probably not in order to change what she already believed. Apart from the one instance in which she stated that students of other religions could be having a discussion just like the one in which she was participating, Amy exhibited few cracks in her defenses. Even minor doubts, such as when she stated, "I don't know if I do or not" in reference to whether God was speaking through commonalities between other sacred texts and the Bible, were quickly resolved. She stated on the questionnaire that there had been no changes in how she viewed her own faith, but only a reinforcement of her existing belief in predestination. It was acceptable to listen to others, but under no circumstances should an evangelical change their beliefs, since "switching over... would be bad for you." This desire to maintain her position within the original tradition by rejecting other traditions (at least the non-Christian ones) is indicative of a closed reaction to relativization (see Campbell, 1999).

CALEB

Boundaries

Although Caleb acknowledged the existence of boundaries between Christians and non-Christians, he did not seem interested in fighting any battles to maintain them. Unlike Amy, he had little use for either distinction from or disapproval of the non-Christian religions he encountered. On the contrary, instead of differentiating himself from those of other traditions, Caleb jokingly associated himself numerous times during the course of our investigations with either Islam or the indigenous American civilizations. Although played for a laugh, in a nonmocking manner, the fact that conversion to another faith was even a joking matter indicates that Caleb did not see encounters with other religions as a threat. At first I wondered whether these repeated associations with the other faiths intimated a desire on Caleb's part to explore beyond the confines of the tradition of his heritage, to "try the other traditions on for size," but later testimony regarding his reasons for learning about other religions led me to reject this interpretation. Although this must still remain a possibility, I believe it was more likely that Caleb's primary purpose for these statements was merely to getting a rise out of his classmates.

Although Caleb acknowledged that there were distinctions between Islam and Christianity, the primary difference he noted was geographical. Like many Americans whose perceptions have been influenced by the national media's focus on the region, Caleb associated Islam with the Middle East and the violence of the Arab–Israeli conflict. Apart from this, Caleb mentioned few differences between Islam and Christianity.

As for the beliefs of indigenous Americans, Caleb noted both similarities and differences when comparing the creation accounts of the Bible and the Popol Vuh. However, he did so in a rather matter-of-fact way, free of loaded words or value judgments. Of particular interest regarding the presence of God in the various traditions is Caleb's capitalization of the word "God" when referring to the Christian divinity, but not the "gods" of the Quiche Maya. In evaluating the statement that Caleb made by doing this, it must be taken into consideration that evangelical Christians are accustomed to seeing this case usage in the Bible, particularly in the Old Testament, where English translations label the Hebrew divinity "God" and those of Israel's neighbors as "gods." Therefore, to follow this example is not the least bit unusual, but to deviate from such a well-established convention would constitute the radical step of equating Christian and Mayan deities, which, despite his openness to seeing divine influence in other traditions, Caleb chose not to make.

With regard to Roman Catholicism, Caleb appeared to distinguish himself quite sharply from it when he wrote on his third essay that "Catholics have a lot in common with Christians." This statement, possibly a remnant from an earlier pattern of exclusive thought, seemed to imply that Caleb did not believe that Catholics were Christians. More likely, however, is that the term "Protestant," like the term "evangelical," is not common parlance for those who usually refer to themselves as "just Christians." Therefore, Caleb was merely using the most familiar self-descriptor in referring to his tradition, and implied no slight of Catholics in the process. Lending support to this interpretation is Caleb's Roman Catholicism montage, in which Christ was present in three of the six foreground images, and a later statement in which he listed Roman Catholicism as one of the many divisions of Christianity. Moreover, when comparing Catholicism with his own tradition, Caleb wrote that, although "they have many more traditions and ceremonies that they must perform, . . . their base beliefs are very similar to ours."

Religious similarity, in Caleb's view, was something that could be found in most of the world's religious traditions. In fact, Caleb saw those things that were the highest priority in his faith—treating others with kindness, loyalty, and understanding—as present in all of the faiths we had studied and not exclusive to either evangelicalism or to Christianity in general. Instead of stressing distinctive characteristics like Amy did, Caleb held that these key moral characteristics were not distinct at all.

Equally noteworthy in all of Caleb's comments was the nearly complete absence of threat rhetoric or disapproval. Muslims, Caleb stated, were "truly dedicated and passionate people. Their religion has standards, and they do their best to live up to them." In fact, apart from the association of Arab–Israeli violence with Islam, the closest he came to disapproving of any of the traditions was that he found reading the Koran and our investigation of Catholicism to be slightly boring. Caleb saw the other traditions not as threats but as "mostly positive." "All these religions, or people involved in them, had their flaws, as do Christians," he wrote, "but for the most part I felt positive about them. They are all in search of something higher and greater than themselves."

In the previous quote, the inclusion of the disclaimer "as do Christians" demonstrates Caleb's mode of defending other traditions by pointing out examples of shortcomings in his own tradition. The polar opposite of a boundary maintenance strategy in which one states how those on the outside are wrong, Caleb several times sought to show critics of negative reference groups that the very things that they were criticizing in other traditions were present in evangelicalism as well. For example, after David had labeled the papal practice of speaking *ex cathedra* as "pretty stupid," Caleb stated, "It's no more stupid than when we believe our pastors when they talk to us in church . . ." Also, following a general discussion in which fellow students depicted the Popol Vuh as outlandish, Caleb stated that "the Bible . . . has a bunch of unbelievable stuff in it too, but we all believe it."

Although not interested in buttressing the walls of a Christian fortress, Caleb did see himself standing within its gates, as evidenced by the words "we all" in the above statement and the possessive adjective in phrases such as "In *our* belief . . ." [emphasis added]. Caleb did not, however, see other Christians as exactly like him. In fact, he saw himself as standing outside of the mainstream. In his definition of salvation, Caleb set himself in opposition to what he termed the only "widely accepted way of gaining salvation." He then cited a verse reference (Romans 10:9–10), implying that he had given this issue some amount of prior thought. In addition, Caleb also saw his views on the prospects for salvation of a hypothetical Muslim neighbor as different from "some Christians" who "wouldn't hesitate to say that he's going to hell, because he isn't saved." He also saw that there were those around him at the school who would view some of what he had expressed in class in a negative light.

A Key Issue for Caleb: Choice

For Caleb, the most important of considerations appeared to be that of free and informed choice. When he affirmed the idea of the Spanish mission endeavor to the New World and stated that "every person deserves to hear the Word of God in their lifetime," Caleb did so because he believed that the American Indians should have been given additional religious options from which to choose. In saying that the missionaries "effectively and rightly brought Christ to the Natives, but they failed in helping the Indians encounter Christ," Caleb affirmed that if an option is presented, it should be a meaningful one. Interestingly, informed personal choice was important not only for non-Christians, but for Christians as well, as evidenced when he stated,

> If . . . you grew up Christian or Muslim, I think it's a really good thing to learn about other religions. Maybe you don't want to spend most of your life as a Christian or a Muslim. If it's a Christian [and he or she converts to another religion], it's a bad thing, but still you have a choice and still get to learn a lot of things to find out for yourself what you think is right.

In this case, Caleb specifically addressed the issue of religious ascription, and, like many fellow modern individuals influenced by the liberal ideal of personal autonomy, found it less authentic than a religious identity validated by choice (see C. Smith, 1998). As has already been stated, choice is also very important for many evangelicals in that the experience of conversion is a voluntary matter. The only difference is that, in the eyes of Caleb, religious choice itself was more important than ending up with the right religion. For Caleb to have held this view indicates that he probably did not believe that the eternal consequences of religious misguidedness were as dire as did many of his classmates.

Although Caleb acknowledged a divine mandate similar to that of Amy when he stated, "In the Bible we are called by God to go into all the world and preach the Gospel," he did not see this as applicable in his case, since one needed a special conviction or call from God to be effective on the mission field. When asked why he did not feel an obligation to evangelize his friends, Caleb could not give an answer beyond "I don't know how to explain it.....Just kind of what I would or wouldn't do. I don't know." He stated that his reticence to evangelize did not stem from a belief that he shouldn't or had no right to, or that Christianity was not a superior form of religion. After all, he had stated before that "If it's a Christian [and he or she converts to another religion], it's a bad thing," and, in reference to the Indians of the New World, "I don't believe that Christ would have already been in them as Christ is in us [Christians]."

The reason, I believe, that Caleb did not want to engage in evangelism was closely tied with his desire not to be judgmental. He wanted to allow others the same freedom to choose that he desired for himself. In his second essay, he placed himself in the shoes of a hypothetical Muslim neighbor and assumed that he or she might share Caleb's own dislike of those who travel door-to-door attempting to gain converts. However, if Caleb and this neighbor "became close friends, I would share with him what I believe," Caleb stated, "and in turn listen to his beliefs. But I would never try to convert him unless he told me he wanted to become a Christian." As the antithesis of the personal influence strategy, the use of a relationship for the purpose of evangelism would be out of place, since, in Caleb's eyes, friends do not attempt to persuade one another toward a point of view, but, at the most, present an option with no expectations whatsoever, and allow for complete self-determination on the part of the listener.

It is also important to note that Caleb saw this process not as a one-way exchange, but as a mutual dialogue in which merit could be found in the opinions of others. In the case of the Spanish missionaries, Caleb chastised them because "They did not listen to what the Indians had to say. They simply preached their message and did not stop to think that the Indians would maybe have something useful to say." In this case, Caleb's acknowledgment that what the American Indians had to say could be of value was, in all likelihood, due to his notion that "God's influence can be seen in all his creations, even people who are non-Christians."

As we have seen, Caleb's lack of urgency or interest in persuading others to accept the Christian faith was closely related to his desire not to judge others. If, in a given society, religious belief was a matter of ascription, and Christianity was not available as an option, Caleb did not see how he or others could be held accountable for following the only road open to them. If he lived in Mayan society in 750 A.D., Caleb said, "I'd be Mayan, and I'd believe in Mayan gods" and would follow the lead of the surrounding society "all the way." Because they could not choose otherwise, Caleb was of the belief that these people who had never heard the gospel would end up in heaven.

As for those who, after hearing a clear presentation of the gospel message, never chose to become Christians, Caleb was not willing to say that they were necessarily damned either. In fact, on the questionnaire he scratched out his initial choice, "In addition to Christians, there is hope for heaven for those who have never heard the gospel of Christ," and in its place he substituted the option

> In addition to Christians, there is hope for heaven both for (a) those who have never heard the gospel of Christ and (b) those who live a moral and spiritual life but do not profess faith in Christ, although they have heard of Him.

Unlike Amy, who felt capable to judge because the Bible had told her how God judges, Caleb did not consider himself qualified to make that determination. He wrote,

> I believe that Christ came for everyone, even those who die not believing in him. I don't think there is any way to know who or what makes someone able to go to heaven without believing in Christ. But I think that God knows, and he has a sense of justice that we could never begin to understand with our finite minds.

The statement that Christ came even for "those who die not believing in him" would lead one to consider Caleb a pluralist when it comes to salvation (see Hick, 1984). If this were the case, however, why did he not choose the broadest option on the questionnaire, which read, "There is hope for heaven for all people, regardless of religious tradition or lifestyle"? I can think of two possible explanations. The first is that Caleb read this final option not in terms of individuals, but in terms of the whole of humanity. However incomprehensible it may be to us, Caleb affirmed that God did have a standard. Although Caleb would not have wanted to judge the fate of any one person, the existence of a standard meant that some would be judged and found lacking, and not everyone therefore would be allowed to enter heaven. It may also be that Caleb did not like the option's second clause, "regardless of religious tradition or lifestyle." Although he did not explicitly state this, it may also be that his focus on those admirable things such as kindness and loyalty that transcended religious boundaries meant that, in some way, he saw these as a symbol of divine influence, and to exhibit a lifestyle in opposition to these things could be evidence of a lack of God's saving presence.

The idea of God having a different standard by which to judge Christians and non-Christians was not troubling for Caleb. In fact, uniformity in general was not something Caleb relished, as evidenced by his disregard of the school dress code and willingness to be a dissenting voice in class discussion. The aspect of Catholicism that he found least attractive was the conformity brought on by the traditions and ceremonies they "must perform." Instead, Caleb preferred variety, as seen when he found it intriguing that the stories of indigenous American peoples didn't always line up or remain the same, and when he saw in the Bible a difference between the God of the Old and the New Testaments.

Caleb's Response to Relativization

Caleb represents, in this study, the student most eager to explore unorthodox ideas. For Caleb, a period of relativization appeared to have already taken place, beginning his freshman year in a class taught by Mr. Weaver. Similar to the cultural investigation in my Spanish 3 class, this *Apologetics/Worldviews* class caused him to "wonder a lot of things and ask a lot of questions," including "questions about the Christian faith and its validity and fairness." Twice during our study he expressed distaste for what he saw as ungrounded emotionality among the parishioners at his church who claimed to have a message from God. To guess which other aspects of the Christian faith Caleb may now have considered invalid or unfair would be speculation, but based on his other responses, they were likely related to the purported harmony or inspiration that evangelicals claimed for Scripture, the exclusive criteria used for judging others' eternal destiny, and the tendency to label as shortcomings things in other traditions that also existed in evangelical Protestant Christianity.

At any rate, these issues were not serious enough to cause him to abandon his faith, but did cause him to make modifications in his belief structure. He recalled coming out of Mr. Weaver's class confused, but by the time he took my Spanish 3 class, he seemed to have reached a point of equilibrium. As to how he had arrived at his new conclusions, Caleb said that they just came to him, although his statement "You don't really ever get answers to the questions any more" indicated that not all of his issues had been resolved, such as his inability to articulate a view of Scripture. Caleb, however, unlike some evangelicals, was able to live with a measure of uncertainty. The fact that he no longer got answers to all of his questions wasn't "a bad thing," and he stated that he "loved that [*Apologetics/World-views*] class," even though it led to a period of confusion.

From what I observed, Caleb was far from a tortured soul desperate to reorient himself within the world around him. On the questionnaire he indicated that he was interested in learning about other religious traditions solely to understand people better, rather than from a desire to enhance his own spiritual journey, presumably because he was already content with where he stood. Although very interested in our discussions, he occasionally nodded off during a video or readings, indicating both sleep deprivation and that he was not hanging on the edge of his seat looking for something to help him work through personal issues. He was even able to joke about the relativization process. When Nathan described his own confusion, Caleb joked, "All my core beliefs just [*makes a "splat" sound with his mouth*]." Whether this feeling of a total loss of core beliefs was something Caleb had actually experienced himself, he did not say. Nonetheless, it was now something about which he could laugh.

It is difficult to know exactly which of Caleb's views was a result of Mr. Weaver's class and which ones he had held prior to that, but it is obvious that the relativization process had wrought changes in the way he viewed his faith and those around him. These included: (1) an openness towards other faith traditions, (2) an expanded view of the scope of salvation, (3) an inability to articulate his view of Scripture and, finally, (4) a realization that his view was only one among many. Instead of saying, "The truth is . . .," Caleb used the words "In our belief. . . ." When he surveyed the panorama of human history and stated that "most civilizations of . . . history . . . have a world underneath theirs of some sort of a hell or underworld," he saw with the eyes of an anthropologist or scholar in religious studies, and not as a believer operating under a taken-for-granted worldview.

For the time being, though, Caleb seemed content to remain within the Christian tradition, but outside of what he perceived as the mainstream. In the year between the end of our investigation and the longitudinal member check, however, Caleb had made a significantly larger number of non-Christian friends. Whether this constituted the first stages in an eventual departure from the evangelical subculture remains to be seen. His disagreement with several key Reformed doctrines and a distaste for the emotionality of charismatic/Pentecostal experientialism, both predominant branches of evangelical Protestantism, may foreshadow a move, not to unbelief, but to either a less institutionalized faith or to another of the Christian traditions.

NATHAN

Boundaries

If Amy was interested in remaining well within the boundaries of orthodoxy while Caleb preferred to explore the periphery and beyond, Nathan fell somewhere in between. He saw Muslims stereotypically as "dark-skinned" and of a particular "race," and yet was aware that the American image of Muslims as "terrorists or violent people" was itself a stereotype. More than just a token addition on the end of his essays, Nathan displayed true admiration for aspects of Islam such as its "good ideas of moral standards," "discipline," the "idea of a single God in control and in charge of creation," and his impression that the Koran "relates closely" to the Bible. However, he also disapproved of Islam because "they are off in their understanding of Jesus Christ and their prophet Mohammed" and stated that "[due to] its inconsistencies with Christianity, [it] isn't acceptable to me as a religion."

Nathan saw the worldviews of the Mayas, Aztecs, and Incas as sharing less in common with Christianity than Islam did. He found himself drawn to those items of indigenous culture such as architecture, dress, and settlement patterns. On the other hand, the only religious similarities with Christianity that Nathan noted were a divine creation and multiple names for the Creator, even when compared to Genesis, the book of the Bible where he would be most likely to find a correlation with what he had read in the Popol Vuh. Differences between the two existed, in part, because of the "faultiness of the [Mayan] gods," although later in our investigation Nathan did acknowledge a similarity between Christ and the Aztec deities who engaged in self-sacrifice on behalf of humanity.

Why did Nathan find some aspects of New World indigenous culture favorable and others unfavorable? Although evangelicals seek to apply the Bible to all areas of life, their penchant for dichotomies dovetails with the tendency of the modern world to categorize and divide activities into those that are "religious" and those that are "nonreligious." For this reason, Nathan could call certain aspects of indigenous American civilization "neat" and, at the same time, choose the "mostly negative" option to describe their belief systems.

In evangelical thought, however, the sacred is usually afforded greater worth than the secular. Why, in this instance, did Nathan view the nonreligious aspects of New World indigenous culture more favorably than the religious ones? Again, this was most likely related to the amount of threat Nathan perceived from each of the two domains. Although he related to the non-Christian religions in a less confrontational manner than did Amy, the eternal consequences of misguided belief were still very grave, and thus, there was less at stake when exploring the secular realm alone. Therefore, it was safe to appreciate vestments or architecture that were different than his own, but once one crossed over into what he perceived as the realm of the sacred, eternal salvation was at risk, and difference was not just unappreciated, but unacceptable.

Although not as foreign as the aforementioned belief systems, Nathan's assessment of Roman Catholicism was at least as unfavorable as it was for the non-Christian traditions. In addition to the unconventional casing of the terms "islamic," "muslim," "indian," and "indians," Nathan continued to deviate from accepted practice during the Catholicism unit, using the lower case for the terms "catholic," "pope," and "virgin Mary." Since he did at times capitalize some of these terms as well, it is difficult without further study to determine exactly how much the slight of Catholicism and the other traditions was intentional, subconscious, due to unfamiliarity with custom, or just an aversion to capital letters. Nevertheless, it was uncannily frequent.

On the questionnaire, Nathan marked the "mostly negative" box, and his comment that Catholicism and the other religions weren't "getting people anywhere because they are ultimately wrong," even though each had their "own way of being close to Christianity" would seem to indicate that Nathan did not see Catholicism as Christian at all. He also contrasted Catholic Spanish missionaries to the New World with "true Christians" and declared that Catholicism itself had many "faults from Christianity." On a case-by-case basis, individual Catholics could be Christians, even if they "believe all that stuff with the saints and Mary and everything" as long as they "still believe Christ as being the savior," but the Catholic Church itself did nothing to encourage this. In fact, proclaiming Mary to be sinless "would take away everything Jesus did," presumably because Christ was the only person to have lived without sin, qualifying him alone to be the atoning sacrifice for the sins of humankind. There could be no other.

Why was Nathan such an outspoken critic of Catholicism? It was obvious that, although he had Catholic acquaintances and had attended one of their religious services, this was a case in which exposure to the Other did not lead to greater acceptance, since he was one of the most vocal critics of Catholicism in the class. The reason for this opposition, according to Nathan, was Catholicism's alleged inconsistency with "the Bible, with its leadership, its members, and its own self!" This inconsistency was extremely bothersome to Nathan, since "none of them...seem to follow the same path." Like Amy, Nathan saw the truth as immutable. For this reason, it was wrong that the Pope "changes things...just randomly, he'll come up with some new law that they have to follow.... How can it just change all the time and always be correct?"

Key Issues for Nathan

Uniformity and Divine Revelation

In addition to questioning how the Pope was the only one who could speak infallibly on matters of faith and morals, Nathan's desire for uniformity of religious experience led him to question a number of "strange phenomena," such as "stigmata and bleeding Mary statues" and Mr. Mandel's photo of the Virgin of Scottsdale. This hesitance to accept that which was paranormal included some forms of divine revelation experienced by those within his own tradition as well. "I don't believe in any audible voice of God," Nathan wrote. "I have heard of experiences, but I don't understand how only a select few can experience them. The Bible can be experienced by everyone." Not only was the Bible equally accessible to all Christians, but the message contained within was consistent. As "inerrant and inspired," the Bible was entirely free of incongruities, for if a text contained any errors, it would not even be "partially inspired," since God would not say different things to different people. For God to behave in a multitude of ways would lead to unpredictability and, therefore, to uncertainty.

During the discussion in which Caleb maintained that the Bible had been assembled by means of criteria made up by men, Nathan said that he had "thought of that point before." As the discussion continued, Nathan declared that "the way it [the compilation of the Bible] happened was the way He [God] wanted it" without giving a reason why he believed that to be true. In fact, two other times during the same discussion Nathan made similar statements without any supporting reasons. Finally, Nathan said that the reason he knew that the Bible "was the way He [God] wanted it" was that "It never contradicts itself, ever.... There's no discrepancy.... There's your proof right there." Nevertheless, it seems that this summary declaration had not completely settled matters for Nathan, since he later asked me whether I thought "the Bible turned out the way God wanted it to."

When it came to interpreting the Bible, Nathan employed a selectively literal hermeneutic, allowing that the book of Revelation, Christ's parables, and the specific number of days of creation in the book of Genesis may have been symbolic, but that historical events including the remaining components of the creation narrative(s) were to be taken literally. This practice of reading texts literally made it difficult for Nathan to recognize and understand myth, as evidenced by the several literal-minded questions he asked during our reading of the Popol Vuh, such as "How does a groundstone talk?" and "How are they [the monkeys] wood?" He also had existential concerns with the text's portrayal of multiple creations, in that "you would think that an almighty creator wouldn't be messing up because that wouldn't give you very much faith as a believer to be sure that your god isn't messing up other things, too." For the Christian

God to have "created the earth in 7 days perfectly, totally in order, and without messing up" was of great importance, since this demonstrated that he was worthy of the trust Nathan had placed in him. In fact, to live without certainty was, to Nathan, an extremely frightening prospect. Regarding salvation, he said that he personally could not "know for sure" whether or not his friends were saved, but he expressed the need for assurance regarding his own salvation, in contrast to Muslims, whom he saw as "a little more unsure" of theirs.

Evangelism

For Nathan, evangelism played a prominent role in his thought through the very end of our investigation. Although he did not quote Scripture to justify his conviction, he did see it as his personal responsibility to spread the gospel. He had done so in the past, on almost a monthly basis, and wished he could do it even more. Whether this referred only to explicit verbalization of the gospel or whether it also included lifestyle evangelism, Nathan saw his own conduct and that of other missionaries as crucial for validation of the gospel message. Employing the same strategy as Amy, evangelism was best "done through example first, and then easily leading them," since it would not be difficult to evangelize someone who had already been drawn to Nathan due to admiration of his virtuous life.

Destroying the sacred books of indigenous peoples, on the other hand, was bad form because it left a negative impression on the people being evangelized. In addition, it hindered effective communication since texts could be studied and used to find a "compromise." By this term, Nathan did not mean taking what those of a target group believed and allowing it to change Christian thought, since any modification of this immutable truth would have been corruption. Rather, compromise meant a one-way transmission of Christian concepts using the target group's own terms and symbols. This, too, was done for strategic reasons, since it was more efficacious "to put God in their lives with what they already know."

Salvation

Near the beginning of the study, Nathan articulated that, in order to be saved, you must "*invite* Christ into your heart" [emphasis added]. This verb choice, expressing human action, along with his rebuttals of Amy's comments regarding predestination, indicated that Nathan viewed himself standing with those who believed that God required humans to exercise free will in deciding whether or not to become Christians. On his second essay, however, he wrote, in a statement with Calvinistic overtones, "God can move anybody to accept Christ." It would appear, then, that Nathan was of two minds regarding what occurred behind the scenes during the salvation experience. This is not uncommon, since proponents of free will also seek to affirm the sovereignty of God, and occasionally make statements like this, even if in the end they state that "God is always at work. He desires relationships. However, if He is continually blocked out of a particular religion, then how can he help them? So it goes both ways." Thus, Nathan acknowledged the persuasive work of God, but affirmed that God allowed his activity to be overridden by human will.

Nathan also expressed the need to "ask Him [God] to come into your life, into your heart, mind, and soul, and accept His free gifts . . . or else you are *like everybody else*" [emphasis added]. Taking this additional step distinguished the Christian from others, who were limited to doing "good works." As in Amy's thought, these actions availed nothing, as they were not an evidence of inner transformation, but rather a futile outward attempt of non-Christians to earn the salvation that God gives freely.

In Nathan's eyes, these non-Christians did not already have God in their lives, even though some were "closer" to believing the truth than others. There were also severe eternal consequences to misplaced belief, since "if they are wrong, then the people are dead wrong." When Nathan attempted to apply this formula to those who had never heard the gospel, his struggles began. If acceptance into God's kingdom was predicated upon the need to "invite Christ into your heart," what was to be done with those who had never heard of him? Unlike Amy, who believed that God revealed himself sufficiently to everyone in some fashion, Nathan initially allowed for the possibility that those who had no access to the Bible would have been ignorant of the requisites for salvation. This prospect bothered Nathan greatly, as seen when he said, "Someone in class said something about, 'You can believe something with all your heart, but if you're wrong, you're dead wrong.' . . . And he's right. I mean, and that bugs me now, when you think about it." It disturbed Nathan because it would be contrary to the loving character of God to eternally condemn someone for ignorance when he or she may not have known of the message of salvation found in the Bible.

Although he could not tell me where it was found or quote it exactly, Nathan insisted that there was a Bible verse that said, "All men have seen." Although he had earlier deemed general revelation incapable of expressing the doctrine of Christ, he later speculated, "There may be a way that they see through nature and they realize, and therefore they accept that and . . . they'll go to heaven." Even if this was not the way, Nathan concluded that "if there's no gospel presented to them exactly," "there has to be" a way they could go to heaven. At this point, Nathan toyed with the idea that people could believe in Jesus without explicitly hearing the gospel, and then hesitatingly chose to lessen the criteria required for salvation. He said,

> [The Bible] doesn't say you have to have heard the gospel to go to heaven. It says you have to believe in Jesus, and if they can get to that point one way or

another, or maybe not even, or close to that point, then God would have a way for them to go to heaven.

This represented a significant shift in Nathan's thinking. When I asked him whether this meant that God had a different standard for those who had not heard the name Jesus, Nathan balked at first, most likely due to the break from uniformity that this entailed, but finally said, "Yeah. I don't know, a different standard, but kind of, sort of like that, yeah." As to how those who had never heard the name Jesus would reach the necessary point of proximity, Nathan said, "I think there's ways for them to figure it out and to accept it. I'm not sure how 'cause I've never been in that situation," echoing his earlier statement, "Maybe we don't understand, but God does."

Nathan's Response to Relativization

One of the reasons Nathan was specifically chosen as the third primary informant was because he most overtly displayed the effects of relativization as the study proceeded. In addition to the shift in the criteria that he held as essential for salvation, Nathan exhibited several other changes as our investigation proceeded.

Nathan began our investigation with traces of a relativized outlook. Already a viewer of the Discovery Channel, he expressed a desire for a larger view of the world than the narrow one he thought was typically held by Americans. He wrote,

> Honestly, sometimes I think we in America we see Christians as predominantly the people we see in our community. I hope that through these studies, I can see how diverse the world is and how God can inhabit anybody for His glory!

At yet an earlier point in our investigation, Nathan, like Caleb, set all religions side by side, relative to one another, and noted that "all major religions have radical groups within themselves that take the words of their religion and misconstrue them."

As demonstrated by his impressions of Catholicism, contact alone was insufficient to bring about a change in Nathan's views of other religious traditions. Although he had a significant amount of previous experience with Catholics, he wrote, "I don't understand the whole thing with the saints either. I think it is weird that they believe these saints are so holy. Even farther out than that...."

At some point during the study, however, Nathan experienced a series of moments in which he began to see through the eyes of the Other. "It makes sense that if the mountains could have water in them they could fill up the earth. I understand that," he said at one point. After fellow students presented a scenario in which polytheism explained the workings of the natural world, Nathan exclaimed, "Now that Popol Vuh thing doesn't seem so weird." This new way of viewing others surprised Nathan. "It's kind of crazy to think," he said, "that's what they thought, and I could see how they could write something like that." This did not mean, however, that he now afforded the indigenous American worldviews equality with his own. They may have been somewhat reasonable, but, as seen in the discussion of Nathan's views on salvation, they were reasonable based on the limited information they had. In this case, the Indians of the New World did not know the entire story, because they had no access to the Bible, but had nevertheless done a fairly reasonable job of explaining the world with what they had at their disposal.

Another of Nathan's responses to relativization was the sacrificing of some of the distinctiveness he had previously accorded his own faith. From the outset of our investigation, Nathan acknowledged similarities between other traditions and "Bible-believing Christians," but as the study progressed this became more frequent. "I'm not saying they're the same," Nathan stated at one point, "but...it [the Koran] parallels, in a lot of ways." Regarding the creation of the world, he added, "It's interesting how diverse the belief systems can be, but yet how they all [are]...really close almost in a way." Near the beginning of the study, Nathan wrote that a hypothetical Muslim would be drawn to him because of the virtuous life that he would display. Presumably this was because it was different than that of the Muslim (although he did admire Muslims' sense of "discipline"). By the end of the study, however, when asked by a fellow student, "Have they changed and everything because of, can you see God in them, or their gods in them?" Nathan responded, "Yeah. Why not? I mean,... They're so close to Christianity, right? I mean, they really are, in a lot of, in a sense." As for the Mayas, Nathan's perception of the Popol Vuh changed from being entirely foreign to something he might have come up with if he had no access to the Bible. Nevertheless, even though they were not as unique as before, Nathan still affirmed the primacy of the Bible and of Christianity. Adherents of those religions whose beliefs were more similar to Christianity, Nathan thought, had "a better chance of figuring out the actual truth."

As the study progressed, Nathan also began to see himself through the eyes of the Other. It came as a new insight to Nathan that those observing him might see his beliefs as outrageous. "I see how other religions can sound completely absurd," Nathan wrote, "but at the same time, those people could see mine the same way." During the second group interview, he asked, "Well, how do these people [Muslims or those of other religions in general] feel about us?" In relation to evangelism, he wondered if there were certain strains of Islam that "might see Christianity better" and, in the case of Muslims who convert to Christianity, Nathan wondered, "What makes them think theirs is wrong then and we're right?" The thought that "maybe they're right and I'm not" never occurred to Nathan, as he affirmed that the only beneficial conversion would be to Christianity. In agreement with Erin, however, he acknowledged that this opinion was "our point of view." At this point Nathan realized that he did not view things from an objective vantage point, but from within his own particular tradition. He noted that those of other religions also claimed to have an exclusive handle on the truth. "To them it's one thing, to us it's one thing," he said, "and everyone thinks they're right." As to why any individuals would convert from one religion to another, Nathan suddenly found the subject difficult to discuss because "you're kind of coming from a biased view." He had moved from the default assumption that his view of "the truth" was objective to the realization that his knowledge was indeed "perspectival and paradigm-dependent" (Olsen, 1995, p. 483).

Since he no longer viewed the world from a position of objectivity, Nathan was reluctant to guess what others thought. He also hesitated because the possibility existed that Muslims might hold a variety of beliefs, just like Christians who don't necessarily "believe the exact same thing even within our own Bible and stuff." Nathan never mentioned the existence of differences of opinion in Protestant Christianity during the early stages of the study, but he instead he chose to criticize Catholicism for its lack of consistency over time. Why then was he not equally critical of Protestants? If asked this question directly, Nathan probably would have affirmed unity for Protestants as preferable to disunity. The likely reason he was harsher on Catholicism, though, was that he saw the longitudinal development of doctrine represented by papal decrees over time as evidence that truth as originally revealed was being tampered with. In the case of Protestants, however, Biblical truth remained unchanged. It was merely that people currently had different interpretations of that one truth.

At any rate, Nathan became much more hesitant to speak authoritatively on the status or the beliefs of others. The jury was still out and Nathan wanted to wait until the facts were in to decide. "I don't think we have enough exposure to the actual people around us to know enough," he said. He was also unsure "where God fits in to everything on different religions.... Somewhere. I don't know. I can't figure it out." Finally, he raised the epistemological question of how one could make judgments about other religions when he asked repeatedly, "How do you know? How do we know? How do we know?"

Twice Nathan comforted himself with the statement that "Maybe we don't understand, but God does." Unlike Caleb, however, who had learned to live with and even to embrace mystery, Nathan had difficulty leaving it at that. The investigation had "made me start thinking a lot more now," he said, and the resulting uncertainty troubled him greatly. He twice asked to know my opinions and declared, "I'm going to have to go to seminary now" to figure things out.

It is important to restate that although he "now wondered many things," the relativization of tradition did not cause Nathan to abandon his faith and slip into a relativistic nihilism. Although he realized that his judgments were subjective, he stated, "I still believe what I believe, but now I wonder about . . . everybody else. I never really thought about everybody else as much."

For Nathan, as with many of his classmates, our investigation was the first time dealing explicitly with the theological issues that shape evangelicals' stance toward "everybody else." Since many of the difficult questions did not have airtight answers immediately provided by the teacher, there was a sense of indeterminacy as we studied and debated. This was more than just learning facts to regurgitate on a test. The answers to the questions had real consequences for how students viewed the world, including their own place within it. Since we are all defined in some measure by our relationship with others (see Volf, 1996), it could be said, to a certain extent, that the students' own personal identity was at stake.

For Amy, the correct course of action was clear. As discomfiting as some of the questions were, she resolved to stand firm in the face of non-Christian worldviews. As adversaries, these alternate enframings of the world were categorically denied the veracity of the Christian faith, and to acknowledge commensurabilities with other religions was to surrender the distinctiveness and significance of her own tradition. In Caleb's eyes, as we have seen, this was the wrong approach. Although he allowed that the religions were different in some ways, and that the possibility of conversion was always present when one encountered other traditions, he thought the benefits of having a wide range of options from which to choose far outweighed the dangers. In fact, Caleb saw little danger in acknowledging what he saw as benign elements in other traditions and deficient ones in his own. Finally, Nathan was of two minds on the matter. In one sense, he steadfastly affirmed the primacy of the evangelical Christian faith, yet he was also undecided on how God fit into the other religious traditions, many of which seemed to contain things that "mirrored the Bible."

One can see from each of these cases the difficulty in stating an unequivocal "evangelical" position on these theological matters. Although there are undoubtedly some very strong impulses in certain directions, within the subculture are different individuals, each of whom picks up on resources from both inside and outside of the subculture and fashions them through dialogue into a mélange that, when examined closely, is notable primarily for its uniqueness. And so it was for the delightful students in the 2000–2001 Spanish 3 class at Midwest Christian Academy. I must say that I enjoyed my time with each of them very much, and consider it an honor to have accompanied them during this particular stretch of their intellectual and spiritual journeys.

CHAPTER 12

EVANGELICALS, CIVIL SOCIETY, AND OTHER RELIGIOUS TRADITIONS

In the preceding chapters, readers were given a glimpse into the setting of an evangelical school and the internal theological debates that go on as members of the evangelical subculture try to establish the proper ways to relate to nonevangelicals within American society. Although my own personal theology looks a bit different now than it did during my time with Amy, Caleb, and Nathan, and I am sure will continue to evolve until the day I die, at this point I do have some observations to make on the topics of religious education, theology, and the relationship of evangelical Christianity with the wider society and its various religious subcultures. Much of what is written in these final two chapters is intended for the eyes and ears of evangelical Christian educators, but I believe that large portions of the discussion are likely to be of interest to a more general audience as well.

EVANGELICALS, MULTICULTURALISM, AND CIVIL SOCIETY

To begin with, as hermeneutical beings we all make some sense of the world by classifying things as similar and dissimilar, positive and negative, and the like. Thus, Amy, Caleb, and Nathan are no different than the rest of us who have conceptual frameworks, narratives, and mental maps that partition the world and the people in it into understandable, segmented

American Evangelicals and Religious Diversity, pages 221–238
Copyright © 2006 by Information Age Publishing
All rights of reproduction in any form reserved.

patterns according to which we direct our lives and our personal interactions. Advocates of cultural diversity recognize this phenomenon as a natural and inevitable occurrence, as something to be celebrated instead of resisted. As theologian Jean Bethke Elshtain (2004) has noted, however, "The danger with such distinction-making is that over time differences may harden into destructive divisions" (p. 39). Racism, sexism, and nationalism are but a few examples of how this propensity for categorizing people can become socially toxic.

A primary strategy that multicultural advocates employ to combat this harmful tendency is to persuade people to value diversity itself and the variety of lifestyles and perspectives it brings. For seeking to avert these destructive divisions, advocates of pluralism should be commended. However, the proposed strategy itself has some deficiencies as well. As we have seen in the case of evangelical Christians, tolerance of others decreases as the amount of perceived threat and the gap in values between ingroups and outgroups increase. In order to deal with the first of these, authors such as Harvard's Diana Eck in her widely circulated book *A New Religious America* (2001) portray recently established religious communities at their best, with very little mention of internecine strife or externally disruptive behavior, as if to say, "Look, you have nothing to fear. See, everyone is so peaceful. All we need is to understand each other."

To the effect that promoting contact with others or learning about other religions can correct misconceptions about those faiths, advocates for diversity should again be commended. However, I must say that I have nearly the same problem with Eck's approach as I do with the presentation of other religions often found in conservative Protestant schools. My Christian faith and my observation of the world tell me that humanity has a dual nature, that we are beings capable of both astonishing generosity and compassion and also of fearful, destructive, and malevolent behavior. Whereas evangelicals in a selectively sheltered enclave commonly accentuate the negative aspects of human nature in portrayals of non-Christian faiths, multicultural educators are sometimes guilty of the opposite crime of overemphasizing the benign aspects of life in America's minority religious communities.

In order to combat intolerance that springs from conflicting values, many multicultural educators promote appreciation of other, differing perspectives. To a certain extent, this can be a very good thing, and I will comment further on this shortly. However, when pushed to its extreme, it has some severe problems, foremost among them that it becomes nearly impossible not to mandate relativism. In asking people to appreciate perspectives that are at odds with their values, it is often required that they ignore the values they already hold or that they modify them to align with more relative standards. For individuals and communities such as the many evangelical Christians who hold to absolute truth, this is entirely unaccept-able, and serves as a primary reason why evangelicals are not favorable to certain strains of multicultural education. Additionally, it has also been said that people are only truly tolerant on issues about which they don't really care much (Almond, 1994), but when their most deeply held ideals are transgressed, almost anyone can become quite intolerant. For example, even typically open-minded individuals with a questing religious orienta-tion display intolerance when their values are violated (Goldfried & Miner, 2002). Likewise, proponents of diversity, some highly tolerant in general, can express rather stern disapproval of fundamentalists and others who do not agree with their principles.

In one sense diametrically opposite to the approaches outlined above, but in an alternative sense very closely related, a second strategy to circum-vent factional strife in modern societies is to encourage those of different communities to focus on the things they hold in common instead of that which divides them. Cognizant of people's propensity to venerate ingroups and to disparage outgroups, proponents of this method call people of dif-ferent communities to see themselves as "more alike than different." Instead of celebrating diversity, this approach downplays particularities and instead seeks to eliminate negative reference groups altogether by encour-aging individuals to view their common humanity as the primary element of their identity. If "human" is the identity characteristic that is most salient in people's psyches, individuals will more often than not see others as shar-ing their identity and will be less likely to engage in adversarial speech or behavior. Some empirical studies lend support to the efficacy of this approach of inducing two disparate groups to focus on a commonly held descriptor (Dovidio, Gaertner, Hodson, Houlette, & Johnson, 2005; Gaert-ner & Dovidio, 2000). There is much to be said in favor of this strategy, since recognition of our common humanity is a good and necessary thing for all of us. One only has to look at the views of many Spaniards toward the Indians of the New World, or of American antebellum whites toward blacks, to see how the imposition of subhuman status on subjugated groups can serve as a powerful justification for their mistreatment.

Like the previous approach, however, this approach does not solve the problem of conflicting values. Rather, it asks people once again to lessen the importance they give to the particular values of their particular com-munities. For example, someone utilizing this method might not encour-age Amy, Caleb, and Nathan at Midwest Christian Academy to view the other traditions themselves as positive, as in the previous approach, but instead tell them that it doesn't really matter what tradition they are a part of because, in the end, all religions are the same anyway. They might point out other similarities such as "These other faiths believe in God too" or "They are very sincere people just like you are." However, the students at

Midwest Christian and most other committed Christians will reject the relativism required by this approach just as they do the former one.

Each of the students at Midwest Christian profiled in the preceding case study differed in the degree to which they acknowledged similarities between evangelical Christianity and the various religions that we studied. However, no matter how much one acknowledges parallels, as long as a Christian takes seriously his or her Christian faith commitment, a contrast is bound to trump all comparisons. This is because Jesus Christ is the core of the Christian faith. While there has developed in recent years a much more conciliatory relationship between the different branches of the Christian faith, the revelation of God in Christ still serves as a formidable boundary between Christians and those of other religions, although obviously this does not hold true for those with only a rudimentary understanding of what their faith requires of them or to liberal Christians who have "notoriously neglected their unique narratives" (Ammerman, 2003, p. 218). Nevertheless, even in the case of many liberal Christians, who see Christ not as divine, but rather as a wise teacher, to call oneself a Christian means that he must still be one's primary teacher (Hall, 1998). In denying the primacy of Christ, one relinquishes one's standing as a Christian and becomes a "theist" or, leaving aside all particular natural or supernatural beliefs in an attempt to exclude no one, a "human."

Even if everyone alive today were to find their primary identity in their humanity, it would still be insufficient. It might eliminate a certain amount of intergroup rivalry, but it would not provide any sort of vision for what humans are supposed to *do* here on earth. For that, we must return to the *different* vision-producing narratives that animate and give direction to our various communities. In a multicultural setting, to be open to those of other faiths does not entail an erasure of boundaries (Volf, 2005a), but rather requires that each of the traditions draws upon the resources in its narratives that promote civil and hospitable behavior toward one another. Although Christians can find things in other religions that are commensurate with the Christian faith if they choose to do so, these elements such as compassion, ethical behavior, and belief in the supernatural are secondary in that they find their grounding for Christians first and foremost in the particular story of God's revelation and reconciliation of the world through Christ. Ironically, in this narrative, humanity is not even the most inclusive, abstracted identity category. The scope can be expanded beyond mankind to the level of carbon-based life forms, or even further to include all components of God's created order.

Of course, many in our nation do not accept the Christian narrative, and some probably find it a bit disconcerting that there are individuals and communities whose primary identity is found in something other than their national citizenry. For those whose allegiance lies first and foremost with the City of God, does any devotion remain for the City of Man? What responsibility do Christians have for our common life together as a nation? While one can recall both historical and contemporary situations in which individuals around the world have been forced to choose, sometimes at the cost of their very lives, between loyalty to Christ and to the state, it must be said that this is far from what one finds in today's America.

In the case of America's evangelicals, they are countercultural enough to have developed their own limited series of institutions committed to preserving their values, but not countercultural enough to threaten the established order. In fact, many evangelicals are among America's most patriotic citizens. At the beginning of Midwest Christian Academy's weekly chapel service, for instance, pledges of allegiance are said to both the American and Christian flags, and during times of private and communal prayer evangelicals frequently thank God for the freedom to be able to worship and practice their faith openly and without fear of persecution. In Midwest City, a quick survey of church parking lots on a Sunday morning will typically find a significantly greater number of American flag decals on car windows in evangelical church parking lots than in those of their liberal counterparts. Additionally, one frequently overhears discussions in Midwest Christian's faculty lounge on both local and national political issues. For most evangelicals, love of country and love of God are not incommensurate. Christians can deeply love human society, their world, and themselves in addition to the ultimate love that is reserved for God. Paradoxically, however, it is because all of these things are creations of a loving God that Christians are able to truly love them in the first place.

Although a Christian's primary allegiance is due only to God, most evangelicals realize that humans are still subject to secondary allegiances, many of which we have not chosen. None of us have selected the families or the nations into which we were born; yet the fact is that we cannot easily dismiss our responsibilities to them. As much as we might wish otherwise sometimes, we are not masters of our own fate. Much of life is ascriptive and part of our calling is to live in such a way as to faithfully honor our obligations to those around us. Although there may be extreme times when one's conscience as a Christian compels one to leave one's family for the sake of the gospel, one is also responsible as a follower of Christ to be a good father, mother, brother, sister, daughter, or son. One may quit one's job in extreme circumstances, but since all of us require sustenance in order to live, we also have responsibilities to the employers who sign our paychecks. Much has been made by certain Christian theologians of how the political disestablishment of Christianity in America has restored the church to its rightful place at the margins of society. However, it is also important to note that to have been born into a representative democracy carries somewhat different responsibilities than did life in the 1st century

Roman world of the New Testament. It is true that Christians should not confuse the well-being of America or liberal democracy with that of the kingdom of God, or the rise and fall of nations with the ultimate meaning of history. Nevertheless, in this time and place, Christians cannot ignore the roles they have been given to play.

As has been stated in an earlier chapter, when individuals enter the public arena, there is often pressure to downplay the particularities of religious commitments, to reserve them for the private sphere. Bishop Leslie Newbigin (1989) identifies in modern societies a conflict between two different ways of viewing the matter, one that treats religious truth claims as *values*, as "what we choose because we want them—either for ourself or for someone else" (p. 17), and *facts*, meaning "the realities which finally govern the world and which we shall in the end have to acknowledge whether we like them or not" (p. 7). Since there is currently no universally accepted standard by which to measure the veracity or falsehood of superempirical claims (Hirst, 1981), many in our society feel that the best they can do is to say that the beliefs they hold are "true for me." For Newbigin, however, since we share the same world, the beliefs that we hold to be true are either true for all or true for none. For those such as evangelical Christians who believe that their faith is not just another culturally constructed item, but rather is based upon the revelation of God, to treat their convictions as purely a private matter that is inapplicable to the individuals and the rest of the world around them is inconceivable.

If religion were merely a matter of personal preference such as a favorite color or flavor of chewing gum, evangelicals would not feel nearly as compelled to spread their faith. By evangelical accounts, though, to share the gospel is to do others the favor of revealing the way the world truly works and giving them the opportunity to align their lives with that revelation. Of course, this can and does create strife with those who hold competing worldviews. In the eyes of some individuals, including many deconstructivists and other postmodern thinkers, evangelical proselytization efforts are at bottom power grabs, attempts to increase evangelicals' hold on the world in order to make it more favorable to evangelical interests and lifestyles. Historically, religious imperialism and holy wars have made it quite clear that social control is something that people will often go to great lengths to obtain. To be fair, there is probably a measure of this in both evangelical political activism and efforts to share the gospel.

However, to view everything through the lens of hegemony, oppression, and the struggle for power is to miss at least half of the story. There is another lens as well, through which Christians see the goodness of God and his residual image found in humanity issuing forth as a means of grace to the world. Not everything we do as humans is done out of self-interest, no matter what rational choice theorists may say. Yes, people may receive benefits from altruistic behavior, but these benefits are always secondary. Certainly people receive satisfaction from helping others, or may even "find it rewarding not to receive any reward" (Sommers, 2001, pp. 48–49), but these gifts are only received as byproducts of pursuing the primary goal, which is the well-being of another.

Viewing evangelistic endeavors through this lens therefore yields a much different picture of the motivation of evangelicals. For some the sharing of their faith may be merely a matter of duty, but for others who have tasted in their own lives the unbounded mercy and grace of God, they unquestionably believe that loved ones, friends, acquaintances, and even complete strangers would be better off, both here on earth and for all eternity, for acknowledging the lordship of the triune God. Thus, they engage others, all the while knowing that many of these people may disagree, even vehemently, with their claims to superiority for the evangelical Christian worldview. As M. Scott Peck (1978) writes,

> For the truly loving person the act of criticism or confrontation does not come easily; to such a person it is evident that the act has great potential for arrogance. To confront one's beloved is to assume a position of moral or intellectual superiority over the loved one, at least so far as the issue at hand is concerned. Yet genuine love recognizes and respects the unique individuality and separate identity of the other person.... The truly loving person, valuing the uniqueness and differentness of his or her beloved, will be reluctant indeed to assume, "I am right, you are wrong; I know better than you what is good for you." But the reality of life is such that at times one person does know better than the other what is good for the other, and in actuality is in a position of superior knowledge or wisdom in regard to the matter at hand. Under these circumstances the wiser of the two does in fact have an obligation out of loving concern for the spiritual growth of the other to confront the other with the problem. The loving person, therefore, is frequently in a dilemma, caught between a loving respect for the beloved's own path in life and a responsibility to exercise loving leadership when the beloved appears to need such leadership. (p. 151)

Although, as a psychiatrist, Peck does not write here specifically about evangelicals, this is precisely the dilemma that the evangelical Christian faces. Evangelicals believe that they know the truth, but most also affirm the right of others to make their own choices and usually try not to offend others with their beliefs. Of course, the sheer act of making exclusive religious claims is for some of their critics an offense in itself.

Before going any further, I must say that I do not believe that evangelicals should be absolved entirely of charges of arrogance. Although it is impractical to go through life subjecting each of one's beliefs to the criticism required by a hermeneutic of suspicion, it is nevertheless imperative to have one's views tempered by a sense of our human finitude and inability to grasp in its entirety the workings of the world or the divine plan for it. In evangelical churches one occasionally hears Isaiah 55:8–9 quoted, which reads, "'For my thoughts are not your thoughts, neither are your ways my ways,' declares the Lord. 'As the heavens are higher than the earth, so are my ways higher than your ways and my thoughts than your thoughts.'" In one sense, many evangelicals are well aware of the limited nature of their knowledge, although this is recognized less in comparing themselves with their neighbor than in comparison to God. It is a central tenet of the Christian gospel that humankind, with its fallen nature, is utterly incapable on its own of achieving salvation and reconciliation with God, but is instead wholly dependent on divine grace. It is this very humility, ironically, that encourages evangelicals to absolutize the Biblical text. If human perception is limited and unable to provide certainty, then a surer standard must be one's guide, namely God's own revelation in the form of Holy Scripture. For those evangelicals who prefer an experiential rather than a propositional faith, religious experiences can be absolutized also if they are viewed as proceeding directly from the Holy Spirit, even if they are bestowed upon fallible men and women. In each of these cases, however, it would do evangelicals well to note that revelation in the Christian tradition is something that is *received* by the grace of God, not something that one has *figured out* or *earned* because of one's own moral or intellectual superiority, a point that some evangelicals tend to forget on occasion.

Additionally, the evangelical propensity for ignoring the role that people play in the process of Biblical interpretation can lead to an epistemological certainty that far exceeds its warrant. If the Bible needs little to no interpretation because it "means what it says," then one cannot misunderstand or improperly use the text, an absurdity considering the many ways in which the Bible has been used to justify atrocities and inanities at various points in the Church's history. Moreover, although many evangelicals such as Amy and Nathan see an immutable Bible as containing everything needed for an unchanging Christian faith, it still holds that the text was written thousands of years ago, and has not yet been fully understood or related to the changing times in which we live. Jesus never gave a sermon on the ethics of genetic cloning, for example, so within the discipline of theology there is needed a great deal of discernment and creative thought on the contents and implications of the sacred book. Theologians do their best, often disagree with one another, and hope that the consensus that emerges is faithful to both the ancient text and the modern context. Furthermore, the fact that the final page has yet to be turned in the story of God's dealings with our world means that there is still much to learn.

To advocate for a measure of epistemological modesty in matters of faith does not mean that evangelicals should abandon absolutes in favor of relativism, but rather that their boldness be tempered by humility. After all, no one is truly a relativist anyway. As C. Smith (2003b) states,

> Scratch hard enough—usually it doesn't take much—and one discovers that hard-core "relativists" are in fact believers and actors in some story or other. That is just the kind of animal we are. Nobody can simply exempt himself or herself from the human condition. (p. 88)

If all of us have a story or stories in which we play a part, whether we are conscious of them or not, it is only right to argue for what each of us currently "knows" to be true. Obviously, we may be wrong about many of the details. We may revise our views in the future based on new discoveries or personal experience. Since we all rely on others for knowledge (Clark, 2005; Coady, 1992), we may find out that someone we trusted as an authority was wrong. Yet for now, we argue, even boldly. It is not out of line for each of us to suggest that others adopt our positions. All ideas have consequences, and in the observable realm of pragmatic experience, it would be foolish to say that all views are equal. To believe that one can survive without food and water, for example, is bound to lead to a premature demise. For helping people to live meaningful and fruitful lives, some worldviews are indeed better than others. Additionally, someone is going to define the parameters in which cultural discourse takes place, and, like others, Christians should argue for their understanding of humanity's proper relation to God and to the surrounding world.

To argue for the Christian position, however, does not mean that everyone who is not a professing Christian must be a fool (or in the case of Muslims, a terrorist). Since none of us has a complete handle on all there is to know, and faith and knowledge are not as easily disentangled as some may say, it is important that we learn to listen to one another. For some evangelicals, including a few of the students at Midwest Christian Academy prior to our investigation, the affirmation of their system of belief as ultimate truth is a result of having been raised in a particular religious tradition and never having experienced the relativization process or having seriously considered alternative views (although one could argue that not to consider the views of others in a pluralistic society is a conscious choice in itself). However, once they do encounter those of other faiths on more than a superficial level, individuals (and their communities) must choose how to respond.

For Christians, the issue of how to relate to the wider culture and the subcultures that constitute it has been a matter of ongoing debate for nearly two millennia. In its formative years as an offshoot of Judaism under the domination of the Roman empire, Christians defined themselves against both Judaism and the paganism of Roman culture, although there are notable exceptions such as the apostle Paul's discourse at Mars Hill and the apologetics of Justin Martyr that display a willingness to see good in at least some elements of non-Christian religion. After the political establishment of Christianity in the 4th century, the role of the church and state changed considerably, as the church came to supply many societal functions that had previously fallen under the auspices of pagan religion. Modern American Christians, once again disestablished yet still able to exert a significant amount of influence within a representative democratic political system, continue to wrestle with how to appropriately relate to "the world."

For some, such as the Old Order Amish, the correct course of action is to remove one's communities as much as possible both geographically and socially from America's other subcultures. Others posit that the Christian church is most faithful to its Lord as a contrast institution, as a prophetic colony of "resident aliens" that eschews all aspirations to power and domination but remains present within society as a witness to the darkness that surrounds it (Hauerwas & Willimon, 1989; Lohfink, 1982/1984). A third position affirms the communal witness of a distinctive Christian way of life and the renouncing of political imposition and social pressure in public affairs, yet holds that Christians can still affirm much that is good in the wider culture and society, which they still call their own (Volf, 1994). A fourth position acknowledges that although boundaries between the church and society are inevitable, this does not preclude Christians from fully participating within the democratic apparatus to bring betterment and justice to the lives of all humanity (Stout, 2004). Still others hold that America has strayed from its Christian moorings and should be returned by means of political influence to its status as a Christian America (Kennedy & Newcombe, 2003). For others, very little distinction is necessary between the church and the world since Christianity is highly compatible with the liberal democratic ideals that currently dominate the American cultural scene (Eck, 2001). Finally, there is yet another position in which to look at the relationship between Christianity and culture is a nonstarter since culture is not a monolithic entity, but rather a conglomeration of varied subcultures, each with their own relationship to Christians and to other societal subgroups (Marsden, 1999).

Although the most powerful philosophical force in American culture may be the liberalism that John Milbank, Stanley Hauerwas, and other prominent "Radical Orthodox" theologians famously despise, it is too simple to limit one's critique to this alone, since culture is never something that is either wholly acceptable or unacceptable to Christians. As John Howard Yoder (1996) has pointed out,

Some elements of culture the church categorically rejects (pornography, tyranny, cultic idolatry). Other dimensions of culture it accepts within clear limits (economic production, commerce, the graphic arts, paying taxes for peacetime civil government). To still other dimensions of culture Christian faith gives a new motivation and coherence (agriculture, family life, literacy, conflict resolution, empowerment). Still others it strips of their claims to possess autonomous truth and value, and uses them as vehicles of communication (philosophy, language, Old Testament ritual, music). Still other forms of culture are *created* by the Christian churches (hospitals, service of the poor, generalized education).... Therefore our need is precisely *not*... a global classification of all of culture in one category. Our need ... is precisely to find categories of *discernment* by virtue of which the several value dimensions of cultural creativeness can be distinguished. (pp. 69–70, original emphasis)

SOME THEOLOGICAL CONSIDERATIONS

In addition to the dominant culture, what do we find when we focus for a moment on the ways in which Christians view different religious subcultures? Although the majority of students in the Midwest Christian Academy Spanish 3 class saw other religious traditions as highly distinct from conservative Protestant Christianity, there were a few who saw various elements of the other traditions as commensurate with their own tradition. For most who rejected the other religions in their entirety, to identify positive elements without immediate qualifications was to embrace relativism and thus to deny the primacy of the Christian faith. However, those who saw similarities did not seem to view the matter in these terms.

Personally, I believe that one must hold both similarity and difference together in creative tension in order to keep from losing something important to the theological understanding of the faithful Christian life. This does not mean affirming and rejecting an equal number of items either in the dominant culture or in other religions. A Christian cannot answer the abstract question "What is the proper ratio of similarity versus difference to be acknowledged?" because each worldview is different. Since each religion "is comprised of a set of loosely related rituals, practices, and metaphysical, historical, and moral claims to truth" (Volf, 2005b, p. 10), each will accord with and diverge from Christianity in unique ways (and accord with and diverge from the different expressions of Christianity as well). Liberal Christianity over the past century or so has been willing to affirm various elements of other religious traditions, but in the process has lost the countercultural aspects it once possessed. Whether this is because they have sacrificed their vision or because they have been victorious in that society now mirrors their vision, it is as if many liberal Christians' only current distinction is that they are indistinct. To stand for inclusiveness, pluralism, and liberal ideals is to stand for little that the rest of the dominant culture does not already supply.

The evangelical wing of American Christianity, however, is in need of a correction in the opposite direction. Although to be commended for "keeping the faith," the tendency to see other religions as entirely counterfeit, misguided, or the work of the devil is a serious theological miscalculation. As with culture at large, there exist within each of society's religious traditions both "patterns of wisdom, beauty, and caring" and "idolatry and exploitation" (Adney, 2001, p. 68). On the one hand, Christians should certainly reject anything in other religions that would deny the central position of Jesus Christ in the story of God's dealings with humankind. However, for other things that seem to line up fairly well with the best in Christian teaching and practice, Christians should not be so quick to turn their backs.

In order to properly affirm items in other religions, I believe one must begin with two premises. The first is that God has not left people of any religious or nonreligious tradition completely devoid of faculties for perception, interpretation, and action. Those in the theological patrimony of John Calvin, Thomas Aquinas, and the Fathers of the Eastern Orthodox Church may disagree on the extent that the image of God has become obscured in the lives of human beings. Nevertheless, the fact that people of all or no religious persuasion find a way to lace up their shoes, multiply numbers in their heads, and notice when their coworkers need a word of encouragement is testimony that people retain the ability to function well enough to make it through the day in one piece. To use this book as an example, many of those cited within these pages would not identify themselves with the Christian faith, yet each has something important to add to our discussion.

This raises a series of questions. When Jesus says in Mark 4:9, "Whoever has ears to hear, let them hear," does this imply that only certain people have ears for spiritual revelation? Does it mean that those who have ears must constantly have them tuned up or risk missing the message? Might those with ears to hear sense the voice of the Spirit speaking in unexpected places? If, as John Stott (1976) states, "the same God is God of creation and of new creation, working out through both his perfect will" (p. 90), in what ways might the original creation still display the marks of the Creator?

The second premise necessary for Christians to affirm elements of other world religions is that everything good in this world is from God. Of course, beginning in the opening chapters of Genesis one finds that the forbidden fruit that appeals to the eye can result in emptiness, misery, and death. Things that people pursue the world over can look good and yet be nothing more than counterfeit or "fool's gold." However, it does not seem to me that this is the sort of thing one finds in each and every element of the world's religions. Rather, I see some things that I believe can help Christians to live more truly in the context of the modern world if they choose to listen. For example, Buddhists, as I understand them, stress the interconnectedness of all things, a notion Christians and others should take very seriously in a world in which it is critical that we serve as good stewards of the natural resources on which all of us depend. Additionally, the Buddhist identification of desire as the source of unhappiness has much to say to Christians and others in a materialistic culture in which hundreds of billions of dollars are spent on advertising to convince people that their lives will be fulfilled if only they buy and consume the correct brand of shampoo, beer, or sports car. To give another example, the Muslim emphasis on religion as a lived response could be a constructive challenge to those Christians for whom religion is primarily assent to a series of intellectual propositions. Moreover, the Muslim focus on the *ummah* can remind Christians steeped in the individualism of American culture of the communal nature of faith. For many North American Indians, there exists the need for purification when one has done harm to others, a reminder for all of us that the thoughtless and cruel things we sometimes do damage not only others, but our own souls as well. Although these elements are bound up with the whole of practicing religious communities, and lose much of their flavor when divorced from the contexts in which they are rooted, I believe that they can serve a purpose not only for their original communities, but for all who heed their message. I do not see these items as antithetical to the Christian faith, but rather as things from which Christians can profit if they have ears to hear.

Of course, as Christians assess the worth of the different elements of the world's religions, they cannot help but measure them according to the standard of their own faith (and of anything else they may have picked up from years of living in a pluralistic society). As much recent philosophy has shown, there is no objective "view from nowhere" by which the value of each tradition can be adjudicated. Each of the world's religious and nonreligious ethical systems provides an account of the true, the good, and the beautiful, but members of one tradition can only judge the tenets of another tradition from their own vantage point.

Nevertheless, to make this comparison can, in my opinion, lead to fruitful discoveries, as the viewpoints of the Other can awaken theological resources in one's own tradition that may have lain dormant for quite some time. Even if one remains within the tradition of one's youth, the conception of the true, the good, and the beautiful can and does change over the course of one's lifetime. As Lamin Sanneh (2004) states, "No faith tradition stands still or alone, except as a relic. Such are the implications of distinction in religious pluralism" (p 36). Though all theologies of response to other faiths are to some extent selective in the matters to which they give their focus (Astley, 2000), to glean insights from other religious traditions does not mean "picking and choosing" from them in the same way that the individualistic practitioners of "religion a la carte" do. Rather, theological reflection is to be done in faithfulness to the community, and the community either recovers those things in its own narratives that have been lost or understands its stories in a new light.

Some theologians suggest that instead of merely recovering neglected elements in one's own tradition, it is also possible to be taught new things that are not already present in the narratives of one's community. Up to this point, it has been stated that we view everything through the lens of our own tradition and that those items in other traditions that we label as "good" coincide with the "good" as identified in our own tradition. However, this is only part of the picture. As Jean Piaget (1947/1950) and others have theorized, we humans both "assimilate" and "accommodate" to our surroundings. In some instances, it may well be that nothing we encounter in life can alter what we already believe. One thinks of a man suffering from paranoia who views all attempts on the part of others to convince him that no one is out to get him as a conspiracy designed to lull him into a false sense of security. When encountering other religious faiths, some postmodernist religious scholars have proposed that, since all human knowing is perspectival, we can never fully understand another religious culture since we cannot step outside of our own frame of reference (see Knitter, 2002). While there is something to be said for our backgrounds affecting what we see or fail to see, it is also true that the things we experience often do reshape the lenses through which we gaze. People do learn and embrace new stories, as evidenced by religious conversions the world over.

I have seen this latter process occur in my own thought regarding the perceived motivations of those who do not explicitly profess faith in Christ. Growing up in the evangelical tradition, I was taught that only God, and not humans, could fully know the heart of an individual man or woman. This never seemed to stop anyone around me though from declaring that whenever non-Christians engaged in altruistic actions they were really trying to "earn their way into heaven through good works." As seen in the case study portion of this work, Amy at Midwest Christian expressed this view quite definitively when she questioned the ulterior motives of those who seemed to be doing worthy acts. As I began to encounter more people who displayed what looked like kindness and generosity, I began to wonder whether this characterization was true. Were certain individuals compassionate in spite of their faith tradition or because of it? I came to realize that in most of the various world religions there do exist cultural and theological resources that promote selfless behavior.

I also came to see how the issues that concern evangelicals are often projected onto others. Most notable among these is a Martin Lutheresque concern with individual salvation, which in an extreme form assumes that everyone who is not a Christian lies awake at night trying to figure out how to reserve a spot in paradise by earning their way into the good graces of a personal Creator and heavenly Judge. When one listens more closely to the voices of non-Christians, though, one realizes that this is not usually what they claim to be after. In this instance, my mental map did not shape what I saw as much as what I experienced led to a redrawing of my map.

If the two premises presented earlier are true, it is impossible for Christians not to affirm that God is still an influence in the lives and cultures of those who do not profess faith in Christ. As George Stroup (1998) puts it,

> Clearly, the Holy Spirit is at work in the world and not just among those who are followers of Jesus. If life itself is a gift of the Holy Spirit, then all human beings and not just Christians have experienced the work of the Spirit, regardless of whether they recognize it as such. Furthermore, the Spirit is at work in the whole world, not just giving life but in many other ways as well. True wisdom is a gift of the Spirit, as are provisional, fragmentary experiences of reconciliation, peace, hope, and justice. (p. 174)

Because of this, evangelicals would do well in my opinion to adopt from their mainline and liberal brothers and sisters the notion of *common grace*, of God's provision for all of his creatures. For me, the need to affirm that which is good in the world (as seen through my Christian lenses, of course) means that I see divine influence in the resources within non-Christian religions that can be employed to promote compassion and giving of oneself for the benefit of others. Though the end itself is not something Christians would fully agree with, some Buddhists emphasize the example of the *bodhisattvas*, who have delayed dissolution into nirvana in order to guide others on the path to cessation. Hindus are sure that their *dharma* calls them to do right by others. The Bahá'í faith has as a primary purpose the alleviation of oppression caused by societal stratification according to race, gender, and class. For all of these things, Christians ought to be grateful and praise God.

So how far does this grace extend? If one is a Christian and assumes that every human being needs what Christians call salvation, does the fact that God seems to be active in non-Christian traditions mean that those of other faiths might also be saved? What about those who have never heard the gospel but have responded to those elements in their culture that Christians would see as true, good, and beautiful? What about people such as American Indians who for so many years experienced a distorted and oppressive version of the gospel wrapped up with cultural and economic imperialism? Will God be merciful to those for whom the message of salvation was not liberation but enslavement? What about those who have heard the gospel but nevertheless have chosen to remain in their own tradition and pursue the goals of that tradition? Might they be saved as well?

Before addressing these questions, it is important to note that the answers depend heavily on how one defines salvation. For quite some time most evangelicals have viewed salvation primarily as something that occurs after we die. However, the New Testament speaks of salvation in the past, present, and future tenses. If one looks at our time here on earth, it is not too much of a stretch for Christians to say that those of other traditions have experienced and continue to experience a measure of God's grace in their lives. A key passage of Scripture, referring specifically to false prophets but used by evangelicals to help them determine whether any particular individual is or is not saved, is Matthew 7:15–20, whose last three verses state, "A good tree cannot bear bad fruit, and a bad tree cannot bear good fruit. Every tree that does not bear good fruit is cut down and thrown into the fire. Thus, by their fruit you will recognize them."

So how does a Christian view the fruit on those trees outside the commonly demarcated boundaries of the Christian orchard? Is the fruit that is appealing to the eye truly good or does its beautiful skin conceal a rotten core? What is going on when non-Christians display what in a Christian's life would be called peace, joy, kindness, self-control, gentleness, and self-giving love?

We do not know for sure. Our actions are so often clouded by self-interest, and even the most openly altruistic acts can be done to bring glory to ourselves. It is possible that some Americans, with distorted vestiges of the nation's Christian heritage shaping their thinking, do engage in noble behavior in an attempt to earn their way into heaven, just as evangelicals suspect. Others may engage in a bit of positive self-image therapy and thus do good so that others will praise them or so that they can regard themselves as a "good person." Yet others may unconsciously (and consciously) find their benevolent actions arising out of the moral orders, both Christian and otherwise, in which they have been raised and enculturated (C. Smith, 2003b).

As for the eternal component of Christian salvation, it has been said that evangelicals have become somewhat uncomfortable with the notion of eternal damnation, as seen among evangelical college students (Hunter, 1987) and in evangelical theological circles (Knitter, 2002). As Paul Knitter (2002) has detailed so well, the New Testament is replete with passages such as Acts 4:12 that state regarding Jesus Christ that "Salvation is found in no one else, for there is no other name given under heaven by which we must be saved." This would seem to disqualify those who either lived before the birth of Christ or those since then who have never heard of him. Yet Christians also have to make sense of Scriptural passages such as the New Testament book of Hebrews in which the Hebrew patriarchs and matriarchs who lived long before Christ are held up as exemplars of faith. Intriguingly, the harlot Rahab and others mentioned in this "faith hall of fame" call into question the evangelical tendency to view faith as intellectual assent to a set of propositions. In the case of Rahab, her defining moment was found not in her agreement with orthodox Christian theology, but in her action of harboring Hebrew spies, which was somehow equivalent to saying "yes" to God.

It is true that much action arises out of the moral orders that we hold and that hold us, and these moral orders are not devoid of content. The obedient individual "still needs to be believing *something* about *someone* (who is God) in order for the fundamental direction of her faith to be properly oriented and fruitful" (Stackhouse, 2001, p. 196, original emphasis). Exactly what that intellectual content must be is something, however, that we cannot inductively piece together based on the exemplars of faith found in the book of Hebrews. I do not believe that I can say whether any given individual has said "yes" to God, or only appears to have done so as a means to some selfish, unspoken end. Again, only God knows the heart. My challenge to evangelicals is to actually live according to the statement that I learned growing up in church. Since no one can know exactly what another's motives are, and there is no apparatus designed to measure such a thing, we are left with educated guesses. The Bible gives some hints as to how God will judge, but the final judgment day is also portrayed as a day of surprises in which those thought to be shoe-ins to enter paradise find themselves on the outside looking in while unknowns surround the table at the heavenly banquet feast (Newbigen, 1989).

This balance between epistemological humility and the willingness to assert the truth of one's worldview should affect the way evangelicals and other Christians encounter the different subcultures of a pluralistic society. Having experienced the love of God, Christians are right to take the good news into the rest of the world, but as they do, they should not assume that they know everything. Of course, even if presented in humility, not everyone is going to like or agree with the message and its particularity. As Noll (2003) has written,

> Evangelicalism at its best is an offensive religion. It claims that human beings cannot be reconciled to God, understand the ultimate purposes of the world, or live a truly virtuous life unless they confess their sin before the living God and receive new life in Christ through the power of the Holy Spirit. Such particularity has always been offensive, and in the multicultural, post-modern world in which we live it is more offensive than ever. But when evangelicalism is at its best, ... that declaration of a particular salvation is its one and only offense. (p. 6)

Thus, as Christians engage the wider society, it is recommendable to listen first and speak second.

Unlike some liberal Christians, however, I do not believe that to respect the dignity of others means that one must respect all of one's interlocutors' ideas as they come. In fact, their ideas may be total rubbish. Numerous scholars have pointed out that to demand that people acknowledge merit in everything another culture produces is to demand praise for things such as wife burning, female circumcision, slavery, and the like. I also do not believe that it is arrogant for me to say that others can have untrue, misguided, and destructive ideas because, in looking back on my life, I can point to some of the ideas that I have held at one time or another that were total rubbish as well. Of course, at the time I thought they were beneficial or I presumably would not have held those ideas in the first place. At any rate, the refusal of people around me to affirm my ideas was a blessing, since the consequences of those ideas were often harmful to me or to others.

On a societal level, what is important is for all groups to acknowledge the *potential* of others to have beneficial ideas, and to listen for those ideas. Of course, dialogue is not a panacea. To use the analogy of marriage, even after years of discussion there remain differences that are irresolvable (Gottman, 1999). To use the example of Nathan, contact with Catholics had not made him any more sympathetic toward their religious practices. However, life together is undoubtedly worse when there is a lack of communication. It has been said already that the dominant society and the subcultures within it can benefit from the critique that other subcultures bring. Modern society, in my opinion, needs the critique of religious subcultures, including Christian ones, and those who disparage evangelical Christians would do well to adopt a measure of humility as well. At times, nonevangelicals have portrayed evangelicals as anti-intellectual, even while holding to unquestioned presuppositions themselves. If all human knowing is limited, then even while one makes truth claims, one must simultaneously question one's ability to fully comprehend that truth. Just as I believe that evangelicals would be well served to consider that in some sense their understanding might be incomplete, it is equally true, if humans are capable of grasping truth at all, that evangelicals may have much to offer.

CHAPTER 13

INGROUPS, OUTGROUPS, AND CHRISTIAN EDUCATION

RELATING TO THE OUTGROUP

In the previous chapter, we explored the challenges that evangelicals face as they encounter the greater society and its various religious subcultures. It was stated that evangelicals would do well to remember the limits of human knowledge in their dealings with those of other faiths, yet this did not mean sacrificing the particular religious character of their own tradition. Assuming that they undergo an initial period of genuine listening and discernment, evangelicals should not be afraid to proclaim their vision of human well-being as defined by the Christian faith. In doing so, they will encounter those with whom they differ sharply, groups whose moral compasses point in nearly opposite directions. There will be those who define themselves in opposition to evangelical objectives, and will serve as negative reference groups for evangelicals' self-definition. Knowing that these groups are hostile to evangelical interests will also generate a degree of perceived threat within the evangelical community.

As was noted earlier in this work, some see this as beneficial for the evangelical subculture. As C. Smith's (1998) subcultural identity theory posits, "Religion survives and can thrive in pluralistic, modern society by embedding itself in subcultures that offer satisfying morally orienting collective identities which provide adherents meaning and belonging" (p. 118). It then adds that those identities are strongest in threatening situations where there are a number of negative reference groups against which one's own group can define itself. This presents evangelicals with a

American Evangelicals and Religious Diversity, pages 239–252
Copyright © 2006 by Information Age Publishing
All rights of reproduction in any form reserved.

dilemma. If subcultural cohesion is dependent on negative reference groups and threat perception, does it diminish if outgroups are suddenly portrayed in a more positive light? Do nuanced presentations of reference groups in which favorable elements are acknowledged weaken the ingroup community? For the sake of honesty, must one sacrifice the vitality of one's tradition?

If C. Smith (1998) is correct, the acknowledgement of positive elements and the lessening of threat rhetoric toward outgroups may cause the cohesion of the ingroup to diminish, but in some instances this is not necessarily a bad thing. As a teacher in a Christian high school, I have seen the blessing that comes when some of the cliques and "roles" that often divide student bodies (e.g., "dumb jocks," "computer nerds," "ditzy cheerleaders," etc.) dissolve as students from different groups take the risk of opening their arms to one another in recognition of their equal value in the eyes of God.

Fear is indeed a great motivator, and there are many harmful things in the physical, emotional, and spiritual dimensions of life of which one should rightly be afraid. One can sense this fear in certain sectors of the evangelical world, particularly with regard to America's religious pluralization, the deterioration of societal morals, and governmental intrusion into the lifeworld of home and family. However, in the Christian narrative, fear does not have the deepest or last word on the matter. As the apostle Paul states in Romans 8:38–39,

> neither death nor life, neither angels nor demons, neither the present nor the future, nor any powers, neither height nor depth, nor anything else in all creation, will be able to separate us from the love of God that is in Christ Jesus our Lord.

This gives Christians a confidence in the midst of fear that even though they may not understand everything with their finite minds, God is ultimately in control and the end of the story will turn out well because of the goodness of its author.

Thus, from a Christian standpoint, for leaders to intentionally heighten the level of threat rhetoric in order to strengthen ingroup commitment cannot be a normative practice (Sommers, 2001). If "perfect love drives out fear" (1 John 4:18) and "the Spirit God gave us does not make us timid, but gives us power, love and self-discipline" (2 Timothy 1:7), then to rally the troops by overemphasizing the shortcomings and ignoring the positive elements of other societal groups is tantamount to a lack of faith. Although self-definition necessarily creates distinction between "us" and "them," the challenge for Christians is instead to build a community "nourished more on its own intrinsic vision than on the deprecatory stories about others" (Volf, 1994, p. 21). As Miroslav Volf (1994) has written, "Fear for oneself and one's identity creates hardness.... People who are secure in themselves—more accurately, who are secure in their God—are able to live the soft difference without fear. They have no need either to subordinate or damn others, but can allow others space to be themselves" (p. 24).

Pragmatically, it is also important to remember that C. Smith's subcultural identity theory is only one explanation for the strength and weakness of religious subcultures. If growth and decline are due to multiple factors whose interrelationships we cannot trace out or understand, then constant preoccupation with subcultural expansion and contraction is not something in which church or religious school leaders should engage. The greatest factor could be fertility rates after all. In a market-driven age in which success is measured in numbers, however, this is a very difficult thing to do. Obviously, a certain amount of people are necessary in that they provide the funds to keep a church's or school's doors open. At some point, however, numbers can become worthless if the mission of the school or church has been abandoned in order to increase enrollment or congregational size. For those churches and religious schools that want to strengthen, unify, and deepen their members' dedication to their Lord, they would be better served by devoting more energy and resources to spiritual formation and discipleship, to telling the religious narratives that have animated the church over the centuries and provided meaning for countless souls. In addition, efforts should be made to relate that story to the modern (and postmodern) world in which we live. If that brings greater numbers of people into church or religious schools, pastors and school administrators can consider it a blessing. If not, so be it. As Mother Teresa remarked countless times during her life, followers of Jesus are called not to be successful, but to be faithful.

It has been said that the uniqueness of the Christian narrative is a wall, keeping the faithful inside and everyone else out. However, if the example of Christ is properly understood, the story is not a barrier, but a gateway. Throughout the gospels, Christ is depicted reaching out to the Other, crossing the societal boundary lines of his day to touch, heal, teach, and eventually give his life for lepers, Samaritans, women, tax collectors, sinners, and a host of other people outside of the religious establishment. The strategy that calls people of different communities to see themselves as "more alike than different" assumes that people will only love someone if they see in the Other a reflection of themselves. While people do gravitate more readily toward those who share their values, spiritual growth comes for the Christian primarily in loving those who are different. To love only those who are "like me" or "like us" sets up the finite human self or community as the measuring stick for worth, an instance of idolatry in its highest form.

To denigrate outgroups is contrary to the example of Christ, who redefined "neighbor" to include even those traditionally seen as one's enemies. The call of Christ to love these enemies is sheer folly to many observers who rightly point out that this is a perfect way to get oneself taken advantage of. As the sixth chapter of the gospel of John so clearly shows, the way of the cross is not for all. Yet no one can doubt the power displayed in the last century by courageous individuals such as Martin Luther King, Jr. and Salvadorian archbishop Oscar Romero.

In order to counteract outgroup denigration, I believe that Christians must do two things. First, since all groups typically relate to other groups (or individuals as group members) on the basis of one defining self-aspect and the secondary characteristics associated with it, Christians must make love, service, and even sacrifice for the Other the key characteristics that accompany the descriptor "Christian." In this way, whenever individuals within the various Christian subcultures compare Christianity with religious outgroups in society, they will do so with the example of Christ's sacrifice as their starting point. Again, this is not done primarily out of convictions of a common humanity or a desire to avoid strife, but out of the love of Christians for their Savior. As Glen Stassen (1996) writes,

> Christian inclusion and Christian opposition to jingoism, racism, classism, and sexism are based not on being ashamed of the particularity of the concrete life and teachings of Jesus, but on loyalty to that historically particular Lord who calls us to practice forgiveness, justice, inclusiveness, transforming initiatives, love of enemies, prayerful acknowledgment of our own sin, and sharing the good news with others while listening to their deeper concerns and acknowledging God's presence among them. We do not become open to others by renouncing Christian particularity and expecting others to renounce their particularity, thus limiting our conversation only to thin and abstract universal principles; we meet one another far more deeply when we affirm each other's own peculiar particularity. (p. 183)

This orientation may surprise those who see Christianity as inherently oppressive, but the example of Jesus himself provides the theological resources to transcend humans' propensity for self-interest. This love for the Other, expressed in a multitude of ways ranging from a simple smile or handshake to risking one's life to defend someone else, cannot help but create bridging capital, those bonds of trust between people of different subcultures. That is not to say that Christians should not still spend significant time nurturing bonding capital, the bonds of trust between individuals within the Christian subculture, since that is in some ways a prerequisite for reaching out to the wider world. We are all limited in the number of relationships that our time and energy can support. Yet there is a place, I believe, for venturing beyond the subcultural walls and for letting others in. In doing so, one hopefully moves beyond unilateral giving, important as that is, to the higher ideal of friendship (Milbank, 1999). This may include forgiving past wrongs as well as asking for pardon for one's own misdeeds. It also may mean, as in the famous parable of the Good Samaritan, humbling oneself enough to allow oneself to be cared for by the "neighbor." To be realistic, these measures may not make Christians everyone's best friends, but I believe it could certainly go a long way toward keeping religious differences from hardening into destructive divisions.

The second element needed for Christians to counteract the harmful deprecation of outgroups is to deal forthrightly with the issues of self-esteem and self-concept. It is theorized that the phenomenon of ingroup bias arises partially from the desire for a positive social identity on the part of ingroup members. Although there are a variety of other motivations that may also underlie human identity dynamics (see Vignoles, 2004; Vignoles, Chryssochoou, & Breakwell, 2002), many people are, as T. S. Eliot (1950) puts it, "absorbed in the endless struggle to think well of themselves" (p. 111). In my mind this statement conjures up images of middle school youth insulting one another, with the putdowns serving to diminish another's status so that the individual issuing the insult looks better in comparison.

The gospel of Christ, however, calls for finding one's ultimate worth not in relation to others at all, but in embracing one's standing before a loving God. In the Christian view, value is not to be found in performance, in the perceptions of society, or in belonging to the right social group, but rather in the knowledge that God has created, reconciled, promised to indwell, and pledged to prepare a place for his people with him when this earthly life draws to a close. To be called the beloved of God, of course, can and has been a source of pride for those who view themselves as the "chosen ones." However, there is no reason for boasting, since, according to the Christian narrative, the love of God is not a result of anything we have done, but free and unmerited grace. This alone should be more than enough to quash any sense of smugness and replace it with a healthy dose of humility. After all, we all still possess that dual nature of both good and evil, and to overstate the virtues of the ingroup is as untruthful as to wrongly degrade the outgroup.

The challenge, then, is not to think well of ourselves, or to think poorly of ourselves, but to think rightly of ourselves (J. B. Smith, 1995). To do so means that we cannot think of the Other as a dragon, or of ourselves as knights on white horses. We cannot be like those addressed by Jesus in Luke 18:9 who "were confident of their own righteousness and looked down on everyone else." As Aleksandr Solzhenitsyn (1974/1975) has written,

> [T]he line separating good and evil passes not through states, nor between classes, nor between political parties either, but right through every human heart, and through all human hearts. This line shifts. Inside us, it oscillates with the years. Even within hearts overwhelmed by evil, one small bridgehead of good is retained; and even in the best of all hearts, there remains a small corner of evil. (p. 615)

It may be true that only some have acknowledged the superintendence of God, but since even the ability to receive grace is itself an undeserved gift of God, Christians can make no claims to be of greater value than the Other. Truly, the gift is for *all.*

CHRISTIAN EDUCATION AND THE VALUE OF RELIGIOUS INSTRUCTION

So what does this mean for private Christian education? If a loving relationship with others plays such a prominent role in Christian ethics, doesn't the formation of private Christian schools sabotage this by limiting contact with those who are different? As much truth as there is to this question, it must be noted that this love of Christians for others does not stand alone or float free of its Christian underpinnings. It arises out of the story of God's self-giving love for those he has created and the call for Christ's followers to do the same. This moral order, by the way, is something that must be *learned.* For those youth already deeply immersed in the ways of Christ at home and in church, it may be that the private Christian school is unnecessary, or even a hindrance to faithful Christian living. However, for many young people who have yet to achieve a full measure of maturity, the opportunity for spiritual formation provided by the Christian school is invaluable, particularly given that full understanding and appropriation of the ways of Christian discipleship can take a lifetime (if not longer).

As we have seen already, there are American citizens who rue the existence of Christian schools. For some of these individuals, the problem is not so much with the content of the Christian faith, but with the limiting of instruction to a single point of view. In this light, any religious socialization is indoctrination since it restricts the autonomy of individual students. However, as long as parents are still allowed a substantive role in the raising of their children, evangelical parents will desire certain things for their children, chief among them a particular religious outlook. As participants in a particular moral order themselves, why wouldn't parents do everything possible to help their children experience what their tradition tells them is true, good, and beautiful? And for evangelical parents, this means that "Christianity should be taught because it is true, because it answers the deepest needs of human nature, and without a knowledge of the love of God and a relationship with him men and women will live impoverished lives" (Goldman, 1965, p. 59).

With that said, I do believe that there are forms of religion that are domineering and repressive, and it has been shown that parents who give their children very little room to develop or express their own views produce offspring for whom religion is relatively less important in their daily lives (C. Smith, 2005). In fact, reaction against these overbearing forms of religion may play a role in the decision of other religious and nonreligious Americans to either abstain from any sort of religious instruction or to introduce their own children to various religious traditions but to promote none of them. However, even this apparent evenhandedness is based on a particular moral vision of the good. Although the goal is religious freedom, I believe that to leave children to explore entirely on their own may be to give them no religion at all or to lead them to believe that religion is something to be taken lightly since all religions are, at bottom, merely subjective preferences instead of visions of the way the world really works.

Others are opposed to Christian or other religious socialization of youth because they disagree with the substance of Christian or other religious faiths. Seen from this angle, Christian or other religious socialization is bad because those who end up as Christians/religious people are not stable, kind, or a benefit to society. If this is the case, the issue is not with subcultural education, but with the specific product it produces. In some cases, this dislike is based on the differing moral visions of the good life between Christians and non-Christians, and, in others, on the inability of some Christians to live up to the ideals of the one who gives them their name. Ironically, to remedy the latter of these requires more, not less, immersion in the teachings of Christ.

Interestingly, from an empirical and pragmatic standpoint it appears that religion *is* good for American children. In the National Study of Youth and Religion (NSYR), the largest study of American teenagers and religion to date, researchers find that

> the differences between more religious and less religious teenagers in the United States are actually significant and consistent across every outcome measure examined: risk behaviors, quality of family and adult relationships, moral reasoning and behavior, community participation, media consumption, sexual activity, and emotional well-being. (C. Smith, 2005, pp. 218, 219)

It would appear that the grounding in religious narratives and communities that youth receive is beneficial for the youth themselves, their communities, and society as a whole. If the statistics and interviews tell the truth, religious socialization is not necessarily oppression, but can be a form of liberation that provides for the existential needs of children such as meaning, belonging, and a vision of what is worth living for in this world. As the NSYR finds, the majority of American adolescents go to church because they want to, not because they are forced to (C. Smith et al., 2004), and many say that they would go more often if they could (C. Smith, 2005).

Douglas (1982) has argued that it is wrong to assume that people are better off with religion than without it since there also exist strains of religious behavior that are "widely regarded as emotionally restrictive, bigoted, fanatical, or psychotic" (p. 2). In the American context, however, this argument is only partially applicable, since the statistics seem to show that the positive forms of religion outweigh the negative ones. Nevertheless, the NSYR does show that although religion on the whole is good for American young people, within the aggregate there are strains of religious expression that are better or worse than others at promoting positive outcomes in the lives of their youth (C. Smith, 2005). Whether this is due to the relative merit of the traditions themselves or to the varying degrees to which adherents devote themselves to their traditions is nearly impossible to determine. At present, those most successful in giving their youth a deep religious sensibility seem to be Mormons and conservative Protestants.

If religion (including much of conservative Protestant religion) is good for America's youth, and if private Christian educational institutions play a role in nurturing religious faith, then a strong case can be made for schools in which religious instruction is a key component of the schools' mission. That the academic outcomes of these institutions often surpass their public school counterparts is an added bonus as well (Jeynes, 2003). As we have seen, these schools are not completely alike. Throughout the United States (and the world, for that matter), one finds different models of private Christian schools, each dictated by combinations of educational philosophy, theology, government guidelines, and the market realities of a given area. In the United States one finds both discipleship schools, in which students (and often their parents) must adhere to the Christian faith in order to be admitted, and evangelistic schools, in which non-Christian students are admitted and presented with instruction from a Christian perspective. As educational administrators and trustees look at what it takes to keep their schools financially solvent, sometimes there is the temptation to move from the former to the latter, to broaden admission requirements in order to increase the tuition base. For financial reasons, one is much less likely to see a move take place in the opposite direction.

Although the context may dictate the possibilities, which of the two options is preferable? Assuming that a school is blessed with sufficient funds, should they take the discipleship or the evangelistic route? Currently, most Protestants have chosen the first option, although many Catholic schools have become increasingly focused on serving the underprivileged of America's inner cities, whether these students are Catholic or not. It must be said that both options have solid support in Christian theology, since strengthening the Christian community and reaching out to the larger world are both goals rooted in the Christian vision. However, it should be noted that both have their weaknesses as well. For schools with wider admissions policies, opening the student body to non-Christians raises issues of how to approach the religious faiths of these students. What responsibilities do Christian schools have to these pupils concerning how their religious traditions are portrayed at the school? As the number of non-Christians grows, does there also grow an implicit pressure to downplay Christian distinctives or to affirm those things in other religions that many Christians would typically be hesitant to support? As Lyndon Furst (2000) suggests, "[T]he state of the art of school leadership has not yet found a way to maintain cultural integrity while having an open door policy" (p. 175).

Within the bounds of Christian institutions it is certainly possible to go too far, to focus so much on common grace that one loses sight of the particular story of the Christian heritage. As Joseph O'Keefe (2000) states, "openness to another faith does not necessitate amnesia about one's own" (p. 85). In a culture of neglected religious narratives, it is imperative that we stop merely "exposing" students to religion and start "teaching" it to them (C. Smith, 2005). As an instructor, I also do not believe that merely presenting an outline of abstract religious options and a set of critical thinking skills is sufficient. Critical thinking is an essential part of religious education, but students also need to see how religious faith makes a difference in the day-to-day affairs of people's lives, including those of their parents and teachers. Otherwise, students are prone to view religion as only hypothetically relevant to hypothetical people in hypothetical times and places.

Besides, to teach at all is a value-laden act. All teachers desire something for their students, even if it begins with something as elementary as learning one's numbers and letters. We all want students to master skills and adopt certain outlooks in the hope that they will turn out a certain way. In a very real sense, every classroom activity is "evangelistic" in that it seeks to impart a change in students toward some end that teachers have in mind for them. We do not sit back and detachedly say, "Well, Johnny, here are the options available to you in life if you choose to learn your numbers and here are the ones available if you don't. Choose wisely, but whatever you pick we will respect your decision since we don't want to restrict your autonomy." Likewise, we don't give our children choices such as whether to wear clothes in public or not. We don't let them decide whether they should attend school or spend all day at home playing video games. The goals of parenting and of teaching are to instill in students all that is necessary to fulfill a particular vision of the good life. If this good life includes submitting oneself to Christ, then it is not surprising that schools have sprung up to encourage the young toward this end. After all, in the Christian tradition, freedom is never simply freedom *from* societal constraints. In the conception of Thomas Aquinas, for example, freedom is *for* excellence, for virtue, for all things that lead to human flourishing as envisioned by the One who created us (Weigel, 2002). In this more complete picture of liberty, if one "autonomously" chooses to live one's life in ways inimical to human spiritual growth and well-being, then one certainly becomes less, not more, free—a concept that is stressed repeatedly in the moral instruction of private Christian schools.

Unlike many European countries that have such a small number of practicing Christians, the United States still has the critical mass to support many of their schools without the need to admit non-Christians. The challenge for these discipleship schools such as Midwest Christian Academy does not lie primarily in the temptation to compromise the school's religious mission, although market realities usually dictate a broad evangelicalism instead of a more narrowly defined one. Rather, I believe the greatest challenge for discipleship schools lies in avoiding insularity. If the Other is not physically present in the school setting, what is to keep the staff and student body from merely guessing at what those outside the school walls think, all the while projecting their own issues onto the Other? At Midwest Christian, for example, most students may know a few Catholics, or have relatives or parents that were once Catholic, but they surely do not know many Muslims or Native Americans. Since the world in which they live will likely become even more global in scope and the United States itself may continue its present diversification, we must prepare them for a future that will include interaction with those of non-Christian traditions. Because of the relativization that diversity brings, for some people it may be "easier to be a Christian without knowing much about other religions" (Wuthnow, 2005b). Yet without an understanding of one's neighbors it is also easier to be a bad Christian. Obviously, devoting resources to one's own religious community is a good thing in that it produces deep and lasting friendships, which usually occur with those who share one's values. All of us could probably use more of these relationships. However, in addition to creating bonding social capital, conservative Protestant discipleship schools need to find a way to engage and relate graciously to those who do not share their faith. At present, I would echo Furst's earlier comment with the statement, "The state of the art of school leadership has not yet found a way to deal openly and genuinely with the Other while having a closed door policy."

I believe that there is a place for both evangelistic and discipleship religious schools, but both types of schools will need to find new ways either to maintain their Christian identity or to engage the Other constructively. I have already argued that schools with closed-door admission policies need to catch a greater glimpse of common grace. Some schools are better at this than others. Enclave and selectively sheltered enclave schools desire that their students flourish as much as other schools do, but to pretend that the Other does not exist or to portray the Other as morally deficient and intellectually bankrupt is to be, in my mind, dishonest. For the Christian, there are things in our world that are undoubtedly harmful to students, not least of these the captivating "hollow and deceptive philosophy" described in Colossians 2:8, "which depends on human tradition and the elemental spiritual forces of this world rather than on Christ." However, to try to shield students entirely from pernicious influences, one of the goals of enclave schools, is not as good as giving students the tools to evaluate them critically and in light of their Christian faith, acknowledging the true, good, and beautiful wherever it may be found, even as one maintains fidelity to the Christian gospel. If the evangelical educational dictum that "all truth is God's truth" (Gaebelein, 1954, p. 20) is correct, then Christians should be grateful for everything that directs their gaze toward their Lord.

Instructionally, there are steps that schools can take to encourage students to embrace the Other as Christ did. At Midwest Christian Academy, for example, I also teach a community service course with a sprinkling of social justice thrown in for good measure. In this course, students spend much of their class time outside of the school, serving others in their local community. For the students' service to satisfy the course requirements, they must serve with organizations whose benefits extend beyond the walls of the school or local church. In addition, students are encouraged to choose places to serve that will bring them in contact with people who are different than they are in age (i.e. service to the elderly), socioeconomic level, ability (i.e. service to the handicapped or infirm), religion, race, and so on. Within the walls of the school it is more difficult to achieve the level of personal contact that the aforementioned class does, although the Other can also be encountered in discipleship Christian schools through classes such as Midwest Christian's Worldview course, as well as through history, literature, and other courses in the humanities.

PEDAGOGICAL ISSUES

Since one of my major reasons for writing this work was to deal with the ways in which religious outgoups are commonly portrayed in private Christian schools, it seems appropriate to address some curricular and other pedagogical issues before concluding. In looking back on the method of instruction used during the case study at Midwest Christian, I believe that I did some things right, and I therefore have continued to use a similar approach in my subsequent years with other Spanish 3 classes. First of all, for the reasons already discussed in these two concluding chapters, I think it was correct to present both commonalities and differences between the various faith traditions and evangelical Christianity.

Second, I believe that it was beneficial for the students to hear from Muslims, Catholics, Mayas, Aztecs, and Incas in their own voices rather than through synopses given by fellow evangelical Christians. Although I did give a brief lecture over each of the religions, often I did so after students had already had the opportunity to read from a tradition's sacred text. Given the tendency we all have to project ourselves and our own issues onto the Other, this served not to eliminate projection altogether, but to remove at least one layer of interpretation that might have stood between the students and the Other. If it had been possible, I would have arranged for guest speakers from all of the traditions we studied to address and interact with the class as well.

Third, I believe that presenting different points of view and withholding my own views for a time did manage to draw more students into our discussions. The more orthodox students felt comfortable sharing because of the prevailing views of the school community as a whole. Those who were less orthodox also felt comfortable expressing themselves because of the rapport they had developed with me and the sense that I would not judge them as less worthy if they held divergent opinions. The fact that answers were not provided immediately was liberating for some students and disconcerting for others. Although teachers do not have to wait until the very end of the study to reveal their viewpoint like I did in the research setting, there is much to be said for letting students wrestle with issues on their own for a while. Sometimes it may be preferable to lay one's cards on the table at the beginning so as to let students know one's biases up front, but there is also a place for concealing one's hand for a time. The urgency created by cognitive disequilibrium can be a powerful motivator for students to engage the topic on a deeper level than they might have if all of the loose ends were tied up and nothing were at stake. As Christian educators, the faith of our students is obviously a precious thing, and we would never want to do anything to damage it, but it is also true that if we keep them too comfortable, they will never grow.

As we have seen, there are many possible responses when one truly realizes that there are other explanatory narratives besides one's own. One is to assume that every option is merely a social construction invented by those living in a particular time and place. None of the students at Midwest Christian, however, adopted this position. Each of them still found it conceivable that a certain narrative had actually occurred in human history. As we have seen, very few religious individuals have their faith shaken by the realization that there are alternate views somewhere in the wider world. With a polysemous nature and a track record of nearly 2,000 years, it does appear that Christianity is fairly capable of holding its own. For this reason, parents and teachers should not fear that other views presented in class are going to defeat it on the grounds that they are more "rational."

After all, even though Christianity has difficulty explaining some things (human free will vs. divine predestination, the existence of evil and suffering in a world created by a good God, etc.), every other explanatory narrative has "cracks" as well (C. Smith, 2003b). In the process of venturing into the unknown, students may encounter things that throw them for a loop for a period of time. Nathan, for example, light-heartedly remarked that he needed to go to seminary to figure things out, but his comment still showed he believed that the Christian tradition could provide the answers that he wanted. As we age, we all encounter things that cause us to reevaluate our mental paradigms, and I believe that this is usually a good thing. To watch our views become more mature and nuanced does not mean that we necessarily give up our original convictions, but rather that we see them molded and shaped to more accurately fit the contours of the world around us. In the case of Caleb, for example, despite his earlier questioning he still saw himself as a Christian, and some onlookers might see in the modifications of his beliefs evidence of a deeper faith than that of certain classmates, whose faith was expressed in somewhat more formulaic terms.

Both educators committed to the appreciation of diversity and Christian educators of my persuasion would be delighted if there existed the perfect curriculum that fostered in all students at least an understanding and sense of respect for the Other. However, there is no such magical formula. Although certain types of contact under certain conditions can increase the odds that any individual will adopt a certain stance toward the Other (Allport, 1954), there is still a large measure of indeterminacy. Just as Nathan's prior contact with flesh-and-blood Catholics had not made him any more understanding or respectful of Roman Catholicism, employing a certain educational method alone does not guarantee a particular response toward other religions or even toward one's own tradition. Whereas our experience together at Midwest Christian led Caleb to question the "validity and fairness" of the Christian faith, it "reaffirmed" Amy's belief in predestination, and another student, Erin, wrote that the investigation made her "more solid in [her] walk with Christ." The variety of ways my students responded to the presence of the Other obviously depended heavily on the subjective framework of prior knowledge and experiences that each brought to our investigation.

I admit that the instructional process employed in the case study was somewhat artificial, in the sense that all worldview or comparative religion classes are artificial when they ask students to systematize beliefs, hold them up side by side, and consider their implications. In doing so, this approach may produce a greater amount of relativization than would normally happen even with certain types of face-to-face contact between adherents of different religious traditions. As much as relativization can occasionally be upsetting to those who have always taken for granted certain aspects of their religious lives, I do not believe that relativization is necessarily a bad thing since it can also serve as a very useful tool in exposing harmful elements of our cultural life that we often accept without a further thought. For example, to realize how notions of desirable body image have changed throughout the centuries and how the Bible presents a different source for human self-worth can be very liberating, especially for female students who have always assumed that there is some objective standard declaring that to be lovely (and therefore loveable) they need to live in the gym and nearly starve themselves to attain a slender frame. To hear that one can find contentedness in one's identity as a beloved child of God can be a refreshing alternative to the pervasive consumerism of Western culture that encourages discontentedness in order to sell more clothes and beauty products. In examples such as this one, I find relativization to be a blessing.

As for this book as a whole, I hope that it has likewise been a blessing for its readers. For those previously unacquainted with the nuances of evangelical thought I hope it has provided an informative view inside the evangelical subculture. I also hope that this work has provided some food for thought for those who teach in schools like Midwest Christian Academy, who face the formidable challenge of how to maintain fidelity to the Christian gospel and to relate truthfully to those who do not share the Christian worldview. I am aware that many of these comments have been made by others before me, but the difficulty we often have in living them out means that they are worth repeating once more. My prayer is that my fellow educators in Christian schools will continue to instruct students in the ways of the Christian faith, with boundaries defined by love for the Other, oneself, the rest of the created order, and the One who made us all.

APPENDIX A

MIDWEST CHRISTIAN ACADEMY STATEMENT OF FAITH

This doctrinal statement is a declaration of our unity around the truths of the Christian faith. Our mission as a Christ-centered, college preparatory high school is to disciple students for Christ by imparting academic knowledge that leads to Christian character.

We believe the Bible to be the only inspired, inerrant and authoritative Word of God, and the proper standard for all human conduct. (11 Timothy 3:16; 2 Peter 1:21)

We believe that there is one God, eternally existing in three Persons: Father, Son, and Holy Spirit. (Genesis 1:1; Matt. 28:19; Jn. 10:30)

We believe in the deity of our Lord Jesus Christ, in His virgin birth, in His sinless life, in His miracles, in His vicarious and atoning death through His shed blood, in His bodily resurrection, in His ascension to the right hand of God the Father, and in his personal return to power and glory. (Jn. 10:33; Matt. 1:23; Heb, 4:15; Jn. 2:11; 1 Cor. 15:3; Eph. 1:7; Jn. 11:25; 1 Cor. 15:4; Acts 1:11; Rev. 19:11)

We believe that man was created in God's image, is a sinner by nature through Adam's sin, and must be born again and recreated in God's image through faith in Christ Jesus. (Gen. 1:27; Rom. 3:23; 2 Cor. 5:17)

American Evangelicals and Religious Diversity, pages 253–254
Copyright © 2006 by Information Age Publishing
253

We believe that for the salvation of sinful man, regeneration by the Holy Spirit is provided by grace, through faith in Christ Jesus. (Jn. 3:16–19; Jn. 5:24; Rom. 5:8–9; Eph. 2:8–10; Titus 3:5)

We believe in the present ministry of the Holy Spirit, by Whose indwelling the Christian is able to live the godly life. (Rom. 8:13–14; 1 Cor. 3:16; 1 Cor. 6:19–20; Eph. 4:30; Eph. 5:18)

We believe in the resurrection of both the saved and the lost, those who are saved unto the Resurrection of Life and those who are lost unto the resurrection of damnation. (Jn. 5:28–29)

We believe in the spiritual unity of believers in our Lord Jesus Christ. (Rom. 8:9; 1 Cor. 12:12–13; Gal. 3:26–28)

We believe that all believers are under the mandate of Jesus Christ to proclaim the Gospel to all the world. (Matt. 28:19–20)

TEACHING OF DOCTRINE. Doctrines that are open to numerous interpretations by sincere, obedient, and loving Christians are not emphasized at Midwest Christian Academy to ensure that the unity and peace in the fellowship of God's people will not be disrupted. When confronted with subordinate doctrinal issues students are encouraged to seek further counsel from their parents and pastor. Within this Biblical perspective, we seek to impart a respect for the sanctity of life and an abhorrence for such sins as abortion, euthanasia, sexual impurity, and substance abuse.

APPENDIX B

PRIMARY DOCUMENT REFERENCES

References on these pages are not always the sources in which the material was originally published, but rather the sources from which they were drawn for the purposes of our investigation. They are not listed alphabetically, but in the order in which they were assigned to students either during the course of class lectures or as reading to be done outside of class.

Koran, The. (4th rev. ed.). (1974). (N. J. Dawood, Trans.). New York: Penguin Books. (Original work published n. d.).
Excerpts include text from the following surahs: 1, 2, 3, 4, 5, 6, 15, 17, 22, 25, 29, 30, 33, 42, 43, 47, 76, 78, 81, 89, 90, 102, 107, 110
Supplemental reading excerpts drawn from the following surrahs: 3, 5, 7, 20, 28

Stewart, D. (1974). *The Alhambra.* New York: Newsweek.
Ibn-al-Katib. (c. 1360). The shining rays of the full moon: On the history of the Nasrid Dynasty (pp. 138–140)
Alvaro. (n. d.). (p. 56)

Taylor, W. B., & Mills, K. (Eds.). (1998). *Colonial Spanish America: A documentary history.* Wilmington, DE: Scholarly Resources.
Excerpts from Coexistence in the medieval Spanish kingdoms (9th to 12th centuries):
Muslims celebrate Christian festivals in mid-9th century (pp. 29–30)
Al-Bakri. A description of Christian Spain from the 10th century (p. 31)
Ibn 'Abdun, Ibn 'Abd al-Ra'uf, & 'Umar al-Jarsifi. Rules for the Christians from the early 12th century (pp. 31–32)

American Evangelicals and Religious Diversity, pages 255–258
Copyright © 2006 by Information Age Publishing

Commager, H. S. (Ed.). (1968). *Documents of American History* (8th ed.). New York: Appleton-Century-Crofts.
  Ferdinand and Isabella. (1492). Privileges and prerogatives granted to Columbus (pp. 1–2)
  Alexander VI. (1493). The papal bull *Inter caetera* (pp. 2–3)

New Oxford annotated Apocrypha, The. (1991). New York: Oxford University Press.
  Excerpts include: Tobit 14, The Wisdom of Solomon 6, Judith 4, Esther (Greek) 13:8–14:19, 1 Maccabees 1-2, Sirach 5:1–6:1, Daniel (Greek) 14 [Bel and the Dragon], Baruch 5
  Supplemental reading excerpts: The Letter of Jeremiah (Baruch 6), Daniel (Greek) 13 [Susanna]

Catholic Church. (1995). *Catechism of the Catholic Church.* New York: Doubleday.
  Entry numbers: Communion of the Church of Heaven and Earth: 954–959
    Immaculate Conception of Mary: 491–492
    Mary—"Ever-virgin": 499–501
    Mary's Assumption into Heaven: 966
    The Mystagogy of the Baptismal Ceremony: 1234–1245
    The Necessity of Baptism (the Unbaptized): 1257–1261
    Purgatory: 1030–1032
    Mortal and Venial Sin: 1854–1864
    Satisfaction (Penance): 1459–1460
    Indulgences: 1471–1473
    Viaticum (Last Sacrament): 1524–1525
    Wounds to Unity: 817–819
    The Church and Non-Christians: 839–848

Vallette, J., Vallette, R. M., & Carrera-Hanley T. (1994). *Spanish for mastery 3: Situaciones* [Spanish for mastery 3: Situations]. Lexington, MA: D. C. Heath.
  Chinchilla, C. S. (1965). El arco de Balam-Acab [The bow of Balam-Acab] (pp. 84–90)

León-Portilla, M. (Ed.). (1980). *Native Mesoamerican spirituality: Ancient myths, discourses, stories, doctrines, hymns, poems from the Aztec, Yucatec, Quiche-Maya and other sacred traditions.* New York: Paulist Press.
  The Popol Vuh: The book of counsel (pp. 101–134)

Bible, The. Genesis chapters 1–11 (version of individual student's choosing).

León-Portilla, M. (Ed.). (1980). *Native Mesoamerican spirituality: Ancient myths, discourses, stories, doctrines, hymns, poems from the Aztec, Yucatec, Quiche-Maya and other sacred traditions.* New York: Paulist Press.
  Teotlatolli, Teocuilcatl: Divine words, divine songs (pp. 135–144)
  The birth of Huitzilopochtli, patron god of the Aztecs (pp. 220–225)

Salomon, F., & Urioste, G. I.. (Eds.). (1991). *The Huarochiri manuscript.* Austin: University of Texas Press.
Excerpts from Chapter 23: The Inca summons all the Huacas (pp. 114–116)

Taylor, W. B., & Mills, K. (Eds.). (1998). *Colonial Spanish America: A documentary history.* Wilmington, DE: Scholarly Resources.
Excerpts from The ancestors of the people called Indians: A view from Huarochirí, Peru (ca. 1598–1608):
Preface (p. 7)
How the idols of old were, and how they warred among themselves, and how the natives existed at that time (pp. 7–8)
What happened to the Indians in ancient times when the water overflowed (pp. 11–12)
How the sun disappeared for five days. In what follows we shall tell the story about the death of the sun (p. 12)
How in ancient times Paria Caca appeared on a mountain named Condor Coto in the form of five eggs, and what followed. Here will begin the account of Paria Caca's emergence (p. 13).

Cobo, B. (1990). *Inca religion and customs* (R. Hamilton, Trans.). Austin: University of Texas Press.
Of the opinions that these Indians had with regard to the soul and the other life after this one (pp. 19–21)

Faces from the past: Incan mummies hold clues to a lost empire. (1999). *Time for Kids, 4*(23), 6.

Leon-Portilla, M. (Ed.). (1992). *The broken spears: The Aztec account of the conquest of Mexico.* Boston: Beacon Press.
The Spaniards see the objects of gold. (pp. 51–52)
The Spaniards take possession of the city (pp. 65–66)
The Spaniards reveal their greed (pp. 66–68)
The seizure of Motecuhzoma's treasures (pp. 68–69)

Keen, B. (Ed.). (1991). *Latin American civilization: History and society, 1492 to the present* (5th rev. ed.). Boulder, CO: Westview Press.
The strange sermon of Father Montesinos (pp. 71–73)

Lockhart, J., & Otte, E. (Eds.). (1976). *Letters and people of the Spanish Indies: Sixteenth century.* New York: Cambridge University Press.
Excerpt from Toribio de Motolinía. (1955). The Franciscan reply (pp. 220–222)

Taylor, W. B., & Mills, K. (Eds.). (1998). *Colonial Spanish America: A documentary history.* Wilmington, DE: Scholarly Resources.
Francisco de los Angeles (1523). Orders given to "the Twelve." (pp. 46–51)
The lords and holy men of Tenochtitlan reply to the Franciscans (1523). (pp. 19–22)

Excerpts from José de Acosta (1588). On the salvation of the Indians: The
Christianity in which the majority of the Indian peoples live (p. 119)
Excerpt from: Despite this, there are great hopes that the Indians will
receive the true faith and salvation; to imagine otherwise is contrary
to theSpirit of God (pp. 119–120)

Prayer for Native Peoples. (Obtained personally from back of church missal at St.
Augustine Parish Community, Isleta Pueblo, New Mexico).

Carrasco, D. (1990). *Religions of Mesoamerica: Cosmovision and ceremonial centers.* San
Francisco: Harper & Row.
When Christ was crucified (pp. 133–134)

Urbina, M. (2001, January). Una experiencia religiosa [A religious experience].
Nuestra Voz, p. 4.

McDonnell, T. P. (1962). *A Thomas Merton Reader.* New York: Harcourt, Brace, &
World.
Excerpt from Conquistador, tourist, and Indian (pp. 328–330)

APPENDIX C

VIDEO REFERENCES

Cromwell Productions Limited (Producer). (1999). *Great adventurers: Christopher Columbus and the New World* [Motion picture]. (Available from Kultur International Films, 195 Highway 36, West Long Branch, NJ 07764)

Duncan Group (Producer). (1996). *Mystic lands: Peru—kingdom in the clouds* [Motion picture]. (Available from the Duncan Group, http://www.duncanentertainment.com)

Evans, T. (Producer) & Ackroyd, D. (Narrator). (1997). *In search of history: The bloody history of human sacrifice.* (Available from the History Channel, http://store.aetv.com/html/h01.jhtml)

Gill, M. (Producer), Fuentes, C. (Writer/Narrator), & Newington, P. (Director). (1991). *The buried mirror: The Virgin and the bull* [Motion picture]. Spain: Sogotel.

Gill, M. (Producer), Fuentes, C. (Writer/Narrator), & Ralling, C. (Director). (1991). *The buried mirror: Conflict of the Gods* [Motion picture]. Spain: Sogotel.

International Video Network. (Producer). (1998). *Beyond borders: Spain* [Motion picture]. (Available from IVN Entertainment, Inc., 1390 Willow Pass Rd., Suite 900, Concord, CA 94520)

Towles, J., & Rich, L. (Producers). (1998). *Central America close-up: El Salvador, Guatemala* [Motion picture]. (Available from Maryknoll World Productions, Maryknoll, NY 10545)

STUDENT DEMOGRAPHIC SURVEY

Name: _____

Age: _____

Circle One:

On a scale from 1 to 10 (with 10 being the highest), how much desire do you have to learn about other cultures?

1   2   3   4   5   6   7   8   9   10

On a scale from 1 to 10 (with 10 being the highest), how important is the Christian faith in your daily life?

1   2   3   4   5   6   7   8   9   10

List cities in which you have lived and how old you were when you lived there:

List countries you have visited:

List schools you have attended and their locations:

List churches you have attended on a regular basis. (Include the church's name, denomination, and location).

Please check any boxes that apply to you. For experiences you have had with religions other than the ones listed, write the name of the religion in the blank and check the appropriate boxes to the right.

	Roman Catholicism	*Islam*	*Aztec*	*Inca*	*Maya*				
Watched a television show about the religion									
Read a book or magazine article about the religion									
"Studied" the religion (read/watched more than two items about it)									
Attended a religious service									
Have an acquaintance who is of the religion (i.e., you know their name)									
Have a friend who is of the religion									
Have a family member who is of the religion									
Used to be a member of the religion yourself									
Are currently a member of the religion									

If you would like, please give additional explanation of the situation(s) you checked above. Use the back of the page if you need more room.

APPENDIX E

REFLECTIVE ESSAY QUESTIONS

1. After our brief study, including the readings from the Koran and the discussion/lecture, what are your impressions of Islam?

2. If you got a new neighbor who happened to be a Muslim, how would you interact with him/her? Do you think he/she would need to hear the Gospel to be saved? Are you the type of person who would feel comfortable trying to encourage him/her to accept Christ?

3. After our brief summary of some of the similarities and differences between Catholicism and Protestantism, and Mr. Mandel's visit, what are your impressions of Catholicism? In addition to anything else you may write, please comment briefly on what you think regarding whether Catholics are saved (and whether or not we should try to share the Gospel with them) and what you think about the placement of the Catholic Church's teaching authority on the same level as Scripture.

4. Compare and contrast the creation account in the Popol Vuh with the first 11 chapters of Genesis. Note any significant similarities or differences. Why are there similarities, do you think? Why are there differences?

5. After our brief study, including class lectures, readings, and videos, what are your impressions of the Mayas, Aztecs, and Incas?

6. Is it okay to take the gospel to a particular cultural group of people when it means that their traditional way of life will be significantly

American Evangelicals and Religious Diversity, pages 263–264
Copyright © 2006 by Information Age Publishing
All rights of reproduction in any form reserved.

modified or, in the case of the Spanish introducing disease into the Americas, the people themselves are physically harmed? Does spiritual peril outweigh physical peril?

7. When the Spanish missionaries first sought to evangelize the Indians, they destroyed many of the sacred books and religious items of the Indians. Today some missionaries encourage people to continue practicing their traditional rituals, even though they may not be in accordance with historical Christian doctrine. Which position do you support, and why?

8. After today's reading, what are your thoughts on Thomas Merton's letter? What about the line in which he says that the conquistadors should have seen Christ already present in the Indian?

STUDENT QUESTIONNAIRE

Name: _____

Circle one:

On a scale from 1 to 10 (with 10 being the highest), how much desire do you have to learn about other cultures?

1 2 3 4 5 6 7 8 9 10

On a scale from 1 to 10 (with 10 being the highest), how important is the Christian faith in your daily life?

1 2 3 4 5 6 7 8 9 10

If you do not think any of the options on the questions below accurately expresses your view or you want to make a comment about the option you have selected, please explain briefly in the blank space after each question.

1. For whom do you think there is hope for heaven? Choose one of the following:

    (a) There is no hope for heaven for anyone, since there is no life after death.
    (b) The only hope for heaven is for those who profess and demonstrate faith in Christ.
    (c) In addition to Christians, there is hope for heaven for those who have never heard the gospel of Christ.

> (d) In addition to Christians, there is hope for heaven both for (1) those who have never heard the gospel of Christ and (2) those who live a moral and spiritual life but do not profess faith in Christ, although they have heard of Him.
> (e) There is hope for heaven for all people, regardless of religious tradition or lifestyle.
> (f) I'm not sure.

Comment(s):

2. Which one of the following best describes where you think God is present and working?

> (a) God is not present or at work in any religious traditions, because He does not exist.
> (b) God is present and at work only in the Christian faith.
> (c) In addition to Christianity, God is also present and at work in some other religious traditions.
> (d) God is present and at work in all religious traditions.
> (e) I'm not sure.

Comment(s):

3. The highest priority for me in my Christian walk is:

> (a) Community involvement
> (b) Evangelism
> (c) Local church
> (d) Political involvement
> (e) Spiritual growth

Comment(s):

4. What percentage of your friends would you say are non-Christians?

    (a) Less than 10 percent
    (b) From 10 to 30 percent
    (c) From 30 to 50 percent
    (d) From 50 to 70 percent
    (e) From 70 to 90 percent
    (f) Over 90 percent

Comment(s):

5. How often do you share the Gospel with people who do not already profess faith in Christ?

    (a) Daily
    (b) Once a week
    (c) Once a month
    (d) Less than monthly
    (e) Never

Comment(s):

6. Which one of the following most accurately describes how you think God speaks to us?

    (a) God does not speak to us.
    (b) The only authoritative way in which God speaks to us is through the Bible.
    (c) God speaks to us in ways other than through the Bible, but the Bible is more authoritative than any of these other ways.
    (d) God speaks to us in other ways that are just as authoritative as the Bible.
    (e) I'm not sure.

Comment(s):

7. Which one of the following most accurately describes your view on the Bible?

    (a) The Bible is without error in everything it says on matters of faith, and is to be taken literally, word for word.

    (b) The Bible is without error in everything it says on matters of faith, but is not always to be read literally on matters such as history and science.

    (c) The Bible contains some errors, but it is still God's word because God still uses it to speak to us.

    (d) The Bible is not inspired by God, but was written by men in their attempt to explain who God is and how He relates to the world.

    (e) I'm not sure.

Comment(s):

8. Choose the option below that best explains your interest in learning about other religious traditions.

    (a) I don't really have much interest in learning about other religious traditions.

    (b) I am interested in learning about other religious traditions so that I can more effectively share the Gospel.

    (c) I am interested in learning about other religious traditions so that I can understand people better, but not necessarily so I can share the Gospel with them.

    (d) I am interested in learning about other religious traditions because I may learn something for my own spiritual journey.

    (e) I am interested in learning about other religious traditions to see if I might want to adopt one of the religions as my own.

Comment(s):

9. Check the box indicating your impressions of each of the religious traditions that we studied in class.

	Entirely positive	Mostly positive	Slightly positive	Slightly negative	Mostly negative	Entirely negative
Islam						
Roman Catholicism						
Maya, Aztec, and Inca						

Comment(s):

10. This study was not meant to be a study of the Protestant Christian faith, but rather the chance to learn about the religions of Islam, Roman Catholicism, and Latin American indigenous religion (Maya, Aztec, and Inca). If, however, what we studied caused you to think about your own faith in a new way, please explain a little bit about that.

11. a) What things did you like about our study of Spain and Latin America? What things did you dislike?

b) What did you find interesting about our study? What did you find boring?

FOCUS GROUP INTERVIEW SCHEDULES

ROUND 1

1. Before we read them in class, which of the three texts (Koran, Apocrypha, and Popol Vuh) had you heard of?

2. Which of them had you read at least a portion of?

3. Choose a word or phrase that best describes how it felt to read each of the sacred texts. Which word or phrase did each of you pick to describe how it felt to read the Koran? The Apocrypha? The Popol Vuh?

4. In what ways would you say our Scriptures (the books that make up the Protestant Bible) are similar and/or different than the Koran, the Apocrypha, and the Popol Vuh?

5. Do you think that God is speaking at all in these other sacred texts?

6. What about God speaking through people, such as the Pope or council of bishops in the Catholic Church, or through people such as our pastors, parents, teachers, friends, etc.?

7. Other than the Bible and the things we've already mentioned, how else do you see God speaking to us?

8. Do you think any of the things we've mentioned as ways that God speaks are "on the same level" as the Bible?

9. Is there anything else you want to say about what we've discussed today?

American Evangelicals and Religious Diversity, pages 271–272
Copyright © 2006 by Information Age Publishing

ROUND 2

1. On a scale from 1 to 10 (with 1 being the lowest and 10 the highest), how much previous experience had you had with each of the religions we studied in class. What number did you choose for Islam? Roman Catholicism? the Mayas, Aztecs, and Incas?

2. Choose a word or phrase that best describes how it felt to study each of the religions. What did you choose for Islam? Roman Catholicism? the Mayas, Aztecs, and Incas?

3. Do you think the worldviews of these three different groups we studied are reasonable? Why or why not?

4. How important is it to learn about other people's religions? Why is it or isn't it important?

> Follow-up to student responses:
> Do you think we should learn about them in order to communicate the gospel more effectively?
>
> Do you think that we as evangelical Christians should seek to learn anything from them?

5. Do you see any danger in learning about other religions?

> Follow-up:
> Do the benefits outweigh the dangers?

6. Mr. Mandel, when he was here to speak to us, said that he'd be glad to have you come visit a mass. What would you think about taking him up on his offer?

> Follow-up:
> What about Islamic or Native American ceremonies? What would you think about attending one of them?

7. Before we close, is there anything else you'd like to add regarding what we've discussed today?

REFERENCES

Acquaviva, S. S. (1979). *The decline of the sacred in industrial society* (P. Lipscomb, Trans.). New York: Harper & Row. (Original work published 1966)

Adherents.com (2005). *Largest religious groups in the United States of America.* Retrieved May 2, 2005, from http://www.adherents.com/rel_USA.html

Adney, M. (2001). Rajah Sulayman was no water buffalo: Gospel, anthropology, and Islam. In J. G. Stackhouse (Ed.), *No other gods before me? Evangelicals and the challenge of world religions* (pp. 65–83). Grand Rapids, MI: Baker Academic.

Alexander, J. C. (1990). Differentiation theory: Problems and prospects. In J. C. Alexander & P. Colomy (Eds.), *Differentiation theory and social change: Comparative and historical perspectives* (pp. 1–15). New York: Columbia University Press.

Allport, G. W. (1954). *The nature of prejudice.* Cambridge, MA: Addison-Wesley.

Allport, G. W. (1966). Religious context of prejudice. *Journal for the Scientific Study of Religion, 5*(3), 447–457.

Almond, B. (1994). New occasions teach new duties? Seven moral myths. *The Expository Times, 105*, 164–167.

Alston, W. P. (1993). *The reliability of sense perception.* Ithaca, NY: Cornell University Press.

Altena, P., Hermans, C. A. M., & van der Ven, J. A. (2000). Towards a narrative theory of religious education: A study of teacher's aims in Catholic primary schools. *International Journal of Education and Religion, 1*, 217–247.

American Anthropological Association. (1998). AAA statement on race. *American Anthropologist, 100*(3), 712–713.

Ammerman, N. T. (1982). Operationalizing evangelicalism: An amendment. *Sociological Analysis, 43*(2), 170–171.

Ammerman, N. T. (1987). *Bible believers: Fundamentalists in the modern world.* New Brunswick, NJ: Rutgers University Press.

Ammerman, N. T. (with Farnsley, A. E., Adams, T., et al.). (1997a). *Congregations and community.* New Brunswick, NJ: Rutgers University Press.

Ammerman, N. T. (1997b). Organized religion in a voluntaristic society. *Sociology of Religion, 58*(3), 203–215.

American Evangelicals and Religious Diversity, pages 273–298
Copyright © 2006 by Information Age Publishing
All rights of reproduction in any form reserved.

Ammerman, N. T. (2002). Connecting mainline Protestant churches with public life. In R. Wuthnow & J. H. Evans (Eds.), *The quiet hand of God: Faith-based activism and the public role of mainline Protestantism* (pp. 129–158). Berkeley: University of California Press.

Ammerman, N. T. (2003). Religious identities and religious institutions. In M. Dillon (Ed.), *Handbook of the sociology of religion* (pp. 207–224). New York: Cambridge University Press.

Anderson, R. M. (1987). Pentecostal and charismatic Christianity. In M. Eliade (Ed.), *The encyclopedia of religion* (Vol. 11, pp. 229–235). New York: Macmillan.

Apple, M. W. (2001). *Educating the "right way": Markets, standards, god, and inequality.* New York: RoutledgeFalmer.

Askew, T. A. (1987). A response to David F. Wells. In A. J. Rudin & M. R. Wilson (Eds.), *A time to speak: The evangelical–Jewish encounter* (pp. 41–43). Grand Rapids, MI: Eerdmans.

Astley, J. (2000). Plurality, dialogue and religious education. *International Journal of Education and Religion, 1,* 198–216.

Astley, J., Francis, L. J., Wilcox, C., & Burton, L. (2000). How different is religious education in Catholic schools? A study of teacher aims in England. *International Journal of Education and Religion, 1,* 267–281.

Baker, D., Han, M., & Keil, C. T. (1996). *How different, how similar? Comparing key organizational qualities of American public and private secondary schools.* Washington, DC: U.S. Department of Education. (NCES No. 96-322)

Ballweg, G. E. (1980). The growth in the number and population of Christian schools since 1966: A profile of parental views concerning factors which led them to enroll their children in a Christian school (Doctoral dissertation, Boston University, 1980). *Dissertation Abstracts International, 41,* 2040.

Balmer, R. (1989). *Mine eyes have seen the glory: A journey into the evangelical subculture in America.* New York: Oxford University Press.

Balmer, R. (2003). Religion in twentieth-century America. In J. Butler, G. Wacker, & R. Balmer (Eds.), *Religion in American life: A short history* (pp. 331–456). New York: Oxford University Press.

Bandow, D. (1995, November/December). Christianity's Parallel Universe. *The American Enterprise Online.* Retrieved February 24, 2005, from http://www.taemag.com/issues/articleid.16460/article_detail.asp

Barna Research Group. (1996). *Christianity has a strong positive image despite fewer active participants.* (Available from Barna Research Group, Ltd., 5528 Everglades St., Ventura, CA 93003 or from http://www.barna.org)

Barna Research Group. (2000). *Asians and the affluent are increasingly likely to be born again.* (Available from Barna Research Group, Ltd., 5528 Everglades St., Ventura, CA 93003 or from http://www.barna.org)

Beatty, K. M., & Walter, O. (1984). Religious preference and practice: Reevaluating their impact on political tolerance. *Public Opinion Quarterly, 48*(1), 318–329.

Becker, P. E., & Dhingra, P. H. (2001). Religious involvement and volunteering: Implications for civil society. *Sociology of Religion, 62*(3), 315–335.

Bell, D. (1980). *The winding passage: Essays and sociological journeys, 1960–1980.* Cambridge, MA: Abt Books.

Bellah, R. N. (1967). Civil religion in America. *Daedalus, 96*(1), 1–21.

Bellah, R. N., Madsen, R., Sullivan, W. M., Swidler, A., & Tipton, S. M. (1985). *Habits of the heart: Individualism and commitment in American life*. New York: Harper & Row.

Berger, P. L. (1969). *The sacred canopy: Elements of a sociological theory of religion*. Garden City, NY: Doubleday.

Berger, P. L. (1979). *The heretical imperative: Contemporary possibilities of religious affirmation*. Garden City, NY: Doubleday.

Berger, P. L. (1998). Protestantism and the quest for certainty. *Christian Century, 115*(23), 782–785, 792–796.

Berger, P. L. (2001). Reflections on the sociology of religion today. *Sociology of Religion, 62*, 443–454.

Beyer, P. (1994). *Religion and globalization*. London: Sage.

Beyerlein, K. (2004). Specifying the impact of conservative Protestantism on educational attainment. *Journal for the Scientific Study of Religion, 43*(4), 505–518.

Bibby, R. W. (1978). Why conservative churches really are growing: Kelley revisited. *Journal for the Scientific Study of Religion, 17*(2), 129–137.

Bibby, R. W. (1987). *Fragmented gods*. Toronto: Irwin.

Bibby, R. W. (1993). Religion in the Canadian 1990s: The paradox of poverty and potential. In D. A. Roozen & C. K. Hadaway (Eds.), *Church and denominational growth* (pp. 278–292). Nashville, TN: Abingdon.

Bibby, R. W. (1999). On boundaries, gates, and circulating saints: A longitudinal look at loyalty and loss. *Review of Religious Research, 41*(2), 149–164.

Bibby, R. W., & Brinkerhoff, M. B. (1973). The circulation of the saints: A study of people who join conservative churches. *Journal for the Scientific Study of Religion, 12*(3), 273–283.

Billig, M. (1996). *Arguing and thinking: A rhetorical approach to social psychology* (2nd ed.). New York: Cambridge University Press.

Blomberg, C. L., & Robinson, S. E. (1997). *How wide the divide? A Mormon and an evangelical in conversation*. Downers Grove, IL: InterVarsity Press.

Bonvillain, N. (1998). *Women and men: Cultural constructs of gender*. Upper Saddle River, NJ: Prentice Hall.

Boone, K. C. (1989). *The Bible tells them so: The discourse of Protestant fundamentalism*. Albany: State University of New York.

Borhek, J. T., & Curtis, R. F. (1975). *A sociology of belief*. New York: Wiley.

Bouma, G. D. (1979). The real reason one conservative church grew. *Review of Religious Research, 20*, 127–137.

Bourdieu, P. (1977). *Outline of a theory of practice* (R. Nice, Trans.). New York: Cambridge University Press. (Original work published 1972)

Brauer, J. C. (1953). *Protestantism in America: A narrative history*. Philadelphia: Westminster.

Brierley, P. (1999). *UK Christian handbook: Religious trends no. 2 (2000/2001 millennium ed.)* London: Christian Research.

Brierley, P. (2000). *The tide is running out*. London: Christian Research.

Brooke, J. H. (1991). *Science and religion: Some historical perspectives*. Cambridge, UK: Cambridge University Press.

Brown, D., & Pinnock, C. H. (1990). *Theological crossfire: An evangelical–liberal dialogue*. Grand Rapids, MI: Zondervan.

Brown, R. K., & Brown, R. E. (2003). Faith and works: Church based social capital resources and African American political activism. *Social Forces, 82*(2), 617–641.

Bruce, S. (1992). Pluralism and religious vitality. In S. Bruce (Ed.), *Religion and modernization: Sociologists and historians debate the secularization thesis* (pp. 170–194). Oxford: Clarendon Press.

Bruce, S. (1999). *Choice and religion: A critique of rational choice theory.* New York: Oxford University Press.

Bruce, S. (2002). *God is dead: Secularization in the West.* Malden, MA: Blackwell.

Busch, B. G. (1998). Faith, truth, and tolerance: Religion and political tolerance in the United States (Doctoral dissertation, University of Nebraska, 1998). *Dissertation Abstracts International, 59,* 2165.

Butler, J. (1990). *Awash in a sea of faith: Christianizing the American people.* Cambridge, MA: Harvard University Press.

Butler, J. (2003). Religion in colonial America. In J. Butler, G. Wacker, & R. Balmer (Eds.), *Religion in American life: A short history* (pp. 1–162). New York: Oxford University Press.

Butler, J., Wacker, G., & Balmer, R. (Eds.). (2003). *Religion in American life: A short history.* New York: Oxford University Press.

Campbell, G. V. P. (1999). The relativization of tradition: A study of the evangelical post–conservative controversy in contemporary American evangelical Protestantism (Doctoral dissertation, University of Pittsburgh, 1999). *Dissertation Abstracts International, 60*(04), 1353A. (UMI No. 9927952)

Carpenter, J. A. (1980). Fundamentalist institutions and the rise of evangelical Protestantism, 1929–1942. *Church History, 16*(1), 62–75.

Carpenter, J. A. (1997). *Revive us again: The reawakening of American fundamentalism.* New York: Oxford.

Carper, J. C. (1984). The Christian day school. In J. C. Carper & T. C. Hunt (Eds.), *Religious schooling in America* (pp. 110–129). Birmingham, AL: Religious Education Press.

Carper, J. C. (1999). Independent Christian schools and the new millennium. *Private School Monitor, 20*(2), 1, 11–12.

Carper, J. C. (2001). The changing landscape of U.S. education. *Kappa Delta Pi Record, 37*(3), 106–110.

Carper. J. C., & Layman, J. (2002). Independent Christian day schools: The maturing of a movement. *Catholic Education: A Journal of Inquiry and Practice, 5*(4), 502–514.

Carroll, J. W. (1979). Continuity and change: The shape of American religion, 1950 to the present. In J. W. Carroll, D. W. Johnson & M. E. Marty (Eds.), *Religion in America: 1950 to the present* (pp. 1–45). New York: Harper & Row.

Casanova, J. (1994). *Public religions in the modern world.* Chicago: University of Chicago Press.

Casanova, J. (2005, April). *Immigration and the new religious pluralism: A EU/US comparison.* Paper presented at "The New Religious Pluralism and Democracy" conference, Georgetown University, Washington, DC.

Chaves, M. (1989). Secularization and religious revival: Evidence from U.S. church attendance rates, 1972–1986. *Journal for the Scientific Study of Religion, 28*(4), 464–477.

Chaves, M. (1994). Secularization as declining religious authority. *Social Forces, 72*(3), 749–774.

Chaves, M. (1999). [Review of the book *American evangelicalism: Embattled and thriving*]. *Christian Century, 116*(5), 227–229.

Chaves, M. (2001). Religious congregations and welfare reform: Assessing the potential. In A. Walsh (Ed.), *Can charitable choice work? Covering religion's impact on urban affairs and social services* (pp. 121–139). Hartford, CT: Leonard E. Greenberg Center on Religion in Public Life, Trinity College.

Chaves, M., Giesel, H. M., & Tsitsos, W. (2002). Religious variations in public presence: Evidence from the National Congregations Study. In R. Wuthnow & J. H. Evans (Eds.), *The quiet hand of God: Faith-based activism and the public role of mainline Protestantism* (pp. 108–128). Berkeley: University of California Press.

Chaves, M., & Gorski, P. S. (2001). Religious pluralism and religious participation. *Annual Review of Sociology, 27*, 261–81.

Chaves, M., & Stephens, L. (2003). Church attendance in the United States. In M. Dillon (Ed.), *Handbook of the sociology of religion* (pp. 85–95). New York: Cambridge University Press.

Clapp, R. (2001). *Border crossings: Christian trespasses on popular culture and public affairs.* Grand Rapids, MI: Brazos.

Clark, K. J. (2005). Without evidence or argument. In J. Feinberg & R. Shafer-Landau (Eds.), *Reason and responsibility: Readings in some basic problems of philosophy* (pp. 110–113). Belmont, CA: Thomson Wadsworth.

Coady, C. A. J. (1992). *Testimony: A philosophical study.* Oxford: Clarendon Press.

Colson, C. W., & Neuhaus, R. J. (Eds.). (1995). *Evangelicals and Catholics together: Toward a common mission.* Dallas: Word.

Compton, S. C. (2003). *Rekindling the mainline: New life through new churches.* Bethesda, MD: Alban Institute.

Conover, P. J. (1988). The role of social groups in political thinking. *British Journal of Political Science, 18*(1), 51–76.

Cooper, B. S., & Dondero, G. (1991). Survival, change, and demands on America's private schools: Trends and policies. *Educational Foundations, 5*(1), 51–74.

Corbett, M. (1991). *American public opinion: Trends, processes, and patterns.* New York: Longman.

Coser, L. A. (1956). *The functions of social conflict.* Glencoe, IL: The Free Press.

Council for American Private Education. (2005). *CAPE member organizations.* Retrieved December 12, 2005, from http://www.capenet.org/member.html

Cromartie, M. (2001). *Religious conservatives in American politics 1980–2000: An assessment.* Retrieved April 6, 2005, from http://www.frc.org/get.cfm?i=WT01D1

Cuddihy, J. M. (1978). *No offense: Civil religion and Protestant taste.* New York: Seabury.

Cupitt, D. (1997). *After God: The future of religion.* New York: Basic Books.

Curran, F. X. (1954). *The churches and the schools: American Protestantism and popular elementary education.* Chicago: Loyola University Press.

Cutsinger, J. S. (Ed.). (1997). *Reclaiming the great tradition: Evangelicals, Catholics and Orthodox in dialogue.* Downers Grove, IL: InterVarsity Press.

Darnell, A., & Sherkat, D. E. (1997). The impact of Protestant fundamentalism on educational attainment. *American Sociological Review, 62*(2), 306–315.

Davidson, J. D. (1985). Mobilizing social movement organizations: The formation, institutionalization, and effectiveness of ecumenical urban ministries. *Society For the Scientific Study of Religion Monograph Series, 6.*

Davie, G. (1994). *Religion in Britain since 1945: Believing without belonging.* Cambridge, MA: Blackwell.

Davie, G. (2002). *Europe: The exceptional case: Parameters for faith in the modern world.* London: Darton, Longman and Todd.

Davis, N. J., & Robinson, R. V. (1996). Are the rumors of war exaggerated? Religious orthodoxy and moral progressivism in America. *American Journal of Sociology, 102*(3), 756–787.

Dayton, D. W., & Johnston, R. K. (Eds.). (1991). *The variety of American evangelicalism.* Knoxville: University of Tennessee Press.

Deckman, M. (2001). Religion makes the difference: Why Christian Right candidates run for school board. *Review of Religious Research, 42*(4), 349–371.

Dein, S. (2001). What really happens when prophecy fails: The case of Lubavitch. *Sociology of Religion, 62*(3), 383–401.

Denzin, N. K. (1978). *The research act: A theoretical introduction to sociological methods* (2nd ed.). New York: McGraw–Hill.

Dobbelaere, K. (1981). Secularization: A multi–dimensional concept. *Current Sociology, 29*, 1–216.

Donahue, M. J., & Benson, P. L. (1993). Belief style, congregational climate, and program quality. In D. A. Roozen & C. K. Hadaway (Eds.), *Church and denominational growth* (pp. 225–240). Nashville, TN: Abingdon.

Dougherty, K. D. (2004). Institutional influences on growth in Southern Baptist congregations. *Review of Religious Research, 46*(2), 117–131.

Douglas, M. (1973). *Natural symbols: Explorations in cosmology.* London: Barrie & Jenkins.

Douglas, M. (1982). The effects of modernization on religious change. *Daedalus, 111*(1), 1–19.

Dovidio, J. G., Gaertner, S. L., Hodson, G., Houlette, M. A., & Johnson, K. M. (2005). Social inclusion and exclusion: Recategorization and the perception of intergroup boundaries. In D. Abrams, M. A. Hogg, & J. M. Marques (Eds.), *The social psychology of inclusion and exclusion* (pp. 245–264). Philadelphia: Psychology Press.

Dowdy, T. E. (1991). Invisibility and plausibility: An analysis of the relationship between forms of privatization and individual religiosity. In M. L. Lynn & D. O. Moberg (Eds.), *Research in the social scientific study of religion* (Vol. 3, pp. 89–114). Greenwich, CT: JAI Press.

Dunn, W. K. (1958). *What happened to religious education? The decline of religious teaching in the public elementary school, 1776–1861.* Baltimore: Johns Hopkins University Press.

Ebaugh, H. R., & Chafetz, J. S. (2000). *Religion and the new immigrants: Continuities and adaptations in immigrant congregations.* Walnut Creek, CA: AltaMira.

Eck, D. L. (2001). *A new religious America: How a "Christian country" has now become the world's most religiously diverse nation.* San Francisco: HarperSanFrancisco.

Eck, D. L. (2002). *On common ground: World religions in America* (2nd ed.) [CD]. New York: Columbia University Press.

Eck, D. L. (2005, April). *American religious pluralism: Civic and theological discourse.* Paper presented at "The New Religious Pluralism and Democracy" conference, Georgetown University, Washington, DC.

Eliot, T. S. (1950). *The cocktail party.* New York: Harcourt, Brace.

Ellison, C. G., & Bartkowski, J. P. (1996). Religion and the legitimization of violence: The case of conservative Protestantism and corporal punishment. In J. Turpin & L. R. Kurtz (Eds.), *The web of violence: From interpersonal to global* (pp. 45–67). Urbana: University of Illinois Press.

Elshtain, J. B. (2004). Anti-Semitism or anti-Judaism? *Christian Century, 121*(10), 39.

Erickson, M. J. (1997). *The evangelical left: Encountering postconservative evangelical theology.* Grand Rapids, MI: Baker.

Ethics and Public Policy Center. (2003, April 7). *Most evangelical leaders favor "evangelizing Muslims abroad": EPPC-Beliefnet survey on evangelizing Muslims.* Retrieved February 8, 2005, from http://www.eppc.org/news/newsID.8/news_detail.asp

Ethridge, F. M., & Feagin, J. R. (1979). Varieties of "fundamentalism": A conceptual and empirical analysis of two Protestant denominations. *Sociological Quarterly, 20*(1), 37–48.

Etzioni, A. (1988). *The moral dimension: Toward a new economics.* New York: Free Press.

Etzioni, A. (1995). *The community of communities: A communitarian position paper.* Retrieved March 26, 2005, from http://www.gwu.edu/~ccps/Comofcom.html

Evans, J. H. (2003). The creation of a distinct subcultural identity and denominational growth. *Journal for the Scientific Study of Religion, 42*(3), 467–477.

Evearitt, T. C. (1979). An analysis of why parents enroll their children in private Christian schools (Doctoral dissertation, Illinois State University, 1979). *Dissertation Abstracts International, 40,* 551.

Festinger, L., Riecken, H. W., & Schachter, S. (1956). *When prophecy fails: A social and psychological study of a modern group that predicted the destruction of the world.* Minneapolis: University of Minnesota Press.

Fine, G. A., & Kleinman, S. (1979). Rethinking subculture: An interactionist analysis. *American Journal of Sociology, 85*(1), 1–20.

Finke, R., & Stark, R. (1988). Religious economies and sacred canopies: Religious mobilization in American cities, 1906. *American Sociological Review, 53,* 41–49.

Finke, R., & Stark, R. (1992). *The churching of America, 1776–1990: Winners and losers in our religious economy.* New Brunswick, NJ: Rutgers University Press.

Fischer, C. S. (1982). *To dwell among friends: Personal networks in town and city.* Chicago: University of Chicago Press.

Fischer, C. S. (1995). The subcultural theory of urbanism: A twentieth-year assessment. *American Journal of Sociology, 101*(3), 543–577.

Fowler, R. B. (1989). *Unconventional partners: Religion and liberal culture in the United States.* Grand Rapids, MI: Eerdmans.

Francis, L. J. (2000). The domestic and the general function of Anglican schools in England and Wales. *International Journal of Education and Religion, 1,* 100–121.

Furst, L. G. (2000). Defining identity in a multicultural society: The challenge to religious schools. *International Journal of Education, 1,* 166–177.

Gaebelein, F. E. (1954). *The pattern of God's truth: Problems of integration in Christian education.* New York: Oxford University Press.

Gaertner, S. L., & Dovidio, J. F. (2000). *Reducing intergroup bias: The common ingroup identity model.* Philadelphia: Psychology Press.

Galli, M. (2004). Evangelicals: Fragmented and thriving. *Books and Culture, 10*(1), 22.

Gallup, G. H. (2004, January 13). *Gallup religious index up from record low.* Retrieved October 15, 2004, from http://www.gallup.com

Garrison, W. E. (1948). Characteristics of American organized religion. *The Annals of the American Academy of Political and Social Science, 256,* 14–24.

Gay, D. A., & Ellison, C. G. (1993). Religious subcultures and political tolerance: Do denominations still matter? *Review of Religious Research, 34*(4), 311–332.

Gleason, B. G. (1980). A study of the Christian school movement (Doctoral dissertation, University of North Dakota, 1980). *Dissertation Abstracts International, 41,* 4670.

Glenn, C. L. (1988). *The myth of the common school.* Amherst: University of Massachusetts Press.

Glenn, N. D. (1987). The trend in "no religion" respondents to U. S. national surveys, late 1950s to early 1980s. *Public Opinion Quarterly, 51*(3), 293–314.

Goldfried, G., & Miner, M. (2002). Quest religion and the problem of limited compassion. *Journal for the Scientific Study of Religion, 41*(4), 685–695.

Goldman, R. (1965). *Readiness for religion: A basis for developmental religious education.* New York: Seabury Press.

Gottman, J. M. (with Silver, N.). (1999). *The seven principles for making marriage work.* New York: Three Rivers Press.

Graves, J. L. (2004). *The race myth: Why we pretend race exists in America.* New York: Dutton.

Greeley, A. M. (1989). *Religious change in America.* Cambridge, MA: Harvard University Press.

Greeley, A. M. (1997). The other civic America: Religion and social capital. *American Prospect, 32,* 68–73.

Greeley, A. M. (2003). The Catholics in the world and in America. In J. Neusner (Ed.), *World religions in America: An introduction* (3rd ed.). Louisville, KY: Westminster/John Knox.

Greeley, A. M., & Hout, M. (1988). Musical chairs: Patterns of denominational change. *Sociology and Social Research, 72*(2), 75–86.

Green, J. C. (1996). *Understanding the Christian right.* New York: American Jewish Committee.

Green, J. C. (2003). Evangelical Protestants and civic engagement: An overview. In M. Cromartie (Ed.), *A public faith: Evangelicals and civic engagement* (pp. 11–29). Lanham, MD: Rowman & Littlefield.

Green, J. C. (2004). Winning numbers: Religion in the 2004 election. *Christian Century, 121*(4), 8–9.

Green, J. C., Guth, J. L., Kellstedt, L. A., & Smidt, C. E. (1994). Uncivil challenges? Support for civil liberties among religious activists. *Journal of Political Science, 22,* 25–49.

Green, J. C., Rozell, M. J., & Wilcox, C. (2003). *The Christian Right in American politics: Marching to the millennium.* Washington, DC: Georgetown University Press.

Green, W. S. (2003). Religion and society in America. In J. Neusner (Ed.), *World religions in America: An introduction* (3rd ed.). Louisville, KY: Westminster/John Knox.

Greenberg Quinlan Rosner Research. (2004). *Re: Evangelicals in America.* Retrieved April 2, 2005, from http://www.pbs.org/wnet/religionandethics/week733/results.pdf

Greer, B. A. (1993). Strategies for evangelism and growth in three denominations, 1965–1990. In D. A. Roozen & C. K. Hadaway (Eds.), *Church and denominational growth* (pp. 87–111). Nashville, TN: Abingdon.

Guth, J. L. (1996). The politics of the Christian Right. In J. C. Green, J. L. Guth, C. E. Smidt, & L. A. Kellstedt (Eds.), *Religion and the culture wars: Dispatches from the front* (pp. 7–29). Lanham, MD: Rowman & Littlefield.

Gutmann, A. (1987). *Democratic education.* Princeton, NJ: Princeton University Press.

Hadaway, C. K. (1982). Church growth (and decline) in a southern city. *Review of Religious Research, 23*(4), 372–386.

Hadaway, C. K. (1993). Is evangelistic activity related to church growth? In D. A. Roozen & C. K. Hadaway (Eds.), *Church and denominational growth* (pp. 169–187). Nashville, TN: Abingdon.

Hadaway, C. K., & Marler, P. L. (1993). All in the family: Religious mobility in America. *Review of Religious Research, 35*(2), 97–116.

Hadaway, C. K., & Marler, P. L. (2005). How many Americans attend worship each week? An alternative approach to measurement. *Journal for the Scientific Study of Religion, 44*(3), 307–322.

Hadaway, C. K., Marler, P. L., & Chaves, M. (1993). What the polls don't show: A closer look at U. S. church attendance. *American Sociological Review, 58*(6), 741–752.

Hadaway, C. K., & Roozen, D. A. (1993). Denominational growth and decline. In D. A. Roozen & C. K. Hadaway (Eds.), *Church and denominational growth* (pp. 37–45). Nashville, TN: Abingdon.

Hall, D. J. (1998). Confessing Christ in the religiously pluralistic context. In W. Brueggemann & G. W. Stroup (Eds.), *Many voices, one God: Being faithful in a pluralistic world* (pp. 65–77). Louisville, KY: Westminster/John Knox.

Hamilton, M. S. (2000). We're in the money: How did evangelicals get so wealthy, and what has it done to us? *Christianity Today, 44*(7), 36–43.

Hammond, P. E., & Hunter, J. D. (1984). On maintaining plausibility: The worldview of evangelical college students. *Journal for the Scientific Study of Religion, 23,* 221–235.

Handy, R. T. (1991). *Undermined establishment: Church–state relations in America, 1880–1920.* Princeton, NJ: Princeton University Press.

Hatch, N. O. (1984). Evangelicalism as a democratic movement. In G. Marsden (Ed.), *Evangelicalism and modern America* (pp. 71–82). Grand Rapids, MI: Eerdmans.

Hatch, N. O. (with Hamilton, M. S.). (1995). Taking the measure of the evangelical resurgence, 1942–1992. In D. G. Hart (Ed.), *Reckoning with the past: Historical essays on American evangelicalism from the Institute for the Study of American Evangelicals* (pp. 395–412). Grand Rapids, MI: Baker Books.

Hauerwas, S., & Willimon, W. H. (1989). *Resident aliens: Life in the Christian colony.* Nashville, TN: Abingdon.

Heelas, P. (1996). *The New Age movement: The celebration of the self and the sacralization of modernity.* Cambridge, MA: Blackwell.

Henry, C. F. H. (1990). Who are the evangelicals? In K. S. Kantzer & C. F. H. Henry (Eds.), *Evangelical affirmations* (pp. 69–94). Grand Rapids, MI: Zondervan.

Herberg, W. (1956). *Protestant, Catholic, Jew: An essay in American religious sociology.* Garden City, NY: Doubleday.

Hermans, C. A. M. (2000a). Analyzing the dialogic construction of identity of religiously affiliated schools in a multicultural society. *International Journal of Education and Religion, 1,* 135–165.

Hermans, C. A. M. (2000b). The challenges of multiculturalism. *International Journal of Education and Religion, 1,* 1–18.

Hermans, C. A. M. (2000c). Conflicting goals for moral education: A study of the behavioral intentions of teachers in Catholic secondary schools in the Netherlands. *International Journal of Education and Religion, 1,* 282–300.

Hick, J. (1984). Religious pluralism. In F. Whaling (Ed.), *The world's religious traditions: Current perspectives in religious studies* (pp. 147–164). New York: Crossroad.

Hick, J. (2001). [Review of the book *The depth of the riches: A Trinitarian theology of religious ends*]. *Reviews in Religion and Theology, 8*(4), 411–414.

Hill, J. P. (2004). *The evangelical advantage: A test of the subcultural identity theory of religious strength.* Unpublished master's thesis, University of Notre Dame, South Bend, IN.

Hill, S. S. (1989). What's in a name? In F. S. Mead & S. S. Hill (Eds.), *Handbook of denominations in the United States.* (9th ed., pp. 251–262). Nashville, TN: Abingdon.

Hirst, P. H. (1972). Christian education: A contradiction in terms? *Learning for Living, 11*(4), 6–11.

Hirst, P. H. (1981). Education, catechesis and the church school. *British Journal of Religious Education, 3,* 85–93.

Hofferth, S. L., & Sandberg, J. F. (2001). Changes in American children's time, 1981–1997. In T. Owens & S. Hofferth (Eds.), *Children at the millennium: Where have we come from, where are we going? Advances in life course research* (pp. 193–229). New York: Elsevier Science.

Hoge, D. R., Johnson, B., & Luidens, D. A. (1994). *Vanishing boundaries: The religion of mainline Protestant Baby Boomers.* Louisville, KY: Westminster/John Knox.

Hoge, D. R., & Noll, M. A. (2000). Levels of contributions and attitudes toward money among evangelicals and non–evangelicals in Canada and the U.S. In L. Eskridge & M. A. Noll (Eds.), *More money, more ministry: Money and evangelicals in recent North American history* (pp. 351–373). Grand Rapids, MI: Eerdmans.

Hoge, D. R., & Roozen, D. A. R(1979). Research on factors influencing church commitment. In D. R. Hoge & D. A. Roozen (Eds.), *Understanding church growth and decline: 1950–1978* (pp. 42–68). New York: Pilgrim Press.

Hogg, M. A. (1992). *The social psychology of group cohesiveness: From attraction to social identity.* New York: New York University Press.

Hogg, M. A., & Abrams, D. (1988). *Social identifications: A social psychology of intergroup relations and group processes.* New York: Routledge.

Hogg, M. A., & Abrams, D. (1990). Social motivation, self–esteem and social identity. In D. Abrams & M. A. Hogg (Eds.), *Social identity theory: Constructive and critical advances* (pp. 28–47). New York: Springer–Verlag.

Holifield, E. B. (1994). Toward a history of American congregations. In J. P. Wind
& J. W. Lewis (Eds.), *American congregations, Vol. 2: New perspectives in the study of
congregations* (pp. 23–53). Chicago: University of Chicago Press.

Holmes, J. C. (1983). *What parents expect of the Christian school.* Santa Fe Springs, CA:
JoHo Publications.

Homans, G. C. (1961). *Social behavior: Its elementary forms.* New York: Harcourt,
Brace, & World.

Hood, R. W., & Morris, R. J. (1985). Boundary maintenance, social–political views,
and presidential preference among high and low fundamentalists. *Review of
Religious Research, 27*(2), 134–145.

Hood, R. W., Morris, R. J., & Watson, P. J. (1986). Maintenance of religious fundamentalism. *Psychological Reports, 59,* 547–559.

Hout, M., & Fischer, C. S. (2002). Why more Americans have no religious preference: Politics and generations. *American Sociological Review, 67,* 165–190.

Hout, M., & Greeley, A. M. (1987). The center doesn't hold: Church attendance in
the United States, 1940–1984. *American Sociological Review, 52*(3), 325–345.

Hout, M., Greeley, A. M., & Wilde, M. J. (2001). The demographic imperative in
religious change in the United States. *American Journal of Sociology, 107*(2),
468–500.

Houtman, D., & Mascini, P. (2002). Why do churches become empty, while New
Age grows? Secularization and religious change in the Netherlands. *Journal for
the Scientific Study of Religion, 41*(3), 455–473.

Hunter, J. D. (1983). *American evangelicalism: Conservative religion and the quandary of
modernity.* New Brunswick, NJ: Rutgers University Press.

Hunter, J. D. (1987). *Evangelicalism: The coming generation.* Chicago: University of
Chicago Press.

Hutchison, W. R. (1976). *The modernist impulse in American Protestantism.* Cambridge,
MA: Harvard University Press.

Hutchison, W. R. (2003). *Religious pluralism in America: The contentious history of a
founding ideal.* New Haven, CT: Yale University Press.

Hyman, H. H., & Wright, C. R. (1979). *Education's lasting influence on values.* Chicago: University of Chicago Press.

Iannaccone, L. R. (1991). The consequences of religious market structure: Adam
Smith and the economics of religion. *Rationality and Society, 3*(2), 156–177.

Iannaccone, L. R. (1994). Why strict churches are strong. *American Journal of Sociology, 99*(5), 1180–1211.

Iannaccone, L., Stark, R., & Finke, R. (1998). Rationality and the "religious mind."
Economic Inquiry, 36(3), 373–389.

Inglehart, R., & Baker, W. E. (2000). Modernization, cultural change and the persistence of traditional values. *American Sociological Review, 65*(1), 19–51.

Inglehart, R., Basañez, M., & Moreno, A. (1998). *Human values and beliefs: A cross-
cultural sourcebook: Political, religious, sexual, and economic norms in 43 societies:
Findings from the 1990–1993 World Values Survey.* Ann Arbor: University of Mich-
igan Press.

Jelen, T. G. (1989). Biblical literalism and inerrancy: Does the difference make a difference? *Sociological Analysis, 49*(4), 421–429.

Jelen, T. G. (1993). The political consequences of religious group attitudes. *Journal of Politics, 55*(1), 178–190.

Jelen, T. G., & Wilcox, C. (1990). Denominational preference and the dimensions of political tolerance. *Sociological Analysis, 51*(1), 69–81.

Jelen, T. G., & Wilcox, C. (1991). Religious dogmatism among white Christians: Causes and effects. *Review of Religious Research, 33*, 32–46.

Jeynes, W. (2003). *Religion, education, and academic success.* Greenwich, CT: Information Age.

Johnson, D. C. (1997). Formal education vs. religious belief: Soliciting new evidence with multinomial logit modeling. *Journal for the Scientific Study of Religion, 36*(2), 231–246.

Johnson, D. W., Picard, P. R., & Quinn, B. (1974). *Churches and church membership in the United States: An enumeration by region, state and county, 1971.* Washington, DC: Glenmary Research Center.

Johnson, P. E. (1993). The Swedish syndrome [Review of the book *The culture of disbelief: How American law and politics trivialize religious devotion*]. *First Things, 38,* 48–50.

Johnston, R. K. (1991). American evangelicalism: An extended family. In D. W. Dayton & R. K. Johnston (Eds.), *The variety of American evangelicalism* (pp. 252–272). Knoxville: University of Tennessee Press.

Jones, D. E., Doty, S., Grammich, C., Horsch, J.E., Houseal, R., Lynn, M., et al. (2002). *Religious congregations and membership in the United States, 2000: An enumeration by region, state and county based on data reported for 149 religious bodies.* Nashville, TN: Glenmary Research Center.

Jorgenson, L. P. (1987). *The state and the non-public school, 1825–1925.* Columbia: University of Missouri Press.

Kalmijn, M. (1991). Shifting boundaries: Trends in religious and educational homogamy. *American Sociological Review, 56*(6), 786–800.

Kantzer, K. S. (1975). Unity and diversity in evangelical faith. In D. F. Wells & J. D. Woodbridge (Eds.), *The evangelicals: What they believe, who they are, where they are changing* (pp. 38–67). Nashville, TN: Abingdon.

Karpov, V. (2002). Religiosity and tolerance in the United States and Poland. *Journal for the Scientific Study of Religion, 41*(2), 267–288.

Kelley, D. M. (1972). *Why conservative churches are growing: A study in sociology of religion.* New York: Harper & Row.

Kellstedt, L. A., & Green, J. C. (1996) The mismeasure of evangelicals. *Books and Culture, 2*(1), 14–15.

Kellstedt, L. A., Green, J. C., Guth, J. L., & Smidt, C. E. (1996). Grasping the essentials: The social embodiment of religion and political behavior. In J. C. Green, J. L. Guth, C. E. Smidt, & L. A. Kellstedt (Eds.), *Religion and the culture wars: Dispatches from the front* (pp. 174–191). Lanham, MD: Rowman & Littlefield.

Kellstedt, L. A., Green, J. C., Smidt, C. E., & Guth, J. L. (1996). The puzzle of evangelical Protestantism: Core, periphery, and political behavior. In J. C. Green, J. L. Guth, C. E. Smidt, & L. A. Kellstedt (Eds.), *Religion and the culture wars: Dispatches from the front* (pp. 240–266). Lanham, MD: Rowman & Littlefield.

Kellstedt, L. A., & Smidt, C. E. (1996). Measuring fundamentalism: An analysis of different operational strategies. In J. C. Green, J. L. Guth, C. E. Smidt, & L. A. Kellstedt (Eds.), *Religion and the culture wars: Dispatches from the front* (pp. 193–218). Lanham, MD: Rowman & Littlefield.

Kennedy, D. J., & Newcombe, J. (2003). *What if America were a Christian nation again?* Nashville, TN: Nelson.

Kennedy, W. B. (1966). *The shaping of Protestant education: An interpretation of the Sunday school and the development of Protestant educational strategy in the United States, 1789–1860.* New York: Association Press.

Keysar, A., & Kosmin, B. A. (1995). The impact of religious identification on differences in educational attainment among American women in 1990. *Journal for the Scientific Study of Religion, 34*(1), 49–62.

Kirkpatrick, L. A. (1993). Fundamentalism, Christian orthodoxy, and intrinsic religious orientation as predictors of discriminatory attitudes. *Journal for the Scientific Study of Religion, 32*(3), 256–268.

Kirn, W. (2002, September). What would Jesus do? *GQ, 72,* 474–479, 495–497.

Knitter, P. F. (2002). *Introducing theologies of religions.* Maryknoll, NY: Orbis Books.

Kohut, A., Green, J. C., Keeter, S., & Toth, R. C. (2000). *The diminishing divide: Religion's changing role in American politics.* Washington, DC: Brooking Institution Press.

Kosmin, B. A., Keysar, A., & Lerer, N. (1992). Secular education and the religious profile of contemporary black and white Americans. *Journal for the Scientific Study of Religion, 31*(4), 523–532.

Kosmin, B. A., & Lachman, S. P. (1991). *The National Survey of Religious Identification 1989–90.* New York: The Graduate School and University Center of the City University of New York.

Kosmin, B. A., Mayer, E., & Keysar, A. (2001). *American religious identification survey 2001.* New York: The Graduate Center, The City University of New York. Retrieved December 12, 2005, from http://www.gc.cuny.edu/faculty/research_briefs/aris/aris_part_two.htm

Kraushaar, O. F. (1972). *American nonpublic schools: Patterns of diversity.* Baltimore: Johns Hopkins University Press.

Lakoff, G. (1973). Hedges: A study in meaning criteria and the logic of fuzzy concepts. *Journal of Philosophical Logic, 2*(4), 458–508.

Lam, P. (2002). As the flocks gather: How religion affects voluntary association participation. *Journal for the Scientific Study of Religion, 41*(3), 405–422.

Lambert, Y. (2004). A turning point in religious evolution in Europe. *Journal of Contemporary Religion, 19*(1), 29–45.

Lamont, M. (1992). *Money, morals, and manners: The culture of the French and American upper-middle class.* Chicago: University of Chicago Press.

Lamont, M., & Fournier, M. (Eds.). (1992). *Cultivating differences: Symbolic boundaries and the making of inequality.* Chicago: University of Chicago Press.

Lechner, F. J. (1991). The case against secularization: A rebuttal. *Social Forces, 69*(4), 1103–1119.

Lehrer, E. L. (1999). Religion as a determinant of educational attainment: An economic perspective. *Social Science Research, 28*(4), 358–379.

Lincoln, Y. S., & Guba, E. G. (1985). *Naturalistic inquiry.* Beverly Hills, CA: Sage.

Lines, P. M. (1988). Treatment of religion in public schools and the impact on private education. In T. James & H. M. Levin (Eds.), *Comparing public and private schools: Vol. 1. Institutions and organizations* (pp. 67–94). New York: The Falmer Press.

Lockerbie, D. B. (1996). *From candy sales to committed donors: A guide to financing Christian schools.* Milwaukee, WI: Christian Stewardship Association.

Lohfink, G. (1984). *Jesus and community: The social dimension of Christian faith* (J. P. Gavin, Trans.). Philadelphia: Fortress Press. (Original work published 1982)

Lopatto, P. (1985). *Religion and the presidential election.* New York: Praeger.

Luckmann, T. (1967). *The invisible religion: The problem of religion in modern society.* New York: Macmillan.

Lynd, R. S., & Lynd, H. M. (1929). *Middletown: A study in American culture.* New York: Harcourt, Brace & Company.

Lynn, R. W. (1964). *Protestant strategies in education.* New York: Association Press.

Lynn, R. W., & Wright, E. (1980). *The big little school: Two hundred years of the Sunday School* (2nd ed.). Birmingham, AL: Religious Education Press.

Macedo, S. (2000). *Diversity and distrust: Civic education in a multicultural democracy.* Cambridge, MA: Harvard University Press.

Manza, J., & Brooks, C. (1997). The religious factor in U.S. presidential elections, 1960–1992. *American Journal of Sociology, 103*(1), 38–81.

Marcum, J. P. (1999). Measuring church attendance: A further look. *Review of Religious Research, 41*(2), 121–129.

Marcus, G. E., Sullivan, J. L., Theiss–Morse, E., & Wood, S. L. (1995). *With malice toward some: How people make civil liberties judgments.* New York: Cambridge University Press.

Marler, P. M., & Hadaway, C. K. (1993). New church development and denominational growth, 1950–1988. In D. A. Roozen & C. K. Hadaway (Eds.), *Church and denominational growth* (pp. 47–86). Nashville, TN: Abingdon.

Marler, P. M., & Hadaway, C. K. (1999). Testing the attendance gap in a conservative church. *Sociology of Religion, 60*(2), 175–186.

Marler, P. M. & Hadaway, C. K. (2002). "Being religious" or "being spiritual" in America: A zero-sum proposition? *Journal for the Scientific Study of Religion, 41*(2), 289–300.

Marler, P. M., & Roozen, D. A. (1993). From church tradition to consumer choice: The Gallup surveys of the unchurched American. In D. A. Roozen & C. K. Hadaway (Eds.), *Church and denominational growth* (pp. 253–277). Nashville, TN: Abingdon.

Marsden, G. M. (1975). From fundamentalism to evangelicalism: A historical analysis. In D. F. Wells & J. D. Woodbridge (Eds.), *The evangelicals: What they believe, who they are, where they are changing* (pp. 122–142). Nashville, TN: Abingdon.

Marsden, G. M. (1980). *Fundamentalism and American culture: The shaping of Twentieth-century evangelicalism 1870–1925.* Oxford: Oxford University Press.

Marsden, G. M. (1991). *Understanding fundamentalism and evangelicalism.* Grand Rapids, MI: Eerdmans.

Marsden, G. M. (1999). Christianity and cultures: Transforming Niebuhr's categories. *Insights, 115*(1), 4–15.

Martin, D. (1969). *The religious and the secular: Studies in secularization.* New York: Schocken Books.

Martin, D. (1978). *A general theory of secularization.* New York: Harper & Row.

Martin, D. (1997). *Reflections on sociology and theology.* Oxford: Clarendon Press.

Marty, M. E. (1979). Forward. In D. R. Hoge & D. A. Roozen (Eds.), *Understanding church growth and decline: 1950–1978* (pp. 9–15). New York: Pilgrim Press.

Mathisen, J. A. (2004). Tell me again: Why do churches grow? *Books and Culture, 10*(3), 18–20, 41–42.

Maykut, P., & Morehouse, R. (1994). *Beginning qualitative research: A philosophic and practical guide.* London: Falmer Press.

McGarty, C. (1999). *Categorization in social psychology.* London: Sage.

McGrath, A. E. (1996). *A passion for truth: The intellectual coherence of evangelicalism.* Downers Grove, IL: InterVarsity Press.

Melton, J. G. (1985). Spiritualization and reaffirmation: What really happens when prophecy fails. *American Studies, 26*(2), 17–29.

Menendez, A. J. (1998). *Who goes to nonpublic schools: A study of U. S. census data.* Silver Spring, MD: Americans for Religious Liberty.

Merrill, R. M., Lyon, J. L., & Jensen, W. J. (2003). Lack of a secularizing influence of education on religious activity and parity among Mormons. *Journal for the Scientific Study of Religion, 41*(1), 113–124.

Miedema, S. (2000). The aims for religiously inspired urban schools: Dialogue, solidarity and personal identity formation. *International Journal of Education and Religion, 1,* 89–99.

Milbank, J. (1999). The ethics of self-sacrifice. *First Things, 91,* 33–38

Miller, S. (2004). Rational choice: Why monotheism makes sense. *Christian Century, 121*(12), 30–36.

Miner, B. (1998). Why I don't vouch for vouchers. *Educational Leadership, 56*(2), 40–42.

Moberg, D. O. (1975). Fundamentalists and evangelicals in society. In D. F. Wells & J. D. Woodbridge (Eds.), *The evangelicals: What they believe, who they are, where they are changing* (pp. 143–169). Nashville, TN: Abingdon.

Moberg, D. O. (1977). *The Great Reversal: Evangelism and social concern* (rev. ed.). Philadelphia: Lippincott.

Monsma, S. V., & Soper, J. C. (1997). *The challenge of pluralism: Church and state in five democracies.* Lanham, MD: Rowman & Littlefield.

Montgomery, J. D. (2003). A formalization and test of the religious economies model. *American Sociological Review, 68*(5), 782–809.

Murphy, C. (1981). Protestantism and the evangelicals. *Wilson Quarterly, 5*(4), 105–116.

Neuhaus, R. J. (1984). *The naked public square: Religion and democracy in America.* Grand Rapids, MI: Eerdmans.

Nevin, D., & Bills, R. E. (1976). *The schools that fear built: Segregationist academies in the South.* Washington, DC: Acropolis Books.

Newbigen, L. (1989). *The gospel in a pluralist society.* Grand Rapids, MI: Eerdmans.

Nietz, J. A. (1952). Some findings from analyses of old textbooks. *History of Education Journal, 4,* 79–87.

Noll, M. A. (1994). *The scandal of the evangelical mind.* Grand Rapids, MI: Eerdmans.

288   *American Evangelicals and Religious Diversity*

Noll, M. A. (1995). The history of an encounter: Roman Catholics and Protestant evangelicals. In C. W. Colson & R. J. Neuhaus (Eds.), *Evangelicals and Catholics together: Toward a common mission* (pp. 81–114). Dallas: Word.

Noll, M. A. (2000a). *American evangelical Christianity: An introduction.* Malden, MA: Blackwell.

Noll, M. A. (2000b). Five years and running. *Books and Culture, 6*(5), 5.

Noll, M. A. (2003). *Understanding American Evangelicals.* Retrieved February 8, 2005, from http://www.eppc.org/printVersion/print_pub.asp?pubID=1943

Nordin, V. D., & Turner, W. L. (1980). More than segregation academies: The growing Protestant fundamentalist schools. *Phi Delta Kappan, 61*(6), 391–394.

Oakes, P. J., Haslam, S. A., & Turner, J. C. (1994). *Stereotyping and social reality.* Cambridge, MA: Blackwell.

O'Keefe, J. M. (2000). The challenge of pluralism: Articulating a rationale for religiously diverse urban Roman Catholic schools in the United States. *International Journal of Education and Religion, 1,* 64–88.

Oldfield, D. M. (1996). *The Right and the righteous: The Christian Right confronts the Republican Party.* Lanham, MD: Rowman & Littlefield.

Olsen, R. E. (1995). Postconservative evangelicals greet the postmodern age. *Christian Century, 112,* 480–483.

Olson, D. V. A. (1993). Fellowship ties and the transmission of religious identity. In J. W. Carroll & W. C. Roof (Eds.), *Beyond establishment: Protestant identity in a post–Protestant age* (pp. 32–53). Louisville, KY: Westminster/John Knox.

Panikkar, R. (1979). The myth of pluralism: The tower of Babel—A meditation on non-violence. *Cross Currents, 29*(2), 197–230.

Park, J. Z., & Smith, C. (2000). "To whom much has been given . . .": Religious capital and community voluntarism among churchgoing Protestants. *Journal for the Scientific Study of Religion, 39*(3), 272–286.

Parsons, P. F. (1987). *Inside America's Christian schools.* Macon, GA: Mercer University Press.

Parsons, T. (1966). *Societies: Evolutionary and comparative perspectives.* Englewood Cliffs, NJ: Prentice Hall.

Peck, M. S. (1978). *The road less traveled: A new psychology of love, traditional values, and spiritual growth.* New York: Simon & Schuster.

Pelikan, J. (1971). *The emergence of the Catholic tradition (100–600).* Chicago: University of Chicago Press.

Penning, J. M., & Smidt, C. E. (2002). *Evangelicalism: The next generation.* Grand Rapids, MI: Baker Academic.

Peshkin, A. (1986). *God's choice: The total world of a fundamentalist Christian school.* Chicago: University of Chicago Press.

Peshkin, A. (1987, Fall). The truth and consequences of fundamentalist Christian schooling. *Free Inquiry, 8,* 5–10.

Pew Forum on Religion and Public Life. (2002). *Religion and politics: Contention and consensus.* Retrieved December 27, 2004, from http://pewforum.org/publications/surveys/religion–politics.pdf

Pew Forum on Religion and Public Life. (2005). *Views of Muslim-Americans hold steady after London bombings.* Retrieved July 27, 2005, from http://pewforum.org/publications/surveys/muslims–survey–2005.pdf

Pfeffer, L., & Stokes, A. P. (1964). *Church and state in the United States.* New York: Harper & Row.

Phillips, T. R., & Okholm, D. L. (Eds.). (1996). *The nature of confession: Evangelicals & postliberals in conversation.* Downers Grove, IL: InterVarsity Press.

Piaget, J. (1950). *The psychology of intelligence.* (M. Piercy & D. E. Berlyne, Trans.). London: Routledge & Paul. (Original work published in 1947)

Presser, S., & Stinson, L. (1998). Data collection mode and social desirability bias in self-reported religious attendance. *American Sociological Review, 63*(1), 137–145.

Princeton Religion Research Center. (1978). *The unchurched American.* Princeton, NJ: The Gallup Organization.

Princeton Religion Research Center. (1996). Just how many evangelicals are there in the U.S. today? *Emerging Trends, 18*(4), 1–2.

Putnam, R. D. (2000). *Bowling alone: The collapse and revival of American community.* New York: Simon & Schuster.

Quebedeaux, R. (1974). *The young evangelicals: Revolution in orthodoxy.* New York: Harper & Row.

Quebedeaux, R., & Sawatsky, R. (Eds.). (1979). *Evangelical–Unification dialogue.* Barytown, NY: Rose of Sharon Press.

Rausch, T. P. (2002). Another step forward: Catholics and evangelicals take a new look at each other. *America, 187*(2), 7–9.

Reese, W. J. (1982). The public schools and the great gates of hell. *Educational Theory, 32*(1), 9–17.

Reese, W. J. (1985). Soldiers for Christ in the army of God: The Christian school movement in America. *Educational Theory, 35,* 175–194.

Reese, T. J. (Ed.). (2000). Gallup Poll explores anti-Catholic bias in U.S. *America, 182*(14), 4–5.

Regnerus, M. D., & Smith, C. (1998). Selective deprivatization among American religious traditions: The reversal of the Great Reversal. *Social Forces, 76*(4), 1347–1372.

Reimer, S. (1996). North American evangelicalism: A look at regional and national variation in evangelical religiosity (Doctoral dissertation, University of Notre Dame, 1996). *Dissertation Abstracts International, 57,* 4156.

Reimer, S., & Park, J. Z. (2001). Tolerant (in)civility? A longitudinal analysis of white conservative Protestants' willingness to grant civil liberties. *Journal for the Scientific Study of Religion, 49*(4), 735–745.

Religion & Ethics NewsWeekly (2004a). *Conversation with Anna Greenberg and John Green.* Retrieved April 2, 2005, from http://www.pbs.org/wnet/religionandethics/week733/p-exclusive.html

Religion & Ethics NewsWeekly (2004b). *Interview: Mark Noll.* Retrieved April 2, 2005, from http://www.pbs.org/wnet/religionandethics/week733/interview.html

Ricoeur, P. (1992). *Oneself as another* (K. Blamey, Trans.). Chicago: University of Chicago Press. (Original work published 1990)

Riesebrodt, M. (2001). Review essay: Sociology for seminarians [Review of the book *The Blackwell companion to sociology of religion*]. *American Journal of Sociology, 107*(3), 808–815.

Riesebrodt, M. (2003). *"Religion": Just another modern Western construction?* Retrieved December 4, 2005, from http://marty-center.uchicago.edu/webforum/122003/commentary.shtml

Rippa, S. A. (1992). *Education in a free society: An American history* (7th ed). New York: Longman.

Robertson, R., & Chirico, J. (1985). Humanity, globalization, and worldwide religious resurgence: A theoretical exploration. *Sociological Analysis, 46*(3), 219–242.

Roof, W. C. (1989). Multiple religious switching: A research note. *Journal for the Scientific Study of Religion, 28*(4), 530–535.

Roof, W. C. (1999). *Spiritual marketplace: Baby Boomers and the remaking of American religion.* Princeton, NJ: Princeton University Press.

Roof, W. C. (2003). Religion and spirituality: Toward an integrated analysis. In M. Dillon (Ed.), *Handbook of the sociology of religion* (pp. 207–224). New York: Cambridge University Press.

Roof, W. C., & McKinney, W. (1987). *American mainline religion: Its changing shape and future.* New Brunswick, NJ: Rutgers University Press.

Roozen, D. A. (1993). Denominations grow as individuals join congregations. In D. A. Roozen & C. K. Hadaway (Eds.), *Church and denominational growth* (pp. 15–35). Nashville, TN: Abingdon.

Roozen, D. A., & Carroll, J. W. (1979). Recent trends in church membership and participation: An introduction. In D. R. Hoge & D. A. Roozen (Eds.), *Understanding church growth and decline: 1950–1978* (pp. 21–41). New York: Pilgrim Press.

Rose, S. D. (1988). *Keeping them out of the hands of Satan: Evangelical schooling in America.* New York: Routledge.

Rudin, A. J., & Wilson, M. R. (Eds.). (1987). *A time to speak: The evangelical–Jewish encounter.* Grand Rapids, MI: Eerdmans.

Sandeen, E. P. (1967). Toward a historical interpretation of fundamentalism. *Church History, 36*(1), 66–83.

Sanneh, L. (2004). Do Christians and Muslims worship the same God? *Christian Century, 121*(9), 35–36.

Schaller, L. E. (1995). Will your congregation be alive in 2025? *The Clergy Journal, 72*(1), 20–23.

Schmalzbauer, J. (1999). [Review of the book *American evangelicalism: Embattled and thriving*]. *Sociology of Religion, 60,* 336–337.

Schneider, H. W. (1952). *Religion in 20th century America.* Cambridge, MA: Harvard University Press.

Schwalbe, M. L., & Mason-Schrock, D. (1996). Identity work as group process. *Advances in Group Processes, 13,* 113–147.

Schweitzer, F. (2000). A stronger case for religion: Perspectives on multicultural education and on religiously affiliated schools. *International Journal of Education and Religion, 1,* 47–63.

Sewell, W. H. (1992). A theory of structure: Duality, agency, and transformation. *American Journal of Sociology, 98*(1), 1–29.

Sherkat, D. E. (1998). Counterculture or continuity? Competing influences on Baby Boomers' religious orientations and participation. *Social Forces, 76*(3), 1087–1114.

Sherkat, D. E. (1999). Tracking the "other": Dynamics and composition of "other" religions in the General Social Survey, 1973–1996. *Journal for the Scientific Study of Religion, 38*(4), 551–560.

Sherkat, D. E. (2001). Tracking the restructuring of American religion: Religious affiliation and patterns of religious mobility, 1973–1998. *Social Forces, 79*(4), 1459–1493.

Sherkat, D. E. (2004). *Beyond belief: Atheism, agnosticism, and theistic certainty in the United States.* Paper presented at the annual meeting of the Society for the Scientific Study of Religion. Kansas City, MO.

Sherkat, D. E., & Blocker, T. J. (1997). Explaining the political and personal consequences of protest. *Social Forces, 75*(3), 1049–1076.

Sherkat, D. F., & Darnell, A. (1999). The effect of parents' fundamentalism on children's educational attainment: Examining differences by gender and children's fundamentalism. *Journal for the Scientific Study of Religion, 38*(1), 23–35.

Shibley, M. (1996). *Resurgent evangelicalism in the United States: Mapping cultural change since 1970.* Columbia: University Press of South Carolina.

Short, C. R. (2001). The stated goals and purposes of Christian schools and the reasons parents give for choosing them (Doctoral dissertation, College of William and Mary, 2001). *Dissertation Abstracts International, 62,* 418.

Sider, R. J. (2005). *The scandal of the evangelical conscience: Why are evangelicals living just like the rest of the world?* Grand Rapids, MI: Baker.

Sikkink, D. (1998). "I just say I'm a Christian": Symbolic boundaries and identity formation among church-going Protestants. In D. Jacobsen & W. V. Trollinger (Eds.), *Re-forming the center: American Protestantism, 1900 to the present* (pp. 49–71). Grand Rapids, MI: Eerdmans.

Sikkink, D. (1999). The social sources of alienation from public schools. *Social Forces, 78*(1), 51–86.

Sikkink, D. (2001). Diversity in Christian schools [Unabridged version]. *Education Matters, 1*(2). Retrieved February 19, 2005, from http://www.educationnext .org/unabridged/20012/sikkink.pdf

Sikkink, D. (2003). The loyal opposition: Evangelicals and public schools. In M. Cromartie (Ed.), *A public faith: Evangelicals and civic engagement* (pp. 173–186). Lanham, MD: Rowman & Littlefield.

Sikkink, D. (2004). The hidden civic lessons of public and private schools. *Catholic Education: A Journal of Inquiry and Practice, 7*(3), 229–365.

Sikkink, D., & Mihut, A. (2000). Religion and the politics of multiculturalism. *Religion and Education, 27*(2), 30–44.

Simmel, G. (1955). *Conflict* (K. H. Wolff, Trans.). Glencoe, IL: Free Press. (Original work published 1923)

Simon, B. (1997). Self and group in modern society: Ten theses on the individual self and the collective self. In R. Spears, P. J. Oakes, N. Ellemers, & S. A. Haslam (Eds.), *The social psychology of stereotyping and group life* (pp. 318–335). Cambridge, MA: Blackwell.

Skerry, P. (1980). Christian schools versus the I.R.S. *Public Interest, 61,* 18–41.

Smedley, A. (1998). "Race" and the construction of human identity. *American Anthropologist, 100*(3), 690–702.

Smidt, C. (1999). Religion and civic engagement: A comparative analysis. *Annals of the American Academy of Political and Social Science, 565,* 176–192.

Smidt, C., & Penning, J. M. (1982). Religious commitment, political conservatism, and political and social tolerance in the United States: A longitudinal analysis. *Sociological Analysis, 43*(3), 231–246.

Smith, C. (with Emerson, M., Gallagher, S., Kennedy, P., & Sikkink, D.). (1997). The myth of culture wars: The case of American Protestantism. In R. H. Williams (Ed.), *Cultural wars in American politics: Critical reviews of a popular myth* (pp. 175–195). New York: Aldine de Gruyter.

Smith, C. (with Emerson, M., Gallagher, S., Kennedy, P., & Sikkink, D.). (1998). *American evangelicalism: Embattled and thriving.* Chicago: University of Chicago Press.

Smith, C. (2000). *Christian America? What evangelicals really want.* Berkeley: University of California Press.

Smith, C. (2003a). Introduction: Rethinking the secularization of American public life. In C. Smith (Ed.), *The secular revolution: Power, interests, and conflict in the secularization of American public life* (pp. 1–96). Berkeley: University of California Press.

Smith, C. (2003b). *Moral, believing animals: Human personhood and culture.* New York: Oxford University Press.

Smith, C. (with Denton, M. L.). (2005). *Soul searching: The religious and spiritual lives of American teenagers.* New York: Oxford University Press.

Smith, C., Denton, M. L, Faris, R., & Regnerus, M. (2002). Mapping American adolescent religious participation. *Journal for the Scientific Study of Religion, 41*(4), 597–612.

Smith, C., Faris, R., & Denton, M. L. (2004). *Are American youth alienated from organized religion? A research report of the National Study of Youth and Religion, Number 6.* Retrieved March 22, 2005, from http://www.youthandreligion.org/publications/docs/Alienation.pdf

Smith, C., & Sikkink, D. (1999). Is private school privatizing? *First Things, 92,* 16–20.

Smith, C., & Sikkink, D. (2003). Social predictors of retention in and switching from the religious faith of family of origin: Another look using religious tradition self–identification. *Review of Religious Research, 45*(2), 188–206.

Smith, C., & Woodberry, R. D. (2001). Sociology of religion. In J. R. Blau (Ed.), *The Blackwell companion to sociology* (pp. 100–113). Malden, MA: Blackwell.

Smith, J. B. (1995). *Embracing the love of God: The path and promise of Christian life.* San Francisco: HarperSanFrancisco.

Smith, T. L. (1957). *Revivalism and social reform: American Protestantism on the eve of the Civil War.* Baltimore: Johns Hopkins University Press.

Smith, T. L. (1967). Protestant schooling and American nationality. *Journal of American History, 53*(4), 679–95.

Smith, T. L. (1980). *Revivalism and social reform* (rev. ed.). Baltimore: Johns Hopkins University Press.

Smith, T. L. (1987). Evangelical Christians and American culture. In A. J. Rudin & M. R. Wilson (Eds.), *A time to speak: The evangelical–Jewish encounter* (pp. 58–74). Grand Rapids, MI: Eerdmans.

Smith, T. W. (1996). *A survey of the religious right: Views on politics, society, Jews and other minorities.* New York: American Jewish Committee.

Smith, T. W. (1998). A review of church attendance measures. *American Sociological Review, 63*(1), 131–136.

Smith, T. W. (2002). Religious diversity in America: The emergence of Muslims, Buddhists, Hindus, and others. *Journal for the Scientific Study of Religion, 41*(3), 577–585.

Snow, D. A., & Machalek, R. (1982). On the presumed fragility of unconventional beliefs. *Journal for the Scientific Study of Religion, 21*(1), 15–26.

Solzhenitsyn, A. I. (1975). *The Gulag Archipelago, 1918–1956: An experiment in literary investigation, Vol. 2.* (T. P. Whitney, Trans.). New York: Harper & Row. (Original work published in 1974)

Somers, M. R. (1994). The narrative constitution of identity: A relational and network approach. *Theory and Society, 23*(5), 605–649.

Sommers, S. C. (2001). Church as subculture: Implications for the pluriform confession of Christ in modern pluralistic contexts (Doctoral dissertation, Fuller Theological Seminary, 2001). *Dissertation Abstracts International, 62,* 642.

Spittler, R. P. (1985). Scripture and the theological enterprise. In R. K. Johnston (Ed.), *The use of the Bible in theology: Evangelical options* (pp. 56–77). Atlanta, GA: John Knox.

Stackhouse, J. G. (2001). Afterword: An agenda for an evangelical theology of religions. In J. G. Stackhouse (Ed.), *No other gods before me? Evangelicals and the challenge of world religions* (pp. 189–201). Grand Rapids, MI: Baker Academic.

Stark, R. (1997). *The rise of Christianity: How the obscure, marginal Jesus movement became the dominant religious force in the Western world in a few centuries.* San Francisco: HarperSanFrancisco.

Stark, R. (1999). Secularization, R. I. P. *Sociology of Religion, 60,* 249–273.

Stark, R., & Bainbridge, W. S. (1985). *The future of religion: Secularization, revival, and cult formation.* Berkeley: University of California Press.

Stark, R., & Finke, R. (2000). *Acts of faith: Explaining the human side of religion.* Berkeley: University of California Press

Stark, R., Finke, R., & Iannaccone, L. R. (1995). Pluralism and piety: England and Wales, 1851. *Journal for the Scientific Study of Religion, 34*(4), 431–444.

Stassen, G. H. (1996). Concrete Christological norms for transformation. In G. H. Stassen (Ed.), *Authentic transformation: A new vision of Christ and culture* (pp. 127–189). Nashville, TN: Abingdon.

Steensland, B., Park, J. Z., Regnerus, M. D., Robinson, L. D., Wilcox, W. B., & Woodberry, R. D. (2000). The measure of American religion: Toward improving the state of the art. *Social Forces, 79*(1), 291–318.

Stokes, A. P. (1950). *Church and state in the United States, Vol. 3.* New York: Harper and Brothers.

Stott, J. R. W. (1976). *Baptism and fullness: The work of the Holy Spirit today* (2nd ed.). Downers Grove, IL: InterVarsity Press.

Stouffer, S. A. (1955). *Communism, conformity, and civil liberties: A cross-section of the nation speaks its mind.* Garden City, NY: Doubleday.

Stout, H. S. (1991). *The divine dramatist: George Whitefield and the rise of modern evangelicalism.* Grand Rapids, MI: Eerdmans.

Stout, J. (2004). *Democracy and tradition.* Princeton, NJ: Princeton University Press.

Stransky, T. F. (1988, March). A look at evangelical Protestantism. *Theology, News and Notes,* pp. 21–26.

Stroup, G. W. (1998). The spirit of pluralism. In W. Brueggemann & G. W. Stroup (Eds.), *Many voices, one God: Being faithful in a pluralistic world* (pp. 167–178). Louisville, KY: Westminster/John Knox.

Stryker, S., & Serpe, R. T. (1982). Commitment, identity salience, and role behavior: Theory and research example. In W. Ickes & E. S. Knowles (Eds.), *Personality, roles, and social behavior* (pp. 199–218). New York: Springer-Verlag.

Stump, R. W. (1998). The effects of geographical variability on Protestant church membership trends, 1980–1990. *Journal for the Scientific Study of Religion, 37*(4), 636–651.

Sullins, D. P. (1993). Switching close to home: Volatility or coherence in Protestant affiliation patterns? *Social Forces, 72*(2), 399–419.

Sullivan, J. L., Piereson, J., & Marcus, G. E. (1982). *Political tolerance and American democracy.* Chicago: University of Chicago Press.

Sumner, W. G. (1906). *Folkways: A study of the sociological importance of usages, manners, customs, mores, and morals.* Boston: Ginn.

Swatos, W. H., & Christiano, K. J. (1999). Secularization theory: The course of a concept. *Sociology of Religion, 60*(3), 209–228.

Swidler, A. (1986). Culture in action: Symbols and strategies. *American Sociological Review, 51*(2), 273–286.

Swidler, A. (2001). *Talk of love: How culture matters.* Chicago: University of Chicago Press.

Tajfel, H. (1981). *Human groups and social categories: Studies in social psychology.* New York: Cambridge University Press.

Tajfel, H., & Turner, J. C. (1979). An integrative theory of intergroup conflict. In W. G. Austin & S. Worchel (Eds.), *The social psychology of intergroup relations* (pp. 33–47). Monterey, CA: Brooks/Cole.

Tamney, J. B., & Johnson, S. D. (1997). Christianity and public book burning. *Review of Religious Research, 38*(3), 263–271.

Taylor, C. (1991). *The ethics of authenticity.* Cambridge, MA: Harvard University Press.

Taylor, C. (1994). The politics of recognition. In A. Gutmann (Ed.), *Multiculturalism: Examining the politics of recognition* (pp. 25–73). Princeton, NJ: Princeton University Press.

Templeton, A. R. (1998). Human races: A genetic and evolutionary perspective. *American Anthropologist, 100*(3), 632–650.

Thompson, W. L., Carroll, J. W., & Hoge, D. R. (1993). Growth or decline in Presbyterian congregations. In D. A. Roozen & C. K. Hadaway (Eds.), *Church and denominational growth* (pp. 188–207). Nashville, TN: Abingdon.

Tilly, C. (2003, February 2). Identities and boundary activation [Msg 1]. Message posted to http://peregrin.jmu.edu/~brysonbp/symbound/conf2003/vforum2 .html

T–NET. (2003). *What is T–Net.* Retrieved February 24, 2003, from http://www.tnetwork .com/WhatIs.htm

Todd, E. M. (2003). [Review of the book *God is dead*]. Retrieved October 12, 2004, from http://www.churchofscotland.org.uk/boards/reviewreform/downloads/ rrgodisdead.txt

Tschannen, O. (1991). The secularization paradigm: A systematization. *Journal for the Scientific Study of Religion, 30*(4), 395–415.

Tumminia, D. (1998). How prophecy never fails: Interpretive reason in a flying–saucer group. *Sociology of Religion, 59*(2), 157–170.

Tuntiya, N. (2005). Fundamentalist religious affiliation and support for civil liberties: A critical reexamination. *Sociological Inquiry, 75*(2), 153–176.

Turner, J. C. (1982). Towards a cognitive redefinition of the social group. In H. Tajfel (Ed.), *Social identity and intergroup relations* (pp. 15–40). New York: Cambridge University Press.

Turner, J. C. (1999). Something to be reckoned with: The evangelical mind awakens. *Commonweal, 126*(1), 11–13.

Turner, J. C. (with Hogg, M. A., Oakes, P. J., Reicher, S. D., & Wetherell, M. S.). (1987). *Rediscovering the social group: A self-categorization theory.* New York: Basil Blackwell.

Turner, J. C., Oakes, P. J., Haslam, S. A., & McGarty, C. (1994). Self and collective: Cognition and social context. *Personality and Social Psychology Bulletin, 20*(5), 454–463.

Turner, W. L. (1979). Reasons for enrollment in religious schools: A case study of three recently established fundamentalist schools in Kentucky and Wisconsin (Doctoral dissertation, University of Wisconsin, 1979). *Dissertation Abstracts International, 40,* 4344.

Tyack, D. (1966). The kingdom of God and the common school. *Harvard Educational Review, 36*(4), 447–469.

Veenstra, G. (2002). Explicating social capital: Trust and participation in the civil space. *Canadian Journal of Sociology, 27*(4), 547–572.

van der Ven, J. A. (2000). Multiculturalism in education: Politics of recognition. *International Journal of Education and Religion, 1,* 19–46.

Verba, S., Schlozman, K. L., & Brady, H. E. (1995). *Voice and equality: Civic voluntarism in American politics.* Cambridge, MA: Harvard University Press.

Vignoles, V. L. (2004). Modelling identity motives using multilevel regression. In G. M. Breakewell (Ed.), *Doing social psychology research* (pp. 174–204). Malden, MA: Blackwell.

Vignoles, V. L., Chryssochoou, X., & Breakwell, G. M. (2002). Evaluating models of identity motivation: Self-esteem is not the whole story. *Self and Identity, 1,* 201–218.

Voas, D., Olson, D. V. A., & Crockett, A. (2002). Religious pluralism and participation: Why previous research is wrong. *American Sociological Review, 67,* 212–230.

Volf, M. (1994). Soft difference: Theological reflections on the relation between church and culture in 1 Peter. *Ex Auditu, 10,* 15–30.

Volf, M. (1996). *Exclusion and embrace: A theological exploration of identity, otherness, and reconciliation.* Nashville, TN: Abingdon.

Volf, M. (2005a, August 4). *Speaking of faith: Religion and our world in crisis—Christianity and violence, Q&A with Miroslav Volf.* Retrieved December 8, 2005, from http://www.publicradio.org/tools/media/player/speakingoffaith/20040311_volf-qa.ram

Volf, M. (2005b, April). *A voice of one's own: Public faith in a pluralistic world.* Paper presented at "The New Religious Pluralism and Democracy" conference, Georgetown University, Washington, DC.

Wacker, G. (1984). Uneasy in Zion: Evangelicals in postmodern society. In G. Marsden (Ed.), *Evangelicalism and modern America* (pp. 16–28). Grand Rapids, MI: Eerdmans.

Wacker, G. (2001). *Heaven below: Early Pentecostals and American culture.* Cambridge, MA: Harvard University Press

Wacker, G. (2003). Religion in nineteenth-century America. In J. Butler, G. Wacker, & R. Balmer (Eds.), *Religion in American life: A short history* (pp. 165–327). New York: Oxford University Press.

Wagner, M. B. (1990). *God's schools: Choice and compromise in American society.* New Brunswick, NJ: Rutgers University Press.

Wagner, M. B. (1997). Generic conservative Christianity: The demise of denominationalism in Christian schools. *Journal for the Scientific Study of Religion, 36*(1), 13–24.

Wald, K. D. (1997). *Religion and politics in the United States* (3rd ed.). Washington, DC: Congressional Quarterly Press.

Wallace, A. F. C. (1966). *Religion: An anthropological view.* New York: Random House.

Warner, R. S. (1988). *New wine in old wineskins: Evangelicals and liberals in a small-town church.* Berkeley: University of California Press.

Warner, R. S. (1991). Starting over: Reflections on American religion. *Christian Century, 108*(25), 811–813.

Warner, R. S. (1993). Work in progress toward a new paradigm for the sociological study of religion in the United States. *American Journal of Sociology, 98*(5), 1044–1093.

Warner, R. S. (1998). Approaching religious diversity: Barriers, byways, and beginnings. *Sociology of Religion, 59*(3), 193–215.

Warner, R. S. (2004). Coming to America: Immigrants and the faith they bring. *Christian Century, 121*(3), 20–23.

Warner, R. S., & Wittner, J. G. (1998). *Gatherings in diaspora: Religious communities and the new immigration.* Philadelphia: Temple University Press.

Warren, R. (2002). *The purpose driven life: What on earth am I here for?* Grand Rapids, MI: Zondervan.

Webber, R. E. (1978). *Common roots: A call to evangelical maturity.* Grand Rapids, MI: Zondervan.

Webber, R. E. (2002). *The younger evangelicals: Facing the challenges of the new world.* Grand Rapids, MI: Baker.

Weber, T. P. (1991). Premillennialism and the branches of evangelicalism. In D. W. Dayton & R. K. Johnston (Eds.), *The variety of American evangelicalism* (pp. 5–17). Knoxville: University of Tennessee Press.

Weigel, G. (2002). A better concept of freedom. *First Things, 121,* 14–20.

Welch, M. R., Sikkink, D., Sartain, E., & Bond, C. (2004). Trust in God and trust in man: The ambivalent role of religion in shaping dimensions of social trust. *Journal for the Scientific Study of Religion, 43*(3), 317–343.

Wells, D. F. (1987). No offense: I am an evangelical. In A. J. Rudin & M. R. Wilson (Eds.), *A time to speak: The evangelical–Jewish encounter* (pp. 20–39). Grand Rapids, MI: Eerdmans.

Wilcox, C. (1988). The Christian right in twentieth century America: Continuity and change. *Review of Politics, 50*(4), 659–681.

Wilcox, C. (1990). Religion and politics among white evangelicals: The impact of religious variables on political attitudes. *Review of Religious Research, 32,* 27–42.

Wilcox, C. (1996). *Onward Christian soldiers: The religious right in American politics.* Boulder, CO: Westview.

Wilcox, C., & Jelen, T. (1990). Evangelicals and political tolerance. *American Politics Quarterly, 18*(1), 25–46.

Wilson, B. (1968). Religion and the churches in contemporary America. In W. G. McLoughlin & R. N. Bellah (Eds.), *Religion in America* (pp. 73–110). Boston: Houghton Mifflin.

Wilson, B. (1976). *Contemporary transformations of religion.* London: Oxford University Press.

Wilson, J. (2003). Correcting misconceptions about evangelicals and civil society. In M. Cromartie (Ed.), *A public faith: Evangelicals and civic engagement* (pp. 1–10). Lanham, MD: Rowman & Littlefield.

Wilson, J., & Janoski, T. (1995). The contribution of religion to volunteer work. *Sociology of Religion, 56*(2), 694–713.

Wilson, J., & Musick, M. (1997). Who cares? Toward an integrated theory of volunteer work. *American Sociological Review, 62*(5), 694–713.

Wilson, J., & Sherkat, D. E. (1994). Returning to the fold. *Journal for the Scientific Study of Religion, 33*(2), 148–161.

Wilson, J. M. (2000). *Group identity and social trust in the American public.* Paper presented at the annual meeting of the American Political Science Association, Washington, DC. August 31–September 3.

Wolfe, A. (2000, October). The opening of the evangelical mind. *Atlantic Monthly, 286,* 55–76.

Wolfe, A. (2003). *The transformation of American religion: How we actually live our faith.* New York: Free Press.

Wolterstorff, N. (1976). *Reason within the bounds of religion.* Grand Rapids, MI: Eerdmans.

Woodberry, R. D., & Smith, C. (1998). Fundamentalism, et al.: Conservative Protestants in America. *Annual Review of Sociology, 24,* 25–56.

Wuthnow, R. (1985). Science and the sacred. In P. E. Hammond (Ed.), *The sacred in a secular age: Toward revision in the scientific study of religion* (pp. 187–203). Berkeley: University of California Press.

Wuthnow, R. (1988a). *The restructuring of American religion: Society and faith since World War II.* Princeton, NJ: Princeton University Press.

Wuthnow, R. (1988b). Sociology of religion. In N. J. Smelser (Ed.), *Handbook of sociology* (pp. 473–509). Newbury Park, CA: Sage.

Wuthnow, R. (1991). *Acts of compassion: Caring for ourselves and helping others.* Princeton, NJ: Princeton University Press.

Wuthnow, R. (1998). *After heaven: Spirituality in America since the 1950s.* Berkeley: University of California Press.

Wuthnow, R. (1999). Mobilizing civic engagement: The changing impact of religious involvement. In T. Skocpol & M. Fiorina (Eds.), *Civic engagement in American democracy.* Washington, DC: Brookings Institution.

Wuthnow, R. (2003). *All in sync: How music and art are revitalizing American religion.* Berkeley: University of California Press.

Wuthnow, R. (2004). Presidential address 2003: The challenge of diversity. *Journal for the Scientific Study of Religion, 43*(2), 159–170.

Wuthnow, R. (2005a). *America and the challenges of religious diversity.* Princeton, NJ: Princeton University Press.

Wuthnow, R. (2005b, February 4). *Hanging in the balance: Sociology and theology.* Lecture presented at Yale Divinity School's Center for Faith and Culture. Retrieved July 23, 2005, from http://www.yale.edu/divinity/video/wuthnow.htm

Yamane, D. (1997). Secularization on trial: In defense of a neosecularization paradigm. *Journal for the Scientific Study of Religion, 36*(1), 109–122.

Yoder, J. H. (1996). How H. Richard Niebuhr reasoned: A critique of Christ and culture. In G. H. Stassen (Ed.), *Authentic transformation: A new vision of Christ and culture* (pp. 31–89). Nashville, TN: Abingdon.

Printed in the United States
72353LV00005B/160-162

9 781593 115173